Domenico Delli Gatti   Mauro Gallegati
Alan Kirman (Eds.)

Interaction and Market Structure

Essays on Heterogeneity in Economics

Springer

Editors

Prof. Domenico Delli Gatti
Catholic University of Milan
ITEMQ
Largo Gemelli, 1
20123 Milan, Italy

Prof. Mauro Gallegati
DSGSS
Viale Crucioli, 120
64100 Teramo, Italy

Prof. Alan Kirman
EHESS, IUF,
Université d'Aix-Marseille III
GREQAM
2 Rue de la Charité
13002 Marseille, France

Library of Congress Cataloging-in-Publication Data

Interaction and market structure : essays on heterogeneity in economics / Domenico
Delli Gatti, Mauro Gallegati, Alan Kirman (Eds.).
    p. cm. -- (Lecture notes in economics and mathematical systems ; 484)
  Includes bibliographical references (p.).
  ISBN 3540669795 (softcover : alk. paper)
    1. Economics--Mathematical models. 2. Markets--Mathematical models. I. Delli Gatti,
Domenico. II. Gallegati, M. (Mauro) III. Kirman, A. P. IV. Series.

HB135 .I55 2000
330'.01'1--dc21

99-462210

ISSN 0075-8442
ISBN 3-540-66979-5 Springer-Verlag Berlin Heidelberg New York

Typesetting: Camera ready by author
Printed on acid-free paper   SPIN: 10734504   42/3143/du   543210

Contents

Introduction

Domenico Delli Gatti, Mauro Gallegati, Alan P.Kirman   1

Learning to Trade and Mediate

Herbert Dawid   9

Learning to Be Loyal. A Study of the Marseille Fish Market

Alan P.Kirman, Nicolaas J. Vriend   33

On New Phenomena in Dynamic Promotional Competition
Models with Homogeneous and Quasi-Homogeneous Firms

Michael Kopel, Gian Italo Bischi, Laura Gardini   57

A Reconsideration of Professor Iwai's Schumpeterian Dynamics

Reiner Franke   89

Agents' Heterogeneity, Aggregation, and Economic Fluctuations

Domenico Delli Gatti, Mauro Gallegati, Antonio Palestrini   133

The Dynamic Interaction of Rational Fundamentalists and Trend
Chasing Chartists in a Monetary Economy

Carl Chiarella, Alexander Khomin   151

Self-Organization in Global Stochastic Models
of Production and Inventory Dynamics

Sergio Focardi, Michele Marchesi   167

Heterogeneous Agents, Complementarities and Diffusion
Do Increasing Returns Imply Convergence
to International Technological Monopolies?
Andrea Bassanini, Giovanni Dosi   185

Market Organization: Noncooperative Models of Coalition Formation
Sylvie Thoron   207

Evolutionary Selection of Correlation Mechanism
for Coordination Games
Angelo Antoci, Marcello Galeotti, Pier Luigi Sacco   225

The Propagation of Cooperation in a Spatial Model
of Learning with Endogenous Aspirations
Paolo Lupi   235

Expectation Formation in a Cobweb Economy:
Some One Person Experiments
Cars Hommes, Joep Sonnemans, Henk van de Velden   253

Fecund, Cheap and Out of Control:
Heterogeneous Economic Agents as Flawed
Computers vs. Markets as Evolving Computational Entities
Phillip Mirowski, Koye Somefun   267

Introduction

Domenico Delli Gatti[1], Mauro Gallegati[2], Alan P. Kirman[3]

[1] ITEMQ, Catholic University, Milan, Italy

[2] MET, University of Teramo, Italy

[3] GREQAM, Université d'Aix-Marseille, Ecole des Hautes Etudes en Sciences Sociales, and Institut Universitaire de France

The economics of heterogeneity

This volume contains a set of papers which pursue the aim of examining how the properties of aggregate economic variables are influenced by the actions and interactions of individuals. This has been the central theme of a series of workshops held at the University of Ancona, Italy, since 1996, whose general title is *Workshops on Economics with Heterogeneous Interactive Agents (WEHIA for short)*.[1]

Considering the economy as a complex evolving system of interacting agents, one has to take seriously three fundamental issues:

- the heterogeneity of the agents in the economy,

- the ways in which agents interact,

- the dynamic process which governs the evolution of the individual and the aggregate variables.

The third issue concerns especially the idea that agents learn and adapt rather than calculate optimally (Anderson et al., 1988; Arthur et al., 1997; Allen, 1988.)

As to the first issue, general equilibrium theory allows, of course, agents to be as heterogeneous as one wants but as the Sonnenschein-Mantel-Debreu results have

---

[1] The papers published in this book are a selected sample of the papers presented at the 3rd WEHIA workshop held at the University of Ancona on May 29-30, 1998.
The SIEC (*Social Interaction Economics and Computing*) Group, at the Dipartimento di Economia, Università di Ancona, manages a web site (http://www.econ.unian/ospiti/siec/) in which one can find papers from the WEHIA 1996-99 workshops. The papers presented at the first workshop are now in M.Gallegati and A.P.Kirman, eds., *Beyond the Representative Agent*, Elgar, 1999.

shown we can say nothing about the stability nor the consequences of the equilibrium and it thus remains a highly abstract concept. The general equilibrium theorist may not feel at ease with the representative agent assumption because some of the assumptions about individuals which form the building blocks of general equilibrium theory do not hold for the average or representative agent (the "Weak Axiom of Revealed Preference" does not hold in the aggregate for example). Furthermore, Arrow (1951) has shown that the proposition according to which the properties of an aggregate function will reflect those of the individual function has no theoretical foundations.

Coming to the second issue, in the Arrow-Debreu benchmark model, agents interact only through the price system and this removes much of the interest of the model as a description of a real-world economy. Thus, ignoring heterogeneity may lead to a fallacy of composition when agents' decisions are not perfectly synchronised (so that composition effects arise, see Caballero, 1992). This undermines the theoretical model and distorts the empirical analysis. Game theory, on the other hand, which might seem to be an attractive alternative, has tended to restrict itself to very restrictive cases in which agents interact strategically in a very sophisticated way (Kirman, 1999). Main stream economic theorising seems to have got itself into a *cul de sac*, and more and more economists reject the straightjacket of the "representative agent" acting in a world capable of functioning, by optimally allocating resources, but not of evolving through agents' interaction.

The representative agent framework has been one of the most successful tools in economic theory, even if its fate has been paradoxical (Scholb, 1998). As Stoker (1993: 1829) notes, "it has proved a tremendous engine for the development of rational choice models over the last two decades, and their empirical application has developed into an ideology for judging aggregate data models". It is the cornerstone of the microfoundations of mainstream macroeconomic literature, since the aggregation process is very simple and allows one to rule out any difference between the behaviour of individually optimising agents and that of the aggregate.[2] If this procedure were correct, the behaviour of the aggregate variable would simply be the reproduction on a larger scale of individual optimising behaviour. Once the search for the elementary particles and their laws of functioning was crowned with success these principles could be applied to aggregate behaviour, analogously to the methodology of the hard sciences before the quantum revolution. However, one of the achievements of the latter has been the rebuttal of the notion that aggregate behaviour can be explained on the basis of the behaviour of a single unit: the elementary particle does not even exist as a single entity but as a network, a system of interacting units (Capra, 1996).

---

[2] The conditions for exact aggregation are very restrictive ; see e.g. Martel, 1996.

The analysis of heterogeneity and interaction leads to a rebuttal of the standard view of what are appropriate microfoundations since one cannot explain aggregate dynamics as the sum of the behaviour of individuals: in fact, because interaction is a sort of externality, the aggregate is different from the sum of its parts and the aggregate network determines individual behaviour. Despite its success, economists are growing more and more dissatisfied with the representative agent framework (Kirman, 1992). Empirical analysis at the panel data level has shown that heterogeneity matters and aggregation of heterogeneous agents is of central relevance, since there is systematic evidence of individual differences in economic behaviour (Stoker, 1993) and neglecting heterogeneity in aggregate equations generates spurious evidence of dynamic structure. Moreover, aggregation of very simple individual behaviour may lead to aggregate complex dynamics (Lippi, 1988; Lewbel, 1992.)

Therefore there are theoretical as well as empirical reasons to question the reliability of the representative agent and the literature on heterogeneous agent is thus burgeoning in several fields, from distribution to economic policy, to employment, capital market imperfections and dynamics (Rioss-Rull, 1995; Delli Gatti and Gallegati, 1999). In particular, the assumption of a constant distribution of income, wealth or endowments over time, which is fundamental to achieving exact aggregation of identical agents, is quite implausible when coping with dynamics: In a sense, agents' heterogeneity is the logical requirement for dynamic analysis.

The papers here examine situations in which the organisation of the economy reflects the direct interaction of the agents, in which agents are only limitedly rational and where the structure of the aggregate evolution may be very different from that of the evolution of individual behaviour.

Perhaps the easiest way to situate these papers is to think of the opposite point of view according to which the behaviour of the economy is described by that of a "representative agent". The basic point of view here is that a complex system such as an economy does not generate aggregate behaviour which is simply related to individual behaviour: aggregate dynamics and individual heterogeneity are intertwined.

Outline of the book

We will now briefly review the contributions in the book and show how they reflect some common themes.

Dawid in *Learning to Trade and Mediate* examines a situation in which agents can either produce and trade or mediate. He shows using simulations that both direct trading and trade via specialised mediators can arise. Thus, an economy organises itself and speculates even though agents are homogeneous to start with. The agents in the model are of two types, yet three types emerge. As in many papers in this spirit agents have very simple learning rules yet the economy as a whole develops considerable structure.

Kirman and Vriend in *Learning to be Loyal: A Study of the Marseille Fish Market*, build a simple model of a wholesale market for a perishable good. The agents are either sellers or buyers. Yet using reinforcement learning agents learn to behave differently and reproduce many of the features of the real market analyzed. Price dispersion, loyalty and differentiated treatment of buyers all appear. Once again, market structure emerges as agents co-evolve.

Bischi, Gardini and Kopel in the paper *On New Phenomena in Dynamic Promotional Competition Models with Homogeneous and Quasi Homogeneous Firms* study a market in which firms compete for market shares. They modify their sales effort by means of a simple updating rule which takes into account the results achieved in previous proofs. Even though firms are homogeneous the evolution of market share over time can exhibit very complicated behaviour. Thus, asymmetric results may occur even though agents are originally symmetric. Heterogeneity here is endogenous rather than assumed, it emerges from the interaction between individuals.

The theme of endogenous heterogeneity is taken up by Franke in *A Reconsideration of Professor Iwai's Schumpeterian Dynamics*. He develops an early model of Iwai and shows that the dynamics of an economy in which innovations and diffusion of innovation are occurring will not lead to an equilibrium in which all firms adopt the most efficient technique available. Instead a non degenerate spectrum of techniques will persist.

Delli Gatti, Gallegati and Palestrini in *Agents' Heterogeneity, Aggregation and Economic Fluctuations* show how heterogeneity endogenously arises when market imperfections are taken into account. The main message of this paper is that aggregate fluctuations can be better understood by analysing the evolution of the cross-sectional distribution at micro level. In their model a shock will trickle down across the whole distribution of agents modifying aggregate behaviour and, since composition effects are large, it may produce very different dynamics. Moreover, since there exist as many steady states as the agents' equilibrium distribution, the concept of a "natural rate" is lost.

In *The Dynamic Interaction of Rational Fundamentalists and Trend Chasing Chartists in a Monetary Economy,* Chiarella and Khomin develop a model of a monetary economy which exhibits heterogeneity of behaviour over time but where at any point in time agents hold either "fundamentalist" or "chartist" views and the fundamentalist view is adopted by more agents as inflation accelerates or decelerates. Thus, the self-reinforcing switching behaviour will lead to complex dynamic behaviour but by no means necessarily to a traditional steady state.

In *Self-Organisation in Global Stochastic Models of Production and Inventory Dynamics*, Focardi and Marchesi examine an economy in which both production and consumption take place. There are random shocks but rather than being wiped out on average they produce endogenous fluctuations and a distribution of production. In this model firms are linked to each other in a rather general structure. Thus, a perturbation effect together with uniform shocks generates persistent heterogeneity.

A theme that has permeated much of the literature on interaction is the diffusion of innovations. Arthur (1989) and David (1985) have argued that there is a tendency for one technique to become monopolistic. In *Heterogeneous Agents, Complementarities and Diffusion*, Bassanini and Dosi show that as soon as there are location specific increasing returns and externalities persistent heterogeneity may arise. This would explain international differentiations in terms of standards and technique. Again, heterogeneity is explained as a result of the nature of the interactive process.

Thoron in *Market Organization : Noncooperative Models of Coalition Formation* pursues the theme of emergent heterogeneity. Using a game theoretic approach she looks at a situation in which agents may want to form coalitions. She shows that which coalition structures will emerge depends on he reactions of coalitions to the loss of a member. The interesting feature that links this paper to the others in the book is that asymmetric coalition structures may emerge even though all the players are symmetric.

Antoci, Galeotti and Sacco in *Evolutionary Selection of Correlation Mechanisms for Coordination Games* also use the game theoretic approach to look at the correlated equilibria of co-ordination games. This sort of equilibrium which has come to be considered as a reasonable solution for such games. It is highly dependent on the choice of correlation mechanisms. In the spirit of this book, they do not look at some sophisticated strategic choice of such a mechanism but rather allowed bounded irrational players to play against each other and use replicator dynamics to select the appropriate correlation mechanism. Thus, the correlation device used to achieve co-ordinate evolves from the interaction amongst players rather than being chosen by the modeller.

It might be thought that all of the authors have tried to show that heterogeneity arises even in symmetric situations but in some cases simple myopic agents may, by interacting together come to co-ordinate as a particular form of behaviour. Lupi in *The Propagation of Co-operation in a Spatial Model of Learning with Endogenous Aspirations* shows how simple minded duopolists playing against each other can learn, by initiating others when they are not satisfied with their profit level, to co-operate. This co-operative behaviour emerges in a situation in which there is no conscious co-ordinations.

In *Expectation Formation in an Cobweb Economy*, Van de Velden, Hommes and Sonnemans show that interaction and co-evaluation may not be necessary to generate heterogeneous behaviour. In their model individuals learned experimentally how to react to the market feed back which was the same for all of them. Only a minority of them learned their way to the "Rational Expectations Equilibrium". A way of interpreting this is to say that individuals faced with the same situation may learn their way to very different results.

In the last chapter in the book, *Fecund, Cheap and Out of Control: Heterogeneous Economic Agents as Flawed Computers versus Markets as Evolving Computational Entities*, Mirowski and Somefun adopt a more radical stance than the rest of the papers in the book and propose that markets themselves should be viewed as computational devices or formal automata. They trace the history of what they call the computational understanding of markets and adopt a consciously evolutionary approach in their analysis. Their approach which is a novel one suggests how heterogeneous agents may be subject to a selection process. Emergent organisation is, as with the other chapters in the book, a central theme but the organisation comes from the market. This approach puts a heavy emphasis on the role of the market something which is perhaps absent from many more standard models.

In conclusion, what can be seen from this collection of papers is the evolution of thinking on the subject of the aggregate behaviour of markets and economies. The chapters in the book are use a variety of mathematical tools and of approaches varying from simple automata to more sophisticated game theoretic analysis. Yet, a common trend is very apparent. The initial approach in the earlier WEHIA conferences was to put the emphasis on the heterogeneity of agents to counteract the omnipresence of the representative individual. Here what we see is the use of more dynamic models with agents acting and interacting according to simple rules and in which heterogeneity may arise endogenously. Thus, once we put on one side more traditional neo-classical analysis heterogeneity of behaviour and of characteristics and the emergence of market organisation can be derived from the interaction of rather simple individuals.

References

Allen, P.M. (1988), "Dynamic Models of Evolving Systems", System Dynamics Review, vol. 4, pp.109-130.

Anderson, P.W., Arrow, K.J., Pines, D. (eds) (1988), "The Economy as a Complex Evolving System", Redwood City: Addison-Wesley.

Arthur, W.B. (1989), "Competing Technologies, Increasing Returns, and Lock-in by Historical Events", Economic Journal, vol. 90, pp. 116-31.

Arthur, W.B., Durlauf, S.N., Lane, D.A. (eds) (1997), "The Economy as a Complex Evolving System II", Redwood City: Addison-Wesley.

Arrow, K.J. (1951), "Social Choice and Individual Values", New Haven, Yale University Press.

Caballero, R. J. (1992), "A Fallacy of Composition", American Economic Review, vol. 82, pp. 1279-1292.

Capra F. (1996), "The Web of Life", New York, Doubleday-Anchor Book.

David, P. (1985), "Clio and the Economics of QWERTY", American Economic Review, vol. 75, pp. 332-7.

Delli Gatti, D., Gallegati, M. (1999), "Heterogeneity, Aggregation, and Capital Market Imperfections", in Punzo, L.F., "Cycle, Growth and Structural Change", Oxford, Clarendon, Forthcoming.

Kirman, A. (1992), "Whom or What Does the Representative Individual Represent?", Journal of Economic Perspectives, vol. 6, pp. 117-36.

Kirman, A.P. (1999), "Interaction and Market", in M.Gallegati and A.P.Kirman (eds.), "Beyond the Representative Agent", Elgar, pp. 1-46.

Lewbel, A. (1992), "Aggregation and Simple Dynamics", mimeo, Brandeis University.

Lippi, M. (1988), "On the Dynamic Shape of Aggregated Error Correction Models", Journal of Economic Dynamics and Control, vol. 12, pp. 561-85.

Martel, R. (1996), "Heterogeneity, Aggregation and a Meaningful Macroeconomics", in Colander, D. (ed.), "Beyond Microfoundations", Cambridge, Cambridge University Press, pp. 127-144.

Rios-Rull, J.V. (1995), "Models with Heterogeneous Agents", in Cooley, T.F. (ed.), "Frontiers of Business Cycle Research", Princeton, Princeton University Press, pp. 98-125.

Scholb, F. (1988), "The Paradoxical Fate of the Representative Firm", mimeo, University of Jena

Stoker, T. (1993), "Empirical Approaches to the Problem of Aggregation over Individuals", Journal of Economic Literature, vol. 21, pp. 1827-1874.

Learning to Trade and Mediate[*]

Herbert Dawid

Department of Economics, University of Southern California, Los Angeles, CA 90089-0253

Abstract. In this paper we study the behavior of boundedly rational agents in a two good economy where trading is costly with respect to time. All individuals have a fixed time budget and may spend time for the production of good one, the production of good two and trading. They update their strategies, which determine their time allocation, according to a simple imitation type learning rule with noise. In a setup with two different type of agents with different production technologies we show by the means of simulations that both direct trade and trade via mediators who specialize in trading can emerge. We can also observe the transition from a pure production economy via direct trade to an economy with mediated trade.

JEL Classification: D83, F10
Keywords: bounded rationality, learning, trade, mediation

1 Introduction

Mediated trade is a phenomenon which can be observed in many different markets in the real world economy. Examples reach from retail stores to real estate agents and stock brokers. In all those cases 'producers' do not directly deal with the 'consumers' of their goods but there are middlemen in-between who facilitate the trades. The basic role of these middlemen is to reduce the search costs of buyers and sellers needed to find an appropriate trading partner. The middlemen profit from these transactions by marking up their selling prices but it is quite obvious that in many instances trading via mediators nevertheless pays off for all agents in the economy. This observation indicates that many goods are not traded on central markets but more complicated structures have developed in order to reduce the transaction costs. However, the question how these structures evolve has not attracted too much attention of economics scholars up to now.

---

[*] This research has highly profited from the suggestions and remarks of Richard Day which are gratefully acknowledged. The author would also like to thank Nick Vriend, James Robinson and the participants of the Workshop on Economics with Heterogenous Interacting Agents in Ancona for helpful comments. Financial support from the Austrian Science Foundation under grant F 01005 "Adaptive Information Systems and Modelling in Economics and Management Science" is gratefully acknowledged.

In most economic models the problem of search and transaction costs in trading is neglected and it is assumed that producers and consumers have no problems finding each other and agreeing on the equilibrium price to carry out the trade[1] There are several exceptions like Rubinstein and Wolinsky (1987), Day (1994) or Pingle (1997) where middlemen are explicitly introduced into a model of trade. Rubinstein and Wolinsky demonstrate how this topic can be dealt with in an equilibrium framework but if we relax the demanding assumption underlying this concept we have to study a decentralized economy consisting of several self interested but boundedly rational individuals. These individuals are not a priori organized and also do not have rational expectations about the actions of other market members. The general question arising in this context is whether a perfectly organized market does indeed emerge in such a model and how the market structure looks like.

In order to study the emergence of market organization an agent based approach using a population of heterogeneous interacting individuals is very well suited. The agents are boundedly rational and determine their actions based on imitation of successful other individuals and own experience. Experiments have shown that such kind of behavior can indeed be observed when people are dealing with an unknown environment [Pingle (1995)]. The setting of the model is a very simple economy with two goods where each agent is able to produce both goods and to trade. The transaction costs of trading are introduced via a fixed time budget and the assumption that finding a trading partner needs some time. We carry out our analysis of this model primarily by the means of computer simulations. This approach has recently gained high importance also in economic research [see e.g. Arifovic (1996), Dawid (1999a), Routledge (1995), Tesfatsion (1997), Vriend (1995)] and chances are they will become even more important in the near future. Although such an approach does not permit exact general results like analytical studies do, it enables us to study complex interactive models which could not be dealt with analytically.

The questions posed in this article are: can boundedly rational agents who all start off as pure producers organize in a way to use the possible profits of production specialization and trading and how does the transition from a production economy to an economy with trade look like? There is an ongoing discussion in the trade literature [e.g. Krugman (1981), Helpman and Krugman (1985)] whether trade is entirely due to comparative advantages and differing factor endowments or may also be explained by economies of scale. Traditionally, these questions are dealt with in an equilibrium framework, but here we will also investigate this question using a learning approach. In Dawid (1999b) we have established the emergence of trade in a model with homogeneous production technologies and increasing returns to scale. Here we are going to compare these results with the findings in a model with de-

---

[1] Note however that there is a some literature dealing with the emergence of a *medium* of exchange in trade; see e.g. Jones (1976) or Marimon et al. (1990).

creasing returns to scale in production and heterogeneities in the production function.

The paper is organized as follows. In section 2 we present the basic simulation model, in section 3 we present our simulation results and in section 4 we discuss these results and carry out a short mathematical analysis which should enhance the understanding of the numerical findings. We end with some final remarks in section 5.

2 The Model

In this section we describe our model. We will first present the basic version where agents cannot hold stocks and thus only engage in direct trade and afterwards introduce the possibility of becoming a mediator, building up stocks and exclusively concentrating on trading.

2.1 The Agents

We model the evolution of a system of n interacting economic agents who may split their available time on production and trading. Each agent has a fixed time budget in each period which is normalized to one. There are two goods in the economy and he may spend his time on producing good 1, producing good 2 or trading. There are two different types of agents in our model. Agents of type I are more efficient in producing good 1 than good 2 and type II agents are more efficient in producing good 2. These different abilities might stem from differing availability of resources, differing training of the agents or just differing talent. For reasons of simplicity we always assume that there is the same number of type I agents in the population as of type II agents. The behavior of agent i is described by his degree of specialization in production, sp^i, and the variable s^i determining the amount of time he invests in trading. The variables may vary with time but we omit the time argument in our notation. The variable $sp^i \in [0,1]$ denotes the fraction of production time agent i invests in producing the good where he is more efficient. If we denote by x_g^i the fraction of time the agent invests in producing good g we have

$$x_1^i = \begin{cases} (1 - s^i)sp^i & \text{type} = I \\ (1 - s^i)(1 - sp^i) & \text{type} = II \end{cases}$$

$$x_2^i = \begin{cases} (1 - s^i)(1 - sp^i) & \text{type} = I \\ (1 - s^i)sp^i & \text{type} = II \end{cases}.$$

Of course, this implies

$$x_1^i + x_2^i + s^i = 1 \quad \forall i = 1 \ldots n.$$

To keep matters as simple as possible we assume the following production technologies. A type I agent has production functions

$$f_1^I(x_1) = a_1 x_1^\alpha, \quad f_2^I(x_2) = a_2 x_2^\alpha$$

whereas a type II agent produces according to

$$f_1^{II} = a_2 x_1^\alpha, \quad f_2^{II}(x_2) = a_1 x_2^\alpha,$$

where $a_1 > a_2$ and $\alpha < 1$. Note that we consider decreasing returns to scale in production[2]. Furthermore, we make the simplifying assumption that the degree of homogeneity is the same in both production functions and, finally, we assume that a type II agent is an exact copy of a type I agent, only with goods 1 and 2 exchanged. The preferences of the agents are represented by the concave utility function

$$U(c_1^i, c_2^i) = b_1(c_1^i)^{\beta_1} + b_2(c_2^i)^{\beta_2}, \quad b_g > 0, \ \beta_g < 1.$$

In what follows we always assume $a_1 \doteq a_2$, $b_1 = b_2$, $\alpha_1 = \alpha_2$ and for computational convenience $\beta_1 = \beta_2 = \frac{1}{2}$. Note that we assume that the two types of agents have different production functions but identical preferences. Introducing heterogeneity also with respect to preferences would be an interesting extension of the model which should be followed up in future research.

The trading behavior of the agents is determined as follows: given a price p of good one (expressed in units of good two) the agent has to determine whether he likes to buy or sell good one. Assuming that an agent currently holds γ^i units of good 1, δ^i units of good 2 and maximizes the utility gained by consuming all the goods, he has excess supply respectively demand for good one in the amount of

$$g(p, \gamma^i, \delta^i) = \frac{\gamma^i p^2 - \delta^i}{p(1+p)}$$

units. Whenever two agents are matched for trading (the mechanism governing this matching is described below) they exchange goods where the price p is determined such that excess demand for good one equals the supply. It is easy to see that with the supply and demand functions given above there is always a unique price with this property.

2.2   Transactions within a Period

Each period t consists of three different stages, namely production, trade and consumption.

---

[2] As mentioned above, we have carried out an analysis of a similar model with homogeneous production technologies in the population and increasing returns to scale in Dawid (1999b).

In the first stage all agents produce according to their production variables x_g^i. After production they might trade the good. We denote by γ^i and δ^i the amounts of goods 1 and 2 agent i is holding during the trading period. The holdings vary during the trading period and these variables always denote the current value. Initially, we have for an agent i of type j

$$\gamma^i = f_1^j(x_1^i), \qquad \delta^i = f_2^j(x_2^i).$$

The trading procedure explicitly introduces search costs into the model. The basic idea is that every agent spends some time looking around and searching for a trading partner. There are some randomly chosen agents in the population he can meet if he invests enough time in trading, but some of these possible matches are never realized because of a lack of time available for search. Think of a producer who has a number of potential trading partners reachable within one day. If he decides to visit one of these agents he might either meet him in the middle, which means that both have to invest time, or – if the other agent does not sacrifice time for trading – go all the way and loose twice as much time. Of course he can also keep producing the whole time and wait for some of his neighbours to come all the way and trade with him.

In our simulations we use the following procedure to determine the trading partners. Two agents i and j can only trade with one another if the sum of the time invested in trading exceeds some given threshold $\chi > 0$. The initial trading budget for each agent is in each period given by $S^i = s^i$ and is reduced step by step during the trading period by the amount of time which has already been used for trading. Interpreting the effort invested in trading as search costs this restriction means that the agents have to invest time for searching for partners if they like to trade. Note, however, that all effort might be invested by one party allowing "professional" traders who can be reached by others without any costs. Defining the "trading pool" as the set of all agents who might trade in the rest of period t the matching algorithm for trading can be described as follows:

1. Choose randomly an agent i from the trading pool where each agent in the pool is chosen with the same probability.
2. If $S^i = 0$ return agent i to the trading pool and go to 1.
3. Choose randomly (again uniformly) an agent j from the rest of the trading pool.
4. If $S^i + S^j < \chi$ goto 5., else determine amount and price for the trade between i and j. If $\delta^i \gamma^j < \delta^j \gamma^i$ good 1 is traded from agent i to agent j, if the inequality holds the other way round good 1 is traded from agent j to agent i. In the case of equality no trade takes place. Let us assume that good 1 is traded from i to j. The amount traded and the trading price are determined by the condition

$$g(p; \gamma^i, \delta^i) + g(p; \gamma^j, \delta^j) = 0$$

which yields the amount

$$y_{ij} = \frac{\gamma^i p_{ij}^2 - \delta^i}{p_{ij}(1 + p_{ij})}, \tag{1}$$

where

$$p_{ij} = \sqrt{\frac{\delta^i + \delta^j}{\gamma^i + \gamma^j}} \tag{2}$$

is the corresponding price. In other words, we assume that if two (producing) agents meet they are able to determine the price which allows them both to buy respectively sell the optimal amount given the trading price. Afterwards, the holdings of both agents are updated accordingly:

$$\gamma^i = \gamma^i - y_{ij}$$
$$\delta^i = \delta^i + p_{ij} y_{ij}$$
$$\gamma^j = \gamma^j + y_{ij}$$
$$\delta^j = \delta^j - p_{ij} y_{ij}.$$

5. Update the time budgets

$$S^k = S^k - \min\left[S^k, \max\left[\frac{\chi}{2}, \chi - S^l\right]\right] \quad k = i, j, \quad l = i, j, \ k \neq l.$$

If $S^j = 0$ eliminate j from the trading pool. If $S^i = 0$ eliminate i from the trading pool and check whether there are still agents with $S^k > 0$ in the trading pool. If this holds true go to 1 else stop trading. If $S^i > 0$ goto 2. The time budget updating can be interpreted as follows: if two agents meet where both are looking for a partner each of them has to invest trading time in the amount of $\frac{\chi}{2}$ to find the partner; however, if an agent does not actively search for a partner or does so only for a short time ($S^i < \frac{\chi}{2}$) he is harder to find and his partner has to invest more time. Note also that this scheme implies that a trader leaves the market as soon as he has invested all his trading time.

Note that the trading scheme described above assumes that passive traders (agents with $s^i = 0$) only trade once and leave the market afterwards.

After the trading period all agents consume their current holding receiving a utility of

$$U^i = b\left(\sqrt{\gamma^i} + \sqrt{\delta^i}\right).$$

2.3   Learning

We consider a learning process where all agents review their current strategy every τ periods. Upon reviewing his strategies an agent i may decide to adopt the strategy of another agent based on the payoff in the previous τ periods.

The probability to adopt the strategy of an agent j increases with the past payoff of j. Let $\bar{U}^j$ denote the average payoff of agent j in the previous T periods. With

$$\pi^j(i) = \begin{cases} \bar{U}^j & j \neq i \\ w\bar{U}^j & j = i \end{cases}$$

the probability that agent i adopts the strategy of agent j is given by

$$\Pi^j(i) = \frac{\pi^j(i)}{\sum_{k=1}^n \pi^k(i)},$$

The parameter $w \geq 1$ governs the inertia of the agent by increasing the probability that he uses his own strategy again in the next τ periods. After all agents have adopted their new strategies these strategies are disrupted by stochastic shocks. These shocks might incorporate implementation errors of the agents but also intended innovations. With some small probability $\mu_v > 0$ an amount ξ_v generated by a normal distribution $N(0, \sigma_v^2)$ is added to the variable $v \in \{sp, s\}$ of agent i. If the shock drives a variable out of $[0,1]$ the variable is set to 0 or 1 respectively. This completes one learning step and all agents use their new strategies for the next τ periods. Afterwards another learning step takes place and so on.

The proposed learning algorithm describes imitation based adaptation of the agents strategies. The individuals do not build any expectations in order to optimize anticipated payoffs but just consider the past success of other individuals and try to imitate the ones with above average utility. Imitational learning rules have been analyzed in several mainly game theoretic contexts [e.g. Schlag (1998), Vega-Redondo (1995) or Björnerstedt and Weibull (1996)]. The learning dynamics may also be interpreted as a stochastic version of the well known replicator dynamics (Taylor and Jonker (1978)) which was thoroughly analyzed in the biological and economic literature [e.g. Hofbauer and Sigmund (1998), Cressman (1992)]. Although this kind of adaptation underestimates the complexity of the actual decision making process of economic agents in most contexts it can nevertheless provide interesting insights into the evolution of a population of boundedly rational agents who do not have enough information about their environment to be able to predict future developments in a sensible way or to determine optimal responses to expected future developments. In situations like this the reliance on strategies which worked well in the past may indeed be rational behavior (see also Pingle (1995)).

2.4   Mediators

The fact that we did not allow the agents to build up stocks so far rules out the possibility of the emergence of agents who exclusively concentrate on trading without producing any goods themselves. We call these agents mediators and will now extend the model by allowing the agents to decide to mediate in the market rather than to produce. This is done by adding three more decision variables to the existing three decision variables of each agent. The first of the three additional variables, id^i describes the identity of agent i. Whenever this variable has value 0 the agent is a producer and behaves in exactly the same way as the agents described above. If $id^i = 1$ the agent is a mediator. This implies that $s^i = 1$ and no time is invested in producing. Furthermore, a mediator has a different kind of trading behavior than the producing agents. Whereas the producing agents trade in a way to maximize their utility from consumption the meditator rather sells and buys good 1 at fixed prices. He sells one unit of good 1 for p_s^i units of good 2 and buys it for p_b^i units of the second good. These two prices are decision variables of the agent and again might change over time. Of course, mediators always markup selling from buying prices and we have $p_s^i > p_b^i$. To be able to mediate, an agent has to possess some stocks of both goods. Thus, we assume that whenever an agent changes due to imitation or innovation from production to mediation he initially produces without trading for four periods (two periods for each good) and afterwards completely stops production and starts trading. The stock of good g agent i holds is denoted by l_g^i. If an agent switches from mediation to production he leaves his stock untouched and is able to use this stock again if he decides to switch back to mediation at some time.

Mediators trade only with producers but never with other mediators. When a mediator i is matched for trading with a producer j an amount of

$$y_{ij} = \min(\max(0, g(p_s^i, \gamma^j, \delta^j)), l_1^i)$$

of good one is traded from i to j at price p_s^i and or amount of

$$y_{ji} = \min\left(\max(0, -g(p_b^i, \gamma^j, \delta^j)), \frac{l_2^i}{p_b^i}\right)$$

of good one is traded from j to i at price p_b^i. Note that $p_s^i > p_b^i$ implies that at most one of these two amounts is positive. On the other hand, it is possible that both amounts equal zero and no trade occurs. The minimum operator used in these expressions ensures that no mediator sells a higher amount of a good than he has on stock. After the trade the current holdings of the producer and the stock of the mediator are updated.

The mediators try to keep their overall size of stock after consumption constant over the periods. However decreasing marginal utilities of both goods makes it profitable for the mediators to smooth their consumption and consume equal amounts of both goods. Thus, they consume the same aggregate amount of goods they have gained by trading in the current period but split consumption equally between the two goods in order to increase utility. Denoting by $l_{g,t-1}^i$ the stock held at the end of period $t-1$ and by $\tilde{l}_{g,t}^i$ the stock held after trading in period t we define $c^i = \tilde{l}_{1,t}^i + \tilde{l}_{2,t}^i - l_{1,t-1}^i - l_{2,t-1}^i$. Every period the consumption of mediator i in period t

$$\gamma^i = \min\left(\frac{c^i}{2}, l^i_1\right), \qquad \delta^i = \min\left(\frac{c^i}{2}, l^i_2\right)$$

is subtracted from the stock.

Learning basically works just like in the model without mediators. The only difference is that innovation effects also the three additional decision variables id^i, p^i_s and p^i_b. The variable id^i is inverted with some small probability μ_{id} and there is some probability that normally distributed noise is added to the prices. In case that innovations would lead to a violation of $p^i_s > p^i_b$ these innovations are neglected.

3   Simulation Results

In this section we present the results of some computer simulations we ran using the model described above. We will only shortly explain our results in this section, but in section 4 we will provide an extensive discussion of our findings and will try to draw a rather general picture of the behavior of a population of boundedly rational agents in this setup.

In all our simulations we use a population of size $n = 100$. The population is initialized homogeneously such that the agents decision variables are given by $x^i_1 = x^i_2 = \frac{1}{2}$, $s^i = 0$. The parameters b and a_2 are set to 1. We always assume that the agents update their strategies every 10 periods ($\tau = 10$). The threshold for trading is given by $\chi = 0.1$ and the inertia parameter for the imitation process was always set to $w = 2$. Concerning the innovations a normally distributed noise term with expectation 0 and variance $\sigma = 0.1$ is added to a continuous decision variables with probability $\mu = 0.02$. The simulations were run for $T = 3000$ generations. Most of our results appear to be robust with respect to changes in these parameters. In cases where we present results of single simulation runs we performed sufficient numbers of runs to check that the results reported here are at least qualitatively robust.

The focus of our studies is the emergence of trade as such, i.e the time evolution of the amount traded, the production and trading strategies and the influence of certain parameter values on the long run outcome of the system. In particular, we will concentrate on the ratio a_1/a_2 describing the degree of heterogeneity in the production functions and the returns to scale parameter α. In most cases we will present simulation results which we got in the model with mediation. In particular in those cases where no significant number of mediators emerge these results are virtually identical to those obtained in the model where agents do not have the option to mediate. In cases where we show results from the model without the possibility of mediation we will point this out.

In our first two figures we show the time trajectories of the crucial variables of the model in dependence of the ration a_1/a_1. In figure 1 we present the trajectories of the average aggregated utility $(\bar{U}_t)$, the average degree of specialization $(\bar{sp}_t)$, the average time invested in trading $(\bar{s}_t)$, the amount of trade in the population (tr_t) measured in units of good 1 and the number of mediators for $a_1 = 2$ and $\alpha = 0.5$. It can be clearly seen that the population basically stays in its initial state where all agents spend all their time for the production of the two goods. No trade emerges and only at the end of the run the agents specialize a little bit and invest more time for their more efficient production technology. Average utility oscillates but no upward trend can bee seen. Furthermore, the number of mediators is insignificant throughout the run. This could be seen as an indicator that the learning rule used is just too weak and does not allow for the adoption of trade or more efficient production strategies. However, if we increase the ratio a_1/a_2 we get quite different results. In figure 2 we show the same variables as in figure 1 for a run with parameter values $a_1 = 8$, $\alpha = 0.5$.

Here learning leads to an increase in average utility in the population. We can see that after about 1000 periods of a pure production economy there is a sudden increase both in $\bar{s}_t$ and the trading volume indicating the emergence of massive direct trade. Afterwards, we can observe a rather slow adaptation of the degree of specialization towards the maximal value of one. Whereas the emergence of direct trade initially does not increase average utility the climbing degree of specialization causes an improvement of average utility from $\bar{U} \approx 32$ to $\bar{U} \approx 36$. Note that the number of mediators is again small throughout the run. However, it is interesting that a little bit of mediation takes place in the periods before direct trade is established in the economy but not any more after the emergence of direct trade.

To get a more systematic picture of the influence of the ratio a_1/a_2 on the long run behavior of our model we have performed 10 simulation runs for any integer value of $a_1 \in [1,8]$ and $\alpha = 0.5$. In figure 3 we depict the average values of the five variables discussed above at the end of the runs[3]. The picture is consistent with the observations we made above. Raising a_1 improves average utility at the end of the run and leads to an intensification of trade. The larger a_1 is, the larger is on average the degree of specialization and the time invested in trading. The number of mediators is always very small which suggests that for these values of χ and α direct trade is the only way of goods exchange which can be established. For $a_1 \leq 3$ the average trading volume and the average degree of specialization is rather small which can be seen as an indicator that for such a small heterogeneity no substantial trading evolved in any of the runs.

So far we have observed only the emergence of direct trade although the framework we are using in our simulations allows also for massive media-tion. At first sight this is quite surprising, in particular if we compare these findings to those in the case of homogeneous production technologies with

---

[3] The superscript 'av' always indicate that these are average results of ten different simulation runs.

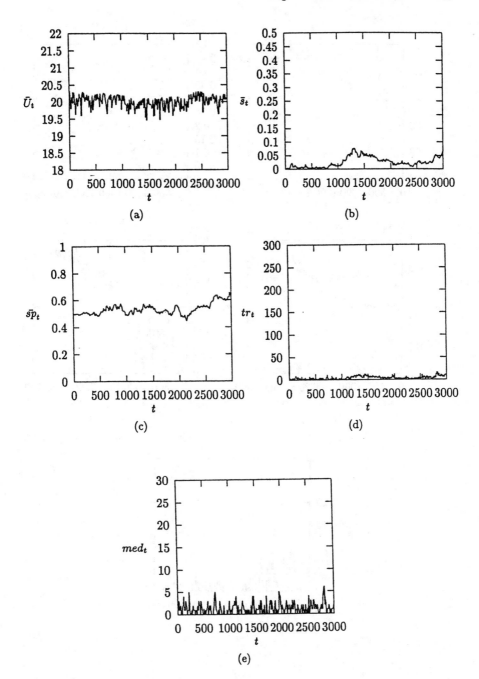

Fig. 1. The development of a pure production economy in the model with small heterogeneity ($a_1 = 2$, $a_2 = 1$) and $\alpha = 0.5$: a) average population utility, b) average time invested in trading by producers, c) average degree of specialization, d) volume of trade, e) number of mediators.

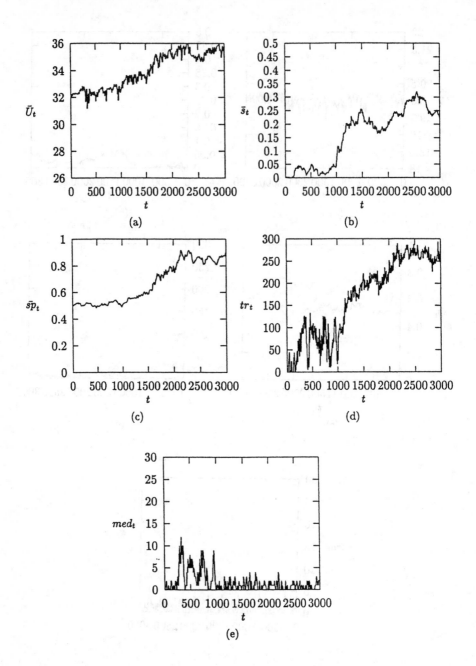

Fig. 2. Emergence of direct trade in the model with parameter values $a_1 = 8$, $a_2 = 1$ and $\alpha = 0.5$: a) average population utility, b) average time invested in trading by producers c) average degree of specialization, d) volume of trade, e) number of mediators.

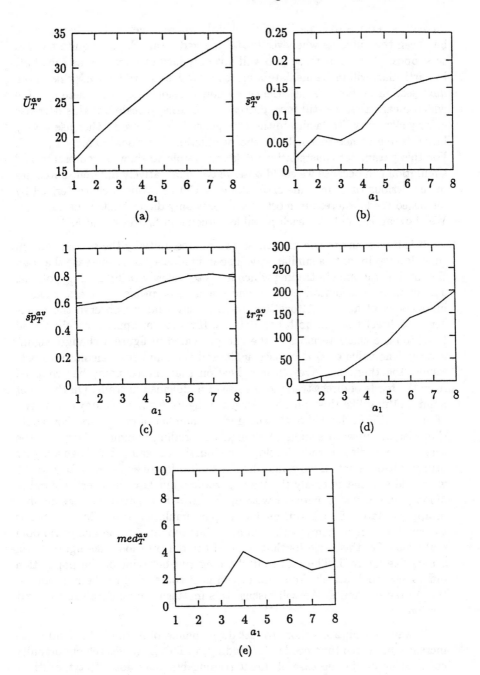

Fig. 3. Long run results after 3000 periods averaged over 10 runs with $\alpha = 0.5$, $a_2 = 1$ and $a_1 \in [1, 8]$: a) average population utility, b) average fraction of time invested in trading by producers, c) average degree of specialization, d) volume of trade, e) number of mediators.

increasing returns to scale (Dawid (1999b)) where in general mediated trade has been the outcome whenever trade emerged at all. So, it is quite natural to suppose that an increase in α will not only facilitate trading as such but, in particular, will make mediation more attractive (we will discuss this in the next section in more detail). Hence we now consider the case where $\alpha = 0.9$ which means that we still have decreasing returns to scale but this decrease is very slow now. To facilitate the emergence of trade we further use a very large degree of heterogeneity in the production functions, namely $a_1 = 8$. For this parameter constellations it is impossible to show a 'representative' simulation run because we could observe two qualitatively different outcomes in the various runs. In some cases the long run behavior is characterized by mediated trade whereas in most of the cases only direct trade is carried out. We show an example for each possible outcome in figures 4 and 5.

It is interesting to compare these two figures. Initially the two simulation runs develop in quite a similar way. The individuals slowly increase the fraction of time invested in trading which leads to a slowly rising trading volume. The number of mediators is small and seems to be primarily due to random innovations of agents. Altogether, we may say that we observe the emergence of direct trade in both populations. However, at approximately period $t = 1500$ the characteristics of the run presented in figure 4 changes significantly. The value of $\bar{s}_t$ decreases again and the number of mediators starts rising. Together, this gives clear indication that the economy has changed from the mode of direct trade to the use of middlemen in trade. On the other hand, nothing like this can be observed in figure 5 where $\bar{s}_t$ stays at a level of about 0.15 till the end of the run and the number of mediators shows only short lasting upward swings. Although the trading volume is larger in the case where mediated trade develops, the individuals gain on average a higher utility if it does not. If we would draw a similar figure as figure 3 for $\alpha = 0.9$ we would see that not only the trading volume but also the average number of long run mediators increases with a_1. For $a_1 = 8$ we get an average number of approximately 8 long run mediators per simulation run. This number is too small for an economy with mediation but too large to be due to random mutations. So, this suggests that some of the ten runs look like figure 4 and others like figure 5. The fact that the long run behavior of the population differs also qualitatively from run to run is of course due to the random nature of the dynamics. We will discuss this matter in more detail in the next section.

A way to facilitate a more robust development of mediation should be to increase the search time needed for trading, χ. This increases the opportunity costs occurring in the case of direct trading but may not affect the utility of mediators if the number of individuals they can trade with is determined by the ratio of mediators to producers rather than by the time constraint. In order to verify this conjecture we have performed simulations for values of χ in the range $[0.05, 0.3]$. The average long run results are depicted in

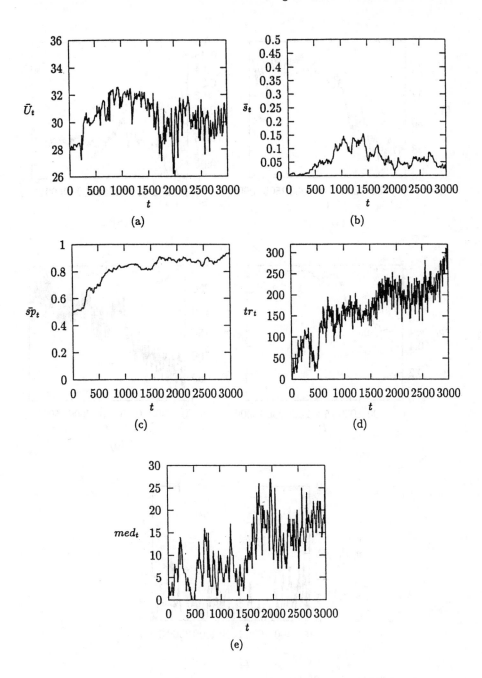

Fig. 4. Emergence of mediated trade in the model with parameter constellation $a_1 = 8$, $a_2 = 1$ and $\alpha = 0.9$: a) average population utility, b) average fraction of time invested in trading by producers, c) average degree of specialization, d) volume of trade, e) number of mediators.

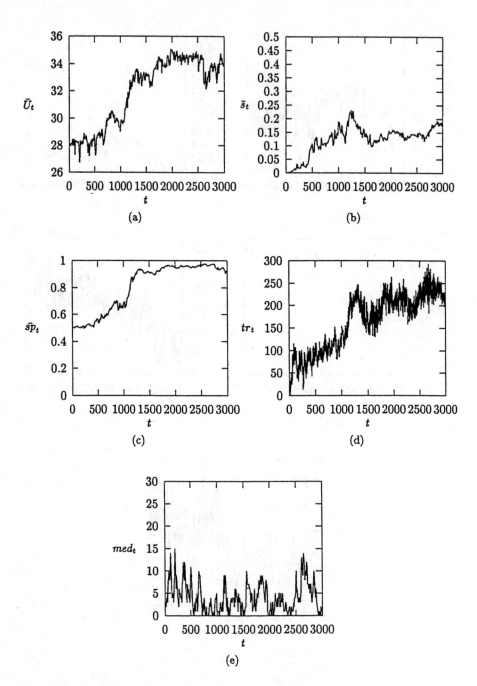

Fig. 5. Emergence of direct trade in the model with the same parameter constellation as in figure 4: a) average population utility, b) average fraction of time invested in trading by producers, c) average degree of specialization, d) volume of trade, e) number of mediators.

figure 6. As expected, the average utility and trading volume decreases with increasing χ. However, the average number of mediators increases with χ as long as the trading time threshold is small. At the same time the fraction of time invested in trading by the producers decreases. This shows that the fraction of cases where mediated trade emerges increases with χ. We have also carried out numerical experiments for the same parameter values in the model without mediators and here we get for larger values of χ significantly smaller trading volumes. In particular, trade basically vanishes for $\chi > 0.2$. Thus, in the presence of such large search costs the possibility of mediated trade seems to be essential for the development of the exchange of goods in the economy.

Finally, we would like to mention that we also examined the influence of other parameters in the model, like the level of inertia or noise. However, sensible variations of these parameters did not change the qualitative behavior of the model and we do not present these numerical experiments here.

4   Discussion

Having presented the simulation results in the previous section we will now use them to gain a better understanding of the dynamic process of self organization in this economy. From a mathematical point of view the evolution of the population state can be described by a time homogeneous Markov process on a continuous state space. Due to the extremely complicated structure of the transition functions a rigorous mathematical analysis seems to be impossible and even approximation results for decreasing mutation probabilities are out of reach[4]. Thus, simulations seem to be the only available means in order to study the dynamic behavior of the system. However, we will discuss the simulation results using very loose comparative static analyses pointing out some properties of the **static** model with completely rational agents. This allows us to make some observations on how successful the self- organization of the population has been.

In the last section we have seen that three qualitatively different population states emerged as the long run outcome of our model. One which exhibits no trade, one with direct trade and one with mediated trade respectively. A goal of this study is to determine how efficient the self organization of the market is with boundedly rational agents. In order to answer this question we have to derive 'benchmarks' of perfectly organized economies of certain types which can be compared to our simulation results. Thus, we will now

---

[4] Kandori and Rob (1995) derive a general theory characterizing the long run outcome of learning dynamics with noise for low levels of noise. However, this theory needs a discrete state space and also a much simpler mode of interaction than we have in our model.

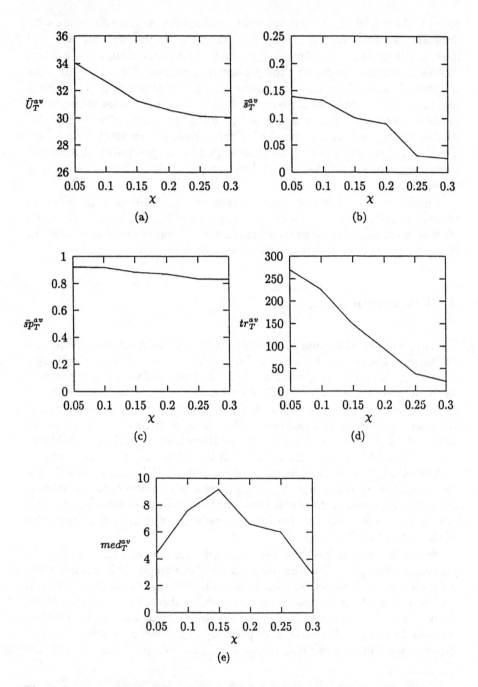

Fig. 6. Long run results after 3000 periods averaged over 10 runs with $\alpha = 0.9$, $a_1 = 8$, $a_2 = 1$ and $\chi \in [0.05, 0.3]$: a) average population utility, b) average fraction of time invested in trading by producers, c) average degree of specialization, d) volume of trade, e) number of mediators.

consider for each of these three cases an 'equilibrium' state[5] which has the corresponding properties and calculate the individuals strategies and payoffs. These calculations will be used to discuss some of the simulation results in more detail.

Let us first consider the case where no trade takes place in the population. A type I agent who does not trade maximizes his payoff by choosing

$$x_1 = \frac{a_1^{\frac{1}{2-\alpha}}}{a_1^{\frac{1}{2-\alpha}} + a_2^{\frac{1}{2-\alpha}}}, \quad x_2 = \frac{a_2^{\frac{1}{2-\alpha}}}{a_1^{\frac{1}{2-\alpha}} + a_2^{\frac{1}{2-\alpha}}}.$$

For an type II agent the optimal allocation of time is exactly the reverse. The corresponding payoff reads

$$U_{pr} = \sqrt{\left(a_1^{\frac{1}{2-\alpha}} + a_2^{\frac{1}{2-\alpha}}\right)^{2-\alpha}}.$$

If the population is indeed organized in such a way it is quite costly to start trading because the whole search costs have to be carried by the individual who is looking for a trading partner. Thus, we might conjecture that such a state is stable as long as the gains from trade are not too large. It is easy to see that the payoff of specialization increases both with α and the ratio a_1/a_2. On the other hand, the opportunity costs of trading depend primarily on α. Increasing the value α makes trading more costly in the sense that the amount of output which could be produced in the time which is invested in trading increases. However, a high α also decreases the payoff of an agent producing both goods because he has to produce in a less efficient part of his production set and his consumption plan gets more skewed towards the good he can produce more efficiently.

Considering figure 1 we realize that the long run outcome of this simulation very closely resembles the state described above. In the end of the run the agents slightly specialize in the production of the good they can produce more efficiently and approach the optimal value $sp \approx 0.6135$. The gained utility is almost identical to U_{tr} which is for these parameter values given by $U_{pr} = 2.04$ (remember that we depict the added utility of 10 periods). On the other hand, we may infer from figure 3 that the no trade states only emerge for values $a_1 \leq 3$. For larger values of a_1 normally trade gets established. For small values of α this is always direct trade.

In order to study a state with direct trade we consider a situation where all individuals invest a fraction 2χ of their time for trading and the rest entirely for producing their more efficient good; i.e. we have $s^i = 2\chi, x_1^i = 1-2\chi, x_2^i = 0$ for all type I agents and $s^i = 2\chi, x_1^i = 0, x_2^i = 1-2\chi$ for all type

---

[5] We are using this term in a rather loose sense here. In particular in the case with direct trade it is not obvious whether the state we consider is indeed an equilibrium in a strict game theoretic sense.

II agents. The theoretical optimal value of s^i is rather difficult to determine because we have to take into account the stochastic matching algorithm. An individual has to trade off the probability not to meet a trading partner of the other type against the loss of production due to excessive investment in trading time. The value used here is suggested by the simulation results. If we make the simplifying assumption that in every period every agent meets at least one agent of the other type who is willing to trade (note that in this setup every agent meets four other individuals per period for trading) we can easily calculate the corresponding expected payoff:

$$U_{tr} = 2\sqrt{\frac{a_1}{2}(1 - 2\chi)^\alpha}$$

Thus, we see that also in the run depicted in figure 2 learning was quite efficient. The utility increases quite significantly due to the trading and reaches a level of $U \approx 35.5$ compared to the maximal possible payoff of $U_{tr} = 37.8$. Part of the gap between the two values is due to the fact that individuals are not completely specialized in production, but it seems that there is also some loss of utility because of failures to trade in a period.

Comparing the values U_{pr} and U_{tr} we realize that the individuals are better off in a state with direct trade than in a pure production state if the fraction a_1/a_2 is large compared to χ. As could be expected from our considerations above the effect of an increase of $\alpha \in [0, 1)$ is ambiguous and depends on a_1, a_2 and χ. Of course we can not infer from the fact that U_{tr} is larger than U_{pr} that direct trade emerges in the population. This does only imply that trading pays off **after** it has been established in the population. But the pure production state could still be evolutionary stable. However, looking at figure 3 we see that direct trade emerges for $a_1 \geq 4$ and $U_{tr} > U_{pr}$ holds under this parameter constellation for $a_1 \geq 3.07$. So the two values are rather close here.

Finally, we also like to consider a perfectly organized state where mediation has already been established and compute the agents' payoff. These findings will be compared to the outcomes of our learning process where mediation did emerge exemplified by the run depicted in figure 4.

We assume that a fraction r of the agents mediate, which means that they use the strategy $x_1 = x_2 = 0, s = 1$. The number of type I and type II agents among the mediators is equal. The rest of type I agents use $x_1 = 1, x_2 = s = 0$ and the rest of type II agents have $x_2 = 1, x_1 = s = 0$. The number of producers a trader can deal with is constrained by the fact that each producer exchanges goods only with one trader per period and the time constraint. Denote by $\mu = \min\left[\frac{r}{1-r}, \frac{2r}{\chi(1+r)}\right]$ the expected number of trading partners per trader. For the sake of simplicity let us assume that exactly half of these partners are of type I and half of them are of type II. Let us further assume that the trader buys good 1 at a price of p and sells it at a price of $\frac{1}{p}$ (such a behavior is optimal due to symmetry) and that he can always deliver the quantity of goods he likes to trade. Given these simplifying assumptions it is easy to see that the income per period of a trader is given by

$$U_{med} = 2b\sqrt{\frac{\mu a_1 p}{2(1+p)}}(1-p).$$

In order to optimize this expression the trader should choose $p = \sqrt{2} - 1$ which gives him a utility of

$$U_{med} = \sqrt{2}(\sqrt{2}-1)b\sqrt{\mu a_1}.$$

Accordingly, an amount of $y = \frac{a_1(\sqrt{2}-1)}{\sqrt{2}}$ of good 1 or good 2 respectively is exchanged in any encounter between a producer and a trader. Since the probability that a producer meets a trader is given by $\frac{1-r}{r}\mu$ the utility of the expected income of a producer per period reads

$$U_{pr} = b\sqrt{a_1}\left[1 - \frac{\mu(1-r)}{r} + \mu\frac{1-r}{r}\sqrt{\frac{1}{1+p}} + \mu\frac{1-r}{r}\sqrt{\frac{p^2}{1+p}}\right]$$

$$= b\sqrt{a_1}\left[1 - \frac{\mu(1-r)}{r} + \mu\sqrt[4]{2}\frac{1-r}{r}\right].$$

Because it is not costly to change from production to mediation and vice versa the long run utility of traders and producers should be equal. Under the assumption that the time constraint is not binding for the traders (i.e. $\mu = \frac{r}{1-r}$) this yields the equation

$$\sqrt{2}(\sqrt{2}-1)\sqrt{\frac{r}{1-r}} = \sqrt[4]{2}.$$

The unique solution is

$$r = \frac{1}{3(\sqrt{2}-1)} = 0.8047.$$

For $\chi < 0.2164$ we have $\mu = \frac{r}{1-r}$. The utility in this state is given by

$$U_{med} = U_{pr} = \sqrt[4]{2}b\sqrt{a_1}.$$

These considerations show that in a perfectly organized population with mediated trade there should be about 20% mediators in the population if a heterogeneous state consisting of producers and mediators emerges. In such a case the expected payoff of producers and mediators would be equal given that the mediators choose an optimal price and the producers indeed use all their time for production.

Comparing these findings with the simulation result shown in figure 4 we realize how well the self organization has worked here. We have indeed about 20 mediators and average utility per period is only slightly smaller than $U_{med} = 33.6$. We now also see that the fact that direct trading as shown in figure 5 leads to a larger long run average utility than mediated trade for this parameter constellation is no accident. Even if mediation is established in the economy in its most efficient way the average utility could still be improved if the population would go back to direct trading. Of course this crucially depends on the parameter values, and in particular does not hold any more if the trading costs χ or the parameter α increase[6]. Thus, it is very interesting to observe that in almost half of our simulation runs with these parameter values mediated trade did emerge. A possible explanation is a 'lock-in' effect. For the first individuals who start mediating in a population of producers who invest also some time in trading the profit of mediation is rather large because the number of individuals they can trade with is only bounded by the time constraint but there is no competition with other mediators. Thus, initially mediation yields large payoffs and accordingly more agents start mediating. However, if producers do not have to look for trading partners they do invest less time in trading. At the same time payoffs of mediators go down because the ratio of producers to mediators decreases. This leads to smaller average utility values than before mediation was initiated, however there is no way back because an agent who likes to start direct trading now is very unlikely to find a trading partner who both produces and invests time in trading. This effect can be seen quite nicely in figure 4 where we have direct trade up to period 1500 and mediation gets established afterwards causing a slight decrease in average utility. Obviously, this lock-in takes place in some of the cases but not in all of them. Thus, it is almost impossible to predict in such a setting whether in the long run mediated trade will be present in the economy or not.

5   Conclusions

In this paper we use an agent based learning model to study the emergence of trade in a production economy. We distinguish between two different kinds of trade, direct trade and mediated trade, and study their emergence in a setup with two types of agents who are distinguished by their production functions. Our learning rule does not involve any foresight whatsoever but only imitation based on past performance coupled with random innovations. Loosely speaking, in this framework a shop has to be profitable right from the start in order to survive.

Depending on the parameter constellations considered we could observe three qualitatively different long run outcomes of the simulation: a pure production state, a state with mediated trade and a state where all exchange is performed via middlemen. Whereas we never encountered the coexistence of significant direct and mediated trade we observed that mediation emerged

---

[6] See Dawid (1999b).

out of a state where direct trade has already been developed. The fact that the long run behavior may look qualitatively different for different runs even if the model and the parameters keep the same stresses the importance an approach where the dynamic process of self organization is explicitly modelled. However, it also suggests that a refined description of the individuals learning behavior may allow additional insights. Also, it should be investigated in how far the results obtained here change in the framework of a multi-good economy or in a spatial model with local interaction. We plan to tackle these questions in future research.

References

Arifovic, J., 1996, The Behavior of the Exchange Rate in the Genetic Algorithm and Experimental Economies, Journal of Political Economy, 104, 510-541.

Björnerstedt, J. and J. Weibull, 1996, Nash equilibrium and evolution by imitation, in: K. Arrow et al., eds., The Rational Foundations of Economic Behavior (Macmillan, London).

Dawid, H., 1999a, Adaptive Learning by Genetic Algorithms: Analytical Results and Applications to Economic Models (Springer, Heidelberg).

Dawid, H., 1999b, The Emergence of Exchange and Mediation in a Production Economy, to be published in *Journal of Economic Behavior and Organization*.

Day, R., 1994, Complex Economic Dynamics, Volume I: An Introduction to Dynamical Systems and Market Mechanisms (MIT Press, Cambridge, MA).

Helpman, E. and P.R. Krugman, 1985, Market Structure and Foreign Trade (MIT Press, Cambridge, MA.).

Hofbauer J. and K. Sigmund, 1998, Evolutionary Games and Population Dynamics (Cambridge University Press, Cambridge).

Jones, R.A., 1976, The Origin and Development of Media of Exchange, Journal of Political Economy, 84, 757-775.

Krugman, P.R., 1981, Intraindustry Specialization and Gains from Trade, Journal of Political Economy, 89, 5, 959-974.

Marimon, R., McGrattan, E. and T. Sargent, 1990, Money as a Medium of Exchange in an Economy with Artificially Intelligent Agents, Journal of Economic Dynamics and Control, 14, 329-373.

Pingle, M., 1995, Imitation versus Rationality: An Experimental Perspective on Decision Making, Journal of Socio-Economics, 24, 281-315.

Pingle, M., 1997, The Endogenous Formation of Market Making Intermediaries: An Experiment, Working Paper, University of Nevada.

Routledge, B.R., 1995, Artificial Selection: Genetic Algorithm and Learning in a Rational Expectations Model, manuscript, University of British Columbia, Vancouver.

Rubinstein, A. and A. Wolinsky, 1987, Middlemen, Quarterly Journal of Economics, CII, 581-593.

Schlag, K., 1998, Why imitate, and, if so, how? A Bounded Rational Approach to Multi-Armed Bandits, to be published in Journal of Economic Theory.

Taylor, P.D. and L.B. Jonker, 1978, Evolutionary Stable Strategies and Game Dynamics, Mathematical Biosciences, 40, 145-156.

Tesfatsion, L., 1997, A Trade Network Game with Endogeneous Partner Selection, in Amman, H., Rustem, B. and Whinston, A.B. (Eds.), *Computational Approaches to Economic Problems*, pp. 249-269, Kluwer.

Vega-Redondo, F., 1995, Expectations, Drift, and Volatility in Evolutionary Games, Games and Economic Behavior, 11, 391-412.

Vriend, N.J. (1995), Self-Organization of Markets: An Example of a Computational Approach, *Computational Economics*, 8, 205-231.

Learning to Be Loyal. A Study of the Marseille Fish Market*

Alan P. Kirman[1] and Nicolaas J. Vriend[2]

[1] E.H.E.S.S., GREQAM, Marseille, France

[2] Queen Mary and Westfield College, University of London, Dept. Economics, Mile End Road, London E1 4NS, UK, <n.vriend@qmw.ac.uk>, http://www.qmw.ac.uk/~ugte173/.

Abstract. We study the wholesale fish market in Marseille. Two of the stylized facts of that market are high loyalty of buyers to sellers, and persistent price dispersion, although the same population of sellers and buyers meets in the same market hall on every day. We build a minimal model of adaptive agents. Sellers decide on quantities to supply, prices to ask, and how to treat loyal customers. Buyers decide which seller to visit, and which prices to accept. Learning takes place through reinforcement. We analyze the emergence of both stylized facts price dispersion and high loyalty. In a coevolutionary process, buyers learn to become loyal as sellers learn to offer higher utility to loyal buyers, while these sellers, in turn, learn to offer higher utility to loyal buyers as they happen to realize higher gross revenues from loyal buyers.

JEL classification: C7, D4, D8, L0, L1, L7

Keywords: Market structure, price dispersion, loyalty, adaptive behavior, coevolution

---

* An earlier version was first presented at the Economic ALife workshop at the Santa Fe Institute, May 1995, and subsequently circulated in several variants. We thank seminar and workshop participants at the Santa Fe Institute, the European University Institute, VPI&SU, UC-Los Angeles, UC-Irvine, and the Universities of Trento, Southern California, George Mason, Pompeu Fabra, London (QMW), Keele, and Ancona, participants at conferences of the SEDC in Barcelona, SCE in Geneva and Cambridge, ESEM and EEA in Istanbul, ASSET in Alicante and Marseille, and IIFET in Tromsø, and Antonio Cabrales, Art De Vany, and Johan Stennek for helpful comments and discussions. All errors and responsibilities are ours. Financial support through TMR grant ERBFMBICT950277 (NJV) from the Commission of the European Community, Brussels is also gratefully acknowledged.

1. Introduction

In this project we study the working of the wholesale fish market in Marseille (France). There are two reasons to study this specific market. First, we have a unique data set containing the records for all single transactions that have taken place in this fish market over a number of years. Rich as such a data set is, this is at the same time one of its limitations, as there are, for example, no data for transactions that did not take place. Second, this wholesale fish market is a relatively simple market. It is well-defined, and well-structured, compared with, for example, a market economy as such, or with a market like the one for second-hand cars. Also, fish is a perishable commodity, implying that there are no inventories carried over (cf. the early literature on market microstructures in finance).

Our real interest as economists is not in fish markets *per se*. But we do believe that some of the insights developed in this study of the fish market might be carried over to other real markets. In particular we believe that if we want to understand the dynamics of interactive market processes, and the emergent properties of the evolving market structures and outcomes, it might pay to analyze explicitly how agents interact with each other, how information spreads through the market, and how adjustments in disequilibrium take place.

In section 2 we will sketch the real fish market, and present two not easily explained stylized facts.[1] In section 3 we present a minimal model with interacting agents. Section 4 reports on some results, and section 5 concludes.

2. The Real Fish Market

The market is open every day from 2am to 6am. The real market has a fixed population of about registered 40 sellers. They buy their supply outside the market before the market opens. There is also a fixed population of buyers; about 400. These buyers are retail sellers or restaurant owners. During the market day, they shop around, visiting individual sellers. Standing face-to-face with a seller, the buyer tells the seller which type of fish and which quantity he is interested in. The seller then informs him about the price. Prices are not posted. And they are individual in a threefold sense. First, each individual seller decides upon his own prices. Second, each seller may have different prices for different buyers. Third, each seller may even ask a different price for a given type and quantity of fish if that is proposed by the same buyer at different times of the day. A price communicated by an individual seller to an individual buyer for a given

---

[1] For another recent paper about a fish market (Fulton), which has a structure similar to the Marseille market, see Graddy [1995].

transaction is not perceived by other buyers or sellers in the market. The prices are take-it-or-leave-it, and there is no bargaining. At the end of the day, unsold fish is thrown away, or sold to the European Union at bottom prices. It is forbidden to sell old fish.[2]

The most remarkable stylized facts of the real market are the following. First, there is a widespread high loyalty of buyers to sellers. Second, there is persistent price dispersion. Further documentation of these stylized facts can be found in Kirman & Vignes [1991], Kirman & McCarthy [1990], Vignes [1993], Härdle & Kirman [1995], and Weisbuch et al. [1996]. Since the same population of sellers and buyers is present every day in the same market hall, at first glance these stylized facts may seem somewhat puzzling. Of course, standard economic reasoning can explain these facts. If these agents behave in this way, they must have good reasons to do so, and the task for the theorist is simply to uncover these reasons. In the remainder of this paper, we will not focus on the empirical details concerning this fish market, but instead on the modeling approach we have chosen to explain the mentioned stylized facts.

For various reasons this turns out to be far from simple. As we will show now, some simple standard arguments do not have much explanatory power. Either they do not apply to this specific market, or they leave open too many possibilities. First, the stylized facts might seem to be related to the quality of the fish. It could be that the price dispersion simply correlates with quality differences of the fish. However, the classification scheme used to distinguish types of fish uses several quality measures. Clearly, there will be some residual quality differences within each type, but the price dispersion observed within each type seems excessive, e.g., when compared with the price dispersion between different types of fish.

Next, the effect of quality differences could seem to be related to the loyalty in case there would be an information asymmetry. Before discussing the contents of the information asymmetry argument, we would like to question whether an information asymmetry would be likely in this market. All buyers are professional traders themselves; retailers or restaurant owners. In any case, even if there were an information asymmetry concerning the quality of the fish, it is not clear what its effect would be. The standard textbook argument would run as follows. If the quality of the fish is not detectable ex ante for the buyers, then a seller has an incentive to deliver good quality with respect to repeat buyers, as an investment in his reputation. That is, the information asymmetry would explain the existence of loyalty of buyers to specific sellers. This seems a too loose application of the textbook argument. Notice that we have a fixed population of buyers in the Marseille fish market. That is, every buyer (loyal or not) is a potential repeat buyer; unlike the standard textbook example of tourists. Hence, a seller would have an incentive to deliver good quality to every single buyer. Clearly, a seller cannot offer higher quality to all buyers. A last attempt to save the causal link

---

[2] This is a simplification since some species can be offered for sale on the succeeding day. Buyers are however capable of recognizing the freshness of the fish.

between quality differences and loyalty would be to argue that non-loyal buyers are intrinsically non-loyal anyway, and that therefore there is no incentive to offer them good quality. But exactly the same argument would tell you that loyal buyers are intrinsically loyal anyway, and that therefore there would be no incentive to deliver them good quality. Hence, with respect to quality differences we must conclude that they may exist, but they are not observable in data, and it is unclear what they could explain, besides a minimal amount of price dispersion.

A second ready-to-use explanation economic theory might seem to offer for the stylized facts is the theory of implicit contracts. Because of the uncertainty related to variation in the daily supply to the fish market, the agents stipulate implicit contracts specifying the loyalty of buyers to specific sellers. This might well be, but the story cannot be that simple. First, on this fish market there are also variations in the daily demand. Given the variation in the daily supply, one might expect that buyers and sellers agree upon an implicit contract in which prices are somewhat higher than otherwise, while the supply to these buyers is guaranteed. With the variation of the demand one might expect an implicit contract in which prices are lower, while the demand to the seller is guaranteed (cf., newspaper subscriptions). With variation on both sides it is not clear what form the implicit contract should take. But also with variation on the supply side only, the form of the implicit contract is not obvious a priori. One contract might be the one mentioned above; with higher prices and better service to the buyers agreeing upon such a contract. Note that there is a trade-off between the price to be paid by those buyers and the service they get. This implies that those buyers might be equally well off under an implicit contract that gives them lower prices and worse service. In other words, there might exist an implicit contract specifying a long-term relationship between a buyer and a seller, in which the buyer is *not* served more frequently than buyers without such a contract. Many examples of explicit contracts of this type exist; for example in the natural gas market, or the market of power supply. In the cases in which such a buyer is not served, he will be forced to visit other sellers. Hence, in the transaction data such a seller might appear as one of the non-loyal buyers, even when there is this long-term relationship characterized by bad service. Hence, it might well be that there exist implicit contracts in the wholesale fish market in Marseille, but, besides the standard problems that it is not clear who should design the contracts and how they should be enforced, in our case the problem is that they might come in many forms, and it is difficult or impossible to indicate some of them in the transaction data. To the extent that implicit contracts might come in many forms, this might explain the existence of price dispersion. The problem, however, is that it leaves open many possibilities. Just as in some static models on price dispersion (Futia [1977], or Burdett & Judd [1983]), there might be multiple equilibria, and it is not clear whether the stable equilibria are characterized by price dispersion. Hopkins [1995] presents a dynamic analysis of such models.

A third standard argument is that it is known that in markets where suppliers first decide on their supply, and then enter a Bertrand game with given fixed stocks, there need not exist a pure-strategy Nash equilibrium, whereas a mixed-strategy Nash equilibrium exists in general (see Stahl [1988], and the references therein). This might explain some of the price dispersion. Although, given that in our market there is price dispersion for a given seller even within one day, this means that we must imagine such a seller flipping coins for every single price asked. Moreover, it leaves open the issue of loyalty.

A more sophisticated approach than these simple arguments would be to design a multi-stage game with an equilibrium characterized by the stylized facts just mentioned. But designing and analyzing such a game is complicated. Moreover, it is easy to imagine such a game will have multiple equilibria; and not only because of the equilibria being asymmetric. Here is a very rudimentary example of the kind of games one could construct. Suppose there are two sellers, and two buyers. A seller's strategy S is a price proposed to buyer 1, and a price proposed to buyer 2. A buyer's strategy S is simply the choice of a seller to visit. Suppose that for both seller 1 and seller 2 we have S=(a, b). And suppose for buyer 1 we have S=(seller 1), and for buyer 2 we have S=(seller 2). Now suppose, a≠b, then we have a Nash equilibrium for the one-period game with loyalty and price dispersion. As we see immediately, many such equilibria may exist. Therefore, what we will do instead is something very simple. We will build a minimal model of an artificial fish market with adaptive agents. Besides being simple, an advantage of this approach is that the evolutionary outcomes of this model might offer some insights as to which of the possible equilibria of a corresponding multi-stage game might be more likely to occur.

With respect to quality, we will focus on one observable quality aspect, the seller's service rate, and analyze its role in the market. With respect to implicit contracts, we will keep these really *implicit*. That is, keeping aggregate demand and supply constant (although individual supply and demand faced may vary), we will analyze whether long lasting trading relationships do emerge in the artificial market, and we will analyze their characteristics. And with respect to the possibility of a mixed-strategy Nash equilibrium, we will not study how introspection may lead to equilibria, but we will instead look for the emergence of patterns in the behavior of adaptive agents.

Our comparison of the artificial and the real world will not be characterized by a quest for a complete model of the fish market. We will not try to build a model fitting all aspects of the real world for the following reasons. First, every model is by definition an abstraction. If enough data can be collected, statistical testing will reject any model. Second, when modeling by building artificial worlds, one might get a very good fit without gaining understanding. There exist economic simulation models with more than 10,000 variables. At some point it might be that one mainly succeeds in building a copy of the real world, about which we have the same degree of understanding as about the real world. Therefore, we will only consider specific questions concerning the stylized facts of the real market that appear remarkable or important. We will try to build a minimal model that generates, and with which to test those stylized facts. This might suggest ways to understand, or not, those phenomena. This understanding is of the same type as with formal mathematical models. The question is whether we might consider the real world to be working `as if' it were like our model.

3. The Artificial Fish Market

The place of action in our minimal model is the market hall. The actors are 10, initially identical sellers, and 100, initially identical buyers. They meet in the market hall for 5000 days, for a morning and afternoon session (see below). The commodity traded is indivisible, and perishable. On each day the sequence of events is the following.

In the morning, before the market opens, the sellers buy their supply outside the market for a given price that is identical to all sellers, and constant through time ($p^{in} = 9$). The market opens, and the buyers enter the market hall. Each buyer wants 1 unit of fish per day. All buyers simultaneously choose the queue of a seller. The sellers, then, handle these queues during the morning session (see below). When all queues have been handled, the end of the morning session is reached. In the afternoon, the market re-opens. All still unsatisfied buyers choose the queue of a seller. The sellers handle these queues, after which the end of the afternoon session is reached. All unsold stocks perish. The buyers re-sell their fish outside market at a given price that is identical for all buyers, and constant through time ($p^{out} = 15$). Notice that each buyer can visit at most one seller in the morning plus one seller in the afternoon. Figures 1 and 2 give a sketch of the market.

On each day, the buyers have to make the following decisions. First, they choose a seller for the morning session. Second, they decide which prices to accept or reject during the morning session. Third, if necessary, they choose a seller for the afternoon. And fourth, they decide which prices to accept or reject during the afternoon. The sellers face four decision problems as well. First, they decide the quantity to supply. Second, they decide how to handle their queues. Third, they decide which prices to ask during the morning. And fourth, they decide which prices to ask during the afternoon.

Each single decision problem is modeled separately for each individual agent by means of a Classifier System. Considering a Classifier System as a `black box' for the moment, this implies that in our artificial fish market each single buyer, and each single seller has 4 decision boxes in his head. Hence, with 10 sellers and 100 buyers we model explicitly 440 decision boxes by separate Classifier Systems. Figure 3 presents one such stylized Classifier System.

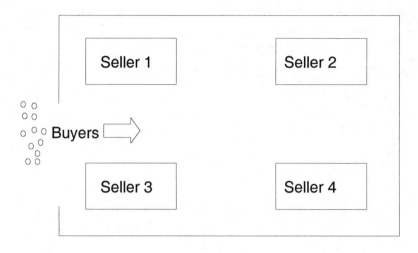

Fig. 1: The Market Hall with Buyers and Sellers

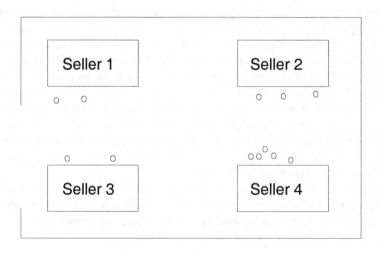

Fig. 2: Each Buyer Has Chosen a Seller

condition	action	strength
if	then	....
.. ....	....	....
.. ....	....	....

Fig. 3: A Classifier System

A Classifier System consists of a set of rules, each rule consisting of a condition `if ...'` part, and an action `then ...'` part, plus to each rule attached a measure of its strength. The Classifier System does two things. First, it decides which of the rules will be the active rule on a given day. Hence, it checks the condition part, and all rules satisfying the `if ...'` condition make a `bid' as follows: bid = strength + $\varepsilon$, where $\varepsilon$ is white noise. The rule with the highest `bid' in this `stochastic auction' wins the right to be active.[3] Second, the Classifier System updates the strength s of a rule that has been active and has generated a reward from the environment on a given day t-1 as follows: $s_t = s_{t-1} - c \cdot s_{t-1} + c \cdot reward_{t-1}$, where $0 < c < 1$. Hence, $\Delta s_t = c \cdot (reward_{t-1} - s_{t-1})$. In other words, as long as the reward generated by the rule on day t-1 is greater than its strength at t-1, its strength will increase. Hence, the strength of each rule converges to the weighted average of the rewards from the environment generated by that rule.[4] In our implementation of this model, the strengths of all rules are equal at the start.

Classifier Systems are a form of reinforcement learning. Reinforcement learning is related to multi-armed bandit problems, and is based on two principles. First, agents try actions. Second, actions that led to better outcomes in the past are

---

[3] Besides through the white noise added to the `bids', the agents experiment through some kind of `trembling hand', disregarding any `bid' with a given small probability.

[4] We presented this specific learning model in Kirman & Vriend [1995]. Sarin & Vahid [1997] analyze the theoretical properties of this model, relating it also to evolutionary explanations. And in Sarin & Vahid [1998] they show its empirical relevance by explaining the data of some laboratory experiments.

more likely to be repeated in the future. Reinforcement learning is among the most basic forms of learning, for which there exist ample support in the psychological literature (see, e.g., Bush & Mosteller [1955], or Roth & Erev [1995]). Moreover, it is a minimal form of modeling learning, in the sense that we do not need to make many assumptions about the reasoning procedures followed by the agents.

We will now specify in a more detailed way the contents of each decision box for each of the types of decisions to be made by the buyers and the sellers.

Buyers

First, the buyer must make the choice of a seller for the morning session. This is the first decision related to the question 'who is going to interact with whom?'. The rules have no condition. The actions are simply: <choose seller 1>, <choose seller 2>, ..., up to <choose seller 10>. The strength of each activated rule is updated once a day using the following payoff as reward from the external environment: payoff = max $\{p^{out} - p^{morning}, 0\}$ if a transaction takes place, and payoff = 0 if no transaction takes place during the morning session. For each seller visited the buyer keeps track of his average experienced payoff. Note that the payoff is greater or equal to zero because whichever seller he chose to visit, whatever price this seller asks him, he has always the fall-back option of rejecting the price. In other words, if a buyer accepts a price giving him a negative payoff, he should not blame the seller he chose to visit, but his decision to accept that price. No transaction takes place in case a buyer is not served, finding only empty shelves, or if he rejects a price.

Second, there is the choice of a seller for the afternoon session. This decision box is specified analogously to the one for the morning session. Note, however, that it is a separate decision box. Some sellers might be good sellers to visit in the morning, but not in the afternoon, or the other way round. Sellers that are sold out during the morning session simply close for the afternoon, and will not be visited by buyers. The strengths of the rules for the afternoon session are updated using the following payoffs: payoff = max $\{p^{out} - p^{afternoon}, 0\}$.

Third, the prices to accept or reject during the morning session. There are 21 possible prices: 0, 1, 2, ..., 20. The rules are of the form: <if p = 0 then reject>, <if p = 0 then accept>, <if p = 1 then reject>, ..., <if p = 20 then accept>. Thus we have a set of 21 x 2 = 42 price acceptance/rejection rules. For the daily update of the strengths of the rules, the following payoff from the environment is used as a reward. If the price is accepted then we have payoff = $p^{out} - p^{morning}$. Note that this payoff will be negative if $p^{morning} > p^{out}$. If the price during the morning session is rejected then the reward for that rejection depends upon what happens during the afternoon session. If during the afternoon session this buyer does not transact, then the rejection during the morning led eventually to a zero payoff. If however the rejection during the morning is followed by a transaction during the afternoon, the reward for the rejection during the morning will be determined as follows: payoff = max $\{p^{out} - p^{afternoon}, 0\}$. Analogous to the reward for the choice of a seller, this payoff is never negative as the buyer has, after a rejection during the morning, always the fall-back option of not buying during the afternoon.

Fourth, there is the choice of which prices to accept or reject during the afternoon session. This is analogous to the morning acceptance/rejection decision, but modeled separately. After the morning session, buyers can retry during the afternoon session, but after the afternoon session the trading day is over. Hence, prices that are unacceptable during the morning session might be acceptable during the afternoon. The reward for the price acceptance/rejection decision during the afternoon is determined by the following payoff: payoff $=p^{out} - p^{afternoon}$ if the price is accepted, and payoff $= 0$ if no transaction takes place, i.e., if the buyer rejects or is not served.

Some readers might wonder, if the buyers know p^{out}, they should know which prices to accept or reject during the afternoon session, and which prices are definitely unacceptable during the morning session. Hence, why do we model buyers who still have to learn this? First, this may be considered as a step towards a more general setting in which p^{out} is not given, and in which the buyers do not know the price for which they can resell outside the market. Second, if the buyers would know which prices to accept/reject, and would actually follow that knowledge, the sellers could work out which prices they should propose. Note that when a seller proposes a price to a buyer during the afternoon session, the situation resembles closely that of an ultimatum game (see, e.g., Güth & Tietz [1990]), with pie size p^{out}. Although the subgame-perfect equilibrium of that game in extensive form is offering the minimum slice size, we know that in laboratory settings many human subjects deviate from the game-theoretically `correct' actions, and that, in general, the outcomes do not converge to this equilibrium. One explanation offered in the literature (e.g., Gale et al. [1995], or Roth & Erev [1995]), is that the point of convergence depends crucially upon the relative speed of learning of the two sides. Therefore, we do not want to impose which actions the players choose. Instead, we will analyze which actions emerge as they happen to have led to better outcomes. We will come back to this point in the next section, when discussing the results.

Sellers

Now we turn to the sellers. First, they decide which quantity to supply. The rules do not have a condition, and specify simply a quantity to supply: <supply 0>, <supply 1>, ..., up to <supply 30>. The strengths are updated daily, using as a reward from the environment: payoff = net profit.

Second, the sellers have to decide how to handle the queues they face. This is an example of a decision related to the `who is going to interact with whom?' question.[5] Basically, facing a crowd of customers, the seller has to decide at any moment which potential buyer to serve. Note that we assume the queues to be

---

[5] Two other papers dealing with this issue are Stanley et al. [1993], and Vriend [1995].

`Italian' rather than `British'. Besides physically `reshuffling' queues, sellers can obtain the same result by, e.g., by putting some of their fish aside for some customers; a common practice for many shop keepers, but not one which is practised in the Marseille fish market. We assume that the buyers differ among each other, as seen by the sellers, in the sense that their faces will have a different degree of familiarity for the sellers. More specifically, this degree of familiarity of the face of buyer i to seller j on day t is indicated by a variable $L_{ij}(t)$ as follows:

$$L_{ij}(t) = \sum_{x=1}^{t} \frac{r_{ij}(t-x)}{(1+\alpha)^{t-x}} \, 1$$

with $r_{ij}(t) = \alpha = 0.25$ if buyer i visits seller j, and $r_{ij}(t) = 0$ otherwise. Hence, $0 \leq L_{ij}(t) \leq 1$. This degree of familiarity of a face of a buyer for a seller is a weighted average of the past presences of this buyer in the seller's queue; assigning more weight to recent visits. The question, then, is, should a seller serve familiar faces first, later, or should he be indifferent? Assume that a seller uses a roulette wheel to decide which buyer to serve, and that the slot size for each buyer i in the queue of seller j is equal to $(1+L_{ij})^b$. If the seller were indifferent between serving loyal or casual customers, he would use a roulette wheel with equal slot sizes for all buyers, which is achieved by setting b=0. If the seller wanted to give advantage to loyal customers, he would assign larger slot sizes to more loyal customers, which is achieved by setting b>0. Finally, disadvantage to loyal customers can be given by assigning them smaller slot sizes, setting b<0. Hence, given the degree of familiarity of the buyers' faces to a seller, the only decision variable needed by a seller to determine whether to give advantage or disadvantage to a loyal buyer, is this variable b. The decision box to decide upon the value for b looks as follows. The rules have no condition, and the action part is simply a value for b: <b = -25>, <b = -20>, ..., <b = 0>, ..., up to <b = 25>. The strengths of these rules are updated daily by using the following reward from the environment: payoff = gross revenue. Note that once the supply decision has been made, supply costs are sunk costs, and the seller's objective is to maximize gross revenue. We do not want to pretend that real sellers actually carry out such calculations, but casual empiricism suggests that sellers are able to distinguish between their customers on the basis of their degree of familiarity. If their behavior coincides with that of the agents in our model, this might suggest that they are behaving `as if' they carry out such calculations.

Once a seller has picked his next customer to be served, his third decision to make is the price to ask. As mentioned above, there are 21 possible prices: 0, 1, 2, ..., 20. The condition part of the rules takes account of the following three state variables. The loyalty of the buyer (3 classes are distinguished, `low', `middle', `high', in order to make the number of rules not too high), the remaining stock of fish, and the remaining queue. In fact, we take the ratio of these last two variables (again distinguishing three classes as above in order to limit the number of rules). This leads to the following set of 3x3x21 price rules: <if loyalty='low' and

ratio='low' then $p^{ask} = 0>$, <if loyalty='low' and ratio='low' then $p^{ask} = 1>$, ..., <if loyalty='high' and ratio='high' then $p^{ask} =20>$. The strengths of these rules are updated using as a reward from the environment: payoff = revenue obtained using that price rule, where the revenue = price if accepted, and 0 if the price is rejected.

The fourth decision for a seller is the prices to ask during the afternoon. This decision box is analogous to the one for the morning session. But again, note that this is a separate decision box, since sellers may learn that it is profitable to charge different prices in the two sessions.

The model we have sketched is a simple model, abstracting from various aspects of the real fish market. The price p^{out} is assumed to be identical for all buyers, and constant through time. The same applies to the price p^{in}. All buyers, and all sellers are always present on the market. There is only one good, which is supposed to be homogeneous. Each buyer wants one unit per day only. There is a strict division of days into morning and afternoon sessions. And buyers can make only one visit per sub-period. These are all abstractions from reality. But even with these simplifications the model is already complicated. The first question is whether, and how, this minimal model can generate the stylized facts of the real market. Note that little of the agents' actions is predetermined. We do not assume a reservation price property. There are no adjustment rules of the form: if demand>supply then p^{ask} increases. The treatment of loyal customers is not predetermined. The adaptive agents have to find out themselves what actions are good ones, and reinforcement learning simply corresponds to the economic idea that agents are seeking to do the best they can, without imposing certain reasoning procedures or heuristics.

4. Results

The results presented here are for one run only. By experimentation and `playing around' with the model we know that the results are representative, but a systematic reporting on this will be postponed till a later version of the paper.[6] Since for each period all actions of all agents are recorded, for example the buyers' decision with respect to any of the 21 prices they might face, including all

---

[6] The results are also robust in the sense that they do not seem to be very sensitive to the exact algorithm used. We have tried alternative algorithms like Genetic Algorithms, hill climbing algorithms, and annealing schedules for the sellers' decisions without observing qualitative changes in the results in any significant sense. This robustness conforms the experience reported by Roth & Erev [1995]. The reinforcement algorithm is based on the idea that actions that have led to better payoffs are more likely to be used in the future. This principle is common to many learning dynamics, like e.g., replicator dynamics and all generalizations thereof.

rejections, and all buyers that were not served, the generated data set is much richer than the one covering the real fish market.

Prices

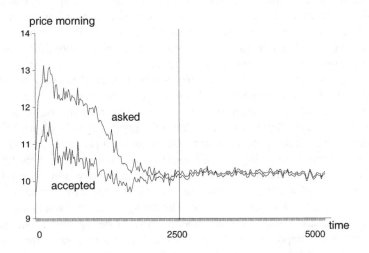

Fig. 4: Time Series Average Prices Asked and Accepted During Morning Sessions

Figure 4 presents the time series of all prices asked and all prices accepted during the morning sessions. For presentational reasons, each observation is the average of 20 days. Note, first, that the series start around 10, the average of the range of possible prices. Second, the prices asked increase faster than the prices accepted. Third, at some point, the latter starts `pulling' down the prices asked. Fourth, prices accepted, then, decrease too much, and at some points are `pulled' up again. Fifth, in the second half of the history there is almost perfect convergence of prices asked and prices accepted. Sixth, average prices are stable at a level of 10.2 during that period. A regression of prices asked in that half against time, gives a coefficient of -0.00001 that is statistically significant, but practically irrelevant (implying a price decrease of only 0.1 over a period of 10,000 days). These qualitative and quantitative features are representative for replications of the simulation.

Why do we not get a convergence of prices asked and prices accepted at a price equal to 14? That is at a price equal to $p^{out}-1$. As mentioned in the previous section, during the afternoon, when a buyer faces a seller, the situation resembles closely that of an ultimatum game. The subgame-perfect equilibrium of that game in extensive form is proposing the minimum slice size of the given pie to the receiver. That is, $p^{afternoon}=p^{out}-1$. Backward induction, then, leads to $p^{morning}=p^{afternoon}=p^{out}-1$. A difference with the ultimatum game is that the interactions between the buyers and sellers are repeated. However, it is not simply a repeated ultimatum game, because the repetition is not enforced; both sellers and buyers can refuse to play the game again with each other. Hence, the effect of repetition is much weaker than in a standard repeated game.

Observe, in figure 4, that the sellers do try to drive the prices up towards this level of 14. But before the buyers learn to accept those prices, the sellers learn not to try them anymore, because they get rejected too often. This conforms to experience with the ultimatum game. Even with perfect information, there is in general no convergence to the subgame-perfect equilibrium; not in a laboratory setting with human subjects, and not in simulations with artificial players (see, e.g., Gale et al. [1995] with replicator dynamics, or Roth & Erev [1995] with reinforcement learning). As mentioned above, an explanation for this result is that the point of convergence depends crucially upon the relative speed of learning of the two sides. Hence, as far as the modeling of the individual players is concerned, there are two extreme possibilities. First, impose on all agents to play right from the start the game-theoretically `correct' actions, although this would be at odds with much real world evidence. Second, do not tell the agents anything about which prices are good to ask, accept, or reject, let the agents learn about this all by themselves, and analyze which actions emerge. Any modeling option between these extremes would impose some of the agents' actions, taking away some of the emergent character of the actions, and breaking the symmetry between buyers and sellers, or between the morning and afternoon sessions. Clearly, if we had imposed on the buyers or sellers which prices to propose, accept, or reject, the emergent price patterns would have been very different.

Notice that a simple demand and supply analysis would have predicted a very different price than the game-theoretic analysis. Market supply is perfectly elastic at $p^{in}=9$, whereas market demand is perfectly inelastic up to $p^{out}=15$, leading to a market clearing equilibrium at $p=9$.

For the afternoon, we get a similar graph for the prices, but as we see in figure 5 with some differences. There is slightly more convergence of prices asked and prices accepted. Almost no price is ever rejected during the afternoon. This convergence occurs at a stable, but somewhat higher price level than in the morning sessions; 11.2 against 10.2.[7] This is in agreement with the real data.[8] The precise pattern during the first half of the 5000 days is somewhat different from the morning sessions.

---

[7] A regression of prices asked in that half against time, gives a coefficient of 0.00007 that is statistically significant (implying a price increase of only 0.7 over a period of 10,000 days).

[8] In the real fish market there is some falling off at the very end of the day when there are mainly transaction of very small sizes. Notice that in our model all transaction have a unit size.

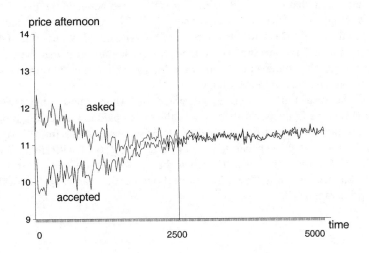

Fig. 5: Time Series Average Prices Asked and Accepted During Afternoon Sessions

Some readers might wonder, if prices are higher in the afternoon than in the morning, then buyers must be boundedly rational in an extreme way. But that would be a wrong observation. Suppose that there is exactly the same distribution of prices *asked* in the morning and in the afternoon, and suppose that those buyers that encounter prices in the upper tail of the distribution reject in the morning. The result will be that the average price *paid* in the morning will be lower than the average price *paid* in the afternoon. And it is only these prices actually *paid* that are available in the real market data. Now, suppose that we shift the morning price distribution somewhat to the left. The same argument used above implies that we could even have that the average price *asked* in the morning is smaller than the average price *asked* in the afternoon; and that with rational agents. The point is that it is not the average price that gets rejected. A sharper observation would seem that if we look at the simulation data, and if buyers are rational, then one should get that the average price *rejected* in the morning should be higher than the average price *asked* in the afternoon (neglecting for the moment the possibility of arriving 'too late'). But even that observation turns out to be incorrect; and that although our agents are so rational that the reinforcement of their acceptance/rejection rules in the morning are as follows: reinforcement accept(price) = payoff morning, and reinforcement reject(price) = payoff afternoon. How is this, then, possible? Suppose that the distribution of prices asked by the sellers adapts to the acceptance behavior of the buyers. The result will be that prices in the morning that are usually rejected will almost never be asked, and the prices asked in the morning will usually be accepted. But the buyers experiment every now and then. Sometimes they reject a low price, although they know that on average accepting it had been better in the past. This brings the average price rejected in the morning down.[9] Note that experimentation is not irrational. Its payoff is partly in the form of information. But the result of the adaptation by the sellers, plus the experimentation by the buyers is that there is a bias which means that the average price *rejected* in the morning may be lower than the average price *asked* in the afternoon.

What is the distribution of prices generated underlying these time series? Figure 6 presents the frequency distribution of the prices paid in the market during the last 2500 days of the artificial fish market. As we see, prices from 9 to 12 occur with frequencies greater than 8%, and prices from 9 to 11 with frequencies greater than 18%. Given the price for which the sellers buy outside the market ($p^{in}=9$), and the price for which the buyers resell outside the market ($p^{out}=15$), the 'effective' price range is 7.

Loyalty

The second stylized fact of the real fish market was the high loyalty of buyers to sellers. In the previous section we presented a measure of the loyalty of a given buyer i to a given seller j: $0 \leq L_{ij}(t) \leq 1$. Hence, for every buyer i, we can construct the following loyalty index: $\Sigma_{\text{seller } j} L_{ij}(t)^2 / \{\Sigma_{\text{seller } j} L_{ij}(t)\}^2$. This loyalty index will have a value equal to 1 if the buyer is perfectly loyal to one seller, and would have a value equal to 1/(number of sellers) if the buyer has 'avoiding' behavior, visiting all sellers in a fixed sequence, and if there were no greater weight put on more recent visits.[10]

In figure 7 we present the time series for the morning sessions of this measure of loyalty averaged over all buyers, and the same series plus or minus two times the standard deviation. Each observation is the average of 20 days. We observe that loyalty does develop, but slowly, and with some variance over the buyers.

---

[9] If buyers would sometimes accept a high price in the morning although they know that rejecting it had been better in the past, this will not influence the comparison given above.

[10] Because of the discounting, the distribution of Lij(t) will not be uniform, but skewed, leading to a loyalty index of 0.14 in case of 'avoiding' behavior.

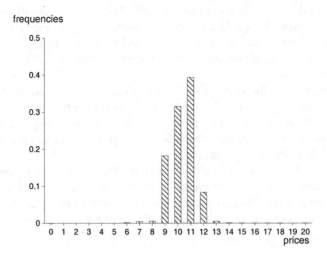

Fig. 6: Price Distribution Last 2500 Days

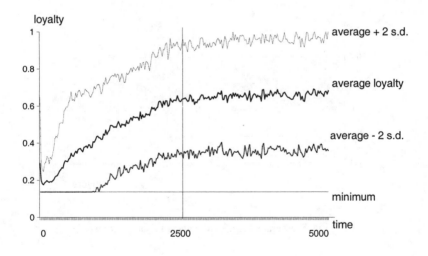

Fig. 7: Time Series Average Loyalty During Morning Sessions

The buyers do not know the concept of `loyalty'. They simply choose a seller during every morning session. We did not impose assumptions which would favor the emergence of loyalty. For example, we could have imposed a `forgetting' mechanism; reducing the strength of the rule to visit a given seller with a fixed fraction every day that rule has not been chosen. Then, sellers not visited for some time will automatically gradually fade out from the buyers menu of potential sellers to be visited. Another assumption would have been to apply a so-called annealing schedule; gradually diminishing the noise added to the 'bids' by which sellers were chosen.

The sellers know the concept of 'loyalty'. They recognize which faces they have seen more often than others recently. But they are indifferent towards loyalty at the start. That is, they have no initial bias towards giving advantage or disadvantage to loyal customers in their queue, and no bias towards higher or lower prices to charge to loyal buyers.

Hence, the first question to ask is, why do buyers learn to become loyal? Figure 8 presents for all 100 buyers the difference in payoff they experience, averaged over the last 2500 mornings, when returning to the same seller as the previous morning, or when switching to a different seller.

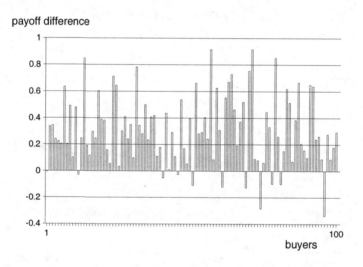

Fig. 8: Average Payoff Advantage Loyal Customers

As we see, 90% of the buyers experience a higher payoff when sticking to their seller than when switching, where the payoff to a buyer depends upon the prices proposed to them and the service rate he gets.[11] Hence, we observe that visiting a seller where a buyer is loyal is simply more reinforced than visiting a different seller.

The next question is, why do sellers offer a higher payoff to loyal buyers than to other buyers? At the start, sellers were indifferent in this respect. Figure 9 presents for all 10 sellers the difference in payoff they experience, averaged over the past 2500 mornings, when dealing with a loyal customer or when dealing with a newcomer.

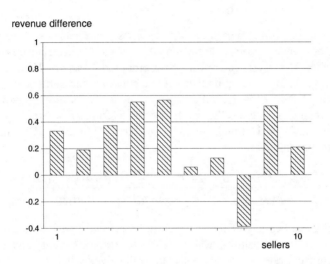

Fig. 9: Average Payoff Advantage Sellers Dealing with Loyal Customers

As we see, all but one sellers realize higher gross revenues when dealing with loyal buyers, where revenue depends upon the prices accepted and the rejection rate. Hence, offering a higher payoff to loyal customers makes sense.

In some sense what emerges here is remarkable. Both buyers and sellers are better off in loyal trading relationships. How is this possible? Note that this is not a constant-sum game. *If* two traders have decided to make a transaction then the determination of the price is a constant-sum game; given the pie size of $p^{out}=15$. The payoff for a buyer is $p^{out}-p^{accepted}$, whereas the payoff for a seller is $p^{accepted}$.

---

[11] Note that we made a simplification here. Loyalty is not a binary variable determined exclusively by the buyer's last visit, but a real-valued index between 0 and 1. It is a convenient approximation to present the results this way.

Hence, if, for a given the number of transactions, loyal buyers are better off on average than non-loyal buyers, then sellers dealing with loyal buyers are necessarily worse off on average. This is confirmed in table 1.

	Buyers	sellers	sum
Loyal	4.83	10.17	15.00
Switching	4.81	10.19	15.00

Table 1 Average Payoff per Transaction for Buyers and Sellers

But this is not the correct measure. In some cases a buyer chooses a seller, or a seller chooses a buyer with no transaction taking place. Sellers can sell out before serving a buyer, and buyers can refuse prices proposed by sellers. Hence, the game of choosing a potential trading partner is not a constant-sum game; the number of pies to be divided depends upon the players' actions. The average payoff offered to a buyer when choosing a seller can be written as follows, where the last factor on the right-hand side is simply the average service rate offered by the sellers chosen by the given buyer:

$$\frac{\Sigma(\, p^{out} - p^{ask}\,)}{\#\,visits} = \frac{\Sigma(\, p^{out} - p^{ask}\,)}{\#\,proposals} \cdot \frac{\#\,proposals}{\#\,visits}$$

Similarly, the average payoff for seller when proposing a price to a buyer in his queue can be written as follows, where the last factor on the right-hand side is the average acceptance rate of the buyers served by the given seller:

$$\frac{\Sigma(\, p^{accepted}\,)}{\#\,proposals} = \frac{\Sigma(\, p^{accepted}\,)}{\#\,transactions} \cdot \frac{\#\,transactions}{\#\,proposals}$$

Notice that a high service rate benefits the buyers without directly hurting the sellers, whereas a high acceptance rate benefits the sellers without directly hurting the buyers. Table 2 gives the average outcomes for the last 2500 mornings for the buyers, and for the sellers, distinguishing loyal and non-loyal interactions. As we see, loyal buyers tend to have a higher acceptance rate, and get a higher service rate than non-loyal buyers. In other words, the total surplus that can be realized is greater with loyal trading relationships, and therefore both sides can be better off through loyalty.

Thus, the important factor of the model is that both sides are learning about a situation which is changing precisely because their counterparts are also learning.

There have been few studies in which analytic results are obtained for such situations, although the reinforcement learning models used in game theory have this feature (see Roth & Erev [1995] for a discussion). Figure 10 presents the coevolutionary process, graphing the simultaneous emergence of the payoff advantage from loyal trading relationships to both buyers and sellers, and the emergence of this loyalty itself.

	#proposals/#visits (service rate)	#transactions/#proposals (acceptance rate)
Loyal	0.83	0.86
Switching	0.79	0.83

Table 2 Average Service and Acceptance Rates for Two Types of Buyers

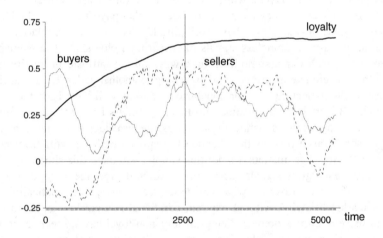

Fig. 10: Coevolution: Emergence Payoff Advantages of Loyalty to Buyers and Sellers, and Loyalty

Each observation is again the average of 20 mornings, and we smoothed the series by taking 25 period moving averages. Note, first, in the beginning sellers get a lower payoff from loyal customers than from new customers. Second, simultaneously, the payoff advantage to loyal buyers collapses. Third, only when a payoff advantage to sellers dealing with loyal customers emerges does the payoff advantage to loyal customers start to rise again. Fourth, in the meantime, loyal buyers had always experienced a positive payoff difference, and loyalty emerged.

Fifth, during the main part of the simulated history, the advantage of loyal relationships is positive to both buyers and sellers, and loyalty develops at a steady level around 0.66. Sixth, at the end, the advantage of loyalty to buyers and sellers collapses simultaneously, and re-emerges, whereas loyalty itself remains constant. Hence, one of the questions to be analyzed will be, what happens in the longer run with the variables in figure 9. For example, it might be that the actual advantage of loyalty to both sellers and buyers vanishes, but that loyalty itself continues simply because the buyers are locked in in their loyal shopping behavior.

5. Concluding Remarks

In our minimal model of the fish market both stylized facts price dispersion and loyalty do emerge during a coevolutionary process, in which both sides adapt to their changing environment. Buyers learn to become loyal, as sellers learn to offer a higher payoff to loyal buyers, while these sellers, in turn, learn to offer a higher payoff to loyal buyers, as they happen to realize a higher payoff from loyal buyers.

In some sense, this suggests that developing loyalty has some similarity with sending intrinsically meaningless signals like wearing a blue shirt. The similarity lies herein that with our assumptions there was nothing intrinsic in loyalty that makes it pay. There are no real costs of switching to another seller. Hence, at first sight one might conjecture that our conclusion could as well have been the other way round: `Buyers learn to become non-loyal, as sellers learn to offer a higher payoff to non-loyal buyers, while these sellers, in turn, learn to offer a higher payoff to non-loyal buyers, as they happen to realize a higher payoff from non-loyal buyers'. However, matters are not this simple. Although this similarity with intrinsically meaningless signals seems true to some degree, there are also some important differences. Loyalty, whatever its degree, develops automatically as a result of market behavior, without explicit, additional non-market decisions like the color of your shirt. Moreover, being loyal or non-loyal has a direct economic meaning. Suppose, for example, that there appears to be serial correlation in a seller's decisions, and that a buyer is satisfied with that seller. Loyalty would pay to that buyer, but continuing to dress blue while shopping around randomly would not. Or suppose that a seller offers a bad service. One of his buyers becoming non-loyal would hurt, but that buyer merely changing the color of his shirt would not. The basic problem here is one of coordination. Loyalty means continuity, and allows buyers and sellers to avoid unproductive meetings.

We have shown how an explicit consideration of market interactions between the individual agents may lead to the explanation of stylized facts that were not easily explained by standard arguments neglecting this interaction. Already with this minimal model, starting with a population of identical buyers and identical sellers, the behavior displayed by the agents is rather rich, and much more has to be analyzed; for example, the exact pricing behavior of the sellers. Also, a cursory examination of the data shows the emergence of heterogeneity among buyers and among sellers, i.e., of `types' of agents, and relationships between `types' of agents. For example, many sellers realize most of their sales in the morning, but some become typical afternoon sellers. And it appears that both types of implicit contracts do emerge. Some sellers offer their loyal customers good service with higher prices, whereas at the same time some other sellers combine lower prices with bad service for their loyal customers.

References

Burdett, K., & Judd, K. (1983). Equilibrium Price Dispersion. *Econometrica*, *51*, 955-969.

Bush, R.R., & Mosteller, F. (1955). *Stochastic Models for Learning*. New York: Wiley.

Futia, C.A. (1977). Excess Supply Equilibria. *Journal of Economic Theory*, *14*, 200-220.

Gale, J., Binmore, K., & Samuelson, L. (1995). Learning to Be Imperfect: The Ultimatum Game. *Games and Economic Behavior*, *8*, 56-90.

Graddy, K. (1995). Testing for Imperfect Competition at the Fulton Fish Market. *Rand Journal of Economics*, *26*, 75-92.

Güth, W., & Tietz, R. (1990). Ultimatum Bargaining Behavior: A Survey and Comparison of Experimental Results. *Journal of Economic Psychology*, *11*, 417-440.

Härdle, W., & Kirman, A.P. (1995). Nonclassical Demand: A Model-Free Examination of Price-Quantity Relations in the Marseille Fish Market. *Journal of Econometrics*, *67*, 227-257.

Hopkins, E. (1995). *Price Dispersion: an Evolutionary Approach* (mimeo).

Kirman, A.P., & McCarthy, M. (1990). *Equilibrium Prices and Market Structure: The Marseille Fish Market*.

Kirman, A.P., & Vignes, A. (1991). Price-Dispersion: Theoretical Considerations and Empirical Evidence from the Marseille Fish Market. In K.J. Arrow (Ed.), *Issues in Contemporary Economics: Proceedings of the Ninth World Congress of the International Economics Association, Athens, Greece*. (Vol. 1. Markets and Welfare, pp. 160-185). London: MacMillan.

Kirman, A.P., & Vriend, N.J. (1995). *Evolving Market Structure: A Model of Price Dispersion and Loyalty* (mimeo) Paper presented at the Workshop Economic ALife, Santa Fe Institute.

Roth, A.E., & Erev, I. (1995). Learning in Extensive-Form Games: Experimental Data and Simple Dynamic Models in the Intermediate Term. *Games and Economic Behavior*, *8*, 164-212.

Sarin, R., & Vahid, F. (1997). *Payoff Assessments without Probabilities: A Simple Dynamic Model of Choice* (mimeo).

Sarin, R., & Vahid, F. (1998). *Predicting How People Play Games: A Procedurally Rational Model of Choice* (mimeo).

Stahl, D.O. (1988). Bertrand Competition for Inputs and Walrasian Outcomes. *American Economic Review, 78,* 189-201.

Stanley, E.A., Ashlock, D., & Tesfatsion, L. (1993). *Iterated Prisoner's Dilemma with Choice and Refusal of Partners* (ISU Economic Report No. 30) Iowa State University.

Vignes, A. (1993). *Dispersion de prix et marchés décentralisés: le cas du marché au poisson de Marseille* (Ph.D. thesis) European University Institute, Florence.

Vriend, N.J. (1995). Self-Organization of Markets: An Example of a Computational Approach. *Computational Economics, 8,* 205-231.

Weisbuch, G., Kirman, A., & Herreiner, D. (1996). *Market Organisation* (mimeo).

On New Phenomena in Dynamic Promotional Competition Models with Homogeneous and Quasi-homogeneous Firms

Michael Kopel[1], Gian Italo Bischi[2], and Laura Gardini[3]

[1] Department of Managerial Economics and Industrial Organization, University of Technology, Theresianumgasse 27, 1040 Vienna, Austria
[2] Istituto di Scienze Economiche, University of Urbino, 61029 Urbino, Italy
[3] Istituto di Matematica "E. Levi", University of Parma, Italy and Istituto di Scienze Economiche, University of Urbino, 61029 Urbino, Italy

Abstract. In this paper we study a class of dynamic promotional competition models, in which firms compete for market share by expending marketing effort. We investigate two main issues. First, we answer the question if it is possible to give a global characterization of the stability of the steady state effort allocation. We show that by using the concept of critical curves and an invariance property of the coordinate axes a characterization of the set of feasible points (points that generate positive trajectories converging to the steady state allocation) and its changes can be given. Second, we deal with the assumption of homogeneous firms, which is often made in the literature. We demonstrate that the symmetric model which derives from this assumption exhibits, in many situations, non-generic dynamical behavior. New phenomena, like Milnor attractors and synchronization of trajectories, arising in the homogeneous case are illustrated. The introduction of small heterogeneities into the model invalidates many of the conclusions derived under the hypothesis of homogeneous firms.

Keywords: Promotional competition, Homogeneous and quasi-homogeneous firms, Global dynamics, Milnor attractors, Synchronization, Symmetry breaking.
JEL Classification: E32, M30

1 Introduction

Market share attraction models specify that the market share of a competitor is equal to its attraction divided by the total attraction of all the competitors in the market, where the firm's attraction is given in terms of competitive effort allocations. Consider the case of two firms, which compete against each other in a market on the basis of both the quality and the magnitude of the marketing effort expended by each competitor. Let B denote the sales potential of the market (in terms of customer market expenditures). If firm 1 expends x dollars of effort and firm 2 expends y dollars, then the share of the market (sales revenue) accruing to firm 1 and to firm 2 is Bs_1 and $Bs_2 = B - Bs_1$, respectively, where

$$s_1 = \frac{ax^{\beta_1}}{ax^{\beta_1} + by^{\beta_2}} \tag{1}$$
$$s_2 = \frac{by^{\beta_2}}{ax^{\beta_1} + by^{\beta_2}}$$

The terms $A_1 = ax^{\beta_1}$ and $A_2 = by^{\beta_2}$ are the attractions of customers to firm 1 and 2, respectively, given the expenditures of x and y units of effort[1]. The parameters a and b denote the relative effectiveness of effort expended by the firms. Since $\frac{dA_1}{dx}\frac{x}{A_1} = \beta_1$ and $\frac{dA_2}{dx}\frac{x}{A_2} = \beta_2$ the parameters β_1 and β_2 denote the elasticity of the attraction of firm (or brand) i with regard to the effort of firm i. Note that the payoff of each firm depends on the actions of both firms. This type of model is theoretically appealing because it is logically consistent: it yields market shares that are between zero and one, and sum to one across all the competitors in the market. Market share attraction models have been used frequently in empirical work; see, e.g., Bultez and Naert (1975), Naert and Weverbergh (1981). Moreover, they are prevalent in the economics, game theory, operations research and marketing literature; see, for example, Monahan and Sobel (1994), Monahan (1987), Friedman (1958), Schmalensee (1976), Case (1979, Ch. 4), Cooper and Nakanishi (1988).

In the existing literature predominantly *static* market share attraction models are used. Questions like the existence and uniqueness of (Nash) equilibria (Friedman 1958, Mills 1961, Schmalensee 1976), and their structure (Schmalensee 1976, Monahan 1987, Karnani 1985) are investigated. Few authors also study the local stability properties of these equilibria (Schmalensee 1976, Balch M. 1971), but global stability properties are completely neglected. This is quite in contrast to the recent interest on global phenomena in the economics literature. See, for example, Brock and Hommes (1997), Kopel (1996), de Vilder (1996). Furthermore, it is often assumed that the elasticities of the attractions of the firms with respect to effort, given by the parameters β_1 and β_2 in (1) are the same for all firms in the industry (often assumed to be equal to one, see Friedman 1958 and Mills 1961). The same can be said for the relative effectiveness of efforts, measured by the parameters a and b. This restrictive assumption of *homogenous* firms is only made to keep the models analytically tractable, but oftentimes lacks empirical evidence.

In this paper several open questions are addressed related to the issues raised in the previous paragraph. In order to do this we use (1) and introduce a dynamic version of a market share attraction model with adaptive adjustment of competitive effort allocations. The first topic we then briefly cover is

---

[1] In marketing theory market share attraction models are used to describe the competition between several brands of a product in the market. The expressions then describe the attractions of the individual brands.

in line with recent research agendas in economics, namely the characterization of the global properties of the (symmetric) model. We will be concerned with the question of how to describe the set of initial effort allocations which will converge to a competitive steady-state effort allocation, and the changes of this set when parameters (slightly) change. This topic has not been covered in the literature and will be one of the main points in the paper. The second issue we will address is the importance of the assumption of homogenous firms (or brands). That is, we ask the question if the introduction of *small heterogeneities* matter or not. If they do (and it will be shown that they do under certain circumstances), then the conclusions derived in the literature under the assumption of symmetry should be applied with caution.

2 A Brand Competition Model for Market Share

In this section we introduce a dynamic version of a market share attraction model with adaptive adjustment of competitive effort allocations following Bischi et al. (1998a). In this model it is assumed that the two competitors change their marketing efforts adaptively in response to the profits achieved in the previous period. In particular, the marketing efforts in period $t+1$ are determined by

$$x_{t+1} = x_t + \lambda_1(Bs_{1t} - x_t)x_t \tag{2}$$
$$y_{t+1} = y_t + \lambda_2(Bs_{2t} - y_t)y_t$$

where the market shares s_{1t} and s_{2t} are determined by (1). The decision rule the firms use is a type of anchoring and adjustment heuristic (Tversky and Kahneman 1975), and is widely used in decision theory (see Wansink et al. 1998, Sterman 1989). The marketing efforts x_{t+1} and y_{t+1} of period $t+1$ are determined by, first, recalling an anchor - the previous allocations x_t and y_t - and then adjusting for the achieved results of the previous period, $Bs_{1t} - x_t$ and $Bs_{2t} - y_t$. Note that this adjustment also depends on how much effort has been expended before. The parameters $\lambda_i > 0, i = 1, 2$, measure the extent of the adjustment or the adjustment speed. If we replace the expressions for the market shares s_{1t} and s_{2t} in (2) by the expressions in (1), the dynamic market share attraction model

$$T: \begin{cases} x_{t+1} = x_t + \lambda_1 x_t \left(B\dfrac{x_t^{\beta_1}}{x_t^{\beta_1} + k y_t^{\beta_2}} - x_t \right) \\[2em] y_{t+1} = y_t + \lambda_2 y_t \left(B\dfrac{k y_t^{\beta_2}}{x_t^{\beta_1} + k y_t^{\beta_2}} - y_t \right) \end{cases} \tag{3}$$

where $k := b/a$, describes the evolution of the marketing efforts and the corresponding market shares of the two firms over time. The local and global properties of the map (3) for the general case of non-homogeneous firms have been studied in Bischi et al. (1998a). Here we are more concerned with the case of homogeneous and almost homogeneous firms, where the firms' parameters differ only slightly. We will describe which new phenomena arise in such situations and how they can be studied.

3   Homogeneous Firms: General Properties

In what follows we will be mainly interested in the homogeneous case of identical firms

$$\lambda_1 = \lambda_2 = \lambda > 0; \quad \beta_1 = \beta_2 = \beta > 0; \quad k = 1 \tag{4}$$

in which the map T in (3) assumes the *symmetric* form

$$T_s : \begin{cases} x_{t+1} = x_t + \lambda x_t \left(B \frac{x_t^\beta}{x_t^\beta + y_t^\beta} - x_t \right) \\[2mm] y_{t+1} = y_t + \lambda y_t \left(B \frac{y_t^\beta}{x_t^\beta + y_t^\beta} - y_t \right) \end{cases} \tag{5}$$

This map is symmetric in the sense that it remains the same if the variables x and y are swapped. We will later deal with the case of quasi-homogeneous firms, where the parameters of the firms are only slightly different. As an example of quasi-homogeneous firms, one might imagine that firms differ only slightly in their relative effectiveness of efforts, captured by a value of the parameter k close to, but different from, one. Hence, k is in effect a measure of the degree of heterogeneity of the two firms. Note that the response parameter β measures the degree of competition in model (5), see also Hibbert and Wilkinson (1994). If $\beta = 0$, there is no competition between the firms and the attractiveness of each firm is constant. The two firms act independently and the market shares are equal. The larger the parameter β, the larger is the effect of an increase in marketing effort exerted by the competitor on the other firms market share and, hence, the larger is the degree of competition. We will use this simple model as a vehicle to cover the topics described at the end of the Introduction.

3.1   The Feasible Set

First note that the map (5) is defined only for nonnegative values of the marketing efforts x and y, because of the presence of the real exponent β. Starting from a given initial effort allocation (x_0, y_0), a *feasible* time evolution of the system is obtained only if the corresponding trajectory $\{(x_t, y_t) = T_s^t(x_0, y_0), \ t = 0, 1, 2...\}$ is entirely contained in the positive orthant. Such a trajectory has been called *feasible trajectory* in Bischi et al. (1998a), and the *feasible set* has been defined as the subset of $\mathbb{R}_+^2$ whose points generate feasible trajectories. The delimitation of the feasible set is a prerequisite for any study of models like (3) and (5). This point has not been addressed in the literature so far, but it has been studied in Bischi et al. (1998a). In that paper it is shown that for the model (3) the invariant coordinate axes and their preimages of any rank form the boundary of the feasible set. We briefly and informally repeat the argument for the case of homogeneous firms. For analytical details (in the non-symmetric case) we refer to Bischi et al. (1998a). An important feature of the model (5) is that the two coordinate lines are invariant, i.e. $x_t = 0$ implies $x_{t+1} = 0$ and $y_t = 0$ implies $y_{t+1} = 0$. This means that if one of the firms expends no resources, it cannot achieve a positive market share, hence, earn any profit, and will not have anything to expend in the next period. If, at the same time, the competitor expends positive marketing effort, it captures the whole market. The decision rule then determines if the marketing effort from one period to the next is raised or lowered, depending on the fact if the competitor made a profit or a loss. Accordingly, the dynamics of the model (5) restricted to one of the axis is governed by a one-dimensional system, $s_{t+1} = f(s_t)$, where

$$f(s) = (1 + \lambda B)s - \lambda s^2 \tag{6}$$

The map f generates the same dynamics as the standard logistic map $z_{t+1} = h(z_t) = \mu z_t(1 - z_t)$, where $\mu = 1 + \lambda B$ and the relation between the two systems is $s = \frac{1+\lambda B}{\lambda} z$. This feature enables us to deduce the possible dynamics of the time evolution of the marketing expenditures along the invariant axes from the well-known properties of the logistic map[2]. Bounded and feasible trajectories along the invariant axes are obtained when $\lambda B \leq 3$ (corresponding to $\mu \leq 4$), provided that the initial effort allocations lie in the segments $\omega_i = 00_{-1}^{(i)}, i = x, y$, where $0_{-1}^{(x)} = (\frac{1+\lambda B}{\lambda}, 0)$ and $0_{-1}^{(y)} = (0, \frac{1+\lambda B}{\lambda})$ are the rank-1 preimages[3] of the origin on the corresponding axis computed using the map f (corresponding to the unit interval for the quadratic map). If the initial effort expenditures along the axes are taken outside the segment ω_i, unfeasible trajectories are obtained. Now consider the region bounded by the segments ω_x and ω_y and their rank-1 preimages $\omega_x^{-1} = T_s^{-1}(\omega_x)$ and $\omega_y^{-1} = T_s^{-1}(\omega_y)$.

Following Bischi et al. (1998a), these preimages can be analytically computed as follows. Let $X = (p, 0)$ be a point of ω_x. Its preimages are the real solutions of the algebraic system obtained from (5) with $(x_{t+1}, y_{t+1}) = (p, 0)$, and it is easy to see that the preimages of the point X are either located on

---

[2] The logistic map has been the object of interest for researchers from various fields for many years, and it is frequently used in applications in economics, see e.g., Day (1994), Baumol and Benhabib (1987). The dynamics generated by the logistic map are well understood, see e.g. Mira (1987) or Devaney (1989).

[3] A preimage of a point $P = (x_p, y_p)$ is a point $P_{-1} = (x, y)$ such that $T_s(x, y) = P$. A point P may have more than one preimages (or no preimages) which are obtained by solving the system $T_s(x, y) = (x_p, y_p)$, with respect to the unknowns x and y, for given values of x_p and y_p.

the same invariant axis $y = 0$ (in the points whose coordinates are the solutions of the equation $f(x) = p$, with f given in (6)) or on the curve of equation

$$x = \left[ky^\beta \left(\frac{\lambda B - \lambda y + 1}{\lambda y - 1} \right) \right]^{\frac{1}{\beta}}. \tag{7}$$

Analogously, the preimages of a point $Y = (0, q)$ of ω_y belong to the same invariant axis $x = 0$, in the points whose coordinates are the solutions of the equation $f(y) = q$, or lie on the curve of equation

$$y = \left[\frac{x^\beta}{k} \left(\frac{\lambda B - \lambda x + 1}{\lambda x - 1} \right) \right]^{\frac{1}{\beta}}. \tag{8}$$

These two curves intersect the axes in the points $0_{-1}^{(i)}, i = x, y$ and intersect each other in the point $0_{-1}^{(d)}$, located on the diagonal (see fig. 1). All points outside the region bounded by $\omega_x, \omega_y, \omega_x^{-1}$ and ω_y^{-1} cannot generate feasible trajectories.

This process can now be iterated: in general, the boundary of the feasible set is given by the union of all the preimages of ω_x and ω_y of any rank. However, as shown in the next subsection, as long as $\lambda B \leq 3$, the boundary of the feasible set has the simple shape shown in fig. 1. This is due to the fact, that the preimages ω_x^{-1} and ω_y^{-1} are entirely contained in a region where points have no preimages. To gain more information about these regions with different numbers of preimages, we have to introduce the concept of critical curves.

3.2   Critical Curves

If we consider a two-dimensional system (3), then the fact that the map T is single-valued does not imply the existence and the uniqueness of its inverse T^{-1}. For a given (x', y') the rank-1 preimage (or backward iterate) $(x, y) = T^{-1}(x', y')$, obtained by solving the system with respect to the unknowns x and y, may not exist or it may be multivalued. In other words, there might be several effort allocations of the two competitors leading to the same marketing expenditures in the following period, or there may be none. In such cases T is said to be a noninvertible map, and the plane can be subdivided into regions Z_k, $k \geq 0$, whose points have k distinct rank-1 preimages. As the point (x', y') varies in the plane $\mathbb{R}^2$, pairs of preimages appear or disappear as this point crosses the boundaries which separate regions of different numbers of preimages. Hence, such boundaries are characterized by the presence of at least two coincident (merging) preimages. This leads to the definition of the critical curves, one of the distinguishing features of noninvertible maps. Following the notations of Gumowski and Mira (1980), Mira et al. (1996), Abraham et al. (1997), the *critical set* LC (from the French

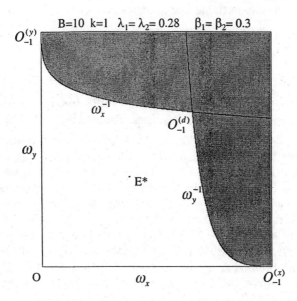

Fig. 1. The boundary of the feasible set is given by the segments $\omega_x = 00^{(x)}_{-1}$ and $\omega_y = 00^{(y)}_{-1}$ on the invariant axes, and their rank-1 preimages ω_x^{-1} and ω_y^{-1}. The curves on which the preimages ω_x^{-1} and ω_y^{-1} are located intersect the diagonal in the point $0^{(d)}_{-1}$.

"Ligne Critique") is defined as the locus of points having two, or more, coincident rank-1 preimages, located on a set (*set of merging preimages*) called LC_{-1}. LC is the two-dimensional generalization of the notion of critical value (a local minimum or maximum value) of a one-dimensional map, LC_{-1} is the generalization of the notion of critical point (a local extremum point)[4]. Arcs of LC separate the regions of the plane characterized by a different number of real rank-1 preimages. The critical sets of rank k are the images of rank k of LC_{-1} denoted by $LC_{k-1} = T^k(LC_{-1}) = T^{k-1}(LC)$, LC_0 being LC. Points of LC_{-1} in which the map is differentiable are necessarily points where the Jacobian determinant vanishes: in any neighborhood of a point of LC_{-1} there are at least two distinct points which are mapped by T in the same point (near LC), hence the map is not locally invertible in these points.

---

[4] This terminology, and notation, originates from the notion of critical points as it is used in the classical works of Julia and Fatou. For the logistic map the critical point is $c_{-1} = 1/2$, and the critical value $c = h(c_{-1}) = \mu/4$.

This implies, for a differentiable map T, that

$$LC_{-1} \subseteq J_0 = \left\{ (x,y) \in \mathbb{R}^2 \,|\, \det DT(x,y) = 0 \right\}. \tag{9}$$

For the symmetric model (5) the locus of points for which $\det DT(x,y) = 0$ is given by the union of two branches, denoted by $LC_{-1}^{(a)}$ and $LC_{-1}^{(b)}$ in fig. 2a. Also LC is the union of two branches, denoted by $LC^{(a)} = T(LC_{-1}^{(a)})$ and $LC^{(b)} = T(LC_{-1}^{(b)})$, see fig. 2b. The branch $LC^{(b)}$ separates the region Z_0, whose points have no preimages, from the region Z_2, whose points have two distinct rank-1 preimages. $LC^{(a)}$ separates the region Z_2 from Z_4, where the points in Z_4 have four distinct preimages. It is then said that (5) is a noninvertible map of $Z_4 - Z_2 - Z_0$ type. Using the critical curves it is now possible to understand why the feasible set has the simple shape as shown in fig. 1 as long as $\lambda B \leq 3$. The branch $LC^{(b)}$ intersects the axes in the points $((1+\lambda B)^2/4\lambda, 0)$ and $(0, (1+\lambda B)^2/4\lambda)$ respectively, where the value $(1+\lambda B)^2/4\lambda$ is obtained as the image of the critical point $1 + \lambda B/2\lambda$ of the map f in (6). Recall, on the other hand, that $\omega_i, i = x, y$ intersect the axes in the points $0_{-1}^{(x)} = (\frac{1+\lambda B}{\lambda}, 0)$ and $0_{-1}^{(y)} = (0, \frac{1+\lambda B}{\lambda})$. These points - and in fact the whole segments $\omega_i, i = x, y$ - lie above $LC^{(b)}$ (and hence in the region Z_0) as long as $\lambda B \leq 3$.

The question naturally arises, what happens when $\lambda B > 3$? An answer is given in Bischi et al. (1998a) where the critical curves of the map (3) are used in order to study the global bifurcations that change the qualitative structure of the boundaries of the feasible set. In that paper it is shown that when a portion of the boundary of the feasible set crosses the critical curve LC passing from Z_0 to Z_2 or from Z_2 to Z_4, new portions of the boundaries are created, resulting in a fractal structure of the boundary.

3.3 Steady State Effort Allocations

We are now ready to get to the first main point in the paper. Our economic interest in studying systems like (3) and (5) is two-folded. First, we want to find out if there is something like a steady state effort allocation, so that we can safely forget studying the transient phase, and investigate the steady states and their structure instead. Second, we are interested in the delimitation of the set of points which converge to it, to gain some insights into the robustness of the model and the dependence of the model's behavior on the initial effort allocations.

Inside the feasible set we described above, one or more attractors of the dynamical system, e.g. several fixed points, cycles of different periods, or more complex attractors, may exist. It can be shown that for the model (3)

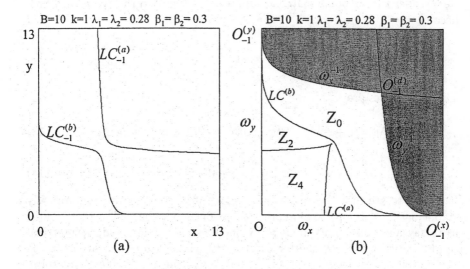

Fig. 2. (a) Critical curves of rank-0, obtained as the locus of pointswhere $det(DT_s(x,y)) = 0$. (b) Critical curves of rank-1,obtained as $LC = T_s(LC_{-1})$. These curves separate the plane into threedistinct regions: Z_0, Z_2, Z_4, whose points have no, two, and fourrank-1 preimages respectively. For this parameter setting the preimages ω_x^{-1} and ω_y^{-1} are competely contained in theregion Z_0, hence they have no further preimages.

for $\beta_i \in (0,1)^5$, $i = 1, 2$, a fixed point

$$E^* = (x^*, B - x^*). \tag{10}$$

exists inside the feasible set, where $x^* \in (0, B)$ is theunique positive solution of the equation $k^{\frac{1}{1-\beta_2}} x^{\frac{1-\beta_1}{1-\beta_2}} + x - B = 0$ (see Bischi et al. , 1998a), and it isunique. A particularly simple solution is obtained in the case ofhomogeneous firms

$$E^* = \left(\frac{B}{2}, \frac{B}{2}\right) \tag{11}$$

Note that this steady state allocation belongs to the diagonal $\Delta = \{(x,y)|x = y\}$. This yields the sensible resultfor the symmetric case that two homogeneous firms competing in the samemarket split the market equally. In

---

[5] Only values of the response parameter belonging to this range are meaningfulin applications, see Cooper and Nakanishi (1988).

order to determine the local stabilityproperties of the steady state allocation, we consider the Jacobian matrix,computed in a point on the diagonal, which becomes

$$DT(x, x; \lambda, B, \beta,) = \begin{bmatrix} 1 - 2\lambda x + \frac{\lambda B(\beta+2)}{4} & -\frac{\lambda B\beta}{4} \\ -\frac{\lambda B\beta}{4} & 1 - 2\lambda x + \frac{\lambda B(\beta+2)}{4} \end{bmatrix} \quad (12)$$

The eigenvalues are

$$\lambda_{\parallel} = 1 + \frac{1}{2}\lambda B - 2\lambda x \text{ , with eigendirectionalong } \Delta; \quad (13)$$

$$\lambda_{\perp} = 1 + \frac{1}{2}\lambda B(1 + \beta) - 2\lambda x \text{ , witheigendirection orthogonal to } \Delta. \quad (14)$$

It is easy to see that the steady state allocation E^* is locallyasymptotically stable for $\lambda B < 4$. Furthermore, the results of theprevious subsections enable us to say also something about the globalbehavior of the model. Numerical results indicate that all the trajectorieswith initial effort allocations inside the feasible set converge to E^*(i. e. , there is no evidence of other attractors). Accordingly, we have aglobal stability result, which says that all the points inside the feasibleset converge to E^* as long as $\lambda B < 4$. One further point deservesmentioning: recall that the feasible set has a simple shape only as long as $\lambda B < 3$. For $\lambda B > 3$ portions of the boundary of the feasible setcross the critical curve $LC^{(b)}$, passing from Z_0 to Z_2 (seethe portions near the axes indicated the arrow in fig. 3a). Hence, portionsof the set of unfeasible points enter the region Z_2. That means thatall the points belonging to these portions suddenly have two preimagesinstead of none. These preimages lie in regions with two and four preimagesrespectively, and lead to further preimages in these regions. This cascadeof preimages lead to a fractal structure of the (boundary of the) feasibleset, which can be clearly observed in the enlargement of fig. 3b (only theregion around the y axis is enlarged). It is a rather surprising fact thatthe set of points which converge to the steady state effort allocation mayhave fractal boundaries. On the other hand, the segments ω_x and ω_y and their preimages ω_x^{-1} and ω_y^{-1}still give a rather good approximation of the feasible set.

4   Homogeneous Firms and Synchronization

If homogeneous firms characterized by identical parameters (4) areconsidered, the evolution of the effort allocations over time is given by (5). In this case it is easy to check that the diagonal Δ isinvariant, i. e. , $T_s(\Delta) \subseteq \Delta$: in adeterministic framework, identical firms starting with identical initialeffort allocations behave identically over time. Formally, $x_0 = y_0$implies $x_t = y_t$ for all $t \geq 0$. We call such trajectories, whichare embedded into Δ, *synchronized trajectories*. The dynamicson the diagonal are governed by a one-dimensional

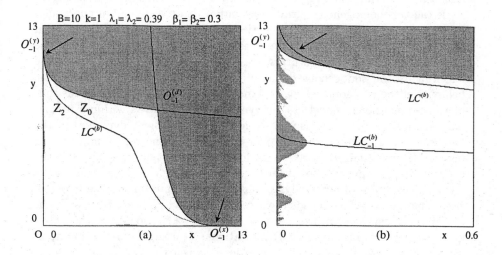

Fig. 3. (a) Feasible set for $3 < \lambda B < 4$. The steady state allocation E^* is asymptotically stable. Numerical evidence suggests that all the feasible trajectories converge to it. The feasible set has fractal boundaries due to the fact that portions of the unfeasible set, indicated by the arrows, entered the region Z_2. (b) Enlargement of (a), obtained by zooming along the x axis by a factor 20, in order to see the fractal structure of the boundary of the feasible set near ω_y. Similar structures also exist along the other portions of the boundaries, i.e. along ω_x, ω_x^{-1} and ω_y^{-1}.

dynamical system $s_{t+1} = f^d(s_t)$, where $f^d = T_s|_\Delta : \Delta \to \Delta$ is the restriction of the two-dimensional map T_s to the invariant submanifold Δ. For our model this restriction yields

$$f^d(s) = (1 + \frac{1}{2}\lambda B)s - \lambda s^2. \tag{15}$$

Again, this one-dimensional system exhibits the same dynamics as the standard logistic map $z = \mu z(1 - z)$, with

$$\mu = 1 + \frac{1}{2}\lambda B \tag{16}$$

by the linear transformation $s = \frac{1+0.5\lambda B}{\lambda}z$. Note that the coordinates of the steady state effort allocation E^* are given by the fixed point of the map

(15). This simpler model can be interpreted as the model of the so-called *representative agent*: it captures the dynamical behavior of both of the two homogeneous firms when the dynamics of these two firms are synchronized.

If the two homogeneous firms start out with different initial effort allocations, the question arises if the trajectories synchronize over time, i.e., if $|x_t - y_t| \to 0$ as $t \to +\infty$. In this case the initial difference between the marketing efforts of the two firms, $|x_0 - y_0,| > 0$, would cancel out in the long-run by the endogenous dynamics of the system, and the asymptotic behavior of the two homogeneous competitors is well-represented by the simpler one-dimensional model (15). If synchronization occurs within a reasonably short time span, we can safely ignore the transient dynamics of the two-dimensional system, and consider the model of the representative firm instead. If synchronization takes very long or does not occur at all, then the concept of the representative firm becomes meaningless. This leads to the second main point of our analysis: under which conditions do the trajectories of marketing efforts of identical competitors which start from different initial effort choices synchronize, and how does this depend on the difference $|x_0 - y_0|$ of the initial effort allocations? Starting from this question, we may then ask, if small heterogeneities between the two firms - a small mismatch of some of the parameters - matter for synchronization or not (see the next section). Answering these questions is not easy, since new dynamic phenomena may appear, especially when the one-dimensional model (15) exhibits chaotic behavior. In this case *chaotic synchronization* may occur, a phenomenon that has been extensively studied in the recent physical and mathematical literature (see e.g. Fujisaka and Yamada (1983), Pecora and Carrol(1990), Pikovsky and Grassberger (1991), Ashwin et al. (1994, 1996), Hasler et al. (1997), Maistrenko et al. (1998))[6]. Before we go on to study our model, we briefly introduce some (mathematical) definitions and notions and present some of the existing results.

4.1 Synchronization in Symmetric Dynamic Models

The question of asymptotic synchronization of the marketing efforts x_t and y_t of the two-dimensional dynamical system (5), possessing a one-dimensional invariant submanifold, can be rephrased as follows. Let $A_s \subseteq \Delta$ be an attractor of the one-dimensional map (15): is it also an attractor of the two-dimensional map T_s? As pointed out above, an answer to this question is not immediate, because measure theoretic attractors, which are not stable according to the usual Lyapunov (or topological) definition, arise quite naturally in this context, and create the conditions for the occurrence of new kinds of dynamic phenomena and bifurcations. Obviously, an attractor A_s of the restriction f^d is stable with respect to perturbations along the invariant diagonal Δ. Accordingly, an answer to the question addressed above can

---

[6] For a first application of these concepts to a dynamic Cournot duopoly game with boundedly rational agents, see Bischi et al. (1998b).

only be given through a study of the stability of A_s with respect to perturbations *transverse* to Δ (*transverse stability*). If $A_s = \{x_1, ..., x_k\}$ is a stable
k-periodic cycle of the map f^d then an answer to the question addressed
above is very simple: in this case $\mathbf{A}_s = \{(x_1, x_1), ..., (x_k, x_k)\}$ is a k-cycle,
embedded into the diagonal Δ, of the two-dimensional map T_s and, due to
the symmetry of T_s, the Jacobian matrix computed in a point $(x, x) \in \Delta$ is
symmetric, with eigenvalues

$$\lambda_{||}(x), \text{ with eigenvector } \mathbf{v}_{||} = (1, 1) \text{ along } \Delta$$
$$\lambda_{\perp}(x), \text{ with eigenvector } \mathbf{v}_{\perp} = (1, -1) \text{ orthogonal to } \Delta \tag{17}$$

Therefore, the multipliers of the k-cycle $\mathbf{A}_s$ are

$$\lambda_{||}(\mathbf{A}_s) = \prod_{i=1}^{k} \lambda_{||}(x_i), \text{ with } \mathbf{v}_{||} = (1, 1) \text{ and}$$
$$\lambda_{\perp}(\mathbf{A}_s) = \prod_{i=1}^{k} \lambda_{\perp}(x_i), \text{ with } \mathbf{v}_{\perp} = (1, -1) \tag{18}$$

Since we assumed that $\mathbf{A}_s$ is attracting along the diagonal Δ, i.e. $|\lambda_{||}(\mathbf{A}_s)| \leq$
1, a sufficient condition for its asymptotic stability[7] in the two-dimensional
phase space of the map T_s is $|\lambda_{\perp}(\mathbf{A}_s)| < 1$.

The situation becomes more complex when $\mathbf{A}_s$ is a chaotic attractor of
f^d, i.e., when chaotic synchronization is considered. In this case results on the
transverse stability are given in terms of the so-called *transverse Lyapunov
exponents*

$$\Lambda_{\perp}(\mathbf{A}_s) = \lim_{N \to \infty} \frac{1}{N} \sum_{i=0}^{N} \ln |\lambda_{\perp}(x_i)| \tag{19}$$

where $\{x_i, i \geq 0\}$ denotes a trajectory embedded into $\mathbf{A}_s$. If x_0 belongs to a
k-cycle then $\Lambda_{\perp} = \ln |\lambda_{\perp}^k|$, so that for each k-cycle embedded into $\mathbf{A}_s$ a par-
ticular value for $\Lambda_{\perp}$ is obtained. In this case $\Lambda_{\perp} < 0$ if and only if $|\lambda_{\perp}^k| < 1$,
that is, if the corresponding cycle is transversely stable. Instead, if x_0 belongs
to a generic aperiodic trajectory of $\mathbf{A}_s$ then $\Lambda_{\perp}$ is independent of x_0, provided
that $\mathbf{A}_s$ is an ergodic chaotic attractor, with absolutely continuous invariant
measure. In this case $\Lambda_{\perp}$ is called *natural transverse Lyapunov exponent*[8],
denoted by $\Lambda_{\perp}^{nat}$. Since infinitely many cycles, all unstable along Δ, are embedded inside a chaotic attractor $\mathbf{A}_s$, a spectrum of transverse Lyapunov
exponents can be defined, see Buescu (1997)

$$\Lambda_{\perp}^{\min} \leq .... \leq \Lambda_{\perp}^{nat} \leq ... \leq \Lambda_{\perp}^{\max} \tag{20}$$

---

[7] By asymptotic stability we refer to the usual topological definition: (i) $\mathbf{A}_s$ must be
Lyapunov stable, i.e., for every neighborhood U of $\mathbf{A}_s$ there exists a neighborhood
V of $\mathbf{A}_s$ such that $T_s^t(V) \subset U \; \forall t \geq 0$ and (ii) for each $x \in V$, $T_s^t(x) \to \mathbf{A}_s$ as
$t \to +\infty$ must hold.

[8] By the term "natural Lyapunov exponent" we mean the Lyapunov exponent
associated with the natural (or SBR) measure, computed for a typical trajectory
along the chaotic attractor A_s.

The meaning of the inequalities in (20) can be intuitively understood on the basis of the property that a chaotic attractor $\mathbf{A}_s$ includes within itself infinitely many periodic orbits which are unstable in the direction along Δ, and $\Lambda_{\perp}^{nat}$ expresses a sort of "weighted balance" (see Nagai and Lai 1997) between transversely stable cycles (characterized by $\Lambda_{\perp} < 0$) and transversely unstable ones (characterized by $\Lambda_{\perp} > 0$).

The one-dimensional chaotic invariant set $\mathbf{A}_s \subseteq \Delta$ is asymptotically stable (in the usual topological sense) for the two-dimensional dynamical system if all the cycles embedded in it are transversely stable (or, equivalently, if $\Lambda_{\perp}^{max} < 0$). However, it may occur that some cycles embedded into the chaotic set $\mathbf{A}_s$ become transversely repelling ($\Lambda_{\perp}^{max} > 0$) even if the *natural transverse Lyapunov exponent* $\Lambda_{\perp}^{nat}$ is still negative; this is due to the presence of many other transversely attracting orbits embedded inside A_s. In this case $\mathbf{A}_s$ is no longer a Lyapunov attractor: a two-dimensional neighborhood U of A_s exists such that in any neighborhood $V \subset U$ there are points (really a set of points of positive measure) that exit U after a finite number of iterations. However, $\mathbf{A}_s$ continues to be attracting "on average". More precisely, it is an attractor in Milnor sense (see Milnor 1985, Ashwin et al. 1996), which means that it attracts a set of points of the two-dimensional phase space of positive (Lebesgue) measure. The transitions between the two different situations, as some parameter is changed, define new kinds of local bifurcations. The change from asymptotic stability to attractiveness only in Milnor sense, occurring when $\Lambda_{\perp}^{max}$ becomes positive, is denoted as *riddling bifurcation* in Lai, Grebogi and Yorke (1996) or *bubbling bifurcation* in Ashwin et al. (1994) and in Venkataramani (1996). Furthermore, when also $\Lambda_{\perp}^{nat}$ becomes positive, due to the fact that the transversely unstable periodic orbits embedded into A_s have a greater weight with respect to the transversely attracting ones (see Nagai and Lai 1997) a so-called *blowout bifurcation* occurs, at which a Milnor attractor becomes a chaotic saddle. In what follows we will mainly focus on the local and global phenomena occurring after riddling and before blowout bifurcations, that is, at a range of parameters in which a non topological Milnor attractor exists. Note that even if the occurrence of riddling and blowout bifurcations is detected through the transverse Lyapunov exponents, that is, by a local analysis of the linear approximation of the map near Δ, their effects are determined by the global properties of the map. The fate of the locally repelled trajectories is determined by the nonlinearities acting far from the diagonal. In fact, in such a situation, two possible scenarios can be observed depending on the evolution of the trajectories that are locally repelled along (or near) the local unstable manifolds of the transversely repelling cycles:

(L) the trajectories may be folded back towards Δ by the action of the nonlinearities acting far from Δ, so that the dynamics are characterized by some bursts far from Δ before the trajectories synchronize on the diagonal (a very long sequence of such bursts, which can be observed when $\Lambda_{\perp}^{nat}$ is close to zero, has been called *on-off intermittency* in Ott and Sommerer 1994);

(**G**) the trajectories may belong to the basin of another attractor, in which case the phenomenon of *riddled basins* is obtained (see Alexander et al. 1992).

The distinction between the two different scenarios (**L**) and (**G**) described above depends on the global properties of the dynamical system[9]. The global dynamical properties can be usefully studied by the method of *critical curves*, which we introduced above. The reinjection of the locally repelled trajectories occurring in local riddling may be described in terms of their folding action[10]. This idea has been recently proposed in Bischi et al. (1998b) for the study of symmetric maps arising in game theory, and in Bischi et al. (1999) for the study of the effects of small asymmetries due to mismatches of the parameters. In these two papers the geometric properties of the critical curves have been used to obtain the boundary of a compact trapping region, called *absorbing area* (see Mira et al. 1996a), inside which intermittency and blowout phenomena are confined. In other words, the critical curves are used to bound a compact region of the phase plane that acts as a trapping bounded vessel inside which the trajectories starting near the diagonal are confined. For further details on the concept of *minimal* and *invariant* absorbing area and its use to give a global characterization of the different dynamical scenarios, see Bischi and Gardini (1998).

4.2 Synchronization and Synchronization Failure of Homogeneous Firms

After these preparations we can now turn back to our model (5). Recall that the steady state allocation E^* is locally asymptotically stable for $\lambda B < 4$. In what follows we are more interested in the situation when E^* is unstable and we investigate the question of synchronization of the marketing efforts of the two competing firms. The point E^* loses stability along Δ (via a so-called period doubling bifurcation) at $\lambda B = 4$. For $\lambda B > 4$ and $1 - \frac{4}{\lambda B} < \beta < 1$ it is a saddle point, with unstable set along Δ and stable set transverse to it. At $\beta = 1 - \frac{4}{\lambda B}$ it also loses transverse stability (again via a period doubling bifurcation) that creates a stable cycle of period 2 out of the diagonal, with periodic points located symmetrically with respect to Δ. In order to determine the transverse stability of a trajectory $\{x_n, x_n\} \in \Delta$ we consider the transverse Lyapunov exponent for the map (5), readily obtained from (19) with (14):

$$\Lambda_{\perp}^{(nat)} = \lim_{N \to \infty} \frac{1}{N} \sum_{n=0}^{N} \ln \left| 1 + \frac{1}{2} \lambda B (1 + \beta) - 2\lambda x_n \right|.$$

---

[9] The term "global" refers in this context to "not in a neighborhood of the diagonal Δ".

[10] See Mira et al. (1996a) or Mira et al. (1996b) for a description of the geometric properties of a noninvertible map related to the folding (or foliation) of its phase space.

It is important to note that in our case only the orthogonal eigenvalue (14) depends on the response parameter β, i.e. β is a *normal parameter*: it has no influence on the dynamical properties of the restriction along the invariant submanifold Δ, and only influences the transverse stability[11]. This feature enables us to consider a certain attractor along the diagonal and observe for which values of β the evolution of marketing efforts of the two firms synchronize or not, and which kind of transient phenomena occur. Recall that β is also a measure of the degree of competition in the market we try to capture with our model and, accordingly, we can determine how the degree of competition affects the dynamical properties, in particular, the synchronization properties, of the model (5). Will the trajectories synchronize for lower or higher degrees of competition between the two firms? Is the relation between the degree of competition and synchronization properties of the system monotone in the sense that higher/lower values of β lead to synchronization/synchronization failure?

We now consider fixed values of the parameters λ and B, such that a chaotic attractor $\mathbf{A}_s \subseteq \Delta$ of the map (15) exists, with absolutely continuous invariant measure on $\mathbf{A}_s$, and we study the transverse stability of $\mathbf{A}_s$ as the degree of competition between the two firms, measured by the parameter β, varies. Suitable values of the aggregate parameter λB, at which chaotic intervals for the restriction (15) exist, are obtained from the relation (16)[12]. In the examples given below we let $\overline{\mu}_2 = 3.5748049387592....$ Using (16) this yields $\lambda B = 2(\overline{\mu}_2 - 1)$, and the attractor $\mathbf{A}_s$ along the diagonal Δ is in this case a four-band chaotic set[13]. Figure 4 shows the result of the computation of the natural transverse Lyapunov exponent $\Lambda_{\perp}^{nat}$ as β varies in the interval $(0, 0.2)$, where we chose the interval for the values of the response parameter to be in line with empirical evidence; see, e.g., Bultez and Naert, (1975). Observe that in fig. 4 a "window" of negative values of $\Lambda_{\perp}^{nat}$ is visible for $0.0575... < \beta < 0.1895....$

Before discussing the effects of the changes of the sign $\Lambda_{\perp}^{nat}$, we first show, by numerical simulation, that for very small degrees of the competition β the evolution of the marketing effort x_t and y_t of two firms appear to be totally uncorrelated over time. This is no surprise since for $\beta = 0$ the payoffs of the two firms only depend on the firm's own marketing effort and, hence, the firms act independently of each other. Fig. 5 has been obtained with the same parameters λ, B, and k as those used in fig. 4, and we set $\beta = 0.0001$.

---

[11] This is a typical property of coupling parameters in symmetrically coupled maps; see Buescu (1997), Maistrenko et al. (1998), Hasler and Maistrenko (1997).

[12] Recall that the mathematical properties of the logistic map are well understood. Hence, we can use these results if we take into account that the relation between the parameter values and the state variables of the two systems is as described by the equations above.

[13] At the parameter value $\overline{\mu}_2$ the period-4 cycle of the quadratic map undergoes the first homoclinic bifurcation, and four cyclic chaotic intervals are obtained by the merging of 8 cyclic chaotic intervals.

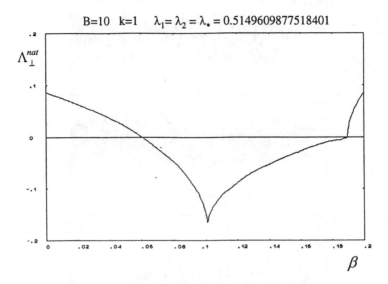

Fig. 4. Natural Lyapunov Exponent $\Lambda_\perp^{(nat)}$ as a function of the degree of competition β, with β ranging from 0 to 0.2, $B = 10$, $\lambda = 0.5149609877518401...$ Each point is obtained by iterating the map (starting from an initial condition along the diagonal) 10.000 times to eliminate transient behavior, and then averaging, according to (19) over another 100.000 iterations.

Due to the particular value of the parameter $\lambda = \lambda_* = 2(\bar\mu_2 - 1)/B = 0.5149609877518401...$ both of the effort time series exhibit a chaotic pattern, as shown in fig. 5a, where the early 300 values of x_t and y_t are represented versus time. The initial effort allocation is $(x_0, y_0) = (5, 5.001)$: the firms start out with almost identical initial marketing efforts and very close to the steady state allocation $E^* = (5, 5)$. Nevertheless, no synchronization takes place. Moreover, the two time patterns are totally uncorrelated, as shown by the graph of fig. 5b, where the difference between the marketing efforts of the competitors, $(x_t - y_t)$, is represented versus time. It is evident that after a very short transient (approximately 20 iterations) the difference between the two variables is of the same order of magnitude as the single variables, even if they are identical and start from quasi-identical initial choices.

A quite different situation is obtained for slightly higher degrees of competition β, where the natural transverse Lyapunov exponent $\Lambda_\perp^{nat}$ is negative. For example, for $\beta = 0.09$ we have $\Lambda_\perp^{nat} = -8.36 \times 10^{-2} < 0$ (see fig. 4), and we expect that synchronization of the marketing efforts of the two firms occurs for a set of initial conditions of positive Lebesgue measure (this implies

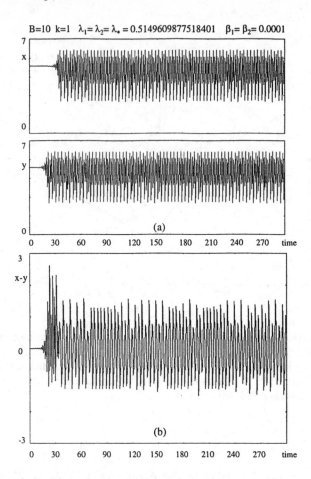

B=10 k=1 $\lambda_1 = \lambda_2 = \lambda_* = 0.5149609877518401$ $\beta_1 = \beta_2 = 0.0001$

Fig. 5. (a) Effort allocations of the firm 1 and 2 respectively over time, shown for the first 300 periods. (b) Difference between the marketing efforts of the two firms for small values of the degree of competition. The decisions of the two firms seem to be independent of each other.

that trajectories that synchronize, even starting out of the diagonal, can be numerically observed). The issue of synchronization gets more complex in this case, however, because for this values of the parameters two coexisting attractors inside the feasible set can be numerically observed: the 4-cyclic chaotic set $\mathbf{A}_s \subset \Delta$ and an attracting cycle of period 2 with periodic points located out of Δ. The cycle $C_2 = ((5.975, 3.371), (3.371, 5.975))$ has been created at $\beta = 1 - \frac{4}{\lambda B} = 0.22$, via a (period doubling) bifurcation of E^* in the transverse direction as explained above. In fig. 6 the coexisting attractors are represented by black points, each with its own basin of attraction: the white points represent the basin $\mathcal{B}(\mathbf{A}_s)$ of the points generating trajectories that synchronize along $\mathbf{A}_s$, whereas the light grey points represent the basin $\mathcal{B}(C_2)$ whose points generate trajectories converging to the stable cycle C_2. The dark-grey region represents the set of points which are not feasible, i.e., which generate unfeasible trajectories. Observe that the issue of synchronization becomes quite complicated now without having any knowledge of the global behavior of the model (5). If we do not have fig. 6 available, it is hard to predict from which initial effort allocations synchronized marketing efforts over time are obtained and for which initial outlays marketing efforts would (two-) cycle. Hence, it is hard to decide when the lower-dimensional model of a representative firm would be a reasonable substitute for the higher-dimensional model (5), and when such a substitution would be misleading. It is interesting to note that (long-run) synchronization of the marketing efforts can also occur starting from initial allocations located very far from the diagonal. In other words, even starting from fairly heterogeneous choices of the two identical competitors, the firms may end up with perfectly synchronized marketing efforts over time, if the initial allocations happen to lie in the white region in fig. 6. On the other hand, and quite counter to one's intuition, even if the initial effort allocations are very close to the diagonal, i.e., $x_0 \cong y_0$, they may not synchronize because they generate trajectories converging to the cycle C_2. Actually, in this case the evolution of marketing efforts exhibits conditions of asynchronous behavior (*phase opposition* between the choices of the two competitors). The reason for this *synchronization failure* is that near the steady state effort allocation E^*, and its preimages along Δ, there are "tongues" formed by initial outlays such that the corresponding trajectory converges to the cycle of period 2. Another important feature to notice is the complex structure of the boundaries that separate $\mathcal{B}(\mathbf{A}_s)$ from $\mathcal{B}(C_2)$. In particular, $\mathcal{B}(\mathbf{A}_s)$ is a non connected set with a fractal structure (self-similarity), a situation which is peculiar of dynamical systems represented by noninvertible maps. Although the feasible set still has a shape similar to the one obtained for $\lambda B < 3$, inside the feasible set we now have two coexisting attractors and, accordingly, two situations might arise - synchronization or synchronization failure of the marketing efforts of the two firms - depending on the fact if initial allocations are chosen from the white or the grey region. This feature is only revealed if we look at the global properties of the system.

For the set of parameters used in preparing fig. 6, the four-band chaotic set $\mathbf{A}_s$, embedded into the invariant diagonal Δ, is not a topological attractor however. In fact, an 8-cycle C_8 embedded inside the diagonal exists, which is transversely repelling[14]. This means that trajectories starting along the local unstable set $W_\perp^u(C_8)$, issuing from the periodic points of C_8, as

---

[14] The 8-cycle is $C_8 = (5.588, 3.894, 6.112, 2.612, 5.824, 3.352, 6.197, 2.378)$ of the map (15) and it has the transverse multiplier $\lambda_\perp(C_8) = -3.0$, as can be easily computed from (18) with (14).

well as those starting from narrow tongues along $W^u_\perp(C_8)$ and from all the infinitely many preimages of the periodic points of C_8 (such preimages are densely distributed along $\mathbf{A}_s$ due to the fact that $\mathbf{A}_s$ is a chaotic set with absolutely continuous invariant measure) are repelled away from the diagonal. These locally repelled trajectories are then folded back by the action of the global dynamical properties of the map (5), and after a transient with some bursts away from Δ occurring, they synchronize in the long-run. The time evolution of the difference of the marketing efforts, $(x_t - y_t)$, during the transient portion of a typical trajectory, starting from the initial allocations $(x_0, y_0) = (6, 6.01)$, is shown in fig. 7, where the early 300 iterates are represented. After about 40 periods the evolution of the system seems to have reached almost complete synchronization. During the next 40 periods the two competitors behave practically in the same way. At this point the trajectory seems to have definitively settled down on the attractor $\mathbf{A}_s$ (this would be the case for a topological attractor), and we would tend to conclude that the two-player-model can be replaced by a one-player-model. However, the trajectory then moves again far away from the diagonal, and the two competitors now act again in a very different fashion. Several bursts of the trajectory, out of Δ, are observed until perfect synchronization of the marketing efforts is eventually obtained. Such an intermittent behavior is a typical characteristic of the convergence to a non-topological Milnor attractor. The pattern of the time series resembles that of a system which is subject to exogenous random shocks, even if the dynamical system that generates such a pattern is completely deterministic. This peculiar dynamical behavior is related to the fact that even if the Milnor attractor attracts "on average" according to the fact that $\Lambda^{nat}_\perp < 0$, the presence of some transversely repelling cycles (even if less influential than the transversely attracting ones) causes sudden bursts when the trajectories happen to get close to them.

The locally repelled trajectories cannot reach the other attractor C_2 however, i.e., the scenario (**L**) of locally riddling (or intermittency) occurs. This is due to the presence of a so-called absorbing area $\mathcal{A}$ around $\mathbf{A}_s$, from which the trajectory starting close to $\mathbf{A}_s$ cannot escape[15]. We briefly describe now how the boundary $\partial\mathcal{A}$ of such an absorbing area can be easily obtained (see Bischi and Gardini 1998 for more details). The boundaries of the region in which the asymptotic dynamics are confined (absorbing and chaotic areas) can be obtained by segments of critical curves and their iterates. It can be used to obtain minimal and invariant absorbing areas which include the Milnor attractor where chaotic synchronization takes place. A practical procedure to

---

[15] An absorbing area $\mathcal{A}$ is a bounded region of the plane, whose boundary is given by critical curves segments of finite rank (segments of the critical curve LC and its images), such that the successive images of the points of a neighborhood of $\mathcal{A}$, say $\mathcal{U}(\mathcal{A})$, enter inside $\mathcal{A}$ after a finite number of iterations, and never exit, being $T(\mathcal{A}) \subseteq \mathcal{A}$. See, e.g., Gumowski and Mira (1980), Mira et al. (1996), Abraham et al. (1997).

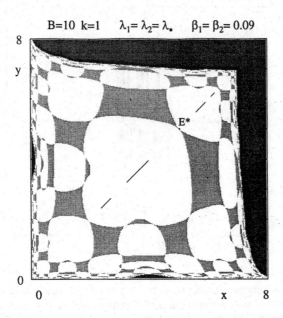

Fig. 6. Two coexisting attractors in the feasible set, a Milnor attractor along the diagonal Δ and a stable period two cycle symmetric with respect to Δ. The white regions indicate points which converge to the Milnor attractor, whereas points in the light-grey region converge to the two-cycle.

obtain the boundary of an absorbing area makes use of the concept of critical curves and can be outlined as follows: starting from a portion of LC_{-1}, approximately taken in the region occupied by the area of interest, its images by T_s of increasing rank are computed until a closed region is obtained. When such a region is mapped into itself, then it is an absorbing area $\mathcal{A}$. The length of the initial segment must be taken, in general, by a trial and error method, although several suggestions are given in the books referenced above. Once an absorbing area $\mathcal{A}$ is found, in order to see if it is invariant or not, the same procedure must be repeated by taking only the portion

$$\gamma = \mathcal{A} \cap LC_{-1} \qquad (21)$$

as the starting segment. In order to obtain the boundary of the absorbing area $\mathcal{A}$ shown in fig. 8, six images of the generating arc $\gamma = \mathcal{A} \cap LC_{-1}$ are sufficient. However, only the portion of γ belonging to the branch $LC_{-1}^{(b)}$ has been used because the images of the other portion, the one belonging to the

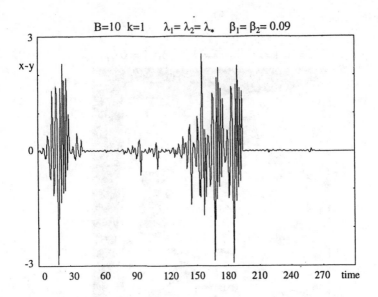

Fig. 7. Typical trajectory converging to a Milnor attrator along the diagonal. Before the marketing efforts of the two firms finally synchronize (i.e. $x_t - y_t = 0$), several bursts can be observed in the transient phase.

upper branch $LC_{-1}^{(a)}$, are always inside the absorbing area, so that they do not form part of the boundary. Hence in fig. 8 we have $\gamma = \mathcal{A} \cap LC_{-1}^{(b)}$ and $\partial\mathcal{A} \subset \bigcup_{k=1}^{6} T^k(\gamma)$.

We remark that $\mathcal{A}$ includes the Milnor chaotic attractor $\mathbf{A}_s \subset \Delta$ (see fig. 6), and all the trajectories starting from a neighborhood of $\mathbf{A}_s$ cannot go out of $\mathcal{A}$. Loosely speaking $\partial\mathcal{A}$ behaves as a bounded vessel for the intermittency phenomena related to the presence of the transversely repelling cycles embedded inside $\mathbf{A}_s$. The local unstable sets of these cycles are folded back (reinjected) by the folding action of the critical curves that form $\partial\mathcal{A}$. A similar transient behavior is observed with lower values of the degree of competition β such that $\Lambda_{\perp}^{nat} < 0$. The only difference is that the absorbing area is smaller (so that the bursts are of smaller amplitude) and longer transients, characterized by intermittency, are observed before the marketing efforts of the two firms synchronize along the diagonal. This is due to the fact that for values of $\Lambda_{\perp}^{nat}$ closer to zero (but negative) the influence of the transversely repelling cycles is stronger and, consequently, the bursts are more frequent and persist longer before the trajectories are eventually captured by $\mathbf{A}_s$ in the long run.

The bottom-line of the investigation so far is this, given the initial allocations are in $\mathcal{B}(\mathbf{A}_s)$: first, the size of the absorbing area containing the Milnor attractor $\mathbf{A}_s$ gives us an idea of the maximal difference between the marketing efforts of the two firms. Second, there is an inverse relationship between the longevity of transients and the values of the natural Lyapunov exponent $\Lambda_\perp^{nat}$. For values of the degree of competition β for which $\Lambda_\perp^{nat}$ is strongly negative, the absorbing area is large (and, hence, the possible difference between the marketing efforts is large), but the transient phase where bursts occur before the trajectories of marketing efforts settle down along the diagonal is relatively short. Neglecting this relatively short transient period we can conclude that the model of the representative player is a good approximation. On the other hand, if $\Lambda_\perp^{nat}$ is close to zero but negative, then the transient phase is rather long. Frequent and persistent bursts occur before the marketing efforts of the competitors synchronize. However, in this case the absorbing area is (very) small, which means that the difference between the marketing effort is (very) small. Neglecting this small difference, again we can conclude that the model of a representative player is a good approximation even in the transient phase. It might seem that this justifies the assumption often made in economic and game theory models, where for analytical convenience it is often assumed that firms are homogeneous. Our analysis so far has shown that even if we consider a dynamic promotional competition model there is either only a relatively short transient before the firms behave in a similar way, or the difference between the choices of the two competitors in the transient phase (which might be long) is negligibly small. Of course, we still have to assume that the initial effort allocations are located inside the basin of attraction of the Milnor attractor.

5   Quasi-Homogeneous Firms and Symmetry Breaking

In the previous subsection we made the very restrictive assumption that the firms' structural parameters are the same and the difference between the competitors lies only in their initial choices of the effort allocations. Although synchronization does not necessarily occur for all initial effort allocations (namely those in the grey region) we can determine for which initial marketing outlays the two-dimensional model (5) can be substituted by the model of a representative player. One question, however, raised in the Introduction, has not been answered yet: Is the assumption of homogeneous firms which is so predominant in the literature an innocuous one? Or do small heterogeneities matter. This is the topic we will now turn to. If a *small heterogeneity* due to a small parameter mismatch is introduced, additional interesting phenomenons occur. Let us assume, for example, that there is a small difference between the two response parameters β_1 and β_2 of the two competitors in the model (3), that is

$$\lambda_1 = \lambda_2 = \lambda; \; k = 1; \; \text{and} \; \beta_2 = \beta_1 + \varepsilon \tag{22}$$

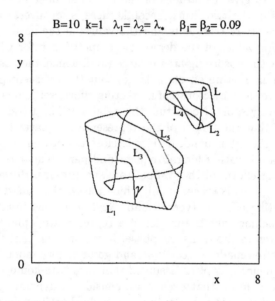

Fig. 8. Boundary of the absorbing are around the Milnor attractor along the diagonal, obtained by arcs of critical curves: $L = T(\gamma)$, with $\gamma \in LC_{-1}$, $L_1 = T(L),...L_k = T(L_{k-1})$, with $k = 2, ..., 5$.

where ε is small with respect to β_1, i.e. $\varepsilon/\beta_1 \ll 1$. Such an assumption should not invalidate the conclusions made in the previous subsection unless these conclusions where only valid under the restrictive assumptions that these results only hold for parameter values which are *exactly* equal. If this would be the case, then these results are not robust to small parameter perturbations and can be questioned on empirical grounds. For any practical purpose we have to make sure that the insights derived from the symmetric model carry over to the model with slightly perturbed parameter values in order to show the robustness of our findings. Unfortunately, as it will turn out, in general the symmetric model does not give rise to a generic behavior. That is, if a small heterogeneity is introduced into the model (3) the evolution of the marketing efforts of the two firms over time may be quite different.

Note, first of all, that such a mismatch of structural parameters causes the destruction of the invariance of Δ, due to the fact that the map is no longer symmetric (this kind of perturbation has been called *symmetry breaking* in Bischi et al. (1999)). The fact that the diagonal is no longer an invariant set also causes the disappearance of the one-dimensional Milnor attractor $\mathbf{A}_s$ along the diagonal. In effect, such a small perturbation may lead to quite different dynamics, since after the symmetry breaking synchronization can no longer occur, and the bursts never stop. The generic trajectory fills up the absorbing area, which now appears to be a two-dimensional chaotic area. Figure 9a is obtained after the introduction of a very small difference between the response parameters of the firms with respect to the set of parameters used in figures 6, 7 and 8: $\beta_2 = 0.09001$ ($\varepsilon = 0.00001$). The evolution of the system (3) starting from the initial effort allocation $(x_0, y_0) = (3.5, 3.5) \in \Delta$, i.e., from homogeneous initial choices, is represented in the phase space (x, y). As in the homogeneous case we have two coexisting attractors, but the two attractors are now a two-dimensional chaotic area and the cycle C_2. In other words, after an apparently negligible heterogeneity has been introduced, the dynamical behavior of the resulting model is quite different: the Milnor chaotic attractor on which asymptotic synchronization occurs is replaced by a two-dimensional chaotic attractor on which on-off intermittency occurs, i.e., bursts never stop. This is clearly visible in fig. 9b, where the difference of the marketing efforts over time, $(x_t - y_t)$, is represented over 10000 periods. It is evident that long time intervals exist in which the two firms show quasi-synchronized behavior, but in-between such intervals asynchronous behavior emerges with an apparently random pattern. As mentioned in Bischi et al. (1999), if the attractor $\mathbf{A}_s$ embedded in the diagonal in the symmetric case is a topological attractor, i.e. no transverse repelling cycles exist, then the introduction of small heterogeneities does not have such a disruptive effect. In this case the symmetric model still serves as a good approximation of the behavior of the two firms.

From an economic point of view, the results of this section make us aware how restrictive the assumptions made in (or almost throughout) the literature are. If the assumption of homogeneity is made for analytical tractability, we should be aware that we solve the model for a very special case. The reason is that for dynamic models the symmetric case is often non-generic, i.e. it exhibits a behavior which is quite different from the model with heterogeneous agents. On the other hand, parameter regions may exist, where the assumptions of homogeneity does not matter at all (see the last remark in the previous paragraph). If the attractor of the symmetric model is a topological attractor, i.e. if all the cycles embedded into the diagonal are attractive, then even after the introduction of a small heterogeneity the evolution of the (now asymmetric) model would still lead to almost perfectly synchronized trajectories. In other words, model builders have to be aware when the assumption of homogeneous players is justified and when it is not. For certain ranges of the structural parameters this assumption might be sensible and valid, whereas for other regions it might be simply wrong and misleading. Assuming homogeneity among all players would in this case give a wrong

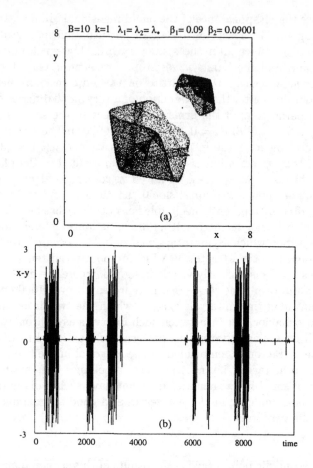

Fig. 9. The introduction of a small heterogeneity in the form of a mismatch of the parameters causes the disappearance of the Milnor attractor along the diagonal; symmetry breaking occurs. Marketing efforts of the two firms no longer synchronize and bursts never stop.

idea of the variety of dynamical phenomena which can be observed for given model.

6   Concluding Remarks and Further Developments

So far we have presented two main ideas. First, we have demonstrated that by using the concept of critical curves and segments on the invariant coordinate axes we can determine the feasible set and the changes of it as some parameters are varied. This gives us the opportunity to derive global stability results, which tells us something about the conditions under which convergence to a steady state allocation is achieved and for which set of initial allocations. Second, we have argued that the assumption of homogeneity, which is so often made in the literature, may lead to wrong conclusions about the resulting dynamical behavior of a model for certain values of the models' parameters.

However, the study of dynamical phenomena of the symmetric model can be continued. As the degree of competition β spans the whole interval $(0, 1)$ other global bifurcations can be evidenced that cause strong qualitative changes of the structure of the set of initial condition which generate trajectories that synchronize. This will be object of further research, and we just give here a brief description of some phenomena that occur as β is further increased. For slightly increased values of the degree of competition β (with respect to the value $\beta = 0.09$), a transition from the scenario (**L**) of locally riddling to the scenario (**G**) of globally riddling is observed. This occurs because the absorbing area $\mathcal{A}$ that includes the Milnor chaotic attractor $\mathbf{A}_s$ where synchronization takes place (fig. 8) becomes larger as β increases, so that finally it has a contact with the boundary that separates $\mathcal{B}(\mathbf{A}_s)$ from $\mathcal{B}(C_2)$. After this contact the absorbing area $\mathcal{A}$ is destroyed, and some trajectories that are locally repelled from $\mathbf{A}_s$ can reach the basin $\mathcal{B}(C_2)$. This leads to a situation of additional uncertainty about the fate of a trajectory starting from a given initial effort allocation, due to the creation of a riddled basin. Given an initial allocation in the feasible set, the evolution of the system may lead to the 2-cycle or it may synchronize, converging to $\mathbf{A}_s$ after a short[16] transient with intermittent behavior. Since the model is deterministic, the fate of the trajectory of marketing efforts is uniquely determined by the initial allocation, but due to the riddled structure of $\mathcal{B}(\mathbf{A}_s)$ the presence of arbitrarily small perturbations or of arbitrarily small errors in measuring the initial outlays makes it practically impossible to forecast the long-run behavior. This would also mean that it is practically impossible to decide, when the model of a representative agent might be used to replace the two-dimensional model. We can say that the contact bifurcation described in this situation marks a transition from a situation in which the model allows to make reasonable forecasts about the long-run behavior of the system (fig. 6) to a situation of complete uncertainty, in which a forecast of the long-run synchronization behavior is impossible. We remark that such a strong qualitative change in the predictability of the time evolution of the system is not related to local properties of the system near the invariant diagonal (i.e., the Lyapunov exponent) but it is due to a global bifurcation, a contact occurring far from Δ.

---

[16] Given an initial allocation which belongs to $\mathcal{B}(A_s)$, the transient before synchronization is shorter with respect to that obtain for $\beta = 0.09$ because the natural Lyapunov exponent is smaller.

If the natural Lyapunov exponent $\Lambda_\perp^{nat}$ changes sign from negative to positive, the chaotic set $\mathbf{A}_s$ becomes a chaotic saddle, i.e., $\mathcal{B}(\mathbf{A}_s)$ has zero measure. This means that the probability for emergence of synchronized behavior is zero, even if the homogeneous firms are starting out with initial allocations arbitrarily close to the diagonal, i.e., $x_0 \cong y_0$. Trajectories after the so-called blowout bifurcation fill up a large chaotic area. Again, this chaotic area is bounded by critical curves: it is the minimal invariant absorbing area that already existed around the Milnor attractor before the occurrence of the blowout bifurcation. However, even if the marketing efforts of the two firms never synchronize, their behavior is not totally uncorrelated. The trajectories remain close to the line of equal choices Δ quite often, that is, the probability that the decisions made by the two firms are similar is higher with respect to a totally uncorrelated competitive system[17].

Acknowledgments: This work has been performed under the under the auspices of CNR, Italy, and under the activity of the national research project "Dinamiche non lineari ed applicazioni alle scienze economiche e sociali", MURST, Italy.

References

Abraham, R., L. Gardini and C. Mira (1997): Chaos in discrete dynamical systems (a visual introduction in two dimension), Springer.

Alexander, J,C., J.A. Yorke, Z. You and I. Kan (1992): Riddled basins, Int. Jou. of Bif. & Chaos 2, 795-813.

Ashwin, P., J. Buescu and I. Stewart (1994): Bubbling of attractors and synchronization of chaotic oscillators, Phys. Lett. A, 193, 126-139.

Ashwin, P., J. Buescu and I. Stewart (1996): From attractor to chaotic saddle: a tale of transverse instability, Nonlinearity, 9, 703-737.

Balch M. (1971): Oligopolies, Advertising, and Non-Cooperative Games, in: H.W. Kuhn, G.P. Szego (Eds.), Differential Games and Related Topics, North-Holland, New York.

Baumol, W.J. and J. Benhabib (1987): Chaos: Significance, mechanism and economic applications, Journal of Economic Perspectives 3, 77-105.

Bischi, G.I., L. Gardini and M. Kopel (1998a): Analysis of Global Bifurcations in a Market Share Attraction Model, forthcoming in: Journal of Economic

---

[17] From a dynamic point of view this is due to the fact that even if $\mathbf{A}_s$ is now a chaotic saddle, i.e. transversely repelling "on average", infinitely many transversely stable cycles still exist embedded into it. $\mathbf{A}_s$ is a chaotic saddle, but not a normally repelling chaotic saddle.

Dynamics and Control.

Bischi, G.I., L. Stefanini and L. Gardini (1998b): Synchronization, intermittency and critical curves in a duopoly game. Mathematics and Computers in Simulation, 44, 559-585.

Bischi, G.I., M. Gallegati and A. Naimzada (1999): Symmetry-Breaking bifurcations and representative firm in dynamic duopoly games", in: Annals of Operations Research.89, 253-272.

Bischi,G. I. and L.Gardini (1998): Role of invariant and minimal absorbing areas in chaos synchronization, Physical Review E 58, 5710-5719.

Brock, W.A. and C.H. Hommes (1997): A Rational Route to Randomness. Econometrica 65, 1059-1095.

Buescu, J. (1997): Exotic Attractors, Birkhäuser.

Bultez, A. V. and P. A. Naert (1975): Consistent Sum-Constrained Models. Journal of the American Statistical Association 70, 529-535.

Case, J.H. (1979): Economics and the Competitive Process, New York University Press, New York.

Cooper, L.G. and M. Nakanishi (1988): Market-Share Analysis. Kluwer Academic Publishers.

Day, R.H. (1994): Complex Economic Dynamics. Vol. I: An Introduction to dynamical Systems and Market Mechanisms, MIT Press.

Devaney, R.L. (1989): An Introduction to Chaotic Dynamical Systems. The Benjamin/Cummings Publishing Co., Menlo Park.

Friedman, L. (1958): Game-Theory Models in the Allocation of Advertising Expenditures, Operations Research 6, 699-709.

Fujisaka, H. and T. Yamada (1983): Stability theory of synchronized motion in coupled-oscillator systems, Progress of Theoretical Physics, 69 (1), 32-47.

Grebogi, C., E. Ott and J.A. Yorke (1983): Crises, sudden changes in chaotic attractors and transient chaos, Physica 7D, 181-200.

Gumowski, I. and C. Mira (1980): Dynamique Chaotique, Cepadues Editions, Toulose.

Hasler, M. and Yu. Maistrenko (1997): An introduction to the synchronization of chaotic systems: coupled skew tent maps, IEEE Trans. Circuits Syst., vol. 44 (10), 856-866.

Hibbert, B., and I.F. Wilkinson (1994): Chaos theory and the dynamics of marketing systems. Journal of the Academy of Marketing Science 22, 218-233.

Karnani, A. (1985): Strategic Implications of Market Share Attraction Models, Management Science 31, 536-547.

Kopel, M. (1996): Periodic and chaotic behavior of a simple R&D model. Ricerche Economiche 50, 235-265.

Lai Y.C., C. Grebogi and J.A. Yorke (1996): Riddling bifurcation in chaotic dynamical systems, Phys. Rev. Lett. 77, 55-58.

Maistrenko, Yu. L., V.L. Maistrenko, A. Popovich and E. Mosekilde (1998): Transverse instability and riddled basins in a system of two coupled logistic maps, Physical Review E, 57 (3), 2713-2724.

Mills (1961): A Study in Promotional Competition, in: F.M. Bass et al. (Eds.), Mathematical Models and Methods in Marketing, R.D. Irwin, Illinois.

Milnor, J. (1985): On the concept of attractor, Commun. Math Phys 99, 177-195.

Mira, C., L. Gardini, A. Barugola and J.C. Cathala (1996a): Chaotic Dynamics in Two-Dimensional Noninvertible Maps, World Scientific, Singapore.

Mira, C. (1987): Chaotic Dynamics, World Scientific, Singapore.

Mira, C., J.-P. Carcasses, G. Millerioux and L. Gardini (1996b): Plane foliation of two-dimensional noninvertible maps, Int. Jou. of Bif. & Chaos, vol.6 (8), 1439-1462.

Monahan, G.E. (1987): The Structure of Equilibria in Market Share Attraction Models, Management Science 33, 228-243.

Monahan, G.E., and Sobel, M.J. (1994): Stochastic Dynamic Market Share Attraction Games, Games and Economic Behavior 6, 130-149.

Naert, Ph., and M. Weverbergh (1981): On the Predition Power of Market Share Attraction Models, Journal of Marketing Research 18, 146-153.

Nagai, Y. and Y.-C. Lai (1997): Periodic-orbit theory of the blowout bifurcation, Physical Review E, 56 (4), 4031-4041.

Ott, E. and J.C. Sommerer (1994): Blowout bifurcations: the occurrence of riddled basins and on-off intermittency, Phys. Lett. A, 188, 39-47.

Pecora, L.M. and T.L. Carrol (1990): Synchronization in chaotic systems, Phisical Review Letters 64 (8), 821-824.

Pikovsky, A. and P. Grassberg (1991): Symmetry breaking bifurcation for coupled chaotic attractors, J. Phys. A: Math Gen. 24, 4587-4597.

Schmalensee, R. (1976): A Model of Promotional Competition in Oligopoly, Review of Economic Studies 43, 493-507.

Sterman, J.D. (1989): Modeling managerial behavior: misperceptions of feedback in a dynamic decision making experiment. Management Science 35, 321-339.

Tversky, A. and D. Kahneman (1975): Judgement und uncertainty: Heuristics and biases. Science 185, 1124-1131.

Venkataramani, S.C., B.R. Hunt, E. Ott, D.J. Gauthier and J.C. Bienfang (1996a): Transition to Bubbling of Chaotic Systems, Phys. Rev. Letters 77, 5361-5364.

Venkataramani, S.C., B.R. Hunt and E. Ott (1996b): Bubbling transition, Phys. Rev. E, 54, 1346-1360.

Vilder, de R. (1996): Complicated endogenous business cycles under gross substitutability. Journal of Economic Theory 71, 416-442.

Wansink, B., R.J. Kent, and S.J. Hoch (1998): An Anchoring and Adjustment Model of Purchase Quantity Decisions, Journal of Marketing Research 35, 71-81.

A Reconsideration of Professor Iwai's Schumpeterian Dynamics

Reiner Franke

University of Bremen, Dept. of Economics, D–28334 Bremen, Germany

Abstract. The paper takes up a Schumpeterian prototype model by K. Iwai (JEBO 1984) on the interplay of technological innovation and diffusion. In a first part, the deterministic version of the model is considered and its long-run equilibrium notion of a wave train is related to Iwai's analysis. The subsequent simulations of the full version of the model with a stochastic arrival of innovations typically yield long oscillations in the growth rates of average productivity. These long waves can be viewed as originating with the frequency distribution of techniques on a wave train, from which the economy is disturbed and back to which it continuously seeks to adapt, where it is in the very nature of this adjustment process to take several decades. Across a wide range of parameter scenarios, the average wave lengths are found to be closely related to the lifetime of techniques in the underlying deterministic economy. Furthermore, the lags between innovation activities and productivity growth are examined.

1 Introduction

While there is a great variety of formal models studying technical change along Schumpeterian lines, these models are seldom put in perspective in the sense that they are related to a benchmark, or prototype, model and its dynamic properties. A model that could provide such a standard has been advanced by K. Iwai [5, 6], whose formulation of the interplay of technological innovation and diffusion is a concise summary of Schumpeter's concept of creative destruction. By extending Iwai's analysis, the present paper seeks to renew interest in this basic frame of reference.

The conceptually most important result at which Iwai arrives is that the economy will never reach a neoclassical state of equilibrium where all firms use the most efficient technique presently available. The model rather suggests another equilibrium notion at a higher level, which can be described as a balance of the centrifugal forces of diffusion with their tendency toward the technological frontier, and the centripetal forces of a never ceasing inflow of new technological knowledge. Thus, in each period the economy is characterized by a bounded but non-degenerate spectrum of coexisting techniques, a multitude of diverse production methods with different units costs. Over time, the least productive vintages are wiped out through evolutionary pressure, while at the other end of the spectrum new techniques with higher efficiencies are continuously added. This process gives rise to a long-run statistical regularity, which is captured by a probability distribution of the cost gaps of the individual techniques to the currently best-practice technique.

Iwai's discussion focusses on the analytical foundations of the notion of a Schumpeterian statistical long-run equilibrium. Another topic worth investigating are the time series characteristics of the economy. This interest originates with the observation that the random process governing the introduction of technological innovations implies that new production methods tend to arrive in clusters. Now, a bunching or clustering of innovations is generally viewed to be at the heart of the phenomenon of long waves (Kuznets [7], Freeman [2]). A model that incorporates this feature and proves able to generate long waves in its aggregate variables has been put forward by Silverberg and Lehnert [9]. In addition, however, their model contains multiplier-accelerator and wage-profit distributional dynamics (cf. [9], p. 12). Their result of long waves is no doubt striking and valuable, but the deeper reasons for this outcome are not exactly clear; the question for the, so to speak, necessary and sufficient conditions for long waves in a Schumpeterian setting remains still open.

A remarkable facet of the Silverberg-Lehnert (SL) model, though it is not hinted at by the authors, is a close relationship to Iwai's second model [6]. In fact, if the Goodwinian distribution dynamics employed by SL are turned off and replaced with the assumption of a constant wage share, then there exists a translation rule from this reduced SL model to the Iwai model that makes the two (almost) equivalent (apart from some minor specification details). It may therefore be suggested that similar long wave phenomena are already obtained in the more elementary Iwai model. Our paper confirms this feeling and, on the basis of a careful reconsideration of Iwai's economy, uncovers the basic logic behind the visible long waves.

Our analysis starts with the approximation procedure by which Iwai [6] derives an explicit formula for the equilibrium probability distribution of the cost gaps mentioned above. To this end, an auxiliary parameter δ is introduced, which Iwai treats as exogenously given. By contrast, we hold that, in order to make it consistent with the approximation concept, δ should be endogenously determined by way of a fixed-point argument. Existence and uniqueness of a fixed-point of δ are no problem, and we call the resulting distribution of cost gaps from then on the 'Iwai distribution'. To calculate the fixed-point, however, one has to resort to numerical methods. This equally holds true for the ensuing investigations.

Before turning to the time series properties of the original Iwai model, it is appropriate to put up a deterministic version where it is assumed that the innovations improve uniformly and are introduced at regular intervals of length T. Here the economy is in long-run equilibrium when the capacity shares of techniques reproduce themselves over time, only at a higher technological scale. This means that the role of technique i at time t is taken over by its successor $i+1$ at time $t+T$. Accordingly, the frequency distribution of the cost gaps remains invariant in the course of time. Such a path of the evolution of the economy is termed a *wave train*. Compared to the Iwai distribution, the wave train distribution of the cost gaps appears to be shifted to the left. This phenomenon can be ascribed to a systematic distortion in Iwai's approximation procedure. Furthermore, the wave train distribution turns out to be remarkably close to a normal distribution.

An important characteristic of a wave train is the lifetime L of techniques, from their birth as best-practice technique until they are weeded out by their more efficient competitors. L depends smoothly on three exogenous parameters: the rate of technical progress (λ), an 'intensity of innovation activities' (ν), and the speed of diffusion (γ). The response surface, i.e. the functional relationship $L = L(\lambda, \nu, \gamma)$, is nonlinear and can be numerically specified by an approximation formula.

The significance of the equilibrium concept of a wave train rests on its global stability, which by all appearances seems to be guaranteed. Hence, however the techniques may be distributed initially, the frequency shares of the cost gaps always converge to the proportions of the wave train distribution. To study the speed at which these adjustments take place, we conduct a stylized experiment. We put the economy on the wave train and then assume a short clustering of innovations, after which the new techniques again arrive at their regular intervals. With respect to the growth rates of average productivity, the adjustment process is characterized by essentially one cyclical motion. Since, as will be shown, the temporary acceleration of technical progress means a shift of the entire frequency distribution of the *level* of unit costs, toward which the economy has to adapt after the perturbation, it is only natural that several decades are needed for convergence. At the aggregate level, the adjustment process therefore manifests itself as one long wave. We find moreover that the length of these waves is initimately related to the lifetime of techniques on the wave train, L.

After this scrutiny of the deterministic economy, we return to the hypothesis that the new techniques are introduced randomly. It was already noticed that this 'innovation noise' entails a repeated clustering of innovations. So the adjustment process never comes to rest, and the oscillations in the aggregate productivity growth rates never die out. Their periods are of similar length as in the stylized experiment just considered, though they vary in the course of time depending on the stochastic variations in the 'degree' of the clustering of innovation activities. The Iwai model thus turns out to be a most elementary Schumpeterian schema to generate long waves in productivity growth.

However, the paper also aims at a theoretical explanation for the occurrence of long waves, for which the deterministic version of the model is a useful device. It is demonstrated that ultimately the long waves originate with the underlying deterministic wave train, from which the economy is disturbed and back to which it continuously seeks to adapt, where it is in the very nature of this adjustment process to take a considerable span of time of several decades.

The insights from the deterministic model are also helpful in assessing the length of the waves in the stochastic model. To this end, the Iwai model is simulated over several thousand years and an average length of its waves is computed, a procedure which is carried out across a wide range of parameter scenarios. Contrasting the average wave length W with the lifetime L of techniques on the corresponding wave trains reveals a close relationship between the two. If we fix the innovation parameter ν, then W results as an almost linear function of L, irrespective of the specific values of λ and γ from which W and L arise.

The fact that a clustering of innovations, with a certain delay, induces rising rates of aggregate productivity growth may suggest that innovation activities observed in the past can be used to 'predict' future productivity growth. In fact, for suitable combinations of lags and the length of the sample periods of innovations, one obtains correlation coefficients as high as 0.80 and more. This may in principle be helpful information, but we also point out that it might involve a statistical artifact.

Lastly, we demonstrate that the frequency distributions of techniques at a point in time are quite distinct from the wave train distributions of the cost gaps or, for that matter, from the mean values of their frequencies over a long period of time. While the distributions of the latter are smooth and well-behaved, it is no exception that, at a given date, the distribution of the capacity shares of techniques is ragged and (essentially) bimodal or trimodal. These 'disequilibrium' phenomena prevail even though the stochastic innovation process is unaltered and the economy experiences no other structural change, either.

The remainder of the paper is organized as follows. Section 2 reconsiders Iwai's approximation by which he obtains an explicit formula for the probability distribution of cost gaps in statistical equilibrium. It then proposes a fixed-point argument as a straightforward device to make the approximation procedure consistent. Section 3 formulates explicitly the laws of motion, that is, the deterministic version of the model with a regular arrival of innovations. It also clarifies the conceptual equivalence with the technological part of the Silverberg-Lehnert model. Section 4 introduces the notion of a wave train and the associated distribution of cost gaps. Since for the investigations to follow a most important characteristic will be the lifetime L of techniques on this equilibrium path, we here undertake a numerical study of the variations of L in response to different values of the model's exogenous parameters.

The ensuing sections involve a clustering in the introduction of new production methods. Section 5 describes the stylized experiment of a one-time clustering of innovations in the deterministic economy. In Section 6 the deterministic hypothesis about the innovation activities is replaced with the usual stochastic one of a Poisson process, so that we are back in the original

Iwai model. The section concentrates on an analysis of the long waves in the productivity growth rates. On the basis of a battery of simulation runs, we study, in particular, the relationship between the average length of these waves and the lifetime of techniques on the equilibrium wave trains. Section 7 contains additional observations on the correlation between productivity growth and innovation activities. It also keeps track of the shape of the frequency distribution of techniques as the dynamic process unfolds. Section 8 concludes. An appendix specifies some details of the translation from the Silverberg-Lehnert model to the Iwai model.

2   Consistency in the Iwai Distribution of Cost Gaps

The outstanding feature of the Iwai model is that even in the long run the process shows no tendency to converge toward a neoclassical equilibrium of uniform technological knowledge. Instead, a spectrum of diverse production methods with a wide range of efficiencies continues to coexist for ever. The model has nevertheless a notion of equilibrium, a state of the industry in which the centripetal forces of technological diffusion and the centrifugal forces of innovation balance. In the given stochastic framework, these forces reproduce over time a relative dispersion of efficiencies which, using expected values, is described by an explicit formula.

The model is based on three exogenous parameters: λ is the the rate of technical progress, i.e., the average growth rate of productivity of the newly invented techniques; the innovation parameter ν is a measure of the effectiveness with which firms introduce these inventions into the economy; γ represents the speed of technological diffusion.[1] The statistical regularity relates to the cost gaps between the production methods and the best-practice technique (BPT) currently in use. Assuming that the production methods are of a fixed-proportion type with constant unit costs c, the cost gaps, denoted by z, are specified as the logarithmic differences to the BPT unit cost C, $z = \ln c - \ln C$. While the level of the BPT unit costs certainly decreases over time (at rate λ on average), the relative frequencies of techniques with a given distance z to the current BPT remain stable. The distribution of the expected values of the corresponding capacity shares in the statistical equilibrium can be described by a density function $\tilde{s} = \tilde{s}(z)$. Introducing another

---

[1] The precise meaning of these parameters is explained in the next section. In the adjustments that are here generally called technological diffusion, Iwai distinguishes between imitation and economic selection of the most profitable techniques. The first concept (represented by a parameter μ) refers to the level of firms, the second (represented by γ) refers to changes in the capacity shares of the production methods (cf., in particular, Iwai [6, pp. 332–336]. For simplicity, our discussion focusses on capacities and neglects the possible role of μ as a mechanism of its own. It may, however, be noted that Iwai's original formula is recovered from the reduced equation (1) below by simply adding μ to each term $\gamma\delta$.

parameter δ, Iwai arrives at the following formula as an approximation to this density function [6, p. 341, eq. (24)],

$$\bar{s}(z) = \bar{s}(z;\delta) = \frac{(\gamma\delta + \nu)^2 / \lambda\gamma\delta}{[A_1\, e^{bz} + A_2\, e^{-bz}]^2}$$

where $A_1 := \sqrt{\nu/\gamma\delta}$, $A_2 := \sqrt{\gamma\delta/\nu}$,

$b := (\gamma\delta + \nu)/2\lambda$, $z \geq 0$

(1)

(Explicit reference to δ is made to ease the exposition below.) Since presumably the dynamic stochastic process set up by Iwai is ergodic, the long-run time averages of the relative frequencies of the cost gaps coincide with these expected values. In the following, we call the distribution given by (1) the 'Iwai distribution'.

Eq. (1) is derived from the solution of a system of differential equations where δ is an auxiliary parameter that serves to approximate several more complicated expressions. The fundamental problem with δ is not the approximation as such, but the fact that the expressions to be approximated are dependent on the distribution $\bar{s}(\cdot;\delta)$ itself. To see this in detail, let us follow Iwai's procedure and, at a given point in time, assume a discrete and finite set of techniques $i = 1, \ldots, n$ ranging in ascending order from the least productive technique $i=1$ to the BPT $i=n$, so that $z_1 > z_2 > \ldots > z_n = 0$ for the corresponding cost gaps. In the description of the motions of the capacity shares $s_t(z_i)$ of these techniques at time t, Iwai has recourse to the following (positive) terms,[2]

$$\delta_t(z_i) := \frac{\sum_{j=1}^{i-1} z_j\, s_t(z_j)}{\sum_{j=1}^{i-1} s_t(z_j)} - \frac{\sum_{j=i}^{n} z_j\, s_t(z_j)}{\sum_{j=i}^{n} s_t(z_j)}, \qquad i = 2, 3, \ldots, n \quad (2)$$

Iwai notes that "although $\delta_t(z_i)$ cannot be treated as a given constant in general, we can still expect it to fluctuate little from one unit cost to another and from one point in time to another." He then goes on with his analysis by substituting for the terms $\delta_t(z_i)$ a constant parameter $\delta > 0$, which he treats as being exogenously given [6, p. 330]. This device is very convenient since it simplifies the abovementioned differential equations to a set of logistic growth equations, for which an explicit solution can be written down; they are also a widely used tool to describe the life-cycles of technological innovations.

Now, even if we accept the hypothesis that on a given time path of innovation and diffusion, the terms $\delta_t(z_i)$ do not greatly vary over time and across techniques, it is less obvious whether they also would remain unaffected when the shape of the equilibrium distributions $\bar{s}$ in (1) changes in

---

[2] It is easily checked that (2) is equivalent to Iwai's equation (7), which refers to the unit costs c_i themselves rather than to the cost gaps z_i [6, p. 330]. Likewise, Iwai's notation $\delta_t(c_i)$ is replaced with $\delta_t(z_i)$ in the ensuing quotation in the text.

response to variations in the other parameters λ, ν, γ. It may therefore be problematic to view δ as an independent variable. To investigate this issue more closely, consider the expressions $\delta_t(z_i)$ in eq. (2). The most reasonable way to approximate them by a single number is to employ the mean value. Clearly, the determination of the latter depends on the capacity shares of the different techniques. Accordingly, we may define the mean value of the δ-terms with respect to a given frequency distribution $s(\cdot) = \{s(z_i)\}_{i=1}^n$ across the set of techniques $z_1, z_2, \ldots, z_n$ by

$$\bar{\delta} = \bar{\delta}[s(\cdot)] := \sum_{i=2}^n \delta(z_i)\, s(z_i) \, / \, \sum_{i=2}^n s(z_i) \qquad (3)$$

where the time index of the $\delta_t(z_i)$ in (2) has been omitted.

While the formulation of eq. (1) is based on the mathematical abstraction of a continuous state space of techniques, it is now more appropriate to adapt this density function to the present setting with a given finite set of cost gaps $z_1, \ldots, z_n$.[3] To this end the values $\bar{s}(z_i; \delta)$ are computed and then renormalized such that they add up to unity,

$$s^I(z_i; \delta) := \bar{s}(z_i; \delta) \, / \, \sum_{j=1}^n \bar{s}(z_j; \delta) \,, \qquad i = 1, \ldots, n \qquad (4)$$

The superscript I is meant to refer to the Iwai distribution in eq. (1).

After these notational preparations, the problem with the exogenous parameter δ can be formulated as follows. A frequency distribution $s^I(\cdot; \delta)$ obtained from eq.s (1) and (4) induces an average value $\bar{\delta}$ according to (3), but it can hardly be expected that $\bar{\delta}$ will be equal to the original δ if this number is freely chosen. A difference between the two values, however, indicates an inconsistency in the use of eq. (1).

The way in which the problem has been presented suggests an endogenous determination of δ by a fixed-point argument. Considering the function that assigns to every δ the distribution of capacity shares $s^I(\cdot; \delta)$ from (1) and (4), and subsequently the resulting average value $\bar{\delta}$ given by (3), consistency prevails for values $\delta^\star$ that entail

$$H(\delta^\star) := \bar{\delta}[s^I(\cdot; \delta^\star)] = \delta^\star \qquad (5)$$

Although the formula for $H(\delta)$ looks very complicated when it is written out, the function $\delta \mapsto H(\delta)$ turns out to be well-behaved in all our numerical calculations.[4] In fact, the function is found to be everywhere decreasing. Since

---

[3] The following argument could have also been applied directly to eq. (1) by replacing the finite sums in (2) with the corresponding integral expressions. However, in the numerical computations below we have to work with a finite set of techniques anyway.

[4] One may wonder how n, the number of cost gaps entering (2–4), makes itself felt in the expressions $H(\delta)$. As n gets large, while the range of the cost gaps is limited though sufficiently wide, this influence practically vanishes, and for this reason we have suppressed reference to the number n. In the simulations below, it will be sufficient to adopt $n = 50$, with the z_i equally spaced along the (essential) support of the Iwai distribution.

it is also positive, there is exactly one point of intersection with the $45°$ line. Existence and uniqueness of the fixed-point δ^* specified in eq. (5) is therefore guaranteed. If, from now on, we speak of the Iwai distribution with respect to given exogenous parameters λ, ν and γ, then this concept of consistency will be understood.

Table 1 presents a selected number of scenarios for λ, ν, γ. The fourth column demonstrates that the fixed-point values δ^* are considerably affected by variations in these exogenous parameters. Thus, there is no single value of δ that could be employed for a reasonable approximation of the terms $\delta_t(z_i)$ in (2).[5]

Various graphs in Iwai's article exhibit a unimodal and quite symmetric shape of the density function $\bar{s}(\cdot)$ of eq. (1). With respect to changes in the diffusion parameter γ, Iwai can analytically show that an increase in $\gamma\delta$ shifts the peak of the density function to the left and also tends to narrow the dispersion of techniques.[6] With the fixed-point concept, it has to be observed that a *ceteris paribus* rise in γ is associated with a fall in δ^*. However, the changes in δ^* happen to be dominated by the changes in γ: the product $\gamma\delta^*$ increases if γ increases. So the conclusion itself remains valid. The fall, reported in Table 1, of the corresponding mean values $\bar{z}$ and standard deviations σ_z of the cost gap distributions confirms the intuition that faster technological diffusion improves average productivity and reduces the range of vintages of production methods still operating.

Iwai furthermore points out a concentration of the distribution with a lower mean $\bar{z}$ if the innovation parameter ν increases or the productivity growth rate λ decreases. In both cases δ^* decreases too, which works in the opposite direction. Again, the so to speak primary effects from ν and λ are dominant and reduce $\bar{z}$ as well as σ_z.

While the effects of variations in γ and λ may be readily appreciated, understanding the response to a change in the innovation parameter ν requires a more specific interpretation of its meaning. A closer discussion in the next section will show that, somewhat loosely speaking, ν can be interpreted as the initial speed of diffusion of the best-practice techniques (if the intervals at which the new tchniques are introduced into the economy are stipulated to be independent of the size of ν). Alternatively (fixing the initial speed of diffusion of the best-practice techniques), ν can be seen to increase proportionately with the frequency at which inventions are introduced. In any case, a rising ν means a higher speed at which innovations become established in the economy. It makes sense from this perspective that an increase in ν diminishes the average cost gap $\bar{z}$ and the standard deviation σ_z, where the

---

[5] The computation of the fixed-points themselves poses no numerical difficulties. By virtue of the pleasant shape of the function $H(\cdot)$, already a simple iteration mechanism like regula falsi is very efficient.

[6] cf. Iwai [6, pp. 341f], together with his first paper [5, p. 178] and the close analogy of his equations (24) and (14), respectively.

Table 1. Statistics of Iwai distribution and wave train.

λ	ν	γ	Iwai Distribution			Wave Train			
			δ^*	$\bar{z}$	σ_z	$\bar{\delta}$	$\bar{z}$	$D(\mathcal{N})$	L
0.03	0.001	0.50	0.437	0.739	0.241	0.436	0.660	0.87	44.0
0.03	0.001	0.30	0.556	0.917	0.307	0.559	0.830	1.11	55.3
0.03	0.001	1.00	0.311	0.554	0.171	0.312	0.481	0.56	32.1
0.03	0.001	5.00	0.140	0.281	0.077	0.146	0.223	0.46	14.9
0.03	0.003	0.30	0.546	0.733	0.302	0.544	0.695	2.48	46.3
0.03	0.003	0.50	0.427	0.600	0.236	0.427	0.559	1.93	37.3
0.03	0.003	1.00	0.305	0.455	0.168	0.306	0.411	1.46	27.4
0.01	0.001	0.50	0.250	0.386	0.138	0.247	0.358	1.56	71.6
0.05	0.001	0.50	0.556	1.006	0.308	0.566	0.871	0.72	34.8

Note: δ^* is the fixed-point defined in eq. (5) which establishes consistency, while $\bar{\delta}$ is the average δ from eq. (3) of the wave train distribution introduced in Section 4; $\bar{z}$ is the mean value of cost gaps, σ_z their standard deviation; $D(\mathcal{N})$ is the deviation of the wave train distribution from the corresponding normal distribution (in % of total area), L is the lifetime of techniques (in years)

dispersion effect is much weaker than the improvement of average productivity.

As for the numerical values of $\bar{z}$ and σ_z themselves, the logarithmic specification of the cost gaps may be recalled. For example, a distribution with $\bar{z} = 0.739$ as in the first row of Table 1 means that the BPT has a unit cost roughly half of the average technique (since $\bar{z} = 0.739$ is equivalent to $\bar{c}/C = e^{0.739} = 2.09$). A production method one standard deviation away from $\bar{z}$ means that the unit costs differ by a factor $e^{0.241} = 1.27$. In view of the empirical example of an industry given by Iwai [6, p. 324], where the ratio of payroll to value added ranges from 0.15 to 0.85, the figures of $\bar{z}$ and σ_z obtained in Table 1 do not seem exaggerated.

At the end of this section on the Iwai distribution, the close relationship between the fixed-point value δ^* and the standard deviation σ_z of the cost gaps may be noted. Across the parameter combinations here considered, the ratios δ^*/σ_z are confined to the narrow range between 1.805 and 1.820 (based on the original numbers with four significant digits); this even holds true for an extreme scenario like $\gamma = 5$ in the fourth row of Table 1.

3   Formulation of the Dynamic Model

In the remaining sections, we study Iwai's Schumpeterian economy and its long-run properties without invoking the approximation procedure.[7] As mentioned above, the equations describing the changes in the capacity shares of techniques i involve distinct terms $\delta(z_i)$ defined in (2), which are subsequently approximated by a constant number δ. Though the previous section has established conditions for a reasonable and consistent choice of δ, by using average values and the fixed-point argument of eq. (5), it might still be felt that this treatment leads to systematic distortions. The usefulness of formula (1) as a summary description of the statistical equilibrium would then be severely undermined.

The suspicion rests on the following observation. The diffusion of techniques i can be described by a set of differential equations in cumulative capacity shares S_i,

$$\dot{S}_i = \gamma\,\delta(z_i)\,S_i\,(1 - S_i) \qquad (6)$$

where S_i is the sum of the relative frequencies of production methods that are at least as productive as technique i; cf. Iwai [6, p. 329]. However, computation of the Iwai distribution $s^I(\cdot; \delta^\star)$ typically yields values of $\delta(z_i)$ considerably above average for both low and high indices i. Hence, if Iwai conveniently replaces the expressions $\delta(z_i)$ with a uniform constant δ, and if in the previous section we suggested to adopt the average value satisfying condition (5) for the approximation, $\delta = \bar{\delta} = \delta^\star$, then a certain bias emerges from this treatment: the thus simplified time derivatives of S_i are systematically smaller for low and high i.

On the one hand, the distortion means that, according to (6), the capacity shares of the most recent vintages rise faster than stated by the approximation. On the other hand, the cumulated frequencies S_i converge more rapidly toward unity, signifying that the least productive techniques (with low indices i) are more rapidly extincted. Since both effects tend to increase average productivity, we may imagine that the average cost gap $\bar{z}$ predicted by the Iwai distribution will somewhat overestimate the mean value of the true equilibrium distribution of cost gaps.

To investigate this problem and, provided the conjecture is confirmed, the seriousness of the approximation errors in the Iwai distribution, we wish to study the dynamics in its purest form. For this purpose, we put up a deterministic version of the Iwai model. In the next three sections we work with the hypothesis that, instead of occurring randomly as in Iwai's original formulation, the innovations are carried out at fixed regular intervals of time. Furthermore, for the numerical simulations later on, we make explicit a

---

[7] While Iwai refers to the technological state of an industry, we prefer the macroeconomic interpretation of a one-sectoral economy. In this way, we can later point out a close relationship to the Silverberg-Lehnert model [9].

discrete-time framework with an adjustment period of h 'years'. The dynamic relationships are specified in such a way that h can be freely chosen and the process of going to the limit, $h \to 0$, is well-defined. In the latter case we obtain the deterministic counterpart of Iwai's differential equations (which refer to expected values).

The dynamic process begins with N_o production methods at starting time $t = 0$. A new technique is introduced into the economy every T years (T being a multiple of h), at dates

$$t \in J := \{ jT : j = 1, 2, \dots \} \tag{7}$$

Productivity of the new techniques grows exponentially at an annual rate λ. Since only (logarithmic) cost differentials will matter, the unit costs may be normalized such that they are given by

$$\ln c_i = -i\lambda T, \qquad i = 1, 2, \dots \tag{8}$$

cf. Iwai [6, p. 338]. Let N_t be the index of the best-practice technique (BPT) at time t, the most productive technique currently in use or just about to be set up in that period. The changes in this variable follow from (7),

$$N_t = \begin{cases} N_{t-h} + 1 & \text{if } t \in J \\ N_{t-h} & \text{else} \end{cases} \tag{9}$$

The time index of N_t will be omitted in the running text whenever this seems possible. The capacity share of technique i at time t is denoted by $s_{i,t}$. To build up the capacity share s_N of the BPT when it comes into existence, we assume a (short) set-up phase of length T_u from time $(N - N_o)T$ until $(N - N_o)T + T_u$. Designate this span of time by

$$U(N_t) := [(N_t - N_o)T, (N_t - N_o)T + T_u] \tag{10}$$

Within the set-up phase, the capacity share s_N of the BPT is supposed to increase autonomously at a given rate q,

$$s_{N,t} = s_{N,t-h} + hq \qquad \text{if } t \in U(N), \text{ where } N = N_t \tag{11}$$

Certainly, $s_{N,t} = 0$ for $t \le (N - N_o)T$. By the end of this transitional stage, at $t = (N - N_o)T + T_u$, the BPT has established a share $s_{N,t} = qT_u$ in total capacity. From then on, the BPT is treated like any other technique, whose changes are governed by the diffusion equation specified below.

As indicated in the preceding section, the innovation process in Iwai's model is characterized by a parameter ν. The present parameters q, T_u, T can be related to ν in the following way. Iwai [5, p. 174] introduces $\nu \cdot \Delta t$ as the probability for a given firm, independently of the age of its capital vintage, to succeed in carrying out an innovation during the small time interval Δt. With M firms, νM is the economy's average rate of innovation per year (ibid.,

p. 175). In other words, $1/\nu M$ is the expected waiting time between two successive innovations, which corresponds to our fixed T. Iwai furthermore assumes that an innovation is implemented instantaneously and is enjoyed by the innovating firm in proportion to its existing capacity [6, pp. 338f]. Thus on average the initial capacity share of the BPT is given by $1/M$. Our analogue of $1/M$ is qT_u.[8] Combining these relationships yields $T = 1/\nu M = qT_u/\nu$, so that Iwai's innovation parameter ν can be reconstructed from our setting as

$$\nu = qT_u/T \tag{12}$$

The analogy also fits in with Iwai's expected rate of change of the BPT capacity share, at a particular instant of time when the production method is just being set up and the other forces of diffusion are not yet at work (expectations concern the dates at which the innovations occur). Denoting this expected value by a superscript 'e', the change is determined in continuous time by the time derivative $\dot{s}_N^e = \nu$ (Iwai [6, p. 339], together with Iwai [5, p. 176]). The counterpart in our model with its innovations at deterministic and discrete intervals is the average rate of change of $s_{N,t}$ (neglecting diffusion) until the next innovation occurs T years later. Over the fraction T_u/T of this period, the rate of change is $[s_{N,t} - s_{N,t-h}]/h = q$, while over the remaining portion it is zero. So the resulting average rate of change of s_N induced by the innovation activities is $q(T_u/T)$. By equation (12), this average change is equal to ν and thus equal to the value of $\dot{s}_N^e$ derived by Iwai.

The process of technological diffusion to which we now turn is governed by differential cost advantages. These adjustments are gradual.[9] The basic idea is that the capacity shares of the techniques change inversely in proportion to the percentage deviations of their unit costs from the economy-wide average unit cost $\bar{c}$. The latter is defined geometrically by

$$\ln \bar{c}_t := \sum_{i \leq N_t} s_{i,t} \cdot \ln c_i \tag{13}$$

The percentage deviations themselves are approximated by logarithmic differences. Assuming a speed of adjustment $\gamma > 0$, the changes in capacity can normally be expressed directly as

$$s_{i,t} = [1 - h\gamma(\ln c_i - \ln \bar{c}_t)]\, s_{i,t-h} \quad \text{for } i \leq N_t, \text{ if } t \notin U(N_t) \tag{14}$$

cf. Iwai [6, p. 328]. By construction, the $s_{i,t}$ add up to unity again. This is, however, no longer ensured over a set-up phase, when the latest technique

---

[8] Note that q has dimension [capacity]/[time], and the dimension [time] cancels out in qT_u.

[9] Retardation factors that prevent firms from adopting the most productive technique immediately are, in particular, adjustment costs, uncertainty, and the often proprietary nature of the newest technology; cf. Soete and Turner [10, p. 617].

N_t is exempted from the diffusion equation. The specification of eq. (14) is maintained for the remaining techniques, but the resulting values have subsequently to be renormalized. Formally,

$$\hat{s}_{i,t} = \{ 1 - h\gamma [\ln c_i - \ln \bar{c}_t] \} \, s_{i,t-h} \quad \text{for } i \leq N-1 \text{ and}$$

$$s_{i,t} = \hat{s}_{i,t} / [s_{N,t} + \sum_{j \leq N-1} \hat{s}_{j,t}] \qquad t \in U(N_t) \quad (N = N_t) \tag{15}$$

Though it is not modelled explicitly, it may be noted that the least productive techniques are likely to have negative net investment, or they may even leave part of their existing capital stocks idle.[10]

For more elevated values of q (or ν, respectively), it might happen that the set-up phase produces an increase in the average unit costs $\ln \bar{c}_t$. The reason is that a strong renormalization in the second equation of (15) may also have a negative impact on some of the more productive techniques, whose costs had been below average shortly before. The relative decline of these techniques is, however, only temporary; after the set-up phase their capacity shares are rising again.

In the numerical investigations to be presented below, we will be particularly interested in variations of the speed of diffusion, γ. It is therefore important to get a feel for its order of magnitude. To this end we point out that with Harrod-neutral technical progress, which leaves the capital-output ratio unaffected, the adjustment equation (14) can be derived from the concept of capital growth rates responding to the profit rate differentials of the techniques. If we let g_i designate the growth rate of the capital stock of technique i, r_i its rate of profit, $\bar{r}$ the average rate of profit, ρ a constant speed of adjustment, and β_s a constant propensity to save out of profits, the investment function of technique i reads

$$g_i = \beta_s \left[\bar{r} + \rho(r_i - \bar{r}) \right] \tag{16}$$

Weighting eq. (16) by the capacity shares and summing across all i yields a classical aggregate investment function $\bar{g} = \beta_s \bar{r}$, where the average capital growth rate equals the average profit rate multiplied by the savings propensity. Furthermore, let us single out wages, which means that the 'unit costs' c_i are interpreted as the physical coefficients of labour input per unit of output of production method i. Introducing ω as the share of wages in national income and κ as the capital-output ratio, which is supposed to be the same for all techniques, the diffusion parameter γ can be approximately expressed as

$$\gamma \approx \beta_s \rho \, \omega / \kappa \tag{17}$$

---

[10] Since old vintages tend to disappear in the long-run, most of the $s_{i,t}$ will be close to zero. For practical reasons, we reset the capacity share of the least productive technique back to zero in the computer simulations when it declines below a benchmark of 0.1%.

(the relationship is proven in the Appendix, which also makes explicit that the goodness of this approximation relies on a symmetric distribution of the techniques.) The Iwai model is thus flexible enough to infer that the speed of diffusion comprises several components. Not only does it depend on the firms' responsiveness to the profitability of alternative technologies, but also on the level of capital productivity, a nation's propensity to save, and even on the distribution of income. In particular, the fact that a *ceteris paribus* increase in the wage share tends to accelerate diffusion, though only weakly so, is perhaps counterintuitive at first sight.

Apart from the general observation about the main factors determining diffusion, eq. (17) is also useful to relate our numerical findings to the computer simulations of the Schumpeterian model put forward by Silverberg and Lehnert [9], which can be briefly characterized as an Iwai model augmented by Goodwinian income distribution dynamics.[11] The central simulations by Silverberg and Lehnert have underlying the tight version of the classical savings hypothesis, $\beta_s = 1$, a capital-output ratio $\kappa = 3$, a wage share (presumably) oscillating around $\omega = 0.61$, and investment reaction intensities $\rho = 1$ and $\rho = 3$.[12] Hence, these simulations typically imply a speed of diffusion, as here defined, of $\gamma \approx 0.20$ and $\gamma \approx 0.60$, respectively. In reality, β_s is certainly less extreme, but also the capital-output ratio might be somewhat overrated. On the other hand, values of the adjustment parameter ρ between 1 and 3 do not seem unreasonable. On the whole, an order of magnitude of γ between 0.20 and 0.60 appears to be an acceptable range for the speed of diffusion to start with, and similar values have already been considered in Table 1 above.

4   Wave Trains

Equations (7–15) describe an evolutionary process that captures the basic Schumpeterian hypotheses on technological diffusion and innovation. While diffusion constitutes an equilibrating force that tends to steer the economy's state of technology toward an equilibrium in which all firms use the most efficient production method, the function of innovation lies precisely in upsetting this equilibrating tendency. The dynamic interaction between the continuous and equilibrating forces of diffusion and the discontinuous and disequilibrating forces of innovation may nevertheless exhibit a certain regularity, which is of a statistical nature in Iwai's stochastic framework and is deterministic in

---

[11] The authors themselves give no reference to Iwai.

[12] The numerical information given by Silverberg and Lehnert is not sufficient to determine the precise value of the steady state wage share ω. Our reasoning by which we arrive at $\omega = 0.61$ is given in the Appendix. As for notational comparability, it may be mentioned that Silverberg and Lehnert [9, p. 12] specify their investment function as $g_i = r_i + s(r_i - \bar{r})$ and discuss the cases $s = 0$ and $s = 2$ in the text. It is easily checked that their parameter s and our ρ in eq. (16) are related by $\rho = s + 1$.

the present setting. In our case, the forces of diffusion and innovation balance if, in regular intervals of time, they reproduce exactly the same spectrum of coexisting techniques, only at a higher scale. This means that the role of technique i at time t is taken over by technique $i+1$ at time $t+T$.

Generally, a solution trajectory of the model is a double sequence $\{s_{i,t}\}$ that, starting from an initial distribution $s_o = (s_{o,1}, \ldots, s_{o,N_o})$ whose components sum up to one, obeys eq.s (7–15). Denote such a trajectory by Φ,

$$\Phi = \{\, s_{i,t} : i \in \mathbb{N}, \ t = 0, h, 2h, \ldots \,\}$$

A solution sequence Φ^e may be said to establish a balanced growth path, or to be an equilibrium trajectory, if its members $s^e_{i,t}$ are related by

$$s^e_{i+1,t+T} = s^e_{i,t}\,, \qquad\qquad i \in \mathbb{N}, \ t = 0, h, 2h, \ldots \qquad (18)$$

Eq. (18) expresses the concept of the self-reproducing spectrum of techniques just mentioned. In effect, an equilibrium Φ^e corresponds to what is known in the literature on partial differential equations (with their continuous state space) as a travelling wave, or a *wave train*. In our context with time and costs measured at discrete intervals, a solution Φ^* can be defined as a wave train if there exists a real number ω and a real function $\phi(\cdot)$ such that

$$s^*_{i,t} = \phi(\ln c_i - \omega t)\,, \quad \text{for all } s^*_{i,t} \in \Phi^*, \ i \in \mathbb{N}, \ t = 0, h, 2h, \ldots \qquad (19)$$

cf. Henkin and Polterovich [3, p. 556]. Compatibility of eq.s (18) and (19) is possible if $\omega = -\lambda$. This derives from (8), since $s^e_{i,t} = s^e_{i+1,t+T} = \phi[\ln c_{i+1} - \omega(t+T)] = \phi[-(i+1)\lambda T - \omega(t+T)] = \phi[-i\lambda T - \omega t - (\lambda+\omega)T] = \phi[\ln c_i - \omega t - (\lambda+\omega)T]$, which equals $s^*_{i,t}$ in (19) if $\lambda + \omega = 0$. In the following we maintain the equality $\omega = -\lambda$ and adopt the star symbol to mark a wave train or equilibrium trajectory, respectively.

The wave train function $\phi(\cdot)$ itself represents the distribution of the cost gaps z_i. In detail, let at a given point in time t the integer number j be determined by the condition $t - T < jT \le t$, which using (7) and (8) implies that the unit cost C_t of the BPT at time t is given by $\ln C_t = -j\lambda T$. Putting $\tau = t - jT$, we then obtain for $i \le j$ and $z_i = \ln c_i - \ln C_t$,

$$\phi(\ln c_i - \omega t) = \phi(\ln c_i + \lambda(jT + \tau)) = \phi(\ln c_i - \ln C_t + \lambda\tau)$$
$$= \phi(z_i + \lambda\tau) \qquad (\text{where } 0 \le \lambda\tau < \lambda T) \qquad (20)$$

It is thus seen that the distribution of the cost gaps remains essentially invariant over time. The distribution shifts slightly between two innovations when the term $\lambda\tau$ increases from 0 to λT, but assumes identical values if we look at it regularly every T years. Obviously, the wave train function $\phi(\cdot)$ corresponds to the Iwai distribution discussed in Section 2.

Applying the concept of a wave train to system (7–15) raises the following four questions: Does a wave train Φ^* exist? Is it uniquely determined? As time progresses, do the frequency distributions of other solutions Φ converge to the distributions that are associated with $\Phi^\star$? Finally, are the Iwai distributions $s^I(\cdot;\delta^\star)$ from eq.s (4, 5) close to the wave train distributions in (19)?

The first three problems have been subjected to a rigorous mathematical analysis by Henkin and Polterovich [3] in another deterministic Schumpeterian model, which was built along similar lines. Under a reasonable set of conditions, the authors prove existence and uniqueness of a wave train $\Phi^\star$ as well as its global stability, so that all other trajectories converge to $\Phi^\star$ irrespective of the shape of their initial distribution s_o. Unfortunately, the (quite elaborated) analysis cannot be readily carried over since the present model differs in a number of specification details. However, existence and the powerful global stability result was fully confirmed in all our numerical simulations. As we have found no reason to harbour any doubts, we do not pursue the mathematical issue any further.[13]

Though the previous section has listed several parameters, it is remarkable that for most practical purposes a study of the wave train distributions needs no more than the same three parameters λ, ν and γ as in the construction of the Iwai distributions in Section 2. Given λ, ν, γ, the characteristics of the wave train distribution ϕ are only marginally affected by different combinations of q, T_u and T yielding the same value of ν in eq. (12).[14] For the numerical simulations to be now presented, we fix the following values for the parameters representing the length of the adjustment period, the set-up period, and the innovation time:

$$h \;=\; 0.10 \qquad\qquad T_u \;=\; 0.10 \qquad\qquad T \;=\; 2 \qquad\qquad (21)$$

As our base scenario, we choose

$$\lambda \;=\; 0.03 \qquad\qquad \nu \;=\; 0.001 \qquad\qquad \gamma \;=\; 0.50 \qquad\qquad (22)$$

Given T_u, T and ν, the speed q for erecting the initial capacities of BPT is residually determined from eq. (12).

Figure 1, which emerges from this base scenario, shows some typical features of the periodic motions that are associated with a wave train. First of all, the time series of the average cost gap $\bar{z}_t$ illustrates, from another point of view, the balance of the centripetal forces of technological diffusion, which gradually diminish the gap to the BPT, and the centrifugal forces of innovations, which show up as a jump in $\bar{z}_t$ every $T=2$ years when a new technique is introduced into the economy. Note that the capacity of the new BPT is still zero at the innovation dates themselves, here at $t = 12, 14, 16$. At these dates the cost gaps of the existing vintages are shifted by one technique,

---

[13] Strictly speaking, our results would be compatible with the existence of another unstable wave train. However, such a phenomenon would have no practical relevance, even if it existed.

[14] For example, an increase in T together with a corresponding reduction of q or T_u means a smaller number of techniques i on the wave train. Nevertheless, the graph connecting the points $(z_i, \phi(z_i))$ as in Figure 2 remains essentially the same.

from $z_{i,t-h} = \ln c_i - \ln C_{t-h} = \ln c_i - \ln c_n = \ln c_i + n\lambda T$ at time $t-h$, say, to $z_{i,t} = \ln c_i - \ln C_t = \ln c_i - \ln c_{n+1} = \ln c_i + (n+1)\lambda T$ at time t (with $n = N_{t-h}$, $n+1 = N_t$; cf. eq.s (8) and (9)). Because of the diffusion effect between $t-h$ and t, the jump in the average cost gap at $t = 12, 14, 16$ is slightly less than $\lambda T = 0.06$.

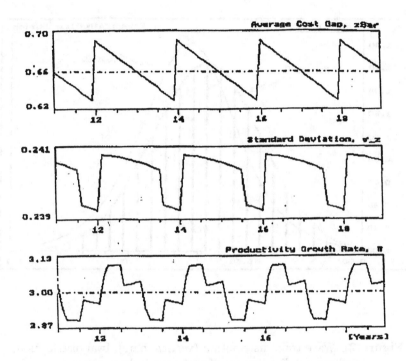

Figure 1. Time series characteristics of a wave train.

The accompanying variations in the standard deviation σ_z of the distribution of techniques are rather limited. The dispersion increases in the set-up phase of an innovation and then decreases, though less steadily than $\bar{z}_t$, when diffusion takes command.

It will certainly be expected that the average growth rate of productivity coincides with the rate of technical progress in the innovations, which is given by $\lambda = 3\%$ per year. This statistical law is brought out in the bottom panel of Figure 1, where π_t is the annual rate of productivity growth,

$$\pi_t = -(\ln \bar{c}_t - \ln \bar{c}_{t-1}) \tag{23}$$

($\ln \bar{c}_t$ the average unit costs at time t as specified by eq. (13)). The movements of π_t are generally less monotonic than those of the average cost gap, which is partly due to the one-year lag in definition (23). The periodic pattern of the changes in π_t can also look quite different in other scenarios. For example, at high values of the innovation parameter ν, π_t may even fall in the set-up phase of an innovation (cf. the remark on eq. (15)).

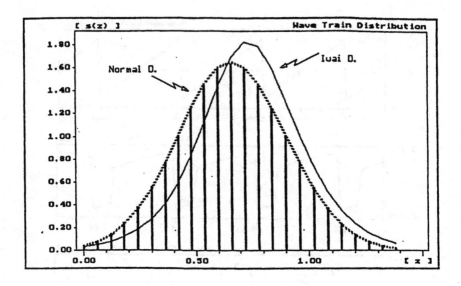

Figure 2. Wave train distribution (vertical bars), Iwai distribution, and normal distribution of cost gaps in base scenario.

After giving an impression of the time series variations of the most important sample statistics on an equilibrium path of system (7–15), we turn to the distribution of the spectrum of techniques in the base scenario. Figure 2 demonstrates the main points we wish to make. The vertical bars indicate the frequencies $s_{i,t}^*$ of the capacity shares just in the middle between two innovations at times $t = (j + 1/2)\,T$, $j = 1, 2, \ldots$ (the capacity shares are not much different at other times). As for scale, the frequencies are renormalized such that the area under the curve connecting these values is unity. (This renormalization will also be understood in the following.) The density function thus obtained can be directly contrasted with the Iwai distribution $s^I = s^I(z_i; \delta^*)$ resulting from the same scenario, where $\delta^* = 0.437$ is the fixed-point of the auxiliary parameter δ that was discussed in Section 2 and reported in Table 1. Incidentally, δ^* is practically identical to the average δ of eq. (3) across the wave train frequencies, which turns out to be given by $\bar{\delta} = 0.436$.

The graph of the Iwai distribution $s^I(\cdot; \delta^*)$ is drawn as the solid line in Figure 2. What leaps to the eye is the systematic deviation from the wave train distribution $\phi(\cdot)$. Apart from minor differences in the shape of the two distributions, the function $\phi(\cdot)$ appears to be shifted to the left of $s^I(\cdot; \delta^*)$. This distortion confirms the reasoning at the beginning of Section 3, according to which the most efficient techniques tend to have higher capacity shares than predicted by the Iwai distribution, while the old vintages have lower shares.

Quantitatively, the wave train and the Iwai distribution overlap on a total of 85.9% of their area, that is, the gap between the two distributions is as large as 14.1%. One needs no statistical procedures to conclude that the two distributions differ significantly from each other.

The systematic difference between the wave train and the Iwai distribution is by no means restricted to the base scenario. Referring to the mean value of the cost gap, Table 1 above documents the discrepancy over a wide range of parameter values λ, ν, γ. In all cases, the wave train is characterized by a lower $\bar{z}$ than the corresponding Iwai distribution. On the other hand, the two distributions remain quite similar in shape, qualitatively and also quantitatively in terms of the standard deviation. This resemblance explains the close values in Table 1 of the fixed-point δ^* of the Iwai distribution and the average $\bar{\delta}$ of the wave train.

The bell-shape character of the vertical bars in Figure 2 suggests to compare the wave train distribution with a normal distribution. The average cost gap is computed as $\bar{z} = 0.660$ (see the top row in Table 1), the standard deviation in the middle between two innovation dates is $\sigma_z = 0.241$ (as indicated by the reference line in Figure 1; σ_z is thus also equal to the standard deviation of the corresponding Iwai distribution). The Gaussian density function constituted by these two parameters is depicted as the dotted bold line in Figure 2. The differences in the frequencies of the normal distribution and the wave train distribution are hardly visible. On the whole, the two distributions have 99.13% of the area below the graph of their density function in common. Accordingly, the gap between these two distributions is just 0.87%. The column $D(\mathcal{N})$ of Table 1 documents that the same gap in the other scenarios is not so much wider, especially if the innovation parameter ν is bounded. We may thus conclude that the distribution of techniques on a wave train is to a remarkably good degree approximated by a normal distribution with the same mean and standard deviation.[15]

If we examine the average cost gap $\bar{z}$ across the different scenarios, the direction of its changes is the same as predicted by the Iwai distribution.

---

[15] Compared to a normal distribution with the same $\bar{z}$ and σ_z, the Iwai distribution function overstates the frequencies around $\bar{z}$. Even if it were corrected for the shift in the average cost gap, the Iwai distribution would therefore still be inferior to a normal distribution as an approximation of the wave train distribution function ϕ.

Specifically, a decrease in the diffusion speed γ increases $\bar{z}$. A closer inspection of a number of additional simulation runs with γ decreasing from 1.00 to 0.20 reveals that the increases in $\bar{z}$ are more than proportionate. The average cost gap also increases as λ rises from 1% to 5%; here the increments in $\bar{z}$ are less than proportionate.

Another feature of wave trains that will play an important role in the following sections is the life-cycle of techniques; that is, the time from their first introduction into the economy over their rise and decline until they are weeded out by their more productive successors. The symmetric shape of the wave train distribution allows us to determine the lifetime of a technique directly by using the average cost gap on the wave train $\bar{z}$ and the growth rate of productivity λ. To this end, specify the total width of gaps as $2\bar{z}$, by which we imply that the capacity share of a technique i with cost gap $z_i > 2\bar{z}$ is considered so low that it may be neglected as being no longer of economic significance.[16] Since by eq. (8) the difference between two cost gaps z_i and z_{i+1} is uniformly given by $\ln c_i - \ln c_{i+1} = \lambda T$, we have $2\bar{z}/\lambda T$ vintages of techniques over the range of cost gaps from $z = 0$ to $z = 2\bar{z}$. As these techniques appear successively in regular intervals of T years, it takes $L = 2\bar{z}/\lambda$ years until the previously best-practice technique is (virtually) eliminated from the market:[17]

$$L \;=\; \text{lifetime of a technique on the wave train} \;=\; 2\,\bar{z}\,/\,\lambda \;\;[\text{years}] \quad (24)$$

Thus, each technique in the base scenario runs through a life-cycle of $2\bar{z}/\lambda = 2 \cdot 0.660 / 0.03 = 44$ years. (On the basis of Figure 2, we may also count the numbers of vertical bars with $z > 0$ and multiply this number by $T = 2$. In this way we get $(24 - 1) \cdot 2 = 46$ years. The difference to the 44 years from eq. (24) is due to our convention to discard old vintages with 'economically insignificant' capacity shares, which here affects the last bar at $z = 1.38$ in Figure 2.)

With the aid of eq. (24) it can now be directly seen that a higher diffusion speed γ and a higher innovation parameter ν not only reduce the average cost gap, but also shorten the life-cycle of techniques. A change in the productivity growth rate λ, on the other hand, works in two directions: an increase in λ raises the average cost gap and so has a positive impact on L, whereas the increase in the denominator has a negative bearing on L. The last column in Table 1 shows that the second effect is dominant; a *ceteris paribus* rise in

---

[16] The 'spread' $2\bar{z}$ of the cost gaps contains the same information as the standard deviation σ_z. As a matter of fact, the relationship between σ_z and $\bar{z}$ can be reasonably well described by the linear approach $\sigma_z = -0.002 + \alpha\,\bar{z}$. Performing this regression for fixed values of ν and over the same 9×9 grid of combinations of γ and λ as in Figure 3 below, we obtain $\alpha = 0.370,\ 0.404,\ 0.428$, respectively, for $\nu = 0.001,\ 0.002,\ 0.003$; the standard error is $0.0069,\ 0.0078,\ 0.0083$, respectively.

[17] Notice that z is unit cost and λ the decrease in unit costs per unit of time. Hence the expression $2\bar{z}/\lambda$ is of dimension [time].

the growth rate of productivity tends to diminish the lifetime of techniques on their wave train. Though this result may not come unexpected, eq. (24) shows that it is not self-evident.

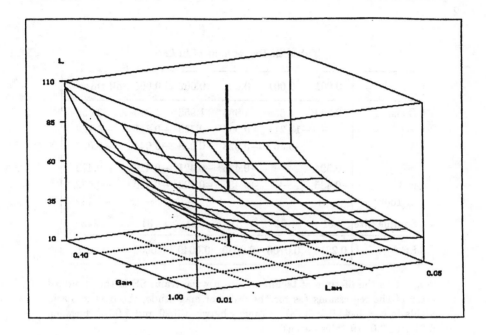

Figure 3. Response surface of the lifetimes $L = L(\gamma, \lambda)$ of techniques on the respective wave trains. ν is fixed at $\nu = 0.001$, the vertical bar indicates the base scenario $\gamma = 0.50$, $\lambda = 0.03$, for which $L = 44$.

Figure 3 represents the variations of the lifetime L as a response surface in a three-dimensional space. While the innovation parameter ν is fixed at $\nu = 0.001$, λ increases from 1% to 5% in one direction in the plane, γ decreases from 1.00 to 0.20 in the other direction. The stepsize for λ is 0.5%, the stepsize for γ is 0.10. We thus have a grid of 9×9 values of λ and γ, and for each pair (γ, λ) the corresponding value of L is plotted. Connecting these points gives the response surface, the graph of the relationship $L = L(\gamma, \lambda)$. The lifetime in our base scenario, $L = L(0.50, 0.03) = 44.0$ is marked by a reference stick.

The smooth shape of the response surface suggests that the lifetimes of techniques can be described by a relatively simple function of the parameters γ, λ, ν. We checked this possibility by a number of elementary regressions. A few explorations made clear that L as the dependent variable should be expressed in logs. The main results of these regressions are collected in Table 2.

Table 2. Regressions of $\ln L$.

$\nu =$	0.001	0.001	0.001	0.002	0.003	all three ν
Const	2.243	4.833	1.988	1.958	1.946	2.055
γ	—	−17.211	−0.594	−0.723	−0.871	−0.729
λ	—	−0.860	−0.028	−0.038	−0.044	−0.037
$\ln \gamma$	−0.594	—	−0.435	−0.421	−0.410	−0.422
$\ln \lambda$	−0.435	—	−0.436	−0.420	−0.410	−0.422
$\ln(1000\,\nu)$	—	—	—	—	—	−0.152
Sample Size	81	81	81	81	81	243
SE	0.2318	0.0706	0.0039	0.0049	0.0055	0.0078

Note: L is the lifetime of techniques on a wave train, SE is the standard error of the regressions (as for the order of magnitude, the base scenario yields $\ln L = \ln 44.0 = 3.78$). γ ranges between 0.20 and 1.00, λ between 0.01 and 0.05 (9 values each).

In the first five columns the innovation parameter ν is fixed and the lifetimes L are computed over the abovementioned 9×9 grid of combinations (γ, λ). The strong improvement in the standard error from the first two columns to the third demonstrates that the regressors γ, λ as well as $\ln \gamma, \ln \lambda$ are definitely inferior to a combination of both types of variables. Adopting the latter approach and comparing the regression coefficients across the three different values of ν, it is seen that an increase in ν not only shifts the response surface of Figure 3 downward but also rotates it somewhat.

Including different values of ν but using (additively) separate regressors $\gamma, \lambda, \ln \gamma, \ln \lambda$, and ν, the rotation effect is averaged out in the coeffcients of the former four variables (cf. $\nu = 0.002$ and the last column in Table 2). Nevertheless, the regression approach reported in the last column of Table 2, which is based on $9 \times 9 \times 3 = 243$ different combinations of (γ, λ, ν), assures us that the functional specification

$$\ln L = a_o + a_1\gamma + a_2\lambda + a_3 \ln \gamma + a_4 \ln \lambda + a_5 \ln(1000\nu) \qquad (25)$$

is an effective numerical description of the relationship between L and γ, λ, ν. To assess the standard error SE $= 0.0078$, recall that the lifetime of techniques in the base scenario was $L = 44.0$. Hence, the standard error associated with (25) is no more than 0.2% of $\ln 44 = 3.78$.

5   Long Waves From a One-Time Clustering of Innovations

The significance of the equilibrium concept of a wave train rests on its global stability. Accordingly, if system (7–15) starts from different initial conditions or is perturbed from its equilibrium path, the relative frequencies of the cost gaps z converge, or return, to the wave train distribution. While this is a result of fundamental importance, it gives no information about the time required for these adjustments. To discuss the speed of convergence toward the wave train in an organized way, consider the following stylized experiment. Suppose that on its evolution on a wave train, the economy is shocked by a short clustering of innovations. In detail, maintain the constant decrease in the unit costs of innovations as specified by eq. (8), $\ln c_{i+1} - \ln c_i = -\lambda T$, but let two techniques arrive on the scene successively after one year instead of the regular two years $(T = 2)$. Say, the innovations are introduced at $t = 6, 8, 10, 11, 12, 14, 16$, etc.

The adjustments in this experiment are of the following kind. With respect to a suitable constant a_o and t being a multiple of $T = 2$, the unit cost of the BPT at time t in the unperturbed economy is determined by $\ln C_t = a_o - \lambda t$. Denoting the unit cost of the BPT in the perturbed economy by $\ln \tilde{C}_t$, we have $\ln \tilde{C}_{10} = \ln C_{10}$, $\ln \tilde{C}_{11} = \ln \tilde{C}_{10} - \lambda T = (a_o - 10\lambda) - 2\lambda$, $\ln \tilde{C}_{12} = \ln \tilde{C}_{11} - \lambda T = (a_o - 12\lambda) - 2\lambda = \ln C_{12} - 2\lambda$. Since afterwards the technical progress proceeds at its regular pace, $\ln \tilde{C}_t = \ln C_t - 2\lambda$ obtains for $t \geq 12$.

When the perturbed economy has converged, its wave train has the same distribution of cost gaps as the unperturbed economy, whereas the best-practice techniques have a lead in the level of unit costs of 2λ. It is thus seen that to each technique in the unperturbed economy there corresponds a technique in the perturbed economy with the same capacity share but a unit cost that is lower by 2λ. At each instant of time, the original distribution of unit costs is shifted by one technique, so to speak.

Given the original time path of innovations with unit costs $\ln C_t = a_o - \lambda t$, the techniques in the unperturbed economy centre around $\ln C_t + \bar{z}$ at time t. The clustering of innovations in the perturbed economy is tantamount to a temporary acceleration of technical progress. The adjustments then setting in have to move an entire distribution of unit costs to a new (moving) centre, which is given by $\ln C_t + \bar{z} - 2\lambda$. However, the adjustment process cannot simply 'skip' one technique; after its introduction into the economy, each technique has to pass through a whole life-cycle. Although in the transition phase the life-cycles will be shorter, the diffusion mechanism of eq. (14) is only gradual and so this reduction of the lifetime of techniques will be rather limited. Recalling from the previous section that techniques are typically operating for 40 years and more, it is easily conceivable that it will take a considerable span of time of several decades until the shift of the entire frequency distribution is completed.

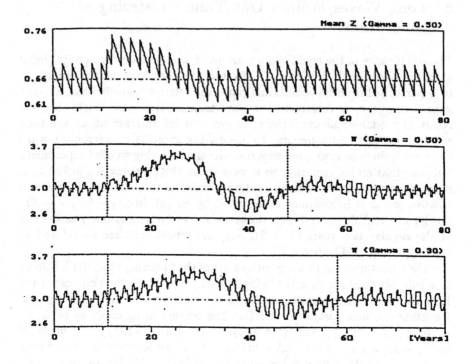

Figure 4. One-time clustering of innovations.

The main statistical properties of the adjustment path are illustrated in Figure 4, where the first two panels refer to the base scenario. The upper panel displays the motions of the average cost gap $\bar{z}_t$. The pattern until $t = 10$ is known from Figure 1. The regular decline in $\bar{z}_t$ after $t = 10$ is interrupted at $t = 11$: the early introduction of the next innovation produces the jump of $\bar{z}_t$ already at that time, from 0.66 to approximately $0.66 + \lambda T = 0.66 + 0.06 = 0.72$. This phenomenon repeats itself at $t = 12$, when $\bar{z}_t$ jumps from 0.69 to 0.75. The average cost gap is here by $\lambda T = 2\lambda = 0.06$ higher than it would have been in the unperturbed economy.

In the readjustments of $\bar{z}_t$ toward the equilibrium fluctuations around $\bar{z} = 0.66$, it is obvious that the forces of diffusion must be more effective than before. This is achieved by the improvement in the average unit costs, which implies a stronger evolutionary pressure on the old vintages than in the unperturbed economy. While the time series of the cost gaps shows that the decrease in $\bar{z}_t$ exceeds the increase from the previous innovation, it is also seen that this difference is not very large. It therefore takes more than 10 years until the fluctuations of $\bar{z}_t$ approach the reference level $\bar{z} = 0.66$.

The process of convergence is characterized by a certain overshooting. The nature of the cyclical adjustments is more clearly visible in the time path of the annual rate of productivity growth π_t in the second panel of Figure 4. As expected, the clustering of the innovations has a positive impact on this growth rate. Note, however, that immediately after the clustering, the improvement in π_t is still quite poor. The technological gains need almost 15 years to work out, a time in which the average cost gaps have already returned close to normal. The delay is due to the time it takes for the two 'extra' techniques introduced at $t=11$ and $t=12$ to gather momentum and to increase their capacity shares such that their weight can become significant in the computation of average costs, or average productivity. In addition, it is worth pointing out that the relatively minor event of two early innovations raises the productivity growth rates by a considerable 0.5% or 0.6% above their equilibrium level. With less knowledge of the microeconomic details, one might perhaps suspect more dramatic, and more direct, causes of the behaviour of the productivity growth rates between $t=20$ and $t=30$.

The oscillation generated by the innovation clustering is obviously a 'long wave' if we neglect the small intermediate fluctuations between two innovations. The two dotted vertical bars in the second panel of Figure 4 indicate the beginning and the end of the first cycle, where the latter is given by the time at which the series of the productivity growth rate cuts the trend line $\lambda = 3\%$ from below.[18] In the base scenario, this cycle has a period of 37.2 years, from $t = 11$ to $t = 48.2$. The bottom panel exemplifies that the wave length increases with slower diffusion. For $\gamma = 0.30$ (and the other parameters fixed), the first cycle extends until $t=58.2$, so that this wave is appreciable 10 years longer.

Maintaining the innovation parameter $\nu = 0.001$, Table 3 reports the wave length F for a couple of other scenarios, most of which have already been considered in Table 1 above. These experiments confirm the observation just

---

[18] To be exact, the timing was obtained in a slightly different manner. Since the standard deviation σ_z of the cost gaps moves synchronously with π_t but its 'short-run' fluctuations are smoother, we took the first significant cutting point of the σ_z-series with its trend line to determine the length of the first cycle. 'Significant' means that if the short-run trough of σ_z following the intersection is again below the equilibrium level, then it must be closer to the trend line than the previous short-run peak.

Table 3. Reaction to a one-time clustering of innovations.

λ	$\lambda = 0.03$	0.01 0.02 0.04 0.05
γ	0.30 0.50 1.00 5.00	$\gamma = 0.50$
F	47.2 37.2 27.2 12.6	61.2 44.9 32.2 29.2
L	55.3 44.0 32.1 14.9	71.6 52.8 38.6 34.8
F/L	0.85 0.84 0.83 0.85	0.83 0.85 0.83 0.84

Note: Clustering as in Figure 4. F is length of first wave, L is lifetime of techniques on the wave train. The underlying innovation parameter is $\nu = 0.001$.

made; the wave length is generally inversely related to the speed of diffusion γ. Another factor producing longer waves is a slower pace of technical progress, i.e., a *ceteris paribus* decrease in the productivity trend rate of growth, λ.

In the general discussion of the readjustments to the wave train distribution it was argued that slow convergence is only natural since all techniques brought into being have to complete a whole life-cycle. We will thus surmise that the longer the lietime L of techniques on the wave train (as determined by eq. (24)), the longer the wave from the innovation clustering. The added computation of L in Table 3 shows that the changes in the wave length F and the lifetime L across the parameter scenarios are indeed in the same direction. The last row of the table reveals that the relationship between F and L is even closer: the ratio F/L is confined to values between 0.83 and 0.85. Given the wide range of parameter values γ and λ investigated, this is a remarkable invariance.[19]

It may finally be noted in Figure 4 that, as compared to the base scenario, the longer wave in the bottom panel is associated with a lower expansion in the productivity growth rate π_t. This is a generally observed phenomenon: a *ceteris paribus* reduction in the speed of diffusion γ as well as in the rate of technical progress λ and the innovation parameter ν, while increasing the length of the wave movement, decreases the amplitude of π_t, i.e., the maximal deviation of π_t from the trend line.

---

[19] The ratio F/L is, however, affected by changes in the innovation parameter ν. On the basis of an extreme value like $\nu = 0.005$, we obtain for $\lambda = 0.03$ and $\gamma = 0.30, 0.50, 1.00$ ratios F/L between 0.98 and 1.00. The waves themselves are moderately shorter than before, namely, $F = 41.2, 33.2,$ and 25.2, respectively.

6   Long Waves From Innovation Noise

The assumption of a deterministic and regular arrival of innovations every T years is a purposeful device to study the evolution of a spectrum of techniques in a pure form. Likewise, a one-time clustering of innovations in this setting is a useful experiment to reveal the basic mechanisms that may build up a long wave in productivity growth. The literature on long waves, however, emphasizes the stochastic nature of the innovation process, which in effect entails repeated clustering of innovations. In general, such a stochastic process will be subject to various feedbacks from the actual growth path of the economy, and there is ongoing research on the determinants of endogenous technical change. In the present paper we neglect the causes of innovation clustering and concentrate on its implications. It will therefore suffice to work with the hypothesis of an autonomous stochastic process that regards an innovation as a point event in time whose probability of occurrence is independent of time and of other innovations. This view leads us directly to the concept of a Poisson process, which is also not too bad as an approximate description of a statistical regularity inherent in the historical time series of innovations.[20]

A time-homogeneous Poisson process is constituted by the following property: the probability that the event occurs at date t, when it has not occurred until date $s < t$, is only dependent on the difference $t - s$, but not on s itself. With respect to a parameter α, the innovation probabilities are then determined by the exponential distribution,

$$\text{Prob(next innov. within } \tau \text{ years)} \ = \ \int_0^\tau \alpha e^{-\alpha s}\, ds \ = \ 1 - e^{-\alpha \tau} \quad (26)$$

Computing expected values, $T := 1/\alpha$ is found to be the mean waiting time between two innovations; equivalently, α is the mean number of innovations per year.

The stochastic hypothesis (26) replaces eq. (7) to determine the set J of the innovation dates. With this respecification of J, the remainder of the equations can be taken over unaltered. System (8–15, 26) with its 'innovation noise' matches Iwai's [5, 6] stochastic model. However, we have a different perspective now. While Iwai sought to derive analytical expressions for the statistical long-run distribution of the cost gaps, we are here in the first place concerned with the time series characteristics of this economy.[21]

---

[20] Silverberg and Lehnert [9, p. 34] conclude their analysis of empirical innovation time series with the summary that "the innovation time series investigated until now in the literature do seem to correspond to a discrete stochastic process of approximately Poisson nature with exponentially increasing trend."

[21] A minor specification detail is that in our eq. (8) the jump in productivity from one innovation to another is constant, whereas Iwai assumes that it is proportional to the time elapsed between the two innovations. These differences should average out in the long-run.

Given the set of parameters, where T now means the *expected* waiting time until the next innovation, each simulation run starts from the corresponding deterministic wave train distribution of unit costs. The innovation dates are obtained from a sequence of pseudo-random numbers.[22] If not stated otherwise, they are always initialized with the same random seed, so that each economy faces the same pattern of innovation dates. The top panel of Figure 5 reports the time series of the number of innovations that, at time t, have been introduced over the past 10 years. Of course, with $T = 2$ the expected number of these innovations is 5. Accordingly, values above this benchmark indicate a clustering of innovations, values below the benchmark summarize a barren period.

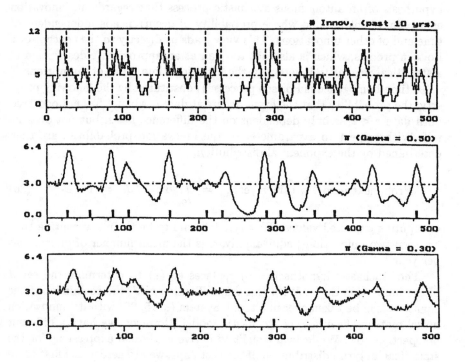

Figure 5. Long waves from innovation noise.

[22] For the implementation of a random mechanism generating the exponential distribution (26), see Press et al.[8, pp. 200f] or any textbook on numerics.

The middle panel of Figure 5 exhibits the series of annual productivity growth rates π_t in the base scenario (plotted once a year). There are many examples where it is clearly seen how a clustering of innovations produces an increase in π_t, usually with a significant delay. The effects of absent innovations are similar in the other direction. Although the fluctuations in productivity growth vary considerably in length and amplitude, the motions can be generally characterized as 'long waves'.

The discussion of the deterministic economy with its equilibrium concept of a wave train helps us to understand the deeper reason for these long waves. Imagining the economy on a wave train, we know that a clustering of innovations disturbs it from this equilibrium path and initiates a rise in the productivity growth rate π_t. If after such a clustering the innovations were to arrive at regular dates, the economy would readjust to the deterministic wave train, where the motions of π_t are of a cyclical nature. The adjustment process toward the original distribution of cost gaps is nevertheless so slow that the first cycle typically takes several decades, while the oscillations soon die out afterwards.

In the stochastic setting, by contrast, a spell of increased innovation activities is easily followed by a period in which the frequency of innovations is below average. On its way back to the wave train, the economy thus experiences another serious perturbation. Especially, this may reinforce the downward adjustment movement of π_t and so counteract the dampening forces just mentioned. Moreover, if the capacity shares of the techniques deviate already significantly from their wave train proportions and the economy is then subjected to new innovation shocks, the changes in the productivity growth rate tend to be stronger than near the wave train.[23]

To summarize, the dynamics of the economy is of an impulse-propagation type. The impulses are given by the irregular introduction of innovations in the economy. We can perceive this innovation noise as continuously destroying the shape of the distribution of cost gaps, in particular, if it were to come close to the equilibrium distribution of the corresponding deterministic economy. The propagation effects can be traced back to the readjustment tendencies toward this hypothetical wave train. Since these adjustments involve an entire distribution of different vintages of techniques, they take place on a time scale that is well beond the ordinary business cycle frequencies. Consequently, the propagation mechanism gives rise to long waves, in the same sense as the

---

[23] We have observed this tendency in the deterministic economy when taking initial distributions of the cost gaps different from the wave train distribution. On the other hand, the random innovations may interfere such as to smooth out the oscillatory adjustments to the wave train. By and large, this phenomenon can be recognized over the time intervals [40, 75] and [175, 225]. However, since sooner or later π_t will again undergo more pronounced variations, these periods of relative tranquillity will appear as part of an even longer wave.

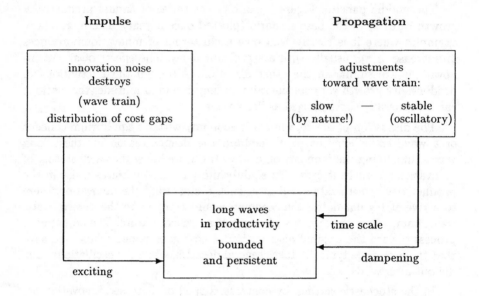

Figure 6. Basic mechanism of the stochastic model,
with reference to the deterministic economy.

expression is used in the literature on technical change. Figure 6 frames this
basic idea about the occurrence of long waves in a schematic diagram.

An average period of cycles in a stochastic series may be measured in
several ways.[24] A direct approach is to determine the time between successive peaks in π_t and take the average of all these intervals. Of course, we will
wish to neglect the tiny ripples in the time series as well as other 'inessential'
turning points. This can be achieved by suitably smoothing the series before
identifying the peaks. The short bold bars in the middle panel of Figure 5
indicate the years for which such a procedure specifies a peak. They reappear
as the dashed vertical bars in the upper panel.[25] Not all peaks thus deter-

---

[24] Silverberg and Lehnert [9, pp. 19–22] compute the spectral density of the productivity growth rate and report the proportion of the spectral variance in the 40–80
year region, which is a more indirect method to obtain a summary assessment of
the average wave length.

[25] In detail, the reference series to compute the peaks was not the productivity
growth rate itself but the series of the σ_z. The reason is that, while σ_z moves
almost perfectly synchronously with π_t in the large, it is less jagged. Furthermore,
the degree of jaggedness does not change very much across the different parameter
scenarios, which may not hold true for π_t. The series of the σ_z was smoothed
by a simple two-sided (arithmetic) moving average extending 10 years in both
directions.

mined coincide exactly with the time at which the actual maximum in π_t occurs, which is due to the smoothing procedure. These shifts in the timing of the peaks will not matter if we are interested in the average length of the waves. Over the 500 years shown, the algorithm dismisses three peaks as inessential: roughly at $t = 180, 405, 455$. The peak-to-peak periods recognized by the algorithm take, in turn, 30, 30, 21, 53, 49, 21, 57, 18, 43, 27, 47, 61 years, so that the average wave length is 38.1 years.

It goes without saying that the algorithm contains an element of arbitrariness. For example, one may argue that $t = 405$ rather than $t = 375$ should be counted as a peak. On the other hand, there are peaks that we may have liked to ignore, possibly at $t = 55$. This ambiguity is the price to be paid for an automatic procedure that is independent of personal judgement. On the whole, we expect that the effects of problematic inclusions and omissions of peaks cancel out. In addition, even if it were felt that the procedure is biased, it would be the same sort of bias across all parameter scenarios.

We are thus ready to evaluate the impact of a change in the parameter values on the average wave length. Consider first a lower speed of diffusion, γ. It has already been noticed in Figure 4 that, with $\gamma = 0.30$, a clustering of innovations needs more time to work out its effects on productivity, and that the amplitude of the resulting wave in π_t is smaller than in the base scenario. In the present context this means that a wave motion just emerging from an innovation clustering may be more or less annihilated by the next clustering. This effect is clearly visible in the bottom panel of Figure 5. For example, the intermediate fluctuations of π_t in the middle panel over the time intervals $[170, 225]$, $[360, 415]$, $[440, 470]$ are here completely smoothed out, so that the previous turning points disappear. Hence, slower diffusion gives rise to longer waves. The bold bars in the bottom panel mark waves that, in turn, extend over 58, 76, 67, 63, 61, 70, 63 years, which yields an average period of 65.4 years. Similar effects are brought about by a reduction in the rate of technical progres, λ, and the innovation parameter, ν.

While 500 years is a vast period in the history of industrialization, in our numerical analysis it can only produce a small number of waves. Furthermore, since especially in the base scenario a considerable dispersion in the single cycles is observed, the average wave length over this sample might be somewhat misleading. If we want to discover a statistical regularity, we need a more reliable measure. To this end we run the simulations over a total of 20 000 years, for all parameter scenarios alike. With the specific random seed adopted, which is the same for each simulation run, the average wave length W in the base scenario turns out to be $W = 43.88$ years. The standard deviation is as high as 15.41 years. It may be added that still 10% of the sample of wave lengths is larger than 65 years, and 10% is less than 26 years. (The distribution of the wave lengths is unimodal but otherwise quite different from a normal distribution.) Hence even under the extremely stylized conditions of our model economy, unconditional expectations about the length of the next wave, without information about the frequencies of innovations in the recent past, would be rather futile.

Regarding the second scenario over the entire sample period of 20 000 years, the difference of $\gamma = 0.30$ to $\gamma = 0.50$ is less dramatic than in Figure 5. Here the waves have an average duration of $W = 49.33$ years (with a standard deviation of 16.51 years). Nevertheless, it is easily checked that the average wave lengths in the two economies differ significantly.[26] Incidentally, the differences in wave lengths remain significant between $\gamma = 0.40$ and $\gamma = 0.50$.

Instead of listing further significant differences between selected parameter scenarios, it is more fruitful to take a wider view. Recall that within the framework of the deterministic economy with a one-time clustering of innovations and the adjustments back to the wave train, the analysis has revealed nearly constant proportions between the length of the first wave and the lifetime of techniques on the equilibrium path (if ν is fixed; cf. Table 2). We now wish to take up the same kind of investigation with respect to the average period of the long waves in the stochastic economy. We compute the average wave length for $9 \times 5 \times 3$ combinations of (γ, λ, ν), where γ varies between 0.20 and 1.00 (stepsize 0.10), λ between 0.01 and 0.05 (stepsize 0.01), and ν assumes the values $\nu = 0.001, 0.002, 0.003$. As for the range of wave lengths across these scenarios, the longest waves with $W = 86.89$ years result for the minimal parameter values $(\gamma, \lambda, \nu) = (0.20, 0.01, 0.001)$, while the maximal values $(\gamma, \lambda, \nu) = (1.00, 0.05, 0.003)$ yield the shortest wave length $W = 36.61$ years.

Comparing the average wave lengths from this battery of simulations with the lifetimes L on the corresponding wave trains, we cannot expect to find the same sort of correlation as in Table 3. But even so, there is still a remarkably close relationship between W and L. First of all, given the innovation parameter ν longer life-cycles are always associated with longer waves, irrespective of the combinations of λ and γ from which L and W result. At least this holds true if the stochastic economies are all faced with the same random sequence of innovation dates. Moreover, the monotonic relationship is also quite regular. Figure 7 plots the pairs (L, W) that are obtained from the 9×5 combinations of (γ, λ) when ν is held constant at 0.001 (hearts), at 0.002 (squares), or at 0.003 (diamonds), where it may be noted that several such pairs (L, W) are close together or even identical. Each of the three sets of (L, W) is seen to trace out a smooth functional relationship $W = f_\nu(L)$.

---

[26] Applying the standard formula for large samples, $t = (W_1 - W_2)/\sqrt{s_1^2/n_1 + s_2^2/n_2}$, yields $t = -5.17$; s_1 and s_2 are the standard deviation, and the sample sizes n_1, n_2 of waves can be recovered from the ratios $20000/43.88$ and $20000/49.33$, respectively. While this result is based on identical sequences of innovations in the two economies, similar values and the same conclusion was obtained for independent simulation runs.

Especially if we neglect the few pairs with a lifetime $L > 80$, these functions are almost linear.

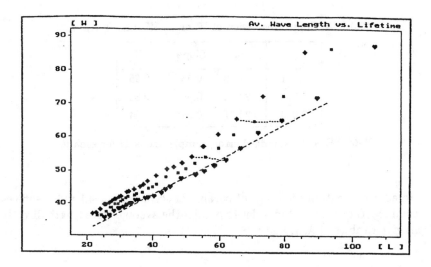

Figure 7. Average wave length in the stochastic economy versus lifetime of techniques on corresponding wave trains. Hearts, squares and diamonds relate to $\nu = 0.001, 0.002, 0.003$.

Fixing (γ, λ) and considering the impact of a rise in ν, we mostly observe a slight increase in W (except perhaps for the extreme values of W and L in the north-east region of the diagram). Figure 7 indicates two examples by the dotted line that connects hearts, squares and diamonds originating from the same pair (γ, λ). In any case, the increase in W is much less than the reduction of L, which implies a steeper slope of the function f_ν as ν increases. The results of fitting a regression line through the three sets of pairs (L, W) are given in Table 4. For each set the maximal pair (L, W) is removed from the sample, so that the three regressions are based on $9 \times 5 - 1 =$

44 pairs. For $\nu = 0.001$, the linear approximation to the function $W = f_\nu(L)$ is drawn as the dashed line in Figure 7.[27] The numerical functional specification in Table 4 and its representation in Figure 7 are the outcome of our endeavour to disclose a concise statistical regularity between the long waves in the stochastic economies and the equilibrium concept of wave trains in their deterministic counterparts.

Table 4. Simple regression of W on L: $W = \alpha_o + \alpha_1 \cdot L$.

ν	Const	Slope	SE
0.001	21.38	0.53	0.95
0.002	22.02	0.59	0.83
0.003	23.37	0.64	0.84

Note: SE is the standard error, sample size is 44 for each ν.

In addition, within the range of parameter scenarios considered it suffices to combine Tables 2 and 4 in order to predict the average wave length directly from given values of λ, γ, and ν.

7 Additional Observations

Apart from the wave motions as such, another feature of the time series shown in Figure 5 above is an apparent correlation between productivity growth rates and innovation activities. An increase in the arrival rate of innovations over the recent past is followed, though with a certain delay, by an increase in productivity growth; likewise with a decrease. This phenomenon was also pointed out by Silverberg and Lehnert [9, pp. 22-26].

We know that the propagation mechanism discussed in the previous section transforms the stochastic Poisson process of innovations into cyclical movements of the productivity growth rates. A look at Figure 5 even seems to suggest that the two series π_t and the number of innovations over the past 10 years exhibit a similar oscillatory pattern, if we abstract from the ragged shape of the latter series. Silverberg and Lehnert, however, subjected this similarity to the more scrupulous examination of a spectral analysis. For their simulation runs, they thus revealed significant differences in the spectral density of the two series. Since the juxtaposition of the series in their

---

[27] Of course, the numerical regression coefficients may slightly shift if we repeat the experiments with a different random number seed, i.e., confronting the economies with a different sequence of innovations. Checking this for another battery of simulation runs with $\nu = 0.001$, we obtained a very similar regression line over most of the relevant range of L.

Figure 9 (p. 24) displays essentially the same qualitative features as our Figure 5 (while their waves and innovation sample periods are longer), we may guess that similar differences in the power spectra can be found in our more elementary model.

Let us rather turn to the 'predictive power' of past innovations for future productivity growth. To this end, Silverberg and Lehnert computed the cross correlation between lagged productivity growth rates and moving averages of different order of the time series of innovations per period. Of course, this yields the same coefficients as using the total number of innovations over the extension of the moving averages. Denote this span of time by T_{Inn} (i.e., $T_{Inn} = 10$ in Figure 5). For an optimal combination of T_{Inn} and the lag in π_t, Silverberg and Lehnert obtained correlation coefficients as high as 0.79 and 0.83. They also briefly mention that, "not unexpectedly", an increase in what in our framework amounts to the speed of diffusion, shortens both the order of the moving average T_{Inn} and the lag leading to maximal correlation [9, p. 23]. In the two experiments with the same mean waiting time between two innovations as ours, $T = 2$, the optimal combination of lag and T_{Inn} is reported as $(24, 28)$ and, for the higher speed of diffusion, $(14, 16)$.

We performed the same computations for our economy across four different scenarios.[28] These are $(\gamma, \lambda) = (1.00, 0.03), (0.50, 0.03), (0.30, 0.03)$, and $(0.50, 0.02)$, for which the corresponding average wave lengths increase as $W = 39.1, 43.9, 49.5$, and 56.3. The maximal corrrelation coefficients are of the same order of magnitude as in Silverberg and Lehnert, that is, 0.81 in the first case and 0.84 in the remaining cases. Also the combinations of T_{Inn} and the lag that give rise to them are quite distinct from one scenario to the next. The dotted sets in Figure 8 show the combinations yielding a correlation coefficient no less than 0.05 from the maximal value. The latter is brought about by the combination marked by the plus sign inside this set in cases $1, 3, 4$, and by the star symbol in the second case. We thus see that, while T_{Inn} is in a similar range, the lag of the optimal combination is much shorter than in the experiments by Silverberg and Lehnert. We may ascribe this differences to the presumably longer waves in their simulations.

To compare our four scenarios with each other, the star symbol of the optimal combination in the second case, which is our base scenario, is repeated in the other three panels. It is seen that the set of good combinations of T_{Inn} and the lag shifts south-west if the scenario generates shorter waves. The converse is only partially true. In economies with longer waves, the T_{Inn} component of the good combinations increases, whereas the lag may increase as well as decrease. The dotted set is consequently enlarged. In particular, and in contrast to the result given by Silverberg and Lehnert, the lag of the optimal combination does not significantly rise.

---

[28] The length of the simulation runs is 1000 years, which is fully sufficient.

Note: Underlying are correlations, across four parameter scenarios with different average wave length W, of the lagged productivity growth rate with the number of innovations over the past T_{Inn} years. The plus symbol indicates the combination of the lag and T_{Inn} yielding the highest correlation (between 0.81 and 0.84), the correlations from the combinations in the dotted area deviate less than 0.05 from the maximal value; the star symbol repeats the optimal pair of the base scenario in the second panel.

If we compare the two time series of the productivity growth rates from $\gamma = 0.50$ and $\gamma = 0.30$ in Figure 5, it is perhaps somewhat surprising that they have the same high correlation coefficient with the innovation series, though on the basis of different values of T_{Inn}. One reason may be that the longer waves which tend to wash out the intermediary fluctuations in scenarios with higher speeds of diffusion, better match up to the smoother time series of the number of past innovations resulting from a longer sample period. In this respect, the relatively good explanatory power of past innovations for future productivity might, to some extent, be a statistical artifact.

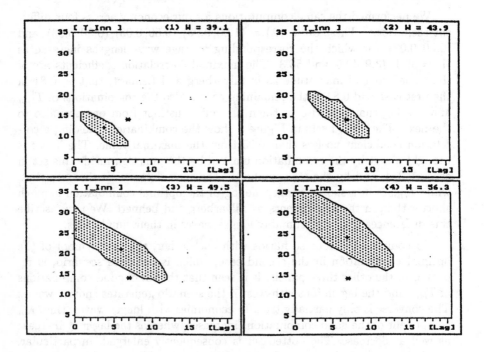

Figure 8. Correlation between productivity and innovation activity.

Apart from this suspicion, the goodness of the correlation measures is not universal but depends on a suitable choice of T_{Inn} and the lag, which in turn are connected to the average length of waves in the economy under investigation (or to the lifetimes of techniques on the wave train). Nevertheless, the dotted sets in Figure 8 indicate that the sensitivity of the correlation coefficients is not too dramatic, so that there may be still some margin for combinations coming sufficiently close to optimal.

In discussing the long-run dynamics of the model, we have so far concentrated on the evolution of average productivity. At the end of the paper, we descend from the aggregate level and return to the distribution of the single techniques. If the economy expands along a wave train, it has been found that the vintages of techniques are distributed smoothly and symmetrically, almost like a normal distribution. Similar distributions are obtained in the stochastic economy if we compute the long-run time averages of the cost gaps.[29] After all, the well-behaved theoretical distribution of expected capacity shares derived by Iwai [6] is an attempt at their approximate description.

To illustrate the persistence of a spectrum of techniques with different efficiencies as a fundamental empirical regularity, Iwai [6, Figure 1, p. 324] presents a typical diagram of an industry in selected years that shows (proxys for) the capacity shares of firms as a function of (proxys for) their unit costs. In an evaluation of the results of his analysis, Iwai [6, p. 341] notes that "it is quite assuring that the shapes of the two 'theoretical' distributions (i.e., the graph of two examples of what we have called the Iwai distribution; R.F.) are not unlike those of the 'empirical' distributions presented in fig. 1"; cf. also Iwai [5, p. 188]. Owing to the small number of empirical data points, the theoretical and empirical distribution can only be compared in qualitative terms. The common feature here is the unimodal shape of the two functions. Taking such a similarity as support of the theoretical model is, however, inadequate. Neglecting the small data basis, a principal reason is that the empirical distribution of unit costs is a distribution at a point in time, while Iwai's analysis is concerned with a probability distribution whose empirical counterpart would be the distribution of cost gaps averaged over a longer period of time.

Figure 9 is more concrete and shows the evolution of the frequency shares (in per cent) of unit costs in the base scenario from $t = 120$ to $t = 210$. It clearly demonstrates that the distributions at a point in time may indeed look very different from the wave train distributions or, for that matter, from the long-run time averages of cost gaps. In particular, the feature of unimodality may easily get lost. Reading Figure 9 across the cost axis, there are many instances of a ragged distribution. We thus see that a bimodal or even trimodal distribution of unit costs at a point in time is by no means an exception, though the economy undergoes no structural change whatsoever.

---

[29] The first and second moments of these distributions do not differ very much from the wave train statistics. We abstained, however, from a more systematic analysis since it seems to be of minor economic relevance only.

To explain the 'irregular' shape of the distribution of unit costs, consider for a moment the case of complete technological stagnation. In the absence of innovations, firms would gradually upgrade their production methods until all mass is concentrated on the most efficient technique. Now, the model's 'innovation noise' is constituted by the randomness of the waiting time between two successive innovations. Hence, every now and then it will happen that a newly introduced technique is granted a longer period during which no other, more productive technique raises its head. Over this, so to speak, close season we are practically in the stagnant economy just mentioned. The new technique can diffuse more rapidly and gain a higher capacity share than under the competitive pressure of an immediate and superior successor. And when better techniques finally arrive, it will still take some time until they become sufficiently influential in the diffusion process.

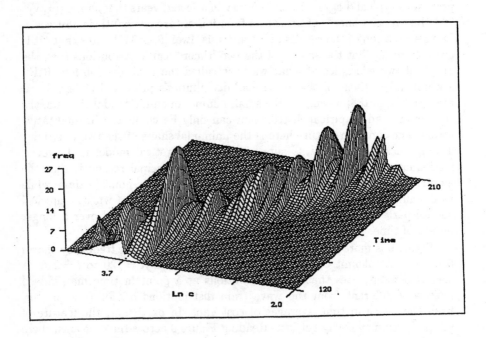

Figure 9. Capacity shares of unit costs over time (base scenario of the stochastic economy, frequencies in per cent).

A converse reasoning applies to a technique that is so unfortunate as to have a lot of early successors. The fast decline of average unit costs in equation (14) admits only moderate growth rates of such a technique, even in the initial stages of above-average productivity. Its economic success will therefore be rather limited. (The life-cycle may or may not be shorter than that of other techniques.) Tracing the frequency of a technique with a given unit cost along the time axis, Figure 9 exhibits examples of both extraordinarily successful techniques and techniques that hardly ever had any chance to grow. From this perspective, a picture of life-cycles of techniques emerges that looks a bit like the backs of a herd of dinosaurs.

8   Conclusion

Iwai [5, 6] has set up a framework that translates the Schumpeterian ideas on the dynamic interaction of technological diffusion and innovation into a formal language. He has done this in a highly stylized way. His model is thus particularly well suited to serve as a basis, or benchmark, against which to evaluate richer and more ambitious modelling work on technical change. Just because of the many creative approaches in this field, reference to such a benchmark model seems almost inevitable unless this sort of theorizing is to fall apart into a collection of unrelated anecdotes. On the one hand, the Iwai model can be a conceptual frame of reference which helps to classify and compare more elaborated versions. On the other hand, these models, most of which have also to resort to computational methods, may be put in perspective by contrasting their properties with the 'stylized facts' generated by the Iwai model, including the numerical features. In our opinion, the Iwai model could, and should, play a similar role as, for example, the well-known Goodwin [4] growth cycle model on employment and income distribution in (non-orthodox) macrodynamic theory.[30]

Iwai's main goal was to question the appropriateness of the neoclassical concept of equilibrium and to demonstrate that, under the Schumpeterian hypotheses on diffusion and innovation, an economy's state of technology will indeed be in a perpetual disequilibrium. Although the evolutionary pressure on profit-seeking firms constitutes a force that steers the economy toward a

---

[30] The importance of a process of "alignment of computational models" as a hallmark of cumulative disciplinary theorizing has been recently emphasized by Axtell el al. [1]; cf. especially p. 22. The Goodwin model is a succint formalization of a basic idea about the macroeconomic distributional conflict between profits and labour income and how it works out over time. While it has stimulated a great variety of generalizations, the conceptual modifications and innovations as well as the dynamic properties are still discussed against the background of the original prototype version. Conversely, a structural analysis of high-dimensional macroeconomic systems can single out subsystems displaying Goodwin-type dynamics.

neoclasssical equilibrium in which all firms use the most efficient production method available, the function of innovation lies precisely in upsetting this equilibrating tendency.

In the long-run, the opposite forces of diffusion and innovation balance, which implies that a multitude of diverse production methods with a wide range of efficiencies will coexist forever. This idea comes most clearly to the fore in a deterministic setting where innovations occur at regular intervals every T years. Compared to the usual neoclassical conception, it may be said that we have here a notion of long-run equilibrium at a higher level. Whereas production methods come into existence, run through a life-cycle and eventually die out, the whole spectrum of different techniques reproduces itself over time, only at an ever increasing scale as time progresses. This means that the role of a technique at some time t is taken over by its more advanced successor at a later point in time, $t+T$. Referring to the differences in unit costs to the currently best-practice techniques, it is the frequency distribution of these cost gaps that remains invariant over time. Drawing on Henkin and Polterovich [3], this steady state evolution of the economy has been called a wave train. The balancing of diffusion and innovation is reflected in the fact that the frequency distribution is non-degenerated (i.e., if all mass were concentrated on the best-practice technique, diffusion would be dominant) as well as limited (i.e., if the distribution did not cease to widen, innovation would be dominant).

Besides their significance as a concept that allows us to capture the balancing of diffusion and innovation in its purest form, wave trains make themselves also felt when the hypothesis of a deterministic arrival of innovations is dropped, so that we are back in the original Iwai model. A basic feature of the deterministic economy is a general tendency of the economy to converge toward the wave train distribution of cost gaps. If now innovations are governed by a stochastic process, we can view the resulting dynamics as a process of impulse and propagation. The impulses from innovation disturb the economy from its wave train distribution, the propagation mechanism drives it back in the direction of this equilibrium path. Thus, the relationship between the stochastic economy and the deterministic economy is akin to the relationship between, say, a stochastic autoregressive system and its deterministic counterpart, the main difference being that in our analysis the state of the economy is characterized by a frequency distribution rather than a vector.[31]

Just as the analysis of a stochastic autoregressive process is intimately related to the analysis of the deterministic difference equations, the time se-

---

[31] More precisely, with discrete vintages of techniques and only finitely many of them 'alive', a frequency distribution is a vector, too. However, we cannot assess in advance the dimension of such a vector, that is, we cannot say in advance how many techniques will be actually operated on a wave train. In particular, this number changes as the exogenous parameters vary.

ries characteristics of the stochastic economy can be much better explained on the basis of a study of the deterministic economy. Our primary interest here was in the phenomenon of low frequency oscillations in the growth rates of average productivity. To elucidate it we refer to the property of the deterministic system that the adjustments toward the wave trains are relatively slow, a result which is not surprising once it is recognized that, in and out of equilibrium, the life-cycles of the techniques typically extend over several decades. It must therefore take a similar span of time until the capacity shares of all the techniques still in existence have converged toward their wave train proportions. Similar motions in productivity growth are bound to occur in the stochastic setting. Though the waves then vary in length, depending on the particular random pattern of clusters in which the innovations occur, the period of the waves is in the same range as the convergence time of the deterministic adjustment paths.

On the whole, the Iwai model with its 'innovation noise' provides a minimal Schumpeterian framework giving rise to long waves in productivity growth. The ultimate reason for this phenomenon can be found in the wave train distribution of the deterministic economy, from which the economy is disturbed and back to which it continuously seeks to adapt. Moreover, the typical time scale of these readjustments is several decades. In this way, the deterministic economy and its wave trains are a useful analytical tool to gain a deeper insight into the causes of long waves. In addition, we have also revealed a quantitative connection from the deterministic economy to the period of the oscillations in the stochastic economy. Across a wide range of parameter scenarios, the lifetime of techniques on the wave train turns out to be closely, almost linearly, related to the average wave length.

One can, of course, conceive of many extensions of the basic Iwai model; in particular, generalizations in which the innovation activities are endogenously determined. Conversely, many existing dynamic models incorporating different vintages of techniques may be related, or 'aligned', to the Iwai model, just as this was possible for the Silverberg-Lehnert [9] model. These models may be better understood — in themselves, in relation to the Iwai model, and in relation to each other — if they are subjected to similar investigations as carried out in the present paper. In this sense, we hope that our paper can be a contribution to cumulative disciplinary theorizing in research on technological change.

Appendix:
The Components of the Speed of Diffusion

Consider a one-sectoral economy producing a good that serves as a consumption good and fixed capital. Let labour be a homogeneous input in the production processes and suppose that all techniques are of the fixed-coefficient type with the same capital-output ratio κ and the same rate of depreciation

δ. Denote the labour coefficients by $\alpha_i = L_i/Y_i$ (L_i labour and Y_i output of production method i), and by s_i the proportion of capital stock K_i in the aggregate capital stock $K = \sum_j K_j$, i.e., $s_i = K_i/K$. Average values, weighted by these capacity shares, are indicated by a bar over the variable, for example, $\bar{\alpha} = \sum_j \alpha_j s_j$. w being the real wage rate, the wage share (or average unit cost) $\omega = wL/Y$ is given by

$$\omega = w\bar{\alpha} \tag{A1}$$

since with $L_i = \alpha_i K_i/\kappa$, we have $Y/L = \sum_j Y_j / \sum_j L_j = (1/\kappa)K/[(1/\kappa)K \cdot \sum_j \alpha_j s_j] = 1/\bar{\alpha}$. The technology-specific profit rates are $r_i = (Y_i - wL_i - \delta K_i)/K_i = (1 - w\alpha_i)/\kappa - \delta$, the average rate of profit is $\bar{r} = \sum_j r_j s_j = (1 - w\bar{\alpha})/\kappa - \delta$. Together with (A1) we obtain

$$r_i - \bar{r} = \frac{-\omega}{\kappa} \frac{\alpha_i - \bar{\alpha}}{\bar{\alpha}} \tag{A2}$$

Using the investment function (16), the change of capacities in continuous time is computed as

$$\dot{s}_i = \frac{d}{dt}\frac{K_i}{K} = \frac{\dot{K}_i}{K_i}\frac{K_i}{K} - \frac{K_i}{K}\sum_j \frac{\dot{K}_j}{K_j}\frac{K_j}{K}$$

$$= (g_i - \sum_j g_j s_j)s_i = \beta_s [\bar{r} + \rho(r_i - \bar{r}) - \bar{r}\sum_j s_j - \rho\sum_j (r_j - \bar{r})s_j]s_i$$

$$= \beta_s \rho (r_i - \bar{r})s_i$$

(the time index has been omitted). Combining this result with (A2) yields

$$\dot{s}_i = \frac{-\beta_s \rho \omega}{\kappa}\frac{\alpha_i - \bar{\alpha}}{\bar{\alpha}}s_i \approx \frac{-\beta_s \rho \omega}{\kappa}(\ln\alpha_i - \ln\bar{\alpha})s_i \tag{A3}$$

Eq. (A3) is to be contrasted with the continuous-time version of eq. (14), which reads $\dot{s}_i = -\gamma(\ln c_i - \ln\bar{c})s_i$. One might be tempted to identify α_i with c_i and $\ln\bar{\alpha}$ with $\ln\bar{c}$. Owing to the slip in notation in eq. (13), however, the latter has to be taken with care, since $\ln\bar{\alpha} = \ln[\sum_j s_j\alpha_j] = \ln[\sum_j s_j c_j]$ and $\ln\bar{c} = \sum_j s_j \ln c_j$ do not generally coincide. The difference between $\ln\bar{\alpha}$ and $\ln\bar{c}$ will nevertheless be limited if we invoke the hypothesis that the distribution of techniques is nearly symmetrical, an assumption that at least is fairly well satisfied for the wave trains discussed in Section 4.

We may then, without loss of generality, rescale the labour coefficients such that $\bar{\alpha} = 1$ and $\ln\bar{\alpha} = 0$. Pairing technique 1 with the best-practive technique N, technique 2 with $N-1$, etc., gives $(c_1 + c_N)/2 \approx (c_2 + c_{N-1})/2 \approx 1$. Since $s_1 \approx s_N$, we have $s_1 \ln c_1 + s_N \ln c_N = s_1 \ln(1 + c_1 - 1) + s_N \ln(1 + c_N - 1) \approx s_1(c_1 - 1 + c_N - 1) \approx 0$. A similar argument applies to $s_2 \ln c_2 + s_{N-1} \ln c_{N-1}$, etc. Thus, $\ln\bar{c} = \sum_j s_j \ln c_j$ will be close to zero, too. Under these provisions, the deviations $(\ln\alpha_i - \ln\bar{\alpha})$ and $(\ln c_i - \ln\bar{c})$ are approximately equal, which finally allows to conclude that $\gamma \approx \beta_s \rho \omega/\kappa$.

It remains to explain our guess that the steady state wage share in the simulations by Silverberg and Lehnert [9] is around $\omega = 0.61$. The argument refers to the aggregate version of the Goodwin part of their model and proceeds as follows. Let π be the constant growth rate of labour productivity, $m = \hat{L}^s$ the constant growth of the labour supply, and $v = L/L^s$ the rate of employment. With the profit rate $r = (1 - \omega)/\kappa - \delta$, the investment identity $\hat{K} = rK$, and $\pi = \hat{Y} - \hat{L}$, one derives for the growth rate of v:
$$\hat{v} = \hat{L} - \hat{L}^s = \hat{Y} - \pi - m = \hat{K} - \pi - m = r - \pi - m = (1 - \omega)/\kappa - \delta - \pi - m.$$
Solving the equilibrium condition $\hat{v} = 0$ for ω yields $\omega = 1 - (\delta + \pi + m)\kappa$. Silverberg and Lehnert (mostly) use $\kappa = 3$ but are not explicit about their base values for δ and m. We may put $\delta = 0.10$ and $\pi + m = 0.03$. This supposition leads to $\omega = 0.61$ as stated in the text. It may also be observed that the profit rate and growth rate in the steady state are given by $g = r = \pi + m = 3\%$.

References

1. AXTELL, R., AXELROD, R., EPSTEIN, J.M., COHEN, M.D. (1995) Aligning simulation models. Santa Fe Institute, Working Paper 95–07–065

2. FREEMAN, C. (1987) Technical innovation, diffusion and long cycles of economic development. In T. Vasko (ed.), The Long-Wave Debate. Springer, Berlin

3. HENKIN, G.M., POLTEROVICH, V.M. (1991) Schumpeterian dynamics as a non-linear wave theory. Journal of Mathematical Economics 20, 551–590

4. GOODWIN, R.M. (1967) A growth cycle. In C.H. Feinstein (ed.), Socialism, Capitalism and Economic Growth. Cambridge University Press, Cambridge

5. IWAI, K. (1984a) Schumpeterian dynamics: An evolutionary model of innovation and imitation. Journal of Economic Behavior and Organization 5, 159–190

6. IWAI, K. (1984b) Schumpeterian dynamics, part II: Technological progress, firm growth and 'economic selection'. Journal of Economic Behavior and Organization 5, 321–351

7. KUZNETS, S. (1940) Schumpeter's business cycles. American Economic Review 30, 257–271

8. PRESS, W.H. ET AL. (1986) Numerical Recipes. Cambridge University Press, Cambridge

9. SILVERBERG, G., LEHNERT, D. (1993) Long waves and 'evolutionary chaos' in a simple Schumpeterian model of embodied technical change. Structural Change and Economic Dynamics 4, 9–37

10. SOETE, L., TURNER, R. (1984) Technology diffusion and the rate of technical change. Economic Journal 94, 612–623

Agents' Heterogeneity, Aggregation, and Economic Fluctuations

Domenico Delli Gatti[1], Mauro Gallegati[2], and Antonio Palestrini[3]

[1] ITEMQ, Università Cattolica, Milano

[2] MET, Università di Teramo

[3] DEA, Università di Ancona

Abstract. We study the implications of agents' heterogeneity for business cycle analysis with the help of a two dimensional non-linear dynamical system derived from a New Keynesian macroeconomic model with imperfect capital markets. In order to analyze the interaction between real and financial variables, we have focussed on the degree of financial fragility of the economy, as proxied by the ratio of corporate net worth to the stock of capital, that is the equity ratio. Our approach allows to analyze both fluctuations due to the impulse-propagation mechanism and self-sustaining endogenous cycles. In the former case, shocks transmitted and amplified by a propagation mechanism, which depends on the degree of agents' heterogeneity. In the latter case self sustained business cycles are generated by the evolution over time of the distribution of heterogeneous agents, classified by the degree of financial fragility.

JEL Classification: E32, E44

Keywords: asymmetric information, heterogeneity, business cycles

1. Introduction

The Representative Agent (RA) framework has a long tradition in economics (Marshall, 1920; an history of the way in which this analytical tool has been employed in economics can be found in Hartley, 1997). Despite the stringency of the logical requirements for consistent aggregation (see, among others, Leontief, 1947; Gorman, 1953; Theil, 1954; Eisenberg, 1961; Green, 1964; Fisher, 1969, 1982), the RA framework has been one of the most successful tools in economics, being the cornerstone of microfoundations in macroeconomics and of aggregation in the mainstream "New" literature ("New Classical" or "New Keynesian": see e.g. Lucas, 1975; Long and Plosser, 1983; Greenwald and Stiglitz, 1993). In such a context aggregation allows to extend the individual rational behavior to the macrorelationships.

Despite its success, economists are growing more and more dissatisfied with this analytical device (Kirman, 1992; Malinvaud, 1993; Grandmont, 1993; Chavas, 1993; see also the essays in Gallegati and Kirman, 1999) for a number of different reasons. First of all, the set of assumptions necessary to reach exact aggregation in a logically consistent way is impressive. Martel (1996: 128) lists the following: homothetic preferences (linear Engel's curve); weakly separable and linearly homogenous production functions, identical for all firms; homogenous and infinitely divisible commodities and factors of production; a common set of prices with constant relative ratios; constant distribution of income and endowments over time. Of course, none of the above mentioned requirements matches the features of the real world economy. In particular, if we relax the assumption of a constant distribution of income or endowments over time, as we have to do when coping with dynamics, agents' heterogeneity becomes the logical requirement for the analysis.

Once we relax the RA hypothesis, fluctuations and cycles may emerge as the result of changes in the distribution of agents rather than the consequence of exogenous shocks to which a "representative" individual reacts, as in the standard literature on the business cycle. Recent research using firms panel-data (Davis and Haltiwanger, 1996; Davis et al. 1996; Caballero et al., 1997) shows that idiosyncratic factors govern the aggregate rates of change of output, investment and employment: the representative firm approach becomes then questionable. Ignoring heterogeneity may lead to a fallacy of composition which may be quite relevant for modeling (Caballero, 1992) and misleading for empirical analysis (Stocker, 1993) also.

Moreover, the RA framework can be unsatisfactory for a wide range of economists, even belonging to opposite sides of the academic spectrum. The general equilibrium theorist may not feel at ease with the RA assumption because some of the building blocks of general equilibrium theory do not hold in the presence of a representative agent (e.g. the "Weak Axiom of Revealed Preferences" or "Arrow's Impossibility Theorem", Kirman, 1992: 122). From a different theoretical perspective, the very idea of asymmetric information of the New Keynesian Economics is inconsistent with the RA hypothesis (Stiglitz, 1992). Recently, Grandmont (1991) has shown that if agents are different, aggregate coherence may hold even if individuals are not rational maximizers. This sheds a different light on the microfoundation issue (in the same vein see Colander, 1996; Hartley, 1997) since aggregate well-behaved relations may be based, e.g., upon heterogeneous non-maximizing individuals which interact.

The adoption of a RA framework also ignores the problem of coordination (which is of a crucial importance when informational imperfections are taken into account: see Leijonhufvud 1981). According to the New Classical view in fact, building an aggregate model upon the RA allows to rule out any difference between the behaviour of individually optimizing agents and that of the aggregate.

In the traditional impulse-propagation approach to fluctuations, if the framework is linear large fluctuations are produced by large shocks or by a sum of small shocks. Since disturbances are characterized by zero mean the latter case is ruled out, and the analysis of fluctuations has to be confined to that of great events (oil shocks, wars, and so). On the contrary, if sufficiently self-reinforcing non-linearities are introduced, small shocks may generate large fluctuations. But whenever a strong non-linearity is present, the "law of strong numbers" does not work, and aggregation becomes a non-trivial matter (Rahn, 1985). If agents are heterogeneous, the propagation mechanism is affected by changes in the distribution of agents. In such a case, it is no longer true that "business cycles are all alike" (Lucas, 1977; see also Zarnowitz, 1998). Whatever the nature of the impulse (Temin, 1998), the propagation mechanism can make the difference if it is large enough to amplify an impulse.

In this paper we explore the implications of agents' heterogeneity for the analysis of the business cycle with the help of a simple New Keynesian model with imperfect capital markets, based on Greenwald and Stiglitz, 1993. In our model firms differ according to their degree of financial fragility (i.e. the ratio of the equity base to the capital stock). As a matter of fact, Greenwald and Stiglitz (1988, 1993), Bernanke and Gertler (1989, 1990), Kyiotaki and Moore (1997), have put forward models in which financial fragility plays an important macroeconomic role in a setting of heterogeneous agents (the pathbreaking approach is Minsky, 1982). These authors, however, don't push the analysis to the point of identifying the law governing the distribution of agents. Our variant of the Greenwald and Stiglitz framework aims precisely at filling this gap, showing how the evolution over time of the distribution of firms according to their degree of financial fragility determines aggregate fluctuations.

Our modeling strategy allows to analyze both fluctuations due to the impulse-propagation mechanism and self-sustaining endogenous cycles. Stochastically generated fluctuations may be due either to individual shocks, i.e. idiosyncratic disturbances, or to aggregate shocks, propagated and amplified by agents' heterogeneity. Endogenous cycles are due to the evolution over time of the distribution of heterogeneous agents, classified by the degree of financial fragility. Therefore, whatever the approach followed in analyzing the business cycle – the linear impulse propagation approach or the non-linear endogenous approach - the main message of this paper is that aggregate fluctuations could be better understood by analyzing the evolution of the cross-sectional distribution at the micro level, i.e. the first two moments of the agents' distribution help explaining fluctuations (see Terasvirta, 1998; Gallegati and Stanca, 1999).

The paper is organized as follows. In section 2 we outline the building blocks of the model. After having identified the laws of motion of the expected value and the variance of the equity ratio, in section 3 we describe the dynamics of these statistics. Section 4 is devoted to simulations of the response of the system to an impulse due to a change in the interest rate. Section 5 concludes. The appendix is devoted to a simple aggregation procedure, which can be adopted to deal with the problem of heterogeneity when interaction is ruled out.

2. The Model

Our economy is characterized by a large number (say z) of firms. Each one of them produces a homogenous good by means of a constant returns to scale technology in which capital is the only input:

$$Y_i = \phi K_i \qquad (2.1)$$

Y_i and K_i are output and capital of the i-th firm, ϕ is the output-capital ratio. Firms sell their output at an uncertain price because of their limited knowledge of market conditions. The individual selling price P_i is a positive random variable with expected value $E(P_i)=P$ and finite variance. P is the market price, uniform across firms. As a consequence, the relative price, $u_i=P_i/P$, is a positive random variable with expected value $E(u_i)=1$ and finite variance.[1]

Moreover we assume, as in Greenwald and Stiglitz, 1993, that firms cannot raise funds on the Stock market because of equity rationing but they have unlimited access to credit. This means that firms do not issue new equities but can obtain from banks all the credit they need to finance production at the (exogenous) rate of interest, r.

Each firm incurs financing costs CF_i equal to debt commitments: $r(qK_i-A_{it-1})$ where q is the real price of capital and A_{it-1} is the net worth or equity base in real terms inherited from the past.[2]

$$CF_i = r(qK_i-A_{it-1}) \qquad (2.2)$$

Assuming that there is no depreciation, capital accumulates according to the investment equation $I_i=K_i-K_{it-1}$.

We assume that the firm incurs capital adjustment cost, CA_i, which is an increasing quadratic function of the ratio of investment to the average capital stock: I_i/K.

$$CA_i = \frac{\gamma}{2} \frac{I_i^2}{K} = \frac{\gamma}{2} \frac{(K_i - K_{it-1})^2}{K} \qquad (2.3)$$

Quadratic adjustment costs are well known in the literature on investment. The novelty of the expression above consists in assuming that adjustment costs are decreasing with the average capital stock: the higher is the average capital stock – i.e. investment activity on the part of other firms – the lower is the level of adjustment costs for the individual firm. This formulation captures a sort of externality in investment activity.

Real profit is the difference between real revenue and real cost, which in turn is the sum of financing and adjustment costs:

---

[1] In a sense we are assuming homogeneous and rational expectations on the part of firms.
[2] Undated variables refer to period t, the current period.

$$\pi_i = u_i Y_i - rq\left(K_i - A_{it-1}\right) - \frac{\gamma}{2}\frac{\left(K_i - K_{it-1}\right)^2}{K} \tag{2.4}$$

Expected real profit therefore is:

$$E\left(\pi_i\right) = Y_i - rq\left(K_i - A_{it-1}\right) - \frac{\gamma}{2}\frac{\left(K_i - K_{it-1}\right)^2}{K} \tag{2.5}$$

In this framework, bankruptcy occurs if net worth becomes negative. Net worth "today" is equal to net worth "yesterday" plus retained profit, which in turn is equal to profit less the flow of dividends (D_i). The bankruptcy condition therefore is:

$$A_i = A_{it-1} + \pi_i < 0 \quad \text{if}$$

$$A_i = A_{it-1} + \pi_i - D_i = A_{it-1} + u_i Y_i - CF_i - CA_i - D_i < 0 \tag{2.6}$$

The inequality (2.6) is verified if the sum of financing costs, adjustment costs and dividends is higher than revenues – thereby generating a loss - and the associated loss is higher than the equity base inherited from the past. In order to simplify the argument, in the following we will assume that the flow of dividends is proportional to net worth inherited from the past:

$$D_i = rA_{it-1} \tag{2.7}$$

In a sense this is tantamount to assuming the net worth is remunerated at the same rate as bank loans.

Substituting (2.2.) (2.3) and (2.7) into (2.6) we get:

$$A_{it} = A_{it-1} + u_i Y_i - rqK_i - \frac{\gamma}{2}\frac{\left(K_i - K_{it-1}\right)^2}{K} < 0$$

Using (2.1) and rearranging, we can write the bankruptcy condition as follows:

$$u_i < r\frac{q}{\phi} - \frac{A_{it-1}}{\phi K_i} + \frac{\gamma}{2}\frac{\left(K_i - K_{it-1}\right)^2}{\phi K_i K} \equiv \overline{u}_i \tag{2.8}$$

In other words, bankruptcy occurs if the realization of the random relative price u_i falls below a critical threshold, $\overline{u}_i$.

Let's assume, for the sake of simplicity, that u_i is a uniform random variable, with support $(0,2)$. In this case, the probability of bankruptcy becomes:

$$\Pr\left(u_i < \overline{u}_i\right) = \frac{\overline{u}_i}{2} = r\frac{q}{2\phi} - \frac{A_{it-1}}{2\phi K_i} + \frac{\gamma}{4}\frac{\left(K_i - K_{it-1}\right)^2}{\phi K_i K} \tag{2.9}$$

Following Greenwald and Stiglitz, moreover, we assume that bankruptcy is costly (Gordon and Malkiel, 1981; Altman, 1984; White, 1989; Gilson, 1990; Kaplan and Reishus, 1990). In particular, bankruptcy costs, CB_i, are a decreasing function of the degree of financial robustness, proxied by the ratio of net worth to the capital stock (equity ratio for short) of the previous period $a_{it-1}=A_{it-1}/K_{it-1}$ and an increasing function of output, Y_i:

$$CB_i = c(a_{it-1})Y_i \qquad (2.10)$$

By assumption bankruptcy costs are linear with respect to a_{it-1}:

$$c(a_{it-1}) = \alpha_1 - \alpha_2 a_{it-1}$$

Substituting this expression into (2.10) we obtain:

$$CB_i = (\alpha_1 - \alpha_2 a_{it-1})Y_i \qquad (2.11)$$

The firm maximizes an objective function, which is equal to the expected profit less bankruptcy cost in case bankruptcy occurs, i.e.:

$$Max \; E(\pi_i) - CB_i \, Pr(u_i < \bar{u}_i) = Y_i - CF_i - CA_i - CB_i \frac{\bar{u}_i}{2}$$

Substituting (2.5) (2.3) (2.8) and (2.10) into the objective function, taking into account (2.1) and rearranging we end up with the following:

$$Max \quad \phi K_i - r_i K_i - \gamma_i \frac{(K_i - K_{it-1})^2}{2K} + B \qquad (P)$$

where

$$r_i = rq \left[1 + \frac{(\alpha_1 - \alpha_2 a_{it-1})}{2} \right]$$

$$\gamma_i = \gamma \left[1 + \frac{(\alpha_1 - \alpha_2 a_{it-1})}{2} \right]$$

$$B = A_{it-1} \left[r + \frac{(\alpha_1 - \alpha_2 a_{it-1})}{2} \right]$$

B is a polynomial of parameters and predetermined variables independent of the capital stock, r_i is the *bankruptcy cost augmented interest rate*. It is determined as a mark-up over the interest rate charged by banks on loans. This mark-up is a decreasing function of the equity ratio: the higher the equity ratio, i.e. the financial robustness of the firm, the lower the bankruptcy cost augmented interest rate. In a sense, this mark-up captures the idea of the risk of the borrower.

Solving (P) with respect to the individual capital stock, we obtain the following First Order Condition:

FOC: $$\phi - r_i - \gamma_i \frac{(K_i - K_{it-1})}{K} = 0$$

The FOC can be interpreted as follows: the expected real marginal revenue must be equal to the real marginal cost, which includes the marginal bankruptcy cost and the marginal adjustment cost.

From the FOC we derive optimal investment:

$$I_i \equiv K_i - K_{it-1} = \frac{\phi - r_i}{\gamma_i} K = \left(\frac{\phi}{\gamma_i} - \frac{r}{\gamma} \right) K$$

The Second Order Condition is satisfied since: $-\gamma_i / K < 0$.

Assuming $\phi > r_i$, we can see from (2.13) that investment is an increasing linear function of the average capital stock. This is a consequence of the externality mentioned above: the higher is the average capital stock – i.e. investment activity on the part of other firms – the lower is marginal adjustment costs for the individual firm and the higher its investment.

The rate of capital accumulation will be:

$$\tau_i = \frac{I_i}{K_i} = 1 - \frac{K_{it-1}}{K_i} = \frac{\phi - r_i}{\gamma} \frac{K}{K} = \left(\frac{\phi}{\gamma_i} - \frac{r}{\gamma} \right) \frac{K}{K_i} \qquad (2.12)$$

It is easy to see that the rate of capital accumulation is an increasing function of the equity ratio:

$$\tau_i = \tau(a_{it-1}) \frac{K}{K_i} = \left[\frac{\phi}{\gamma \left(1 + \frac{\alpha_1 - \alpha_2 a_{it-1}}{2} \right)} - \frac{r}{\gamma} \right] \frac{K}{K_i} \qquad (2.13)$$

3. Dynamics

Since the issue of new equities is ruled out by the assumption of equity rationing, in this framework each firm can increase its net worth inasmuch as it accumulates internal funds. The change of the equity base, therefore, coincides with retained profits. The law of motion of the equity base of the i-th firm can be formulated as follows:

$$A_{it} = A_{it-1} + u_i Y_i - rqK_i - \frac{\gamma}{2}\frac{\left(K_i - K_{it-1}\right)^2}{K} \tag{3.1}$$

Substituting (2.1) into (3.1) and dividing by the individual capital stock we get:

$$a_{it} = a_{it-1}\frac{K_{it-1}}{K_{it}} + u_i\phi - rq - \frac{\gamma}{2}\frac{\left(K_{it} - K_{it-1}\right)^2}{KK_{it}} = a_{it-1}(1-\tau_i) + u_i\phi - rq - \frac{\gamma}{2}\tau_i^2\frac{K_i}{K} \tag{3.2}$$

Taking into account (2.13) we can write:

$$a_{it} = a_{it-1}\left[1 - \tau(a_{it-1})\frac{K}{K_i}\right] + u_i\phi - rq - \frac{\gamma}{2}\left[\tau(a_{it-1})\frac{K}{K_i}\right]^2\frac{K_i}{K} \tag{3.3}$$

(3.3) is the law of motion of the individual equity ratio. It is a fairly complicated expression, which must be radically simplified in order to make the analysis feasible. We propose two shortcuts. The first one concerns $\tau(.)$, which is a non-linear function. In order to simplify the argument, we linearize $\tau(.)$. Instead of following the usual linearization procedure we adopt a radical shortcut and write the rate of capital accumulation as follows:

$$\tau_i = \frac{\phi - r_i}{\gamma}\frac{K}{K_i} \tag{2.13'}$$

Comparing (2.13) with (2.13') it is easy to see that the shortcut consists in substituting γ to γ' in the denominator of the expression. This is tantamount to ignoring the capital adjustment costs in the bankruptcy condition.

The second shortcut concerns the ratio K/K_i. Assuming that the individual capital stock is not too different from the average, this ratio boils down to one.

After these changes it turns out that:

$$\tau_i = \left(\alpha_3 + \alpha_4 a_{it-1}\right) \tag{2.13''}$$

$$\alpha_3 = \frac{1}{\gamma}\left[\phi - rq\left(1 + \frac{\alpha_1}{2}\right)\right]; \quad \alpha_4 = \frac{r\alpha_2}{2\gamma}$$

Therefore we can rewrite (3.2) as follows:

$$a_{it} = a_{it-1}(1-\tau_i) + u_i\phi - rq - \frac{\gamma}{2}\tau_i^2 \tag{3.3}$$

$$a_{it} = a_{it-1}(1-\tau_i) + u^e\phi - iq - \frac{\gamma}{2}\tau_i^2$$

Substituting (2.13'') into (3.3) we get:

$$a_{it} = \left(1 - \frac{u_i\phi}{\gamma} + \frac{rq}{\gamma} + \frac{\alpha_1 rq}{2\gamma} - \frac{u_i\phi\alpha_1 rq}{2\gamma} + \frac{\alpha_2 (rq)^2}{2\gamma} + \frac{\alpha_1\alpha_2 (rq)^2}{4\gamma}\right) a_{it-1} +$$

$$- \left(\frac{\alpha_2 rq}{2\gamma} + \frac{\alpha_2^2 (rq)^2}{8\gamma}\right) a_{it-1}^2 + \left(\phi - rq - \frac{\phi^2}{2\gamma} - \frac{(rq)^2}{2\gamma} - \frac{\alpha_1^2 (rq)^2}{8\gamma} + \frac{\phi rq}{\gamma} + \frac{\phi\alpha_1 rq}{2\gamma} + - \frac{\alpha_1 (rq)^2}{2\gamma}\right) \qquad (3.4)$$

Let:

$$\Gamma_1 = 1 - \frac{\phi}{\gamma} + \frac{rq}{\gamma} + \frac{\alpha_1 rq}{2\gamma} - \frac{\phi\alpha_1 rq}{2\gamma} + \frac{\alpha_2 (rq)^2}{2\gamma} + \frac{\alpha_1\alpha_2 (rq)^2}{4\gamma}$$

$$\Gamma_2 = \frac{\alpha_2 rq}{2\gamma} + \frac{\alpha_2^2 (rq)^2}{8\gamma}$$

$$\Gamma_0 = \phi - rq - \frac{\phi^2}{2\gamma} - \frac{(rq)^2}{2\gamma} - \frac{\alpha_1^2 (rq)^2}{8\gamma} + \frac{\phi rq}{\gamma} + \frac{\phi\alpha_1 rq}{2\gamma} \frac{\alpha_1 (rq)^2}{2\gamma}$$

Therefore we can write (3.4) as:

$$a_{it} = \Gamma_1 a_{it-1} - \Gamma_2 a_{it-1}^2 + \Gamma_0 \qquad (3.4')$$

Aggregating and using the law of the large numbers:

$$a_t = \Gamma_1 a_{t-1} - \Gamma_2 a_{t-1}^2 + \Gamma_0 - \Gamma_2 V_{t-1} \qquad (3.5)$$

The variance of the equity ratio is:

$$V_t = E(a_{it} - a_t)^2 = E(\Gamma_1 a_{it-1} - \Gamma_2 a_{it-1}^2 + \Gamma_0 - a_t)^2$$

or:

$$V_t = \Gamma_2^2(\beta_{t-1} - 1)V_{t-1}^2 + 2\Gamma_1\Gamma_0\mu_{t-1}^3 + 4\Gamma_2^2 a_{t-1}^2 V_{t-1} +$$
$$- 4\Gamma_1\Gamma_2 a_{t-1}V_{t-1} + \Gamma_1^2 V_{t-1} + 4\Gamma_2^2\mu_{t-1}^3 a_{t-1} \qquad (3.6)$$

where a_t is the average equity base; V_t its variance; $\beta_t = E(a_{it} - a_t)^4/V_t^2$ the kurtosis coefficient and $\mu_t^3 = E(a_{it} - a_t)^3/V_t^{3/2}$ the skewness coefficient.

Equations (3.5)-(3.6) describe a non-linear two-dimensional discrete dynamical system that can exhibit very rich dynamics.

It is well known that if i) agents were identical and ii) the system was linear, the dynamical behavior of the system could be analyzed through changes of the behavior of the average, representative agent. In such a case, each cyclical phase would be similar to every other phase, at the macro level and as far as the co-movements are concerned, differing only for amplitude of the standard deviation and period of time. In this case Lucas' claim, according to which "business cycles are all alike", would be correct. It is worth emphasizing, however, that Lucas' claim is true *iff* assumption i) and ii) are maintained[3].

We will show how heterogeneity affects business cycles in a particular version of the model.

Let's start, in analyzing the system, from a convenient special case. If agents are identical - i.e. if the Representative Agent Hypothesis holds true - the law of motion of the equity ratio of the representative firm is:

$$a_t = \Gamma_1 a_{t-1} - \Gamma_2 a_{t-1}^2 + \Gamma_0 \qquad (3.7)$$

(3.7) is obtained from (3.5) assuming that the variance of the equity ratio is zero. In this case, of course, equation (3.6) must be ignored by construction. (3.7) is a quadratic map, topologically conjugated to the logistic map.[4] The dynamical properties of the logistic map are well known and we will not recall them here (for a comprehensive survey see Day, 1994). It is worth mentioning, however, that there are configurations of the parameters such that the dynamics are chaotic, i.e. the equity ratio oscillates apparently at random around the steady state. In this case the economy follows a path of endogenously determined fluctuating growth.

In the following the analysis focuses on the density functions for which $\beta_t = \beta$, $\mu_t^3 = \mu^3$. In other words, for the class of density functions that, like the normal density, has constant skewness and kurtosis. If agents are heterogeneous, the evolution over time of the mean and the variance of the equity ratio is obtained by the iteration of a two-dimensional map $T : (a_{t-1}, V_{t-1}) \to (a_t, V_t)$ given by:

$$a_t = \Gamma_1 a_{t-1} - \Gamma_2 a_{t-1}^2 + \Gamma_0 - \Gamma_2 V_{t-1} \qquad (3.8)$$

$$V_t = \Gamma_2^2(\beta-1)V_{t-1}^2 + 2\Gamma_1\Gamma_0\mu^3 + 4\Gamma_2^2 a_{t-1}^2 V_{t-1} - 4\Gamma_1\Gamma_2 a_{t-1}V_{t-1} + \Gamma_1^2 V_{t-1} + 4\Gamma_2^2\mu^3 a_{t-1} \qquad (3.9)$$

T is a non-invertible map of the plane, that is, starting from some initial conditions, the iteration of the map uniquely defines the trajectory whereas the backward iteration of is not uniquely defined. The study of the dynamical properties of map T is not an easy task.[5] In order to find the fixed points we have to impose the steady state conditions:

$$a = \Gamma_1 a - \Gamma_2 a^2 + \Gamma_0 - \Gamma_2 V \qquad (3.8')$$

$$V = \Gamma_2^2(\beta-1)V^2 + 2\Gamma_1\Gamma_0\mu^3 + 4\Gamma_2^2 a^2 V - 4\Gamma_1\Gamma_2 aV + \Gamma_1^2 V + 4\Gamma_2^2\mu^3 a \qquad (3.9')$$

---

3 If one remove assumption ii) alone, fluctuations become time dependent and non-ergodic (as the literature on non-linear systems has showed). We also maintain that assumption i) has to be removed once one assumes that markets are incomplete: it is a matter of logic rather than realism, which would be relevant per se anyway as we showed in the introductive part.

4 Notice that in this case K=Ki is not an approximation

5 The study of the dynamics of the system such as (3.8)(3.9) has been carried out elsewhere. See Agliari et al., 1999.

Substituting the expression for V obtained from the first equation into the second one, we obtain a 4-th degree equation in a. Of course, some of the solutions may be complex or have no economic interpretation at all.

In the system (3.8')-(3.9'), as shown in Agliari et al. (1999), endogenous irregular fluctuations (self-sustained business cycles) - observationally equivalent to the oscillations produced by random shocks - may arise for many different sets of parameter values. According to the model, self-sustained business cycles are characterised by the asymmetrical behaviour between expansion and contractions, which in turn follow the evolution of the degree of financial fragility (Minsky, 1982; Bernanke et al., 1998).

In this work we focus on the relation between a macroeconomic shock (e.g., monetary shocks) and the agents distribution. We shall consider first the special case $\mu^3 = 0$. This implies a symmetric distribution and the system above specializes to:

$$a_t = \Gamma_1 a_{t-1} - \Gamma_2 a_{t-1}^2 + \Gamma_0 - \Gamma_2 V_{t-1} \qquad (3.10)$$

$$V_t = \Gamma_2^2 (\beta-1) V_{t-1}^2 + (2\Gamma_2 a_{t-1} - \Gamma_1)^2 V_{t-1} \qquad (3.11)$$

Notice that $V_{t-1} = 0$ implies $V_t = 0$. If we represent the initial conditions on the (a,V) plane, this property means that the coordinate axis V=0 (i.e. the a-axis) is trapping. In other words, starting from an initial condition on the a-axis, say -i.e. a situation in which the Representative Agent Hypothesis holds true - the dynamics are confined to the same axis for each t, governed by the restriction of the map to that axis. This restriction is the quadratic map obtained from (3.10)-(3.11) imposing V=0, which coincides with equation (3.7).

In order to implement our simulation we fix the parameter values $\phi = 0.2$, $\gamma = 0.1$, $\alpha_1 = 3$, $\alpha_2 = 0.4$, $\beta = 1.8$ and using the symmetric distribution hypothesis it is possible to find two steady states. The first, with $V = 0$ and $a = 0.432$ (figure 1), is stable and the second is an unstable node. In other words, with this set of parameters the system converges to the representative agent distribution, in the long run.

We can observe what happen to this system, if we allow the distribution to be symmetric, changing the skewness parameter from 0 to 1. The a-axis now is losing its trapping property and the stable steady state has a positive variance (Figure 2).

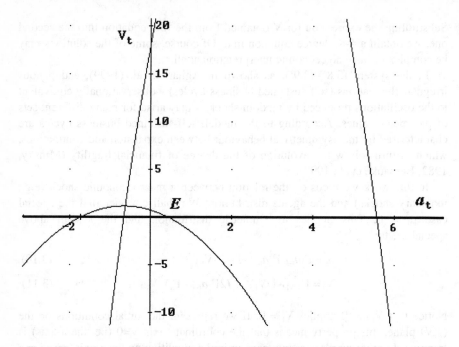

Fig. 1: The steady-states with simmetric distribution. Note that the stable steady-state (point E) is the intersection between the lower parabola and the a-axis (the trapping set).

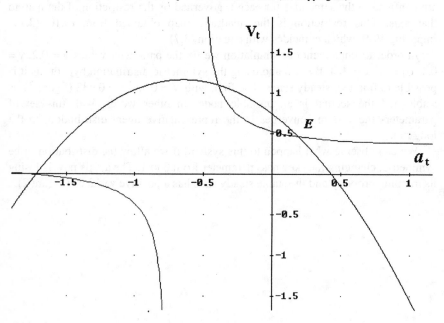

Fig. 2: The steady states with $\mu^3 = 1$. The stable one (point E) is a = 0.192, V = 0.459.

4. The Impulse-Propagation Mechanism and Business Fluctuations

In our framework, we can generate fluctuations of the Slutsky-Frisch type by forcing an exogenous shock upon the system in the vicinity of a stable steady state. If agents are heterogeneous, the propagation mechanism is affected by changes in the distribution of agents. In particular, to analyze the propagation mechanism we have to take into account the higher moments of the distribution. As a consequence, fluctuations associated to the same impulse will differ if the variance is different. In this context there is not such a thing as a unique "natural" or "equilibrium" state but a sequence of states of the distribution over time.

Let's analyze the consequences of an aggregate nominal shock. We model a nominal shock as a monetary innovation that has a short run effect on the interest rate. Figure 3 shows a simulation of the adjustment process following an aggregate price nominal shock[6]. The two patterns show the response to a 1% increase in the interest rate.

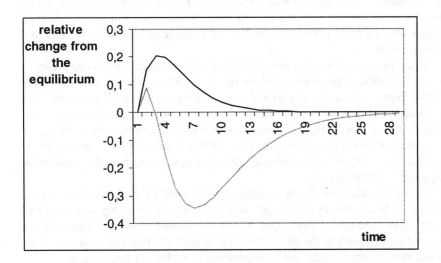

Fig. 3: Impulse response functions for the two distributions. The grey line is the response of the distribution with positive variance.

This simulation shows that when agents' equity ratio distribution changes, the amplification mechanism changes, and consequently the dynamical properties of

---

6 We suppose that it has a stationary distribution with unconditional mean 10%. In this experiment an AR(1), $(i_t - 0.1) = 0.8(i_{t-1} - 0.1) + \varepsilon_t$.

the system change. The change of the distribution modifies the qualitative behaviour of the system: a redistributive policy may, e.g., decrease the variance of the equity ratio, keeping the mean unaltered, producing a change in dynamical behaviour. The reason is that changes in equity base distribution affects the financial soundness of the system; i.e. changes the financial fragility, which is the amplification mechanism of the economy. In the simulation above the shock affects not only the first moment, the aggregate equity ratio, but the variance also. This is the reason of different impulse response function. The shock changes, at the same time, the distribution of equities and the amplification mechanism, so it is likely that business cycles should not be all alike.

4. Conclusive Remarks

In this paper we have tried to assess the implications of agents' heterogeneity for business cycle analysis with the help of a two dimensional non-linear dynamical system derived from a New Keynesian macroeconomic model with imperfect capital markets.

This type of system can generate a wide range of dynamic paths depending on the configuration of parameters and the initial conditions. Our approach allows to analyze both fluctuations due to the impulse-propagation mechanism and self-sustaining endogenous cycles. In the former case, shocks transmitted and amplified by a propagation mechanism, which depends on the degree of agents' heterogeneity. In the latter case self-sustained business cycles are generated by the evolution over time of the distribution of heterogeneous agents, classified by the degree of financial fragility.

Therefore, whatever the basic approach followed in analyzing the business cycle – the linear Slutsky-Frisch approach or the non-linear endogenous approach – the main message of this paper is that the evolution of the cross-sectional distribution of agents at the micro level, i.e. at least the first two moments of the agents' distribution is of the utmost importance in explaining fluctuations.

References

Agliari, A., Delli Gatti, D., Gallegati, M., Gardini, L. (1999), "Global Dynamics in a Non-linear Model of the Equity Ratio", Journal of Chaos, Solitons and Fractals, forthcoming.

Altman, E.I. (1984), "A Further Empirical Investigation of the Bankruptcy Cost Question", Journal of Finance, vol. 39, pp. 1067-1089.

Bernanke, B., Gertler, M. (1989), "Agency Costs, Net Worth and Business Fluctuations", American Economic Review , vol. 79, pp. 14-31.

Bernanke, B., Gertler, M. (1990), "Financial Fragility and Economic Performance", Quarterly Journal of Economics, vol. 105, pp. 87-114.

Bernanke, B., Gertler, M., Gilchrist, S.G. (1998), "The Financial Accelerator in a Quantitative Business Cycle Approach", NBER working paper, 6455.

Caballero R.J. (1992), "A Fallacy of Composition", American Economic Review, vol. 82, pp. 1279-92.

Caballero, R., Engel, E., Haltiwanger, J. (1997), "Aggregate Employment Dynamics", American Economic Review, vol. 87, pp 115-137.

Chavas, J. P. (1993), "On Aggregation and Its Implication for Aggregate Behaviour", Ricerche Economiche, vol 47, pp 201-214.

Colander, D., ed. (1996), "Beyond Microfoundation", Cambridge, Cambridge University Press.

Davis S.J., Haltinwanger, J.C. (1996), "Driving Forces and Employment Fluctuations: New Evidence and Alternative Fluctuations", working paper NBER 5775.

Davis S.J., Haltinwanger, J.C., Schuh, S. (1996) "Job Creation and Destruction", Cambridge, MIT Press.

Day, R. (1994), "Complex Economic Dynamics", Cambridge, MIT Press..

Eisemberg, B. (1961), "Aggregation of Utility Function", Management Science, vol. 6, pp. 337-50.

Fisher, F. M. (1969), "The Existence of Production Function", Econometrica, vol. 37, pp. 453-477.

Fisher, F. M. (1982), "Aggregate Production Function Revisited", Review of Economics Statistics, vol. 49, pp. 615-626.

Gallegati, M., Stanca, L.M. (1999), "The Dynamic Relations between Financial Positions and Investment: Evidence from Company Account Data", Industrial and Corporate Change, forthcoming.

Gallegati, M. , Kirman, A. P., eds. (1999), "Beyond the Representative Agent", Adelshot, Elgar.

Gilson, S.C. (1990), "Bankruptcy, Boards, Banks and Blockholder: Evidence on Changes in corporate Ownership and Control when Firms Default", Journal of Financial Economics, vol. 27, pp.355-388.

Gordon, R.H., Malkiel, B.G. (1981), "Corporation Finance" in Aaron H.A. and Pechman J.A., eds., "How Taxes Affect Economic Behaviour", Washington D.C., Brookings Institution.

Gorman, W. (1953), "Community Preference Field", Econometrica, vol. 21, pp. 63-80.

Grandmont, J. M., (1993), "Behavioural heterogeneity and Cournot Oligopoly Equilibrium", Ricerche Economiche, vol 47, pp 167-187.

Grandmont, J. M. (1991), "Transformations of the Commodity Spaces, Behavioural Heterogeneity and the Aggregation Problem", mimeo, CEPREMAP Paris.

Green, H. A. J. (1964), "The Aggregation in Economics Analysis", Princeton, Princeton University Press.

Greenwald, B.C., Stiglitz, J.E. (1988), "Imperfect Information, Finance Constraints and Business Fluctuations", in Kohn, M. and Tsiang, S.C., eds., "Finance Constraints, Expectations and Macroeconomics", Oxford, Oxford University Press.

Greenwald, B.C., Stiglitz, J.E. (1993), "Financial Market Imperfections and Business Cycles", Quarterly Journal of Economics, vol. 108, pp. 77-114.

Hartley, J. E., (1997), "The representative Agent in Macroeconomics", London Routledege.

Kaplan, S.N., Reishus, D. (1990), "Outside Directorship and Corporate Performance", Journal of Financial Economics, vol. 27, 389-410.

Kirman, A. P. (1992), "Whom or What Does The Representative Individual Represent", Journal of Economic Perspective, vol. 6, pp 117-136.

Kiyotaki, N., Moore, G. (1997), "Credit Cycles", Journal of Political Economy, vol. 105, pp. 211-48.

Leijonhufvud, A. (1981), "Information and Coordination", Oxford, Oxford University Press.

Leontief, W. W. (1947), "Introduction to a Theory of The internal Structure of Functional Relationship", Econometrica, vol. 15, pp. 361-73.

Long, J.B., Plosser, J. B. (1983), "Real Business Cycles", Journal of Political Economy, vol 91, pp. 39-69.

Lucas, R. (1975), "An Equilibrium Model of the Business Cycle", Journal of Political Economy, vol. 83, pp. 1113-1144.

Lucas, R. (1977), "Understanding Business Cycles", in D. Brunner, A. Meltzer, eds, "Stabilizations of the Domestic and International Economy", Amsterdam, North Holland.

Marshall, A. (1920), "Principles of Economics", London, Macmillan.

Malinvaud, E. (1993), "A framework for Aggregation Theory", Ricerche Economiche, vol. 47, pp. 107-135.

Martel, R. J., (1996), "Heterogeneity Aggregation and Meaningful Macroeconomics", in D. Colander, ed, "Beyond Microfoundation", Cambridge, Cambridge University Press, pp. 127-144.

Minsky, H.P. (1982), "Can "It" Happen Again? Essays on Instability and Finance", Armonk N.Y., M.E. Sharpe.

Rahn R.J., (1985), "Aggregation in System Dynamics", System Dynamic Review, vol.. 1, pp. 111-22.

Stiglitz, J.E. (1992), "Methodological Issues and the New Keynesian Economics", in A.Vercelli and N.Dimitri, eds., "Macroeconomics: A Survey of Research Strategies", Oxford, Oxford University Press, pp. 38-86.

Stocker, T. (1993), "Empirical Approaches to the Problem of Aggregation over Individuals", Journal of Economic Literature, vol. 21, pp. 1827-74.

Temin P., (1998), "The Causes of Americam Business Cycle: an Essay in Economic Historiography", in "Beyond Shocks: What Causes Business Cycle", Fuhrer J.C. and S.Schuh, eds., Conference Series, N. 42, Federal Reserve Bank of Boston, pp. 37-59.

Teräsvirta, T., Lundbergh, S. (1998), "Modeling Economic High-Frequency Time Series with STAR-STGARCH Models", SSE/EFI working paper n. 291, Stockholm.

Theil, H. (1954), "Linear Aggregation of Economic Relation", Amsterdam, North Holland.

White, M.J. (1989), "The Corporate Bankruptcy Decision", Journal of Economic Perspectives, vol. 3, pp.129-151.

Zarnowitz V., (1998), "Has the Business Cycle Been Abolished?", Business Economics, vol. 33, pp. 39-45.

The Dynamic Interaction of Rational Fundamentalists and Trend Chasing Chartists in a Monetary Economy

Carl Chiarella and Alexander Khomin

School of Finance and Economics University of Technology,
Sydney PO Box 123 Broadway, NSW 2007 Australia
Fax: +61 2 9514 7711
E-mail: Carl.Chiarella@uts.edu.au

Abstract. In a basic model of monetary dynamics we allow inflationary expectations to be formed as a weighted average of fundamentalist and chartists expectations. The fundamentalists form inflationary expectations rationally in the traditional sense in that they have full knowledge of the economic environment. The chartists form expectations by using standard trend chasing expectations schemes. As inflation accelerates/deccelerates an increasing proportion of agents switch from chartism to fundamentalism and fundamentalists put increasing weight on a reversion towards the fundamental value. The study the dynamics of the resulting economic system and show that it can exhibit a range of complex dynamic behaviour.

1 Introduction

The introduction of the concept of rational expectations into dynamic economic models has been one of the significant developments in economic theory over the last twenty five years. Whilst the use of rational expectations has been widely embraced by the profession there nevertheless remain a number of criticisms of the technique. Firstly the strong informational requirements on the part of the agents who inhabit the models under discussion. To some extent this criticism is being addressed by the developing literature on learning; see eg. [12]. Secondly the saddle point dynamic structure of rational expectations models which necessitates the imposition of arbitrary jumps on certain of the state variables for which the model at hand provides no theoretical justification; the so-called jump-variable technique. Early authors were apparently bothered by this troublesome feature; eg [3] and [1]. The latter author, in invoking the jump-variable technique in his model of output, stock market and interest rates states "... following a standard if not entirely convincing practice..". [13] and [20] give a critique of the jump-variable technique which leads to the conclusion that it should be rejected on methodological grounds alone. [4] and [5] shows how the adoption of a nonlinear modelling framework obviates the need to impose the arbitrary jumps of the jump-variable technique since such models can exhibit local instability but remain globally stable. The nonlinear framework introduced by

Chiarella was based on a portfolio adjustment argument that imposed nonlinear asset demand functions. However a different type of dynamic behaviour then emerges. Thirdly the rational expectations framework generally assumes the existence of a rational representative agent. Recently the central role of the representative agent has been questioned (eg. [14]) and models involving heterogeneous agents have begun to be analysed, see eg. [6], [15], [16], [17], [18], [19], [21] and [2]. In such models there are at least two groups of agents one of which is as well informed (or almost) about the economic model that they inhabit as the traditional rational representative agent, the others are assumed to be less well informed and are only able to make predictions of future values of prices from observations of past price time series.

The traditional argument justifying the use of the jump variable technique is that agents realise that the process of movement away from the equilibrium must eventually come to an end. Hence somehow the market mechanism will come into play in such a way as to place the economic state variables onto the stable manifold of the economy. In this way divergent paths are avoided. To our knowledge there has been no formal modelling of how this process would come about. Our aim in this paper is provide one such formal scenario in which the belief of agents that a period of accelerating inflation or deflation in a monetary economy will eventually come to an end will in fact stabilise the economy without the introduction of any other nonlinear effects such as the portfolio adjustment mechanism introduced by Chiarella. However we do find that a far richer set of stable attractors is possible than is assumed in the standard jump-variable approach. A simpler version of this model in which the fundamentalists only have knowledge of the equilibrium but not the model itself has been studied by [11].

We consider the basic model of monetary dynamics of the Cagan type, as studied by [4]. We allow two groups of agents, fundamentalists (who possess varying degrees of information about their economic environment and use this in forming expectations about next period prices) and chartists (who only use past price time series to form their expectations). As the process of accelerating inflation or deflation progresses, the fundamentalists put more weight on their belief in a reversion to the fundamental value. At the same time the ratio of fundamentalists to chartists moves towards the fundamentalist end of the spectrum as market participants generally believe that a reversion towards the fundamental is increasingly inevitable. We adapt the mechanism used by [2] to model the evolution of the fundamentalist/chartisit ratio. The reason we focus on the Cagan type monetary dynamics model is twofold. Firstly the study of the dynamic behaviour of this model played an important role in the early evolution of the rational expectations literature, in particular in the development of the jump variable technique, see e.g. [3]. It therefore seems important to understand how the dynamics of this basic model is modified under the scenario of heterogeneous agents and evolving beliefs outlined above. Secondly its cycle generating mechanism is at work in a broad class of disequilibrium models of monetary growth dynamics studied by [8] and [9]. It is in particular present in the Keynes-Wicksell model of the real and financial sector studied by [7]. Our aim is to study the effect of evolving beliefs on this mechanism in isolation before moving on in later work to incorporate it systematically into the models discussed in [8], [9] and [10] .

The plan of the paper is as follows. In section 2 we introduce the monetary dynamics model with heterogeneous agents and discuss the mechanism by which the proportions of these evolve . In section 3 we discuss the expectations scheme used by each group of agents and in particular how the fundamentalists switch their expectations towards the fundamental value as inflation/deflation accelerates. In section 4 analyse by numerical simulations the dynamic behaviour of the resulting monetary dynamics model. Section 5 offers some conclusions and proposes future directions for research. Our principal finding is that prices exhibit bifurcating behaviour as the speed of market adjustment and the speed of chartists adaptation increase. For all the simulations we have run, processes of accelerating inflation or deflation always come to an end so that the fluctuations of the model always remain bounded. Even so for a stylised model the fluctuations are unrealistically large so the model can be regarded as being mathematically viable rather than economically viable. To obtain economic viability we would need to introduce some portfolio adjustment mechanism such as in [4]. This task we leave for future research.

2   The Model

We start with the basic elements of the Cagan model of monetary dynamics.
Money demand at time t is assumed to be given by

$$m_t^d = p_t + f(\pi_t),$$ (1)

The money supply is assumed to vary stochastically from period to period according to

$$m_t^s = m_{t-h}^s + \sigma \sqrt{h}\,\tilde{\xi}_t, \quad m_o^s = \bar{m},$$ (2)

where h is the length of the time interval, σ is the volatility of the money supply and $\tilde{\xi}_t \sim N(0,1)$ is a standard random normal variate. Here $m_t = ln(M_t)$, $M_t =$ nominal money at time t, $p_t = lnP_t$, $P_t =$ aggregate price level at time t, $\pi_t = E(\dot{p}_t) =$ expected inflation rate at time t.
In this study the function f is taken to be linear viz.

$$f(\pi) = b - a\pi, \quad (a > 0).$$ (3)

In his critique of the jump-variable technique [4] took f as a nonlinear function (based on a portfolio adjustment argument) in order to ensure global stability. Here we remain with a linear money demand function and seek to determine whether the adaptively evolving expectations of the fundamentalists and chartists can lead to global stability

We assume lagged price adjustment to excess money demand, which we write in discrete time as

$$p_{t+h} - p_t = \beta h[m_t^s - p_t - f(\pi_t)], \tag{4}$$

$$m_{t+h}^s - m_t^s = \sigma\sqrt{h}\,\tilde{\xi}_t, \quad m_o^s = \bar{m}. \tag{5}$$

We have given only sketchy details of the modelling of the stochastic term which is based on [5]. This stochastic set-up gives a consistent stochastic differential equation system in the limit $h \to 0$ and also a consistent stochastic equilibrium when $\beta \to \infty$ and $h \to 0$.

To complete the model we need to specify how expectations are formed. As stated above, we postulate two groups of agents, fundamentalists and chartists who have different information about the economic system and hence use different procedures to form expectations. The fundamentalists have greater knowledge of the economic system as a result of incurring higher costs in calculating their expectations. In particular they have full or partial knowledge of the model as well as knowledge of the expectations mechanism of the chartists. Following [2] we take market expectations as a weighted average of the expectations of these two groups. The weighting of these two groups evolves according to the difference between their most recent estimate of inflation and actual inflation and to their costs. As this difference increases there is a growing belief amongst agents that there will be a return towards the fundamental (or equilibrium) price level, hence more agents switch to fundamentalism. At the same time fundamentalists are putting less weight on the expectation of inflation based on their knowledge of the model, but rather put more weight on price movement towards the equilibrium price.

To clarify the notation we refer to the time line in figure 1. Here subscript 1 refers to the chartists and subscript 2 to the fundamentalists. Thus

$$\pi_{t,t+h}^i = \begin{cases} \text{the expected rate of inflation over the} \\ \text{time interval } (t, t+h) \text{ formed by group } i \\ \text{at time } t, \end{cases}$$

$$p_t = \text{the value of p at time } t,$$

$$g_{t,t+h} = \begin{cases} \text{the actual rate of inflation over the} \\ \text{time interval } (t, t+h) \end{cases} = \frac{p_{t+h} - p_t}{h}.$$

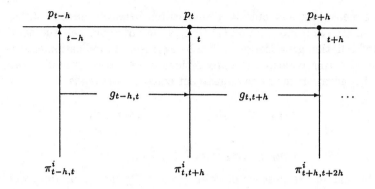

Fig. 1. Time Line

The market expectation of inflation over the time interval $(t, t + h)$ is given by[1]

$$\pi_{t,t+h} = n_t^1 \pi_{t,t+h}^1 + n_t^2 \pi_{t,t+h}^2, \tag{6}$$

where the proportions n_t^1, n_t^2 evolve according to the following scheme which has the effect of switching the proportion towards fundamentalists as the difference between expected and realised inflation increases. This increase being taken as a signal of accelerating inflation/deflation. This mechanism is mathematically equivalent to the one employed by [2], however the economic interpretation is different. In the models considered by Brock and Hommes the prediction error could be related to profit or return which drove the change in proportions. Here the concept of profit or return is not explicitly modelled and any event it is the growing belief of a reversion to the fundamental that is driving the change in proportions. Thus

$$n_t^i = N_t^i / Z, \qquad (i = 1, 2) \tag{7}$$

where

$$N_t^i = exp\left\{ \lambda \left[\left(g_{t-h,t} - \pi_{t-h,t}^i\right)^2 + c^i \right] \right\}, \qquad (i = 1, 2) \tag{8}$$

and

$$Z = N_t^1 + N_t^2.$$

Here c^i are the costs incurred by each group in forming expectations. We assume $c^2 > c^1$, i.e. the fundamentalists incur a greater relative costs in forming their expectations. The quantity $\lambda(> 0)$ is the intensity of choice

---

[1] Given that we are assuming a linear money demand function we could equally assume different money demands for each group, aggregate these using the proportions n_t^i and arrive at the same model as the one we analyse below.

variable measuring how quickly agents switch between fundamentalism and chartism. We see from equation (7) that as the difference between actual and expected inflation grows larger (taken by agents as an indication of accelerating/deccelerating inflation) the proportions evolve towards fundamentalism.

In this notation the price adjustment equation (4) reads

$$p_{t+h} - p_t = \beta h[m_t - p_t - f(\pi_{t,t+h})], \tag{9}$$

$$m_{t+h} - m_t = \sigma\sqrt{h}\,\tilde{\xi}_t, \quad m_o^s = \bar{m}. \tag{10}$$

Note that in the absence of noise (i.e. $\sigma = 0$) the equilibrium would be given by

$$\bar{p} = \bar{m} - b, \quad \bar{\pi} = 0 \tag{11}$$

In the following analysis we take this value of $\bar{p}$ as the equilibrium or fundamental value expected by the fundamentalists.

Following Brock and Hommes we introduce

$$x_t = n_t^2 - n_t^1,$$

so that $x_t = 1(-1)$ corresponds to all agents being fundamentalists (chartists). Some simple algebra shows that

$$x_t = \tanh\left(\frac{\lambda}{2}\left[\left(g_{t-h,t} - \pi_{t-h,t}^2\right)^2 - \left(g_{t-h,t} - \pi_{t-h,t}^1\right)^2 + c^2 - c^1\right]\right) \tag{12}$$

with

$$n_t^1 = (1 - x_t)/2, \quad \text{and} \quad n_t^2 = (1 + x_t)/2.$$

Thus the expression for $\pi_{t,t+h}$ becomes

$$\pi_{t,t+h} = \frac{(1 - x_t)}{2}\pi_{t,t+h}^1 + \frac{(1 + x_t)}{2}\pi_{t,t+h}^2 \tag{13}$$

The dynamical system in this case consists of the difference equations (9), (10) together with the algebraic equations (12) and (13) and some specification as to how the expectations $\pi_{t,t+h}^1$ and $\pi_{t,t+h}^2$ are formed.

3   Expectation Mechanisms

In this section we consider the expectations mechanisms for each group. These are forward looking or rational (in the sense of knowledge of the equilibrium and knowledge of the model) on the part of the fundamentalists and adaptive expectations on the part of the chartists.

For the chartists we assume the classical adaptive scheme of a weighted average [2] of the most recently observed inflation rate and the most recently formed expectation,

$$\pi^1_{t,t+h} = (1 - h\beta_{\pi_1}) \, \pi^1_{t-h,t} + h\beta_{\pi_1} \left(\frac{p_t - p_{t-h}}{h} \right). \tag{14}$$

According to this behaviour chartists are using a geometrically declining weighted average of past inflation rates. Here $0 < h\beta_{\pi_1} \leq 1$.

The fundamentalists form an estimate of the rate of inflation $g^{est}_{t,t+h}$ based on knowledge of the model. Thus for this group we postulate the expectations mechanism

$$\pi^2_{t,t+h} = (1 - h\beta_{\pi_2})(\bar{p} - p_t) + h\beta_{\pi_2} g^{est}_{t,t+h}. \tag{15}$$

According to this scheme the fundamentalists form their expectation of inflation as a weighted average of the forecast of the model, $g^{est}_{t,t,t+h}$ and the deviation of the price level from its equilibrium or fundamental level. The fundamentalists anticipate that the further the price deviates from its fundamental value the more likely is it to revert towards its fundamental value (i.e. equilibrium). Thus the weighting function $h\beta_{\pi_2}$ is a function of $(p_t - \bar{p})$. In particular in this study we take

$$h\beta_{\pi_2} = exp \left[-\frac{(p_t - \bar{p})^2}{s} \right]. \tag{16}$$

The parameter s allows us to vary the rate at which the fundamentalists switch between $g^{est}_{t,t+h}$ and $(p_t - \bar{p})$. For the moment we will assume that the fundamentalists know or have learnt the model i.e. equation (9). However in order to use this information they need to know the expectation rule of the chartists as well as their cost structure so that they can form the weights in equation (4). Here we assume that the fundamentalists know equation (13) and the parameter β_{π_1} and the initial value of $\pi^1_{t,t+h}$. Subsequent research will need to focus on how they learn both these parameters as well as the model.

Thus fundamentalists form $g^{est}_{t,t+h}$ according to

$$g^{est}_{t,t+h} = \beta(m^s_t - p_t - f(\pi_{t,t+h})), \tag{17}$$

$$\pi_{t,t+h} = n^1_t \pi^{1(est)}_{t,t+h} + n^2_t \pi^2_{t,t+h}, \tag{18}$$

$$\pi^{1(est)}_{t,t+h} = \pi^{1(est)}_{t-h,t} + h\beta_{\pi_1}\left(\frac{p_t - p_{t-h}}{h} - \pi^{1(est)}_{t-h,h}\right), \tag{19}$$

$$\pi^2_{t,t+h} = (1 - h\beta_{\pi_2})(\bar{p} - p_t) + h\beta_{\pi_2}g^{est}_{t,t+h}. \tag{20}$$

$$m^s_{t+h} = m^s_t + \sigma\sqrt{h}\tilde{\xi}_t, \qquad m_0 = \bar{m}. \tag{21}$$

Here we write $\pi^{1(est)}_{t,t+h}$ to indicate that this is group 2's estimate of group 1's prediction of inflation in the next period. Since we assume that the fundamentalists have full knowledge of equation (13) $\pi^{1(est)}_{t,t+h}$ will in fact equal $\pi^1_{t,t+h}$. However this notation would allow us at a later stage to incorporate learning by the fundamentalists of the parameter β_{π_1}. Note that $g^{est}_{t,t+h}$ appears on the LHS and RHS of equation (17) and hence will be the solution of an algebraic equation. In fact it turns out that

$$g^{est}_{t,t+h} = \beta\left[m^s_t - p_t - b + \frac{a(1-x_t)}{2}\left\{h\beta_{\pi_1}\left(\frac{p_t - p_{t-h}}{h}\right)\right.\right.$$
$$\left.\left. + (1 - h\beta_{\pi_1})\pi^1_{t-h,t}\right\} + \frac{a(1+x_t)}{2}(1 - h\beta_{\pi_2})(\bar{p} - p_t)\right] /$$
$$\left(1 - \beta\frac{a(1+x_t)}{2}h\beta_{\pi_2}\right). \tag{22}$$

The proportions n^1_t, n^2_t evolve according to equations (7) and (8). According to this scheme the greater the deviation of expected inflation from predicted inflation, the more agents switch to fundamentalism as there is a growing anticipation that the market will turn back towards the fundamental value.

In order to see the order of the dynamical system with which we are dealing we introduce the subsidiary variables

$$u^1_t \equiv \pi^1_{t-h,t}, \quad u^2_t \equiv \pi^2_{t-h,t} \text{ and } v_t \equiv p_{t-h}. \tag{23}$$

The dynamics of our monetary economy can then be written

$$u^1_{t+h} = \beta_{\pi_1}(p_t - v_t) + (1 - h\beta_{\pi_1})u^1_t, \tag{24}$$

$$u^2_{t+h} = h\beta_{\pi_2}g^{est}_{t,t+h} + (1 - h\beta_{\pi_2})u^2_t, \tag{25}$$

$$v_{t+h} = p_t, \tag{26}$$

$$p_{t+h} = p_t + \beta h\left[m^s_t - p_t - f\left(\frac{(1-x_t)}{2}u^1_{t+h} + \frac{(1+x_t)}{2}u^2_{t+h}\right)\right], \tag{27}$$

$$m^2_{t+h} = m^s_t + \sigma\sqrt{h}\tilde{\xi}_t, \tag{28}$$

together with the algebraic equations (11) for x_t, (16) for $h\beta_{\pi_2}$ and (22) for $g^{est}_{t,t+h}$. In all we have a fourth order difference equation system in the no noise (i.e. $\sigma = 0$) case, and a fifth order stochastic difference equation system when $\sigma > 0$ is considered.

4   Numerical Analysis of the Dynamics

We have not been successful in obtaining analytically any tractable expression for the Jacobian of the dynamical system (24) - (28) at its equilibrium from which we could obtain information about possible bifurcation points. Therefore in this section we seek to obtain some insights into the dynamics of the model by performing various numerical simulations[3]

In table 1 we display the basic parameter set used in numerical investigations of the model.

$$a = 0.5, b = 1, h = 0.01$$
$$\lambda = 0.5, c_1 = 0.0, c_2 = 0.5$$
$$\beta_{\pi_1} = 50, s = 1$$
$$\bar{m} = 2, \bar{\pi} = 0, \beta = 2.15$$

Table 1

In figures 2a and 2c we display the pseudo-phase plots of the log-price p and proportions x for the speed of price adjustment β equal to 2.15 and 2.70 respectively. These attractors exhibit typical behaviour observed in a wide range of simulations. As β increases the fluctuations in p become larger and x bounces more and more rapidly between +1 and -1 (ie the fundamentalist and chartist extremes). For values of β below about 2 trajectories are stable to the equilibrium point. As β increases the size of the price fluctuations becomes quite large as can be seen in figure 2c. In spite of the large fluctuations the evolving beliefs mechanism we have described in the previous section succeeds in bringing to an end periods of accelerating inflation/deflation. In figure 2b we show p as a function of time when $\beta = 2.15$. In figure 2d-f we show the effect of the noise term in the money supply when $\beta = 2.15$. This has the effect(see figure 2d) of smearing somewhat the pseudo-phase plot compared to the non-noise picture. In figure 2e we see the effect of noise on the time series for p, which essentially drifts with the stochastic time path of m. Figure 2f shows the time path for the proportions x under the effect of the noise term. This picture is similar to the no noise situation. At this value of β the fraction is concentrated at a value slightly to the chartist end of the spectrum. As we have already pointed out, as β increases the fraction x concentrates at both extremes of the spectrum. We obtained similar results for the effect of noise on all the later simulations and hence do not discuss it further in this paper.

Figure 3 shows the effect of varying β_{π_1} with β held fixed at 3.0. Figures 3a and 3d show the (x, p) pseudo-phase plots at β_{π_1} equal to 70 and 90. The principal effect of increasing β_{π_1} is to increase the range of fluctuations of p as can be readily seen from the time series plots in figures 3b and 3e.

---

[3] The computer programs used to generate the simulations reported here are available upon request from the authors.

Finally figure 4 displays the effect on the (p, x) phase plane of varying the parameter s at $\beta = 2.15$. We recall that s measures the rate at which fundamentalists switch their beliefs to a return towards the fundamental. The higher s the more slowly do they switch to a belief in return towards the fundamental.Thus we see from figure 4 that fluctuations in p are less pronounced and less complex the lower is s. The phase diagrams also indicate how the proportions fluctuate from one extreme to the other in a more pronounced fashion as s increases.

5   Conclusions

We have seen that the introduction of fundamentalists and chartists with adaptively evolving expectations into the basic Cagan model of monetary dynamics can yield complex dynamic behaviour in various parameter regions. Furthermore the model remains globally stable over a wide region of parameter space without the introduction of nonlinear money demand functions of the type considered by [4] and [5]. We recall that the basic mechanism is one whereby the fundamentalists put increasing weight on a reversion to the fundamental as inflation/deflation accelerates, with at the same time an increasing fraction of chartists switching to fundamentalism. We have seen that this mechanism is able to render Cagan type models globally stable over a wide range of parameter space. Our analysis thus provides one possible scenario behind the jump-variable technique. However we hasten to stress that the dynamic outcome is far richer and more complex than what is currently assumed by those who employ that technique in their economic modelling. In essence the jump variable technique only allows for dynamic outcomes which are stable to the equilibrium point of the model, which in terms of the parameters of our model means low values of β, β_{π_1} and s. In our view the price fluctuations to which the model gives rise are unrealistic even for such a highly stylised model. Portfolio adjustment mechanisms at high and low levels of expected inflation along the lines considered by [4] would need to be incorporated to make the model more appropriate for use in more fully integrated macrodynamic models.

Further work on the model at hand needs to be done, in particular calculation of bifurcation diagrams, investigation of Lyapunov exponents, calculation of the long run average and dispersion of the proportions of fundamentalists and chartists and numerical investigation of any homoclinic behaviour along the lines of [22]. Future research will lead in two directions. Firstly the incorporation of learning dynamics into the model structure introduced here. We need to investigate whether and how the fundamentalists can learn about the model and the expectations rules of the chartists. Secondly the adaptively evolving expectations mechanism studied here will be placed into the monetary sector of consistently specified macrodynamic models of the real and financial sectors, for example the hierarchy of disequilibrium monetary growth models studied by [8], [9] and [10]. In these models the proportions of chartists and fundamentalists were held fixed. The introduction of adaptively evolving expectations should thus lead to a greater degree of realism in these models.

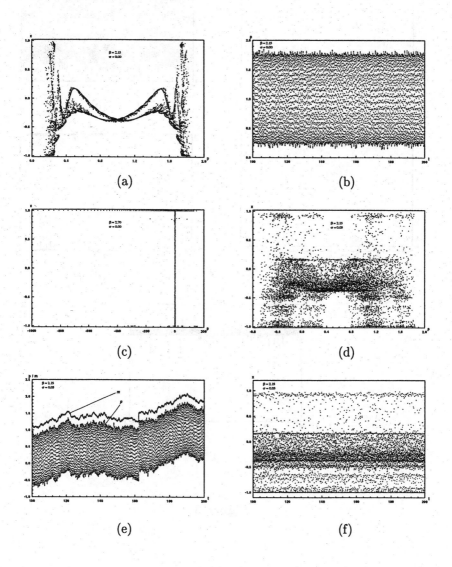

Figure 2

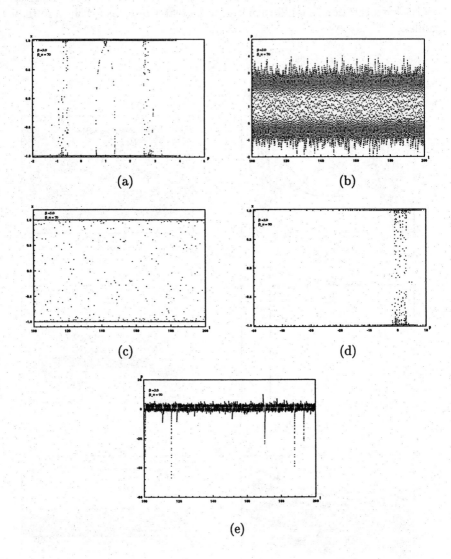

Figure 3

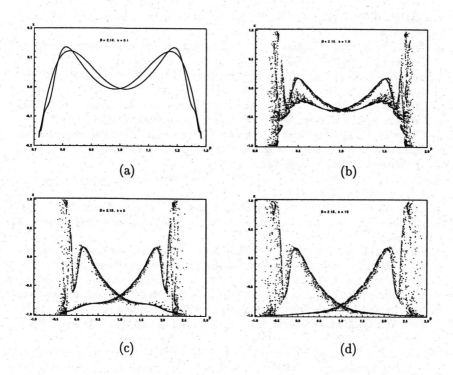

(a)

(b)

(c)

(d)

Figure 4

References

1. Blanchard, O. J. (1981), "Output, the Stock Market and Interest Rates", *American Economic Review*, **71**, 132–143.
2. Brock, W.A. and Hommes, C.H. (1997) "A Rational Route to Randomness", *Econometrica*, **65**(5), 1059-1095
3. Burmeister, E. (1980), "On Some Conceptual Issues in Rational Expectations Modelling", *Journal of Money, Credit and Banking*, **12**, 217–228.
4. Chiarella, C. (1986), "Perfect Foresight Models and the Dynamic Instability Problem from a Higher Viewpoint", *Economic Modelling*, **4**, 283–292.
5. Chiarella, C. (1991), "The Bifurcation of Probability Distributions in a Nonlinear Rational Expectations Model of a Monetary Economy", *European Journal of Political Economy*, **7**, 65-78.
6. Chiarella, C. (1992), "The Dynamics of Speculative Behaviour", *Annals of Operations Research*, **37**, 101-123.
7. Chiarella, C. and Flaschel, P. (1996), "Real and Monetary Cycles in Models of Keynes-Wicksell Type", *Journal of Economic Behaviour and Organisation*, **30**, 327–351.
8. Chiarella, C. and Flaschel, P. (1999a), "Keynesian Monetary Growth Dynamics: Macro-foundations", forthcoming, Cambridge University Press, 1998.
9. Chiarella, C. and Flaschel, P. (1999b), "The Emergence of Complex Dynamics in a 'Naturally' Nonlinear Integrated Keynesian Model of Monetary Growth", forthcoming in *Commerce, Complexity, and Evolution and Economics*, eds Barnett, W., Chiarella, C., Keen, S., Marks, R. and Schabl, H., Cambridge University Press.
10. Chiarella, C. and Flaschel, P. (1999c), "Keynesian Monetary Growth Dynamics in Open Economies", Department of Economics, University of Bielefeld, Bielefeld.
11. Chiarella, C. and Khomin, A. (1999), "An Analysis of Adaptively Evolving Expectations in Models of Monetary Dynamics: The Fundamentalists Forward Looking", forthcoming, *Annals of Operations Research*, 1999.
12. Evans, G. W. and Honkapohja, S. (1995), "Adaptive Learning and Expectational Stability: An Introduction", in *Learning and Rationality in Economics*, eds A. Kirman and M. Salmon, Basil Blackwell, Oxford.
13. George, D. A. R. and Oxley, L. T. (1985), "Structural Stability and Model Design", *Economic Modelling*, **2**, 307–316.
14. Kirman, A.P. (1992), "Whom or What Does the Representative Agent Represent?", *Journal of Economic Perspectives*, **6**, 117-136.
15. Kirman, A.P. (1993), "Ants, Rationality and Recruitment", *Quarterly Journal of Economics*, **108**, 137-156.
16. Lux,T (1995), "Herd Behaviour, Bubbles and Crashes", *Economic Journal*, **105**, 881-896.
17. Lux, T. (1996), "A Master Equation Approach to the Modelling of Financial Markets Microstructure", in Vlacic, L.T., Nguyen, T. and D. Cecez-Kecmanovic, eds., Modelling and Control of National and Regional Economies, Pergamon, Oxford, 409-414.
18. Lux, T. (1997), "Time Variation of Second Moments from a Noise Trader/Infection Model", *Journal of Economic Dynamics and Control*, **22**, 1-38.

19. Lux, T. (1998), "The Socio-Economic Dynamics of Speculative Markets: Interacting Agents, Chaos and the Fat Tails of Return Distributions", *Journal of Economic Behaviour and Organization*, **33**, 143-165.
20. Oxley, L. and George, D. A. R. (1994), "Linear Saddlepoint Dynamics 'On Their Head'. The Scientific Content of the New Orthodoxy in Macroeconomics", *European Journal of Political Economy*, **10**, 389–400.
21. Sethi, R. (1996), "Endogenous Regime Switching in Speculative Markets", *Structural Change and Economic Dynamics*, **7**, 99-118.
22. Vilder, de R. (1995), "Endogenous Business Cycles", Tinbergen Institute Research Series, No. 96.

Self-Organization in Global Stochastic Models of Production and Inventory Dynamics

Sergio Focardi[1] and Michele Marchesi[2]

[1] The Intertek Group, Paris, France

[2] DIEE, University of Cagliari, Italy

Abstract. This paper proposes an extension of the inventory production model developed in Bak, Chen, Scheinkman, and Woodford (BCSW, 1993). We show how the Pareto-Levy type of aggregate distributions emerge in global models as well as in local models. We extend the BCSW model by allowing random connections between firms. The distribution of production in the economy follows a power law probability distribution. In addition, the long-run frequency distribution follows the same law.

Keywords: *Critical state, self-organization, self-similarity, global interaction, stable laws*

Introduction

The concept of self-organizing criticalities (SOC) was introduced as a physical model to explain a vast class of self-similar behavior often found in physical systems. Bak, Tang, and Wiesenfeld (1987) developed a sand pile model as a prototype model of self-organizing criticalities.

The sand pile model is a cellular automata that mimics the behavior of a real sand pile. If grains of sand are randomly added to a sand pile, the pile self-organizes into one of a specific and stable steepness, regardless of its initial steepness. In addition, the stable shape is maintained in a situation of criticality, producing avalanches of any size. The distribution of avalanche size is of the Pareto-Levy type and shows invariance of scale. Since the introduction of the first model of a sand pile, other structures showing similar behavior have been studied.

Self-organizing criticalities are characterized by several key properties. First, they are phenomena of statistical equilibrium. The equilibrium, however, is critical as there are fluctuations of any size, driven by random shocks, around the equilibrium position. Second, the critical equilibrium is self-organizing as the system automatically reaches the critical equilibrium position from any initial configuration. Third, fluctuations show self-similar behavior with fat-tailed distributions of the Pareto-Levy type and power spectrum decaying as ω^b. This type of behavior has to be distinguished from other types of critical equilibrium that depend on fine tuning some parameters of the system.

Bak, Chen, Scheinkman, and Woodford (BCSW) (1993) used the Bak sand pile model to build a model of a production and inventory economy that shows large endogenous fluctuations, even in the limit of external stimuli of constant mean. They thus demonstrate that random shocks to the economy do not average out in aggregate but might produce significant aggregate fluctuations.

BCSW considered a simple square economy made of L layers with L nodes each. Each node is a producer/warehouse that produces/stores only one type of good. A warehouse can store only one unit. Each producer is characterized by a nonlinear production schedule so that it produces either zero or two units of product. Each producer receives orders from the two nearest producers one layer above and gives orders only to the two nearest producers one layer below.

BCSW showed that each final consumer order might create production avalanches whose sizes follow a Pareto-Levy type of distribution. Using the special aggregation properties of Pareto-Levy stable distributions, they then showed that the aggregate behavior follows the same distribution. Even in the limit of an infinite economy, aggregate production - scaled by a suitable factor of scale such that the average of total production remains constant when the economy approaches infinity - shows the same fat-tailed distribution and scale invariance.

The generation of power laws

The objective of the BCSW model is to show that there are endogenous fluctuations in the economy even in situations of constant external stimuli. This objective is reached by showing that random noise applied to the economy translates into stochastic processes characterized by power law distributions.

To extend the BCSW model, we need to consider two mathematical components: 1) the generation of power laws as ensemble distribution and 2) the SOC behavior that translates these power laws into long run frequencies.

One class of probabilistic models that generate power law distributions are percolation models at or near the critical percolation probability. In the BCSW system, both the distances traveled by orders and the global level of production follow a power law distribution. BCSW explicitly compute the exponent of such a distribution using a previous analysis of a directed percolation model done by Dhar and Ramaswamy (1989).

Percolation models translate the idea that economic influence propagates through a nearest neighbor mechanism. The definition of nearest neighbors need not, however, be restricted to topological proximity. A nearest neighbor might be defined in much broader terms, for instance allowing randomness in the choice of the nearest neighbors. Moreover, percolation models need not be restricted to the special model of directed percolation used in the BCSW model.

Very few percolation models have been analyzed rigorously. Among those that can be solved exactly is the one used by BCSW. We will make use of another exactly solvable mode, percolation on a Cayley tree. Simulations and semi-rigorous arguments suggest, however, that percolation models, in general, exhibit power law distributions at and near the critical percolation threshold.

A global model

Following Kirman (1997) we distinguish between local and global models. The fixed nearest-neighbor topology of the BCSW model is typical of local models. We will show, however, that SOC behavior and power laws also appear in global models. We will therefore allow for more general links between firms and for some randomness in the way orders are transferred from one layer to the next. The ensuing model is no longer local as units can communicate with any other unit in the next layer.

The configuration of our model is the following: the system is made up of a finite number M of layers; each layer is made of L nodes. The adoption of a rectangular model of the economy avoids the restriction that the depth of the supplier chain should be equal to the width of the economy. In our global model, the ratio of the width of the economy and its depth is arbitrary.

We shall see, however, that in order to obtain meaningful results it is convenient that width be much bigger than depth. This is because an infinite economy is better represented as the limit of a sequence of economies when L and M become arbitrarily large with the constraint $L>>M$.

Each node has the same configuration as in the BCSW model. In brief, each node represents a firm that produces and stores one good. Each firm is characterized by a nonlinear production schedule such that it either produces zero or two units. Its warehouse can store only one unit of the good.

We say that a node is full if the corresponding firm has one unit in stock and can therefore satisfy one order. We say that a node is empty if the corresponding firm does not have any unit in stock and must therefore start production to satisfy an order. A state C of the system is the configuration of its nodes.

If, on receiving an order, a firm has one unit in its warehouse, it satisfies the order from its inventory which is thus emptied. If the firm has no unit in inventory, it produces two units. One of the units is delivered to satisfy the order, the other remains in inventory. When it produces two units, a firm simultaneously issues two orders to two firms in the next layer. In both cases, the corresponding node changes state.

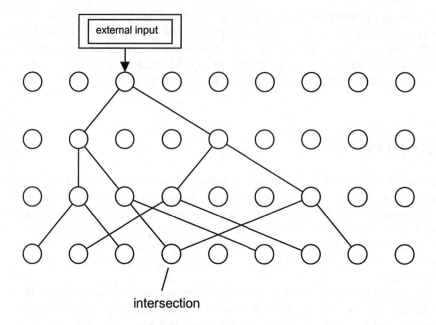

Fig. 1. The layout of the model.

We depart from BCSW by allowing random connections between each layer and the one immediately following. Although we allow each firm to pass orders only to firms in the next layer, we randomly select the path through which orders propagate. We therefore represent the order propagation process as follows:

When an order hits the first layer, a path of connections is randomly selected among all possible paths. A generic connection path is a graph z that connects one node in the top layer with two nodes in the second layer and successively connects each of these two nodes with two nodes in the third layer and so on. Connections might overlap, i.e., the two branches leaving a node might overlap and hit the same node in the layer below. In the third layer, the corresponding graph might then exhibit one, two, three or four links, and so on in the subsequent ones. Figure 1 illustrates the layout of the model.

A path is a graph that connects a set of firms in the lattice. If the firm hit by the first order has an empty stock, two orders are passed on to the firms connected by the chosen path. The process is then repeated by issuing two orders from those sites that are empty to the sites in the following layer that are connected by the path. Orders propagate along the chosen path until all terminal nodes are full and orders can be satisfied from stock, or until the last layer is reached. It is easy to verify that the above process is equivalent to the random choice of firms to which orders are passed from layer to layer.

What is the probability that two branches of a path intersect, i.e., what is the probability that a randomly selected path has at least one intersection in its branches? In absence of intersection, there is one branch in the first layer, two branches in the second layer and so on. Therefore there are 2^i branches in the i_{th} layer.

It is clear that if $2^M>L$, i.e., if $M>log_2L$, every path must have intersecting branches. In fact, after the first log_2L layers, there are more branches than nodes and therefore at least two branches must intersect on the same node. Suppose, therefore, that $M<log_2L$.

Consider a path. Suppose that there is no intersection in the branches of the first

$(j-1)$ layers. Therefore, $k=2^j$ branches hit the j_{th} layer. Suppose that $k<M$. The probability P_j that there is no intersection in the j_{th} layer (given that there was no intersection before) is given by:

$$P_j = L(L-1)\ldots(L-k+1)/L^k. \tag{1}$$

In fact, the number of possible non-intersecting connections is $L(L-1) \ldots (L-k+1)$, because there are L possibilities for the first connection, $L-1$ for the second, and so on. On the other hand, the total number of possible connection, intersecting or not, is L^k. Thus the above probability.

For a given L, P_j is clearly a decreasing function of $k=2^j$ because the number of possibilities of intersection grows with the number of branches; the probability of no intersection therefore decreases. The probability P that there are no intersecting branches in the first j layers of a randomly chosen path is obtained factorizing the probabilities $P = P_1P_2 \; P_j$. Clearly $P>P^j$, as P_j is a decreasing function of j.

We can rewrite P_j as:

$$P_j=(1-1/L)(1-2/L) \quad (1-k/L). \tag{2}$$

Given j, it is evident that we can choose $L=L(j)$ so that P^j is arbitrarily close to 1. Therefore, if we let the economy go to infinity under the constraint $L=L(M)$ we can keep the probability of intersecting branches arbitrarily close to zero (i.e. the probability of non intersecting branches arbitrarily close to one).

In the limit of an infinite economy, the probability that two branches of a path intersect is zero. In fact, for each layer there is only a finite number of possible intersections, each with zero probability. The probability of intersection between branches of the entire graph, therefore, is the countable union of events of probability zero which is itself an event of probability zero.

If we consider a large economy with appropriately chosen ratios between width and depth and such that, in any case, $L>>2^M$, we can assume that the set of paths with intersecting branches is negligible. This assumption allows a significant simplification because we can then adopt the model of percolation on a Cayley tree as we will see below.

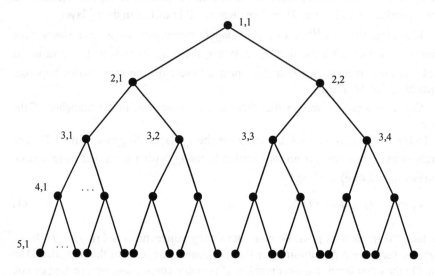

Fig. 2. A Cayley tree.

with intersecting branches is negligible. This assumption allows a significant simplification because we can then adopt the model of percolation on a Cayley tree as we will see below.

Cayley trees

Cayley trees (Grimmet, 1989) are directed and hierarchical trees as the one in Figure 2. In general, a Cayley tree can be an ennary tree, with $\underline{n}$ branches leaving each node but we need to consider here only binary trees. Branches connecting two nodes are called bonds. Each bond can be open or closed independently with probability p.

The appropriate probability space of a percolation lattice, and in particular of a Cayley tree can be constructed rigorously as a product space with an associated σ-algebra of events. For brevity, we will not carry on this construction which can be found in textbooks. (See Grimmet, 1989)

Cayley trees are one of the few percolation models that can be solved exactly. It can be demonstrated that the percolation threshold is exactly 1/2. At the percolation threshold, the size of connected clusters follows a power law distribution with exponent 3/2. Let's call S the size of a connected cluster at the origin, i.e., $\underline{S}$ is the number of nodes in a connected cluster that includes the origin. If $P(S=n)$ is the probability that the size of a connected cluster that includes the origin is exactly n, we can therefore write:

$$P(S=n) = \alpha n^{-3/2} \tag{3}$$

for large values of n and where α is a proportionality constant.

The finite economy case

Let's first analyze a finite economy under the assumptions that $L >> 2^M$ and that, therefore, intersecting paths are negligible. Suppose an order is received at the randomly selected i_{th} node of the top layer, i.e. $a_{1,i}$. At the same time, a path z of connections is randomly selected from the set Z of all possible non intersecting paths.

If node $a_{1,i}$ has units in inventory, it can satisfy the order from inventory and it changes state to empty inventory. If the node $a_{1,i}$ has no unit in inventory, it issues two orders to the next layer, satisfies the incoming order and it is left with one unit in inventory, i.e. it changes state. The two orders follow the branches of the path. The process goes on until either every order can be satisfied from existing inventories or until the last row is reached.

Let $X_{i,z}$ be the random variable that represents the size of the production avalanche corresponding to an order received at site $a_{1,i}$ and following the path z. $X_{i,z}$ is the sum of all production activated at each site. $X_{i,z}$ is therefore equal to the sum of all orders issued in the process of order propagation.

Let's first observe that, by placing an order on site $a_{1,i}$ and by selecting a path, one univocally determines a mapping of the set of the states onto itself. In fact, given a path of connections without intersecting branches and given any state C_l of the nodes, the propagation of orders has the effect of changing every connected sequence of empty sites starting at $a_{1,i}$ into a connected sequence of full sites, while every limiting full site is changed into an empty = site. Let's call C_m the resulting state.

Given a state C_l, a starting site $a_{1,i}$, and a corresponding randomly chosen path z, the propagation of orders uniquely determines the transformation $T_{i,l,z}$ from the state C_l to the state $C_m = T_{i,l,z}(C_l)$ as described in the above paragraph. This transformation is also invertible as the state C_m such that $C_m = T_{i,l,z}(C_l)$ is obviously uniquely determined. In fact, at each layer a number of couples of sites exchange their states while others remain unchanged.

As a consequence of the above, the uniform distribution of states is an invariant distribution for each of the $T_{i,l,z}$. Given a probability distribution of the paths, for instance if paths are randomly chosen with uniform probabilities (as we are analyzing a finite system, the set of paths is finite), and a distribution of the sites where orders are initially placed, the set of states evolves as a Markov chain. In addition, the uniform distribution of states is an invariant distribution for this Markov chain.

The uniform distribution of states implies that sites are, in turn, uniformly and independently distributed with probability 1/2. In fact, the probability space is formed by all possible configurations of sites. If configurations are equiprobable, sites must have the same independent probability 1/2. Suppose then that sites are uniformly and independently distributed with probability 1/2.

We can thus represent the process of order propagation as percolation on a finite Cayley tree. This can be seen in different ways. Each order propagation path, with the exception of a negligibly small number of intersecting paths, is isomorphic to a binary tree, i.e. to a Cayley tree. At each node, orders propagate or stop in function of the occupancy state of the node. Under the assumption of uniform distribution of states, each node is empty/full independently with probability 1/2. Order propagation is therefore a realization of percolation on a Cayley tree with probability 1/2.

More formally, suppose that the state space of all configurations is given together with a non intersecting order path z. We can therefore partition the space of states into classes formed by all configurations that share the same set of empty/full nodes in the given order path z. Each configuration of node occupancy on the order path is isomorphic to a corresponding configuration on a binary tree.

Given that the state space is uniformly distributed, each class contains the same number of members (we are considering a finite case) with a uniform probability distribution. In addition, we can make a one to one correspondence between these classes and a configuration of states on a Cayley tree (limited to a finite size).

Under the assumptions made, production $X_{i,z}$ is numerically the same as the size S of the corresponding connected cluster on the Cayley tree. Therefore, the probability distribution of the random variable $X_{i,z}$ is the same as the probability distribution of the size S of connected clusters at the origin in a Cayley tree. Such distribution is obviously truncated given the finite size of the system and, therefore, of the tree.

As the uniform distribution of states is an invariant distribution, we can conclude that the unconditional distribution of production consequent to orders at any site i and for any given path z exists and follows the same power law with exponent -3/2. Such a power law is independent of the site and path. We can therefore write:

$$P(X_{i,z}=x) = \alpha x^{-3/2} \tag{4}$$

for sufficiently large values of x and where α is a proportionality constant.

As the uniform distribution of states is invariant, the process $X(t)$ is characterized by a uniform distribution of states at each time step. The variable $X(t)$ follows a power law distribution with exponent $-3/2$ at each time t:

$$P(X=x) = \alpha x^{-3/2} \tag{5}$$

We have now to understand how to represent the long-run frequency distribution of values of $X(t)$. The process that represents the evolution of states is not ergodic; the $X(t)$ are not an IID sequence. Ensemble distributions can therefore not be simply exchanged with long-run frequencies. A different type of reasoning is required.

As the model is finite, a number of approximations will have to be made. Let's first study the probability distribution of production consequent to orders propagating through a randomly chosen path given a state C of the system, i.e., a configuration of sites. Let Y_C be the random variable that represents production consequent to orders that follow randomly chosen paths in configuration C.

This problem is dual with respect to the problem of finding the distribution of production over the ensemble of all possible configurations given a path of order propagation. Of course the probability spaces relative to the two cases are different. In one case, the probability space is the set of all configurations and the associated order propagation relative to one given order path. In the other case, we start with a fixed configuration and explore the space of all possible order propagations on every possible path. The formal construction of probability spaces is avoided.

As in the previous case, each path is isomorphic to a Cayley tree. The probability that any given site is full or empty, however, depends on the fraction of occupied sites in each row.

Consider the first row. Suppose that there are p_1 occupied sites and q_1 empty sites, $L = p_1 + q_1$. The first order has a probability p_1/L of hitting an occupied site and a probability q_1/L of hitting an empty site. For the second order, probabilities are slightly different and depend on whether the first order hit a full or an empty site. The same reasoning can be repeated for each branch and for each layer.

The first approximation is made assuming that all orders in a given layer i have the same probability p_i/L of hitting an occupied site and a probability q_i/L of hitting an empty site. This is a good approximation insofar the economy is large and $M<<L$ so that the number of branches is small in comparison with the number of sites.

Using the same reasoning as above, we can conclude that the probability distribution of the random variable Y_C for a configuration C with p_i full sites and q_i empty sites in layer i, is the same as the distribution of connected clusters at the origin on a Cayley tree with the same probabilities.

In general, therefore, the probability distribution of Y_C will depend on the ratio of empty to full sites in each layer of the given configuration. If all ratios p_i/q_i are

1/2 we can conclude that the variable Y_C has a power law distribution with exponent
-3/2:

$$P(Y_C=y) = \alpha y^{-3/2} \tag{6}$$

If we keep the state C constant and apply a sequence of independent random orders with independently randomly selected paths to the state C, then the ensuing $X(t)$ is a sequence of independent random draws from the above distribution. This sequence thus has a frequency distribution that is approximated by the probability distribution.

In our system, however, the order propagation process changes the state of the system. If the process starts with an arbitrary configuration, the ratios p_i/q_i will fluctuate. We can make a reasonable approximation by assuming that the ratios p_i/q_i are constant for each order but we cannot assume that they do not vary from order to order. We will show that the long-run frequency distribution is, however, not affected by these fluctuations.

The key to the reasoning is that the proportion of empty to full sites can be represented as an Ehrenfest process. In fact, consider the numbers p_i and $q_i = L - p_i$. At the arrival of each order, the transition probability from p_i to $p_i + 1$ is q_i/L and the transition probability from p_i to $p_i - 1$ is p_i/L. This is a Markov process known in physics literature as an Ehrenfest process. (See Cox and Miller, 1994)

The Ehrenfest process is an irreducible periodic Markov chain. The long-run frequency distribution of p and q is approximated by a binomial distribution centered around the average $L/2$. Therefore the probabilities $P(p_i=L/2+y)$ and $P(p_i=L/2-y)$ are the same.

Let's now consider the evolution of the system starting from an initial arbitrary configuration. The system receives a random sequence of orders; to each order a randomly selected path is associated. In consequence of the order propagation process, the site occupation varies. As paths are randomly and independently chosen, the random variables that give the proportion of occupied sites per row are independent.

Now consider a given row. The number of occupied sites in the row follows an Ehrenfest process. The long-run distribution of site occupancy is therefore a binomial distribution centered around $L/2$. As a consequence, the long-run distribution of site occupancy is $L/2$ as it is obtained by randomly sampling a symmetrical binomial distribution. Site occupancy probability is therefore 1/2.

As rows are independent, we can conclude that the distribution of Cayley trees obtained through order propagation are a random sampling from Cayley trees with independent probabilities of site occupancy 1/2. The long-run frequency distribution of order cascades therefore follows the same distribution of the ensemble probability.

The SOC behavior is a consequence of the fact that the long-run distribution of the ratios of full/empty sites for each layer is the same that would result from sampling from a uniform distribution of states. In addition, random order paths generate a power law distribution of production. We can conclude that the long-run frequency distribution of production is approximately identical to the power law unconditional ensemble distribution.

It is worth noting that there is a subtle difference between this behavior and the behavior of a sand pile. In a sand pile, we might start from a steepness value that will never be reached again in the SOC behavior. More in general, we might ideally start from an initial non equilibrium shape that will not reoccur in the SOC behavior.

In the above model, however, every state can be reached and every possible production value will be visited. The self-organizing behavior manifests itself as a long-run frequency distribution of states which is the same regardless of the initial state of the system. Essentially, the SOC behavior means that the system maintains itself at a critical percolation threshold.

The infinite economy case

Let's now analyze an infinite economy, i.e., let's take the limit of infinite L, M. Suppose that the initial configuration of the system is characterized by a uniform probability p that a node is empty and a probability $q=1-p$ that the node is full. Suppose, in addition, that each node is full or empty independently of any other node. These probabilities are obviously ensemble probabilities.

Suppose that the zeroth layer receives one order at node i which is randomly selected. There is therefore a probability p that this node is empty and a probability q that the node is full. There is a probability p that two new orders are issued. The state of the node is changed from full to empty or vice versa.

If two orders are issued, they hit two randomly selected nodes at the first layer. Each order hit a node independently of the previous one. As the system is infinite, the two orders hit distinct nodes with probability one. Therefore, each has a probability p of generating two new orders independent of the other order. The state of the sites hit by orders are changed.

This process can be repeated for each subsequent layer. As the system is infinite and orders hit randomly and independently chosen nodes, the probability that two orders hit the same site is zero for each layer. It is easy to see that this stochastic process can be represented exactly as percolation on an infinite Cayley tree.

Below the percolation probability threshold 1/2, the probability of an infinite cascade of orders is zero. The probability distribution of the size of the connected cluster at the origin decays exponentially. At the percolation probability threshold 1/2, there is an infinite cluster in the network but the probability that the connected cluster at the origin be infinite is still zero. (Grimmet, 1989) Therefore, the probability of an infinite cascade of orders remains zero.

Let's call S the number of nodes affected by a cascade, i.e. the size of a connected cluster. For Cayley trees, it is known that at the percolation threshold the number S, for large S, is distributed according to a power law with exponent 3/2:

$$P(S=n) = \alpha n^{-3/2} \tag{7}$$

for large values of n and where α is a proportionality constant.

Above the percolation threshold, for values of p close to 1/2, the probability of an infinite connected cluster at the origin, $P(\theta)$ is finite. Such probabilities scales as $(p-1/2)$:

$$P(\theta)=\alpha(p-1/2). \tag{8}$$

Therefore, in the previous infinite production and inventory model, if nodes are randomly and independently occupied with probability ½, each order generates a production cascade characterized by a tail distributed with a power law with exponent 3/2. If the probability to find empty inventories is above ½, there is a finite probability $p-1/2$ that an order originate an infinite production cascade.

Given that an order has been received and has propagated, what happens to the following order? As the system is infinite and sites are randomly and independently chosen, uniform and independent probability distributions of site occupancy are invariant with respect to the propagation of orders. The propagation of any order is therefore independent of the propagation of previous orders. As a consequence, the distribution of order sizes is a sequence of IID variables and long-run frequency distributions are the same as the ensemble distribution.

One might observe, as a consequence of the above, that the concept of self-organization does not apply to infinite systems as far as a denumerable sequence of shocks is applied to the system. In fact, the order propagation process does not change the probability distribution of site occupancy. The key property of self-organization is the self-mapping of the ensemble of states consequent to the propagation of orders. In infinite systems, however, the propagation of orders generally only interests a set of measure zero. A finite or even a denumerably infinite sequence of orders is not sufficient to change the probability distribution of an infinite system.

The infinite economy as a limit case of a finite economy

We have explored above the two cases of a finite economy LxM and of an infinite economy represented by an infinite lattice. We can now explore the limiting behavior of finite economies. This means, for instance, exploring the limit behavior of the sequence of production random variables when L,M tend to infinite.

Each finite economy is characterized by random variables with power law distributions in a certain range of values. These distributions are then truncated (see below) given the finite size of the model. As the economy tends to infinity, i.e. as L and M tend to infinity under the constraint $L >> M$, the truncated laws tend to a Pareto-Levy distribution of the same law.

Simulations

Results of simulations show that the aggregate orders and production follow a power law distribution with an exponent very close to 3/2. In practice, simulations are made difficult by the combinatorial explosion of rows even for a modest number of layers. In fact, given i layers we need a number L of rows much larger than 2^i. This rapidly becomes a formidable number even for computer simulation.

We performed numerical simulations with 10 layers and 10,000 rows, and with 15 layers and 100,000 rows. Both cases satisfy the condition: $M < log_2 L$, reducing to a minimum overlapping branches. Simulation results are shown in Figure 3.

In both cases, the distribution of production shows an initial section with a power law with exponent -3/2. This is clearly visible in the log/log plot of the distribution. Before decaying rapidly because of finite truncation, all simulations show a pronounced bump. This is simply an artifact of the finite dimension of the simulated systems. In fact, clusters that would continue beyond the finite boundary are counted as clusters of smaller size. Thus the bump. This fact significantly reduces the actual area of power law distribution in the simulation with 10 layers.

We have also done, for comparison, a number of simulations with a smaller number of rows ($L=1000$) and a larger number of layers ($M=100$). Simulation results are shown in Figure 4.

In this system, there are overlapping branches in most layers. Branch intersections do not seem to have much affect on distributions that remain very close to a power law even in the latter cases. These, however, do not lend themselves to mathematical analysis.

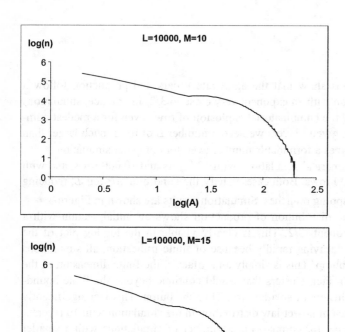

Fig. 3   Simulation results for two systems with increasing dimensions. The logarithm of the activity of the system (A) is plotted versus the logarithm of its frequency (n). Both plots refer to simulations of 2 millions single stimulations.

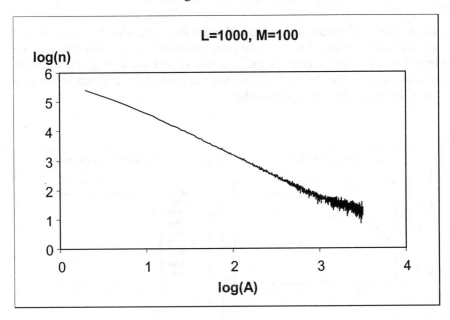

Fig. 4   Simulation results for a system with branch intersections, with 2 millions single stimulations. The distribution of activity is still a power law.

Correlations between weakly coupled economies

Following an idea of the economist Krugman, we want to explore dependencies between economies or sectors. Krugman (1996) observes that the size of exchanges between large economic blocks, for instance Europe and the USA, is of small size in comparison with the size of their internal economies. Still, these exchanges might have large effects on the respective internal economies.

Krugman suggests that there might be a synchronization effect, similar to the phase locking effect between physical resonant systems. Using our previous models, we have performed a number of simulations of small interaction between economies.

Taking advantage of the free connection structure of our models, we let a small fraction of orders at each layer be randomly exchanged between the two economies. We consider only small exchange probability, p, for the orders issued by each layer; numerical simulations were performed with exchange probability varying from 0 to 0.2.

The level of sinchronization is measured in the following way. We form two vectors with all the production values for each simulation run for each economy. We form the dot products between the two vectors and we average over 200,000 simulation runs. Then we plot this average dot product for different values of p, i.e. of the probability to exchange orders.

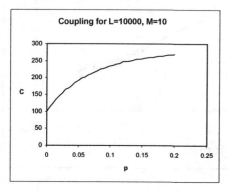
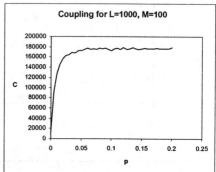

Fig. 5   Coupling among "economies" for different system topologies, as a function of the exchange probability, p, between them.

Figure 5 shows results of simulations for different system topologies. It is clear that there is a strong syncronization effect that grows with the probability p. In the L=1,000, M=100 case, correlations reach a near saturation around 4% of order exchanges. In the case L=10,000, M=10 the saturation effect is much less evident.

This syncronization effect can be explained heuristically observing that, although the exchange of orders is numerically small, orders are exchanged, however, in each layer. The syncronization effect is reinforced at each layer. It is therefore understandable that the number of layers play an important role and that a larger number of layers magnifies the level of syncronization for each coupling coefficient.

Conclusions

We have generalized the BCSW model, showing that economic variables such as orders and production might propagate through global models of a production-inventory economy with significant long-range correlations due to the distribution of the state of the economy which is driven by the propagation itself.

We performed an exact analysis of the proposed system in the case that the size of layers is much bigger than 2 raised to the number of layers, so that overlapping among order paths are negligible. In this case the order propagation is isomorphic to a percolation on a Cayley tree and the activity of the system follows a power law distribution with exponent $-3/2$.

We generalized these results to the infinite case, and performed extensive simulations of the model. The simulation results confir the theory for systems with $L \gg 2^M$, and show similar behavior even for systems that do not comply with this constraint.

Taking advantage of the free connection structure of our model we also empirically studied the coupling between two systems, showing strong synchronization effects even for very low exchange probabilities. This indicates that other types of long-range correlations might be at work, when systems are coupled together.

References

Bak, P., C. Tang and K. Wiesenfeld (1987): Self-Organized Criticality: An Explanation of $1/f$ noise. Physical Review Letters, 59, 4, 381-384

Bak, P., K. Chen, J. Scheinkman and M. Woodford (1993): Aggregate fluctuations from independent sectoral shocks: self-organized criticality in a model of production and inventory dynamics. Ricerche Economiche, 47, 3-30

Carlson, J.M., Chayes, J.T., Grannan, E.R. and Swindle, G.H. (1990): Self-Organized criticality in sand piles: Nature of the critical phenomenon. Physical Review A, 42, 4, 2467-70

Cox, D.R. and H.D. Miller (1965): The Theory of Stochastic Processes, Chapman and Hall, London

Dhar, D. and R. Ramaswamy (1989): Exactly solved model of self-organized critical phenomena. Physical Review Letters, 63, 1659-1662

Grimmett, G.R. (1989): Percolation, Springer-Verlag, New York

Kirman A.P. (1997): The Market as an Interactive System, GREQAM, EHESS, Marseille

Johansen, A. and D. Sornette (1998): Stock Market Crashes Are Outliers. European Physics Journal, B 1, 141, 1998

Krugman, P. (1996): The Self-Organizing Economy, Blackwell, Malden, Massachusetts

Mandelbrot, B.B. and J. W. Van Ness (1968): Fractional Brownian Motions, Fractional Noises and Applications. SIAM Review, 10, 4, 422-437

Heterogeneous Agents, Complementarities, and Diffusion
Do Increasing Returns Imply Convergence to International Technological Monopolies? *

Andrea P. Bassanini[1] and Giovanni Dosi[2]

[1] OECD, Paris, France. E-mail: andrea.bassanini@oecd.org
[2] Sant'Anna School for advanced Studies, Pisa, Italy. E-mail: g.dosi@sssup.it

Abstract. The work analyses the properties of international technological diffusion with interdependent markets in presence of some form of dynamic increasing returns and externalities, heterogenous agents and stochastic adoptions. We build and refine upon previous results from Bassanini and Dosi (1998), where a) we show the conditions of convergence to either technological monopoly or market sharing ultimately depending on the balance between increasing returns and degrees of agents' heterogeneity, and b) we establish the (different) rates of convergence to either limit states. In the multi-market, international, extension considered here we determine the conditions yielding to world monopoly or conversely to world market sharing cum local monopolies. Together, the model accounts also for the rare empirical occurence of stable market sharing in each single market on the grounds of the (slower) rates of convergence that such a limit configuration entails.

1 Introduction

This work concerns some generic properties of the international diffusion of technologies and products in markets which are interdependent but display, to varying degrees, location specific forms of dynamic increasing returns and externalities.

Building on a related paper [Bassanini and Dosi (1998)], in the following we study the ways the spatial dimension of positive feedback in adoption affects the long-run properties of the diffusion processes, especially with regards to the possible emergence of either region-specific or global monopolies

---

* The views expressed here do not reflect those of the OECD Secretariat or itsMember Countries. We are indebted to Yuri Kaniovski for very helpfulsuggestions. We thank also Brian Arthur, Robin Cowan, Klaus Desmet, JudithGebauer, Michael Horvath, Andrea Prat, Aldo Rustichini, Valter Sorana, andparticipants to the 3rd Workshop on Economics with Heterogeneous InteractingAgents, Ancona, Italy, May 1998, and to the Conference on Economic Models ofEvolutionary Dynamics and Interacting Agents, Trieste, Italy, September1998, for their comments. Financial support from International Institute forApplied Systems Analysis (IIASA), Banca Nazionale del Lavoro (BNL), ItalianResearch Council (CNR), and Italian Ministry of University and ScientificResearch (MURST) is gratefully acknowledged. All errors are ours.

(dominant designs) of particular technologies[1]. Two stylized facts are at the origin of this work[2]:

a) A stable pattern of market sharing between competing technologies with no overwhelming dominant position has been rarely observed in markets with increasing returns (or positive feedbacks) of some kind [see Tushman and Murmann (1998)]. For example, even in the case of operating systems, which is often quoted as a case of market sharing, Apple MacIntosh has never held a market share larger than 20% (a partial exception being the submarket of personal computer for educational institutions). This fact has also triggered suspicion of market inefficiencies: Single dominant designs or technological paradigms may prevail even when the survival of more than one technology may be socially optimal [Dosi (1982), Katz and Shapiro (1986), David (1992)]. Think for example to the competition between Java-based architectures and ActiveX architectures for web-based applets: Given that with any of the two paradigms the standard tasks that can be performed are different, the general impression of experts is that society would benefit from the survival of both.

b) International diffusion may sometimes lead to different standards in different countries or conversely to the diffusion of the same standard in every country. For example, while in all the English-speaking world the QWERTY keyboard represents the standard, in the French-speaking world a slightly different version (the AZERTY keyboard) is by far the more adopted one. On the contrary in the VCR market VHS is the worldwide technological leader while the original competitor, Beta, has disappeared.

To explain these two stylized facts we analyze properties of a fairly general and nowadays rather standard class of models of competing technologies, originally suggested by Arthur (1983) and Arthur et al. (1983) and subsequently made popular by Arthur (1989) [and further explored by Cowan (1991), Dosi et al. (1994), Dosi and Kaniovski (1994) and Kaniovski and Young (1995) among others]. This class of models will be presented in details in section 2.

Despite mixed results of some pioneering work on the dynamics of markets with network effects [e.g. Katz and Shapiro (1986)], unbounded increasing returns are commonly called for as an explanation of the emergence of technological monopolies. In a related paper [Bassanini and Dosi (1998)] we show that the emergence of technological monopolies depends on the nature of increasing returns with respect to the degree of heterogeneity of the population: Given a sufficiently high heterogeneity amongst economic agents, limit market sharing may occur even in the presence of unbounded increasing returns. Furthermore we suggest that the observation of the widespread

---

[1] Here the terms monopolies and market sharing are referred to competing technologies without any reference to who is producing what. For instance, a technological monopoly occurs when all users adopt the same technology, even when it is produced by many different suppliers.

[2] For more thorough discussions of the evidence on patterns of innovation and diffusion, see, among others, Dosi (1988, 1992) and Freeman (1992, 1994).

emergence of monopolies is intimately related to properties of different rates of convergence (to monopoly and to market sharing respectively) more than to properties of limit states as such. It is shown that a market can approach a monopoly with a higher speed than it approaches any feasible limit market shares where both technologies coexist. When convergence is too slow the external environment is likely to change before any sufficiently small neighborhood of the limit can be attained. The empirical implication is that among markets with high turnover of basic technologies and increasing returns to adoption, a prevalence of stable monopolies over stable market-sharing should be observed.

Clearly this result also challenges the ideas that internationally unbounded increasing returns are necessary and sufficient to yield global dominance of particular technologies, and by the same token, the emergence of overwhelmingly dominant locational clusters in production.

In order to analyze the international diffusion dynamics and account for the foregoing stylized facts it is useful to start with distinguishing three interrelated processes.

At a first level, diffusion is driven by microdecisions concerning the adoption or not of a new technology. This is what Katz and Shapiro (1994) in their review of the literature on systems competition and dynamics of adoption under increasing returns call *technology adoption decision*. It basically to the decision of a potential user to place a demand in a particular market (or, relatedly, of a producer to start investing in a new technology). Indeed a good deal of literature on determinants of diffusion patterns, and, relatedly, the observed "retardation factors", pertain to this domain of analysis [see Dosi (1992)]. Moreover, relevant questions in this case are the conditions for an actual market of positive size and the conditions allowing penetration of a new (more advanced) technology into the market of an already established one [Rohlfs (1974), Oren and Smith (1981), Farrell and Saloner (1985,1986), Silverberg et al. (1988), Katz and Shapiro (1992)]. For example purchasing or not a fax or substituting a compact disc player for an analogical record player are technology adoption decisions.

Second, following again the terminology of Katz and Shapiro (1994), call *product selection* the choice between different technological solutions which perform (approximately) the same function and are therefore close substitutes. Relevant questions here are whether the market enhances variety or standardization, whether the emerging market structure is normatively desirable and what is the role of history in the selection of market structure [Arthur (1983,1989), Katz and Shapiro (1985,1986), David (1985), Church and Gandal (1993), Dosi et al. (1994), Brock and Durlauf (1995,1998), An and Kiefer (1995), Bryniolfsson and Kemerer (1996), Durlauf (1997)]. Choosing between VHS or Beta in the VCR market or between Word or Wordperfect in the wordprocessors market are typical examples of product selection decisions. However it is easy to extend this domain to include the choice between alternative technological systems (e.g. in energy generation, solar vs. nuclear energy and within the latter, PWR vs. gas-cooled reactors, etc...).

A third level concerns the spatial dimensions (either literally geographical or institution-related) which influence the above decision processes, or, more than that, straightforwardly represent a distinct domain of decision for micro agents. So, for example, an expanding literature on "national systems of innovation" [Lundvall (1992), Nelson (1993) and Freeman (1995), among others] emphasizes the long-term impact of the diverse architectures of national institutional systems as drivers of technological learning. Partly overlapping analyses of incentives and constraints to the location of investments by capital-mobile firm across heterogeneous environments focus upon the interaction between firm-specific capabilities and location-specific advantages in MNCs investments [Cantwell (1989)]. Call the latter *location selection decisions*, which in the model presented below will refer to the choice between different locations where to make an investment in a specific technology, or, more metaphorically, the choice of spatially-bound agents across different technologies, production processes and outputs. This has been for a long time a field rich of qualitative investigation by economic geography and regional economics, recently discovered, at the cost of a lot of institutional simplification by economic theory [e.g. Arthur (1990), Krugman (1991a, 1991b), Rauch (1993), Krugman and Venables (1996), Venables (1996)].

In the following we bring together the three domains of analysis and explore some formal properties of the dynamics of competition among alternative products and technologies diffusing across heterogeneous environments. We consider conditions of convergence to different market structures in a world where there are many regional markets and many different technologies. Agents choose both technology and location. Regional markets are institutional entities which cannot disappear (although their relative size can grow or shrink). Rather a diffusion pattern is realized for every region. This leads to a natural question which underlies the second stylized fact recalled above: What drives convergence to the same or different market structures in different interrelated regional markets?

Intuitively convergence to the same standard is an outcome of the relative weight and strength of international spillovers as compared to nationwide (or regional) increasing returns. For example, in the case of typewriter keyboards, geographical areas with the same language tend to be reflected in spillover clusters due to free "migration" of typists, similar training institutions, etc.... On the other hand, historically, gaining leadership in the European market, with the consequent bias in the related home video market, was crucial to VHS to resolve in its favor the battle for leadership in the Japanese market as well [Cusumano et al. (1992)]. However very little modeling effort has been made so far to formally explore this intuitive explanation. Below we will indeed consider a generalization of one-market models of competing technologies in order to establish conditions of convergence to the same or different technological monopolies in different but interrelated markets.

If one does not disaggregate a system made of many regional markets, the emergence of stable but different dominant designs would look like technological market sharing. How does one reconcile "stylized facts" and theoretical statements on the emergence of different technological monopolies in different interdependent regional markets with "stylized facts" and theoretical statements on overwhelming emergence of dominant designs?

Of course it is trivially true that, with mutually independent markets, different trajectories could emerge in different markets as if they were different realizations of the same experiment. In this paper we show that results on speed of convergence stated in Bassanini and Dosi (1998) can be extended also to the case when markets are interdependent: Even though at high level of aggregation a system of different local monopolies looks like a stable market sharing, we show that it has the same rate-of-convergence properties of a "univariate" system converging to a monopoly.

The remainder of the paper is divided as follows. Section 2 provides one motivating example, formally defines the standard class of models of competing technologies we refer to and summarizes results on rate of convergence to a stable market structure in univariate models. Section 3 establishes our main results on convergence to a stable market structure in multi-markets models. Section 4 briefly summarizes the results.

2   Unbounded Returns and Dominant Designs: A Sample Selection Bias

The class of competing technology dynamics models that we consider takes as the only basic assumption the fact that adopters enter the market in a sequence which is assumed to be exogenous. More than one agent can enter the market in each period [see e.g. Katz and Shapiro (1986) and Dosi and Kaniovski (1994)], but in order to simplify the treatment we abstract from this complication. The simple theoretical tale that underlies these models can be summarized as follows:

Every period a new agent enters the market and chooses the technology which is best suited to its requirements, given its preferences, information structure and the available technologies. Preferences can be heterogeneous and a distribution of preferences in the population is given. Information and preferences determine a vector of payoff functions (whose dimension is equal to the number of available technologies) for every type of agent. Because of positive (negative) feedbacks, these functions depend on the number of previous adoptions. When an agent enters the market it compares the values of these functions (given its preferences, the available information, and previous adoptions) and chooses the technology which yields the maximum perceived payoff. Which "type" of agent enters the market at any given time is a stochastic event whose probability depends on the distribution of types (i.e. of preferences) in the population. Because of positive (negative) feedbacks, the probability of adoption of a particular technology is an increasing (decreasing) function of the number of previous adoptions of that technology.

More formally we can write a general reduced form of payoff functions of the following type:

$$\Pi_j^i(n(t)) = h_i(a_j^i, n(t)),$$

where $j \in D$, D is the set of possible technologies, $i \in S$, S is the set of possible types, $n(t)$ is vector denoting number of adoptions for each technology at time t ($n^j(t)$ is the number of adoptions of technology j at time t), a_i represents the network-independent components of agent i's preferences (a_i^j identifies a baseline payoff for agents of type i from technology j), and $h_i(.)$ is an increasing function (that can differ across agents) capturing increasing returns to adoption. If, at time t, an agent of type i comes to the market, it compares the payoff functions choosing A if and only if[3]:

$$\Pi_A^i(n^A) = \arg\max_{j \in D} \left\{ \Pi_j^i(n) \right\}. \tag{1}$$

Strategic behaviors (including sponsoring activities from the suppliers of technologies) and expectations can be considered as already implicitly included in the foregoing formalization.

In the remainder of this paper we assume that the order of agents entering the market is random, hence $i(t)$ can be considered as an iid sequence of random variables whose distribution depends on the distribution of the population of potential adopters. With this assumption, the dynamics of the foregoing model can be seen in terms of generalized urn schemes:

Consider the simplest case where two technologies, say A and B, compete for a market. Let us denote A's market share with $X(t)$. Given the relationships between (a) total number of adoptions of both technologies $n(t) = t - 1 + n^A(0) + n^B(0)$, (b) the current market share $X(t)$ of A, and (c) number of adoptions of one specific technology, $n^i(t)$, $i = A, B$, that is, $n^A(t) = n(t)X(t)$, the dynamics of $X(t)$ is given by the recursive identity

$$X(t+1) = X(t) + \frac{\xi^t(X(t)) - X(t)}{t + n^A(0) + n^B(0)}.$$

Here $\xi^t(x), t \geq 1$ are random variables independent in t such that

$$\xi^t(x) = \begin{cases} 1 \text{ with probability } f(t,x) \\ 0 \text{ with probability } 1 - f(t,x) \end{cases},$$

and $\xi^t(\cdot)$ is a function of market shares dependent on the feedbacks in adoption. $f(t,x)$ equals the probability that (1) is true when $X(t) = x$ and is

---

[3] We assume that, if there is a tie, agents choose technology A. Qualitatively, breaking the tie in a different way would not make any difference.

sometimes called *urn function*. Designating $\xi^t(x) - E(\xi^t(x)) = \xi^t(x) - f(t,x)$ by $\zeta^t(x)$ we have

$$X(t+1) = X(t) + \frac{[f(t, X(t)) - X(t)] + \zeta^t(X(t))}{t + n^A(0) + n^B(0)}. \tag{2}$$

Provided that there exist a limit urn function $f(\cdot)$ (defined as that function $f(.)$ such that $f(t,.)$ tends to it as t tends to ∞) and the following condition is satisfied

$$\sum_{t \geq 1} t^{-1} \sup_{x \in [0,1] \cap R(0,1)} \mid f(t,x) - f(x) \mid < \infty, \tag{3}$$

asymptotic patterns of this process can be studied by analyzing the properties of the function

$$g(x) = \lim_{t \to \infty} f(t,x) - x.$$

Particularly, treating $g(x)$ in the same way of the right hand side of an ordinary differential equation, it is possible to show that the process (2) converges with positive probability to every stable zero[4]. The foregoing formal representation is employed for every result of the present paper.

In some cases, eq. (1) can be expressed directly in terms of shares rather than total numbers[5]; in this case $f(.,.)$ is independent of t and (3) is trivially verified. In this respect note that, from an interpretative point of view, *total numbers* and *shares* are likely to capture quite distinct economic and technological phenomena. For example, network externalities are often well-captured by the shares dynamics, while more idiosyncratic, cumulative and type-specific processes of learning are more naturally represented as functions of varying numbers of adopters.

As we noticed in the introduction, there seems to be a general consensus that the widespread emergence of dominant designs should be explained on the basis of the presence of unbounded increasing returns to adoption[6]. Unbounded increasing returns to adoption are neither necessary nor sufficient to lead to the emergence of technological monopolies. Let us start with an example drawn from Bassanini and Dosi (1998).

Example 1. Consider payoff functions of this type:

$$\Pi_j(n^j) = a_j + r_j n^j,$$

where r_j, a_j, $j = A, B$, are bounded random variables which admit density. Such a function allows agents to be heterogeneous also in terms of the

---

[4] A convenient review of analytical results on generalized urn schemes can be found in Dosi et al. (1994). The reader is referred to that for the results that are not proved in this paper.

[5] This is particularly relevant in the frequent case when product selection sequentially follows technology adoption [see Bassanini and Dosi (1998)].

[6] See Bassanini and Dosi (1998) for references on this debate.

degree of increasing returns which they experience. By applying (1), dividing payoff functions by total number of adoptions, and rearranging we have that A is chosen if and only if:

$$X(t) \geq \frac{r_B}{r_A + r_B} + \frac{a_B - a_A}{(t + n^A(0) + n^B(0))(r_A + r_B)}. \tag{4}$$

Denoting the random variables on the right hand side with $\varsigma(t)$, from (4) we have that the adoption process can be seen as a generalized urn scheme with urn function $f(t, x) = F_{\varsigma(t)}(x)$, where $F_{\varsigma(t)}(\cdot)$ is the distribution function of $\varsigma(t)$. Now suppose that r_A and r_B are highly correlated and both have bimodal distributions very concentrated around the two modes, in such a way that the distribution of r_A/r_B is also bimodal and very concentrated around the two modes too. Furthermore suppose that the two modes are far away from each other. To fix the ideas say that for a percentage α of the population r_A/r_B is uniformly distributed on the interval $\left[\frac{1}{1-b}, \frac{1}{1-a}\right]$, while for a percentage $1 - \alpha$ of the population r_A/r_B is uniformly distributed on the interval $\left[\frac{1}{1-d}, \frac{1}{1-c}\right]$, with obviously $0 < a < b < c < d$. First, let us consider the case of $a_j = 0$, $j = A, B$. F_ς is by construction independent of t, implying the following urn function:

$$f(x) = F_{\varsigma(t)}(x) = \begin{cases} 0 & \text{if } y \leq a \\ \alpha \frac{1}{b-a}(y - a) & \text{if } a < y \leq b \\ \alpha & \text{if } b < y \leq c \\ \alpha + (1 - \alpha)\left[\frac{1}{d-c}(y - c)\right] & \text{if } c < y \leq d \\ 1 & \text{if } y > d \end{cases}$$

If $b < \alpha < c$, then there are three stable fixed point of $f(x)$ and, as said above, it can be shown that there is a set of initial conditions (that imply giving both technologies a chance to be chosen "at the beginning of history") for which market sharing is asymptotically attainable with positive probability. If $a_j \neq 0$ but have bounded support and admit density, then condition (3) applies and the same argument holds: In fact, relying on the fact that r_j, a_j are bounded it is easy to show that $\sup_{x \in [0,1] \cap R(0,1)} | f(t, x) - f(x) | < K/t$, where $K > 0$ is a constant. The essential ingredient of this example is that the distribution of r_A/r_B is bimodal and very concentrated around the two modes. The argument has nothing to do with the particular (and extreme) distributional form assumed here: Following the same constructive procedure adopted here it is easy to build examples with any other distributional form. The only requirement is that the two modes are sufficiently distant. In other words the only requirement is a sufficient degree of heterogeneity in the population to counterbalance the pro-standardization effects of increasing returns to adoption.

The argument so far suggests that, the distribution of the fine characteristics and preferences of the population of agents might determine the very nature of the attainable asymptotic states themselves. Short of empirically convincing restrictions on the distribution of agents' (usually unobservable) characteristics, Bassanini and Dosi (1998) propose instead an interpretation of the general occurrence of technological monopolies (*cum* increasing returns of some kind) grounded on the relative speed of convergence to the underlying (but unobservable) limit states. When convergence is too slow the external environment is likely to change before any sufficiently small neighborhood of the limit can be attained. Theorems 1 and 2 recalled below show that convergence to technological monopolies tends to be (in probabilistic terms) much faster than to a limit where both technologies coexist. The empirical implication is that in markets with high turnover of basic technologies, when market structure dynamics shows a relatively stable pattern, a prevalence of technological monopolies over stable market sharing is likely to be observed. Therefore the emergence of dominant designs, at a careful look, appears to come out of a sample selection bias: Including cases where market share turbulence never seem to settle down would provide a more mixed picture.

Theorem 1 (Bassanini and Dosi (1998, theorem 2)). *Let $\epsilon > 0$ and $c < 1$ be such that*

$$f(t,x) \leq cx \text{ for } x \in (0,\epsilon) \quad (f(t,x) \geq 1 - c(1-x) \text{ for } x \in (1-\epsilon,1)).$$

Then for any $\delta \in (0, 1-c)$ and $\tau > 0$

$$\lim_{t\to\infty} \mathcal{P}\{t^{1-c-\delta}X(t) < \tau | X(t) \to 0\} = 1$$
$$\left(\lim_{t\to\infty} \mathcal{P}\{t^{1-c-\delta}[1 - X(t)] < \tau | X(t) \to 1\} = 1\right),$$

where $X(\cdot)$ stands for the random process given by (2).

Theorem 2 (Bassanini and Dosi (1998), theorem 5). *Let $\theta \in (0,1)$ be a stable root and $f(\cdot)$ be differentiable at θ with $\frac{d}{dx}f(\theta) < 1/2$. Then for every $\delta, \tau > 0$*

$$\lim_{t\to\infty} \mathcal{P}\{t^{1/2+\delta}|X(t) - \theta| < \tau | X(t) \to \theta\} = 0.$$

Theorems 1 and 2 show that convergence to 0 and 1 can be much faster (almost of order $1/t$ as $t \to \infty$) than to an interior limit (which can be almost of order $1/\sqrt{t}$ only)[7]. Furthermore, if we use L^2 convergence, instead of weak convergence, we can dispose of the assumption of differentiability of the urn function and obtain similar results[8].

Let us now extend the analysis to the international area where, as mentioned earlier, we do observe emergence of different standards and dominant

---

[7] Note that, provided that the number of asymptotic steady states is finite, theorem 2 and 5 do not provide only a statement on conditional convergence but also on absolute convergence.

[8] see Bassanini and Dosi (1998), lemma 1.

designs in different countries. Moreover, note that at high level of aggregation a system of different local monopolies looks like a stable market sharing.
However in the next section we shall show that the foregoing results can be
extended also to the case of many interdependent markets. We prove that a
system of locally dominant designs has the same rate-of-convergence properties of a "univariate" system converging to a single dominant designs. Furthermore we provide a characterization of different convergence patterns. Not
contrary to the intuition, it is the balance between local and global feedbacks
which determines whether the system can converge to the same or different
monopolies in every market.

3 International Diffusion and the Emergence of Technological Monopolies

Suppose that two technologies, say A and B, compete for a complex market
which consists of m interacting parts (which can be thought of as economic
regions or even countries) of infinite capacity. At any time $t = 1, 2, \ldots$ a new
agent enters one of the markets and has to adopt one unit of one technology.
The type of agent and the region are randomly determined on the basis of
the distribution of agents in the population. There can be positive (negative)
feedbacks not only inside every single region but also across them. Thus the
probability of adoption is a function of the vector of previous adoptions in all
regions. For the i-th region we consider the following indicators: $x_i(1 - x_i)$
– the current market share of $A(B)$; γ_i – the frequency of additions to the
region (i.e. this is the ratio of the current number of units of the technologies
in the region to the total current number of units of the technologies in the
market). We assume also that initially, at $t = 0$, there are $n_i^A(n_i^B)$ units of
the technology $A(B)$ in the i-th region and $n_i^A, n_i^B \geq 1$. Finally n stands
for the initial number of units of the technologies on the market, i.e. $n =
n_1^A + n_1^B + n_2^A + n_2^B + \ldots + n_m^A + n_m^B$.

Similarly to the setup above we can say, with no loss of generality, that
at time instants $t = 1, 2 \ldots$. a unit of technology (either A or B) will be
adopted with probability $f_i(t, X(t), \gamma(t))$ in the i-th region. Also it will be A
with probability $f_i^A(t, X(t), \gamma(t))$ and B with probability $f_i^B(t, X(t), \gamma(t))$.
Here $f(., ., .)$ is a vector function which maps $N \times R(0, 1) \times R(S_m)$ in S_m
and $f(., ., .) = f^A(., ., .) + f^B(., ., .)$. By $R(0, 1)$ we designate the Cartesian
product of m copies of $R(0, 1)$, S_m is defined by the following relation

$$S_m = \{x \in R^m : x_i \geq 0, \sum_{i=1}^m x_i = 1\}. \tag{5}$$

Here $R(0, 1)$ and $R(S_m)$ stand for the sets of rational numbers from $[0, 1]$
and, correspondingly, vectors with rational coordinates from S_m. By $X(t)$ we
designate the m-dimensional vector whose i-th coordinate $X_i(t)$ represents

the share of technology A in the i-th region at time t. Also $\gamma(t)$ stands for the m-dimensional vector whose i-th coordinate $\gamma_i(t)$ is the frequency of total adoptions to the i-th urn by the time t. The dynamics of $X(\cdot)$ and $\gamma(\cdot)$ can be described as a generalized scheme of multiple urns with balls of two colors, in analogy with to the one-dimensional case[9].

Consider the process of adoptions of technology A at time t in market i, which is obviously a stochastic variable. We can define the following "conditional adoption" stochastic variable:

$$\xi_i^t(x,\gamma) = E[\xi_{i,A}^t(x,\gamma)|\xi_{i,A}^t(x,\gamma) + \xi_{i,B}^t(x,\gamma) = 1]. \tag{6}$$

$\xi_{i,j}^t(x,\gamma)$, $j = A, B$, stands for adoption of technology j at time t in market i. Then

$$\xi_i^t(x,\gamma) = \begin{cases} 1 \text{ with probability } g_i(t,x,\gamma) \\ 0 \text{ with probability } 1 - g_i(t,x,\gamma) \end{cases} \tag{7}$$

where $g_i(t,x,\gamma) = f_i^A(x,\gamma)[f_i(x,\gamma)]^{-1}$[10].

Hereafter we assume that the functions $g_i(t,.,.) = g_i(.,.)$, that is, the conditional probability of adoption, is independent of t. Let us ignore the time instants t when $X_i(\cdot)$ does not undergo any changes. Then we obtain a new process $Y_i(\cdot)$ which has the same convergence properties as $X_i(\cdot)$ providing that technologies are adopted in the i-th region infinitely many times with probability one. We will implicitly assume the latter condition throughout this section[11]. For particular cases $Y_i(\cdot)$ turns out to be a conventional urn process, or anyhow can be studied by means of some associated univariate generalized urn process.

To implement this idea, introduce $\tau_i(k)$ – the moment of the k-th addition of a technology to the i-th region, i.e.

$$\tau_i(1) = \min \left\{ t : \xi_{i,1}^t(X(t),\gamma(t)) + \xi_{i,2}^t(X(t),\gamma(t)) = 1 \right\},$$

$$\tau_i(k) = \min \left\{ \begin{array}{c} t : t > \tau_i(k-1), \\ \xi_{i,1}^t(X(t),\gamma(t)) + \xi_{i,2}^t(X(t),\gamma(t)) = 1 \end{array} \right\}, k \geq 2. \tag{8}$$

Designate $X_i(\tau_i(k))$ by $Y_i(k)$ and $\xi_i^{\tau_i(k)}(X(\tau_i(k)),\gamma(\tau_i(k)))$ by $\zeta_i^k(Y_i(k))$. Then for $Y_i(\cdot)$ we have the following recursion

$$Y_i(k+1) = Y_i(k) + \frac{1}{k+G_i}[\zeta_i^k(Y_i(k)) - Y_i(k)], \quad k \geq 1, \quad Y_i(1) = \frac{n_i^w}{G_i}. \tag{9}$$

Note the $Y_i(\cdot)$ indeed carries all information about changes of $X_i(\cdot)$. By definition $Y_i(k) = X_i(\tau_i(k))$, but between $\tau_i(k)$ and $\tau_i(k+1)$ the process $X_i(\cdot)$

---

[9] See also Dosi and Kaniovski (1994).

[10] Throughout this section we assume that $f_i(t,x,\gamma) > 0$ for all possible x and γ.

[11] This assumption, which in the spirit of the population models does not appear to be too strong, is needed in order to obtain asymptotic results.

preserves its value. Consequently, should we know that $Y_i(k)$ converges with probability one (or converges with positive probability to a certain value, or converges to a certain value with zero probability, i.e. does not converge) as $k \to \infty$, the same would be true for $X_i(t)$ as $t \to \infty$. (We will systematically use this observation below without further explicit mention).

The next theorem provides sufficient conditions for convergence of $Y_i(\cdot)$ (and consequently $X_i(\cdot)$) to 0 and 1 with positive (zero) probability.

Theorem 3. *Let* $g_i(.) : R(0,1) \to [0,1]$ *be a function such that for all possible* $x \in R(0,1)$ *and* $\gamma \in R(S_m)$

$$g_i(x,\gamma) \leq g_i(x_i). \tag{10}$$

Designate by $Z_i(\cdot)$ *a conventional urn process with* $g_i(\cdot)$ *as the urn-function and* n_i^A, n_i^B *as the initial numbers of balls. Then* $P\{Y_i(k) \to 0\} > 0$ $(P\{Y_i(k) \to 1\} = 0)$ *if* $P\{Z_i(k) \to 0\} > 0$ $(P\{Z_i(k) \to 1\} = 0)$. *Also, when*

$$g_i(x,\gamma) \geq g_i(x_i), \tag{11}$$

the statement reads: if $P\{Z_i(k) \to 1\} > 0$ $(P\{Z_i(k) \to 0\} = 0)$, *then* $P\{Y_i(k) \to 1\} > 0$ $(P\{Y_i(k) \to 0\} = 0)$.

The theorem is proved in the appendix.

The next statement gives slightly more sophisticated conditions of convergence and nonconvergence to 0 and 1 of the process (9) and, consequently, $X_i(\cdot)$.

Theorem 4. *Set* $U_i(x) = \sup_\gamma \{g_i(x,\gamma)\}$, $L_i(x) = \inf_\gamma \{g_i(x,\gamma)\}$. *If there is* $\epsilon > 0$ *such that* $L_i(x) \geq x_i$ $(U_i(x) \leq x_i)$ *for* $x_i \in (0,\epsilon)$ $(x_i \in (1-\epsilon,1))$, *then* $P\{X_i(t) \to 0\} = 0$ $(P\{X_i(t) \to 1\} = 0)$ *for any initial combination of balls in the urn. Let* $g_i(x,\gamma) < 1$ $(g_i(x,\gamma) > 0)$ *for all* $x \in R(0,1)$ *and* $\gamma \in R(S_m)$. *Also let* $\epsilon > 0$, $c < 1$ *and a function* $f_i(\cdot)$ *be such that* $U_i(x) \leq f_i(x_i) \leq cx_i$ $(L_i(x) \geq f_i(x_i) \geq 1 - c(1-x_i))$ *for* $x_i \in (0,\epsilon)$ $(x_i \in (1-\epsilon,1))$. *Then* $P\{X_i(t) \to 0\} > 0$ $(P\{X_i(t) \to 1\} > 0)$ *for any initial numbers of balls in the i-th urn.*

The theorem is proved in the appendix.

Theorem 4 gives sufficient conditions of convergence with positive probability to 0 and 1. The assumptions of theorem, however, are compatible with the case of independent urns (independent markets) as a particular case. More generally they represent conditions of weak feedbacks across markets (across regions) as compared to the extent of intramarket (intraregion) spillovers: Local feedbacks in that case are so important that a single market may converge to one technology, say A, even though all the related markets converge to the other one. In a sense, for the function $g_i(x,\gamma)$, the most important argument is x_i.

Conversely let us now consider the case of strong positive cross-regional feedbacks. Strong positive feedbacks can be characterized in terms of the urn function as follows: We can say that spillovers are strong if $\exists \delta, \chi, \delta > 0, \chi < 1$, such that $\delta < g(x, \gamma) < \chi$ when $x_j = 0$ and $x_k = 1$ for some $k \neq i$. In other words strong positive spatial feedbacks are such that adoptions of one type in other regions can be a partial substitute for adoptions of that type in the same region: even if a region has always chosen technology $A(B)$ in the past, technology $B(A)$ can still be chosen in the future, if it has been frequently chosen in at least another region.

Let us define a set $A \subset [0, 1]^m$ as *reachable* if there exists t such that $P\{X(t) \in A \mid X(0) \text{ given}\} > 0$. We can derive the following result:

Theorem 5. *If $g(0, .) = 0$ and $\forall i = 1, \ldots, m \; \exists \eta_i > 0$ and $c_i \in [0, 1)$, such that $0 < g_i(x, .) \leq c_i x_i, \forall x \in \prod_{i=1}^m [0, \eta_i]$ and $\prod_{i=1}^m [0, \eta_i]$ is reachable, then $P\{X_i(t) \to 0\} > 0$. If $g(1, .) = 1$ and $\forall i = 1, \ldots, m \; \exists \eta_i > 0$ and $c_i \in (0, 1)$, such that $1 > g_i(x, .) \geq 1 - c_i(1 - x_i), \forall x \in \prod_{i=1}^m [1 - \eta_i, 1]$ and $\prod_{i=1}^m [1 - \eta_i, 1]$ is reachable, then $P\{X_i(t) \to 1\} > 0$. Also if $g_i(x, .) \geq \alpha > 0$ in a neighborhood of every y such that $y_i = 0, y_k = 1$ for some $k \neq i$, then $P\{X_k(t) \to 1, X_i(t) \to 0\} = 0$ and if $g_i(x, .) \leq \beta < 1$ in a neighborhood of every y such that $y_i = 1, y_k = 0$ for some $k \neq i$, then $P\{X_i(t) \to 1, X_k(t) \to 0\} = 0$.*

The theorem is proved in the appendix.

If $0 < g(x, \gamma) < 1$ when $x \in [R(0, 1)]^m$ then any neighborhood of $x = 0$ and $x = 1$ are reachable and therefore complete worldwide monopoly of technology A or B may emerge with positive probability. Moreover theorem 5 tells us that, if feedbacks are strong, asymptotically either one technology emerges everywhere, or the other does, or market sharing is the only other possible outcome.

Subject to these conditions of weak or strong spillovers we can provide a generalization of theorem 1 to study the rate of convergence to technological monopolies.

Theorem 6. *Let $\epsilon, \eta_i > 0$ and $c, c_i < 1$ be such that either the assumptions of theorem 4 or those of theorem 5 hold. (In the second case, denote $\max_i\{c_i\}$ with c). Then for any $\delta \in (0, 1 - c)$ and $\tau > 0$*

$$\lim_{n \to \infty} P\{n^{1-c-\delta} Y_i(n) < \tau \mid Y_i(t) \to 0\} = 1$$
$$\left(\lim_{n \to \infty} P\{n^{1-c-\delta}[1 - Y_i(n)] < \tau \mid Y_i(t) \to 1\} = 1 \right),$$

where $Y_i(\cdot)$ stands for the random process given by (9).

The theorem is proved in the appendix.

Again, as in section 2, an important observation, which theorems 6 provides, is that convergence to 0 and 1 can be much faster (almost of order $1/t$ as $t \to \infty$) than to an interior limit (which can be almost of order $1/\sqrt{t}$ only).

An intuitive explanation, that holds rigorously only when $g_i(x, \gamma) = g_i(x_i)$, is that the variance of $\zeta_i^k(x)$, which characterizes the level of random disturbances in the process (9), is $g_i(x)[1 - g_i(x)]$. This value vanishes at 0 and 1 but it does not vanish at θ, being equal to $\theta(1 - \theta)$.

4   Conclusions

This paper has been motivated by two 'stylized facts' concerning the dynamics of diffusion of different technologies competing for the same market niche and a stylized fact concerning the international location of production.

a) A stable pattern of market sharing with no overwhelming dominant position is rarely observed in markets with network esternalities. Unbounded increasing returns to adoption are often called for an explanation of this fact. However the argument is generally based on an incorrect interpretation of the popular Brian Arthur (1989) model. We recalled a simple counterexample, drawn from Bassanini and Dosi (1998), to show that unbounded increasing returns are neither necessary nor sufficient to lead to technological monopolies even in a stable external environment.

b) International diffusion may lead sometimes to different standards in different countries or to the diffusion of the same standard in every country, even without intervention of any regulatory agency. Intuitively when convergence to the same standard is not an accident of history, it is an outcome of the relative weight of international spillovers as compared to nationwide esternalities.

The crucial question we tried to address in this paper is: can a model that account for the former fact accomodate also the latter? By establishing some mathematical properties of generalized urn schemes, we build on a class of competing technology dynamics models to develop an explanation for the former "fact" and to provide sufficient conditions for convergence to the same or to different technological monopolies in different countries. Our explanation for the empirical tendency to converge to technological monopoly relies on convergence rate differentials to limit market shares. In a related paper [Bassanini and Dosi (1998)] we show that a market can approach a monopoly with a higher speed than it approaches any feasible limit market share where both technologies coexist: Convergence to market sharing is in general so slow that the environment changes before the market share trajectory becomes stable in a neighborhood of its limit. In this paper we have shown that this result hold also in a multi-market model where convergence to different local monopolies can occur, even though, at a high level of aggregation, this system may seem to converge to market-sharing. The empirical implication is again that among markets with high rate of technological change and increasing returns to adoption, a prevalence of stable monopolies over stable market sharing should be expected.

5 Appendix

Proof of theorem 3. The theorem is a straightforward consequence of the following lemma which generalizes lemma 2.2 from Hill et al. (1980):

Lemma 1. *Assume that we have a scheme of multiple urns, given by a set of the functions $f_i^A(\cdot, \cdot)$ and $f_i^B(\cdot, \cdot)$, $i = 1, 2, \ldots, m$. Let for some i a function $g_i(\cdot)$ be such that (10) or (11) holds true. Then there is a probability space, where the process (9) and a conventional urn process $Z_i(\cdot)$ can be realized and $Y_i(k) \leq Z_i(k)$ or $Y_i(k) \geq Z_i(k)$ with probability 1 for $k \geq 1$ depending upon whether (10) or (11) holds. The process $Z_i(\cdot)$ has $g_i(\cdot)$ as urn-functions and n_i^A, n_i^B as initial numbers of balls.*

Proof. Fix a probability space with $r_t, t \geq 1$, a sequence of independent random variables having the uniform distribution on $[0, 1]$. For given $x \in R(0, 1)$ and $\gamma \in R(S_m)$ introduce a partition of $[0, 1]$ by the points

$$t_0 = 0, \ t_1 = f_1^A(x, \gamma), \ t_2 = f_1(x, \gamma),$$

$$t_3 = f_1(x, \gamma) + f_2^A(x, \gamma), \ t_4 = f_1(x, \gamma) + f_2(x, \gamma), \ \ldots,$$

$$t_{2m-1} = f_1(x, \gamma) + f_2(x, \gamma) + \ldots + f_{m-1}(x, \gamma) + f_m^A(x, \gamma), \ t_{2m} = 1.$$

Set

$$\xi_{i,A}^n(x, \gamma) = \chi_{\{r_n \in (t_{2(i-1)}, t_{2i-1})\}}, \ \xi_{i,B}^n(x, \gamma) = \chi_{\{r_n \in (t_{2i-1}, t_{2i})\}},$$

where χ_A stands for the indicator of the event A. If $\tau_i(\cdot)$ are defined as above, set

$$\tilde{\zeta}_i^k(x_i) = \chi_{\{r_{\tau_i(k)} \in (t_{2(i-1)}, t_{2(i-1)} + g_i(x_i) f_i(x, \gamma))\}} \tag{12}$$

and

$$Z_i(k+1) = Z_i(k) + \frac{1}{k + G_i}[\tilde{\zeta}_i^k(Z_i(k)) - Z_i(k)], \ k \geq 1, \ Z_i(1) = \frac{n_i^w}{G_i}.$$

Hence $Y_i(\cdot)$ and $Z_i(\cdot)$ are given on the same probability space. If we denote with $\bar{F}_k^i$ the σ-algebra generated by $r_t, : t \leq \tau_i(k)$, then $E[\tilde{\zeta}_i^k(Z_i(k))|\bar{F}_k^i] = g_i(Z_i(k))$. Hence $Z_i(\cdot)$ is a conventional urn process with $g_i(\cdot)$ as urn-function.

Notice that

$$\zeta_i^k(x_i) = \chi_{\{r_{\tau_i(k)} \in (t_{2(i-1)}, t_{2(i-1)} + g(x, \gamma) f_i(x, \gamma))\}},$$

which, from (12), implies that $\zeta_i^t(x_i) \leq \tilde{\zeta}_i^t(x_i)$ or $\zeta_i^t(x_i) \geq \tilde{\zeta}_i^t(x_i)$ with probability 1 depending whether (10) or (11) holds. Now to accomplish the proof it is enough to check that

$$Y_i(t+1) = \frac{(t + G_i - 1)Y_i(t) + \zeta_i^t(Y_i(t))}{t + G_i},$$

$$Z_i(t+1) = \frac{(t+G_i-1)Z_i(t) + \tilde{\zeta}_i^t(Z_i(t))}{t+G_i}.$$

The lemma is proved. ∎

Proof of theorem 4. We need the following lemma:

Lemma 2. *Let $X(\cdot)$ be a conventional urn process with $f(\cdot)$ as urn-function. If there is $\epsilon > 0$ such that*

$$f(x) \geq x \text{ for } x \in (0, \epsilon) \quad (f(x) \leq x \text{ for } x \in (1 - \epsilon, 1)),$$

then $\mathcal{P}\{X(t) \to 0\} = 0$ $(\mathcal{P}\{X(t) \to 1\} = 0)$ for any initial numbers of balls. Also, if $f(x) < 1$ $(f(x) > 0)$ for $x \in (0, 1)$ and there is $\epsilon > 0$ such that

$$f(x) < x \text{ for } x \in (0, \epsilon) \quad (f(x) > x \text{ for } x \in (1 - \epsilon, 1)),$$

then $\mathcal{P}\{X(t) \to 0\} > 0$ $(\mathcal{P}\{X(t) \to 1\} > 0)$ for any initial numbers of balls.

Proof. Set that all conventional urn processes appearing here start from the same numbers of balls in the urn. Let $f(x) > x$ for $x \in (0, \epsilon)$. Set $g(x) = \max(f(x), x)$. Define $Y(\cdot)(Z(\cdot))$ a conventional urn process corresponding to the urn-function x $(g(x))$. Since $x \leq g(x)$, then due to lemma 2.2 from Hill et al. (1980) one has $Y(t) \leq Z(t)$, $t \geq 1$. Consequently $\mathcal{P}\{Z(t) \to 0\} \leq \mathcal{P}\{Y(t) \to 0\}$. But $Y(\cdot)$ is a Polya process, i.e. it converges a.s. to a random variable with a beta distribution. The limit, having a density with respect to the Lebesgue measure, takes every particular value from $[0, 1]$ with probability 0. Hence $\mathcal{P}\{Y(t) \to 0\} = 0$ and, consequently, $\mathcal{P}\{Z(t) \to 0\} = 0$. But the urn-functions $f(\cdot)$ and $g(\cdot)$ agree in $(0, \epsilon)$, which due to lemma 4.1 from Hill et al. (1980) implies that $\mathcal{P}\{X(t) \to 0\} = 0$. Let $f(x) < x$ for $x \in (0, \epsilon)$ and $f(x) < 1$ for all $x \in (0, 1)$. Set $g(x) = \max(f(x), x/2)$. Then $f(x) \leq g(x)$ and due to arguments similar to those given above $\mathcal{P}\{X(t) \to 0\} \geq \mathcal{P}\{Z(t) \to 0\}$, where $Z(\cdot)$ stands for a conventional urn process corresponding to $g(\cdot)$. Finally let us prove that $\mathcal{P}\{Z(t) \to 0\} > 0$. Put $d(x) = \min(g(x), g(\epsilon/2))$. The equation $d(x) - x = 0$ has the only root 0. Hence there is a conventional urn process corresponding to $d(\cdot)$ which converges to 0 with probability 1. Since $g(x) \in (0, 1)$ and $d(x) \in (0, 1)$ for all $x \in (0, 1)$, this implies that $\mathcal{P}\{Z(t) \to 0\} > 0$ for any initial numbers of balls, because of lemma 4.1 of Hill et al. (1980).

Other cases can be handled by similar arguments. ∎

Due to the aforementioned relationship between convergence of $X_i(\cdot)$ and $Y_i(\cdot)$, it is enough to establish the corresponding facts for $Y_i(\cdot)$.

The first statement follows by considering a conventional urn process with

$$d_i(y) = \inf_{x:\, x_i = y} \{L_i(x)\} \quad (d_i(y) = \sup_{x:\, x_i = y} \{U_i(x)\})$$

as the urn-function and applying lemma 2 and theorem 3.

Since convergence to 1 with positive probability can be studied by the same means, let us prove convergence with positive probability to 0 only. Let $Z_i(\cdot)$ be a conventional urn process having

$$d_i(x) = \begin{cases} f(x) & \text{if } x < \epsilon/2 \\ f(\epsilon/2) & \text{if } x \geq \epsilon/2 \end{cases}$$

as urn-function and starting from the same numbers of balls. Then

$$P\{Z_i(t) \to 0\} = 1. \tag{13}$$

Set $l_i(t) = n_i^A (n_i^A + n_i^B + t - 1)^{-1}$, $t \geq 1$. Since we assume that $g_i(x, \gamma) < 1$ for all possible x and γ, the process $Y_i(\cdot)$ can move with a positive probability to the left from any point. Hence

$$P\{Y_i(t) = l_i(t)\} > 0 \text{ for } t \geq 1. \tag{14}$$

For any t such that $l_i(t) < \epsilon/2$ introduce $\mu_i(t)$ as the first instant after t such that $Z_i(\cdot)$ exits from $(0, \epsilon/2)$ providing that $Z_i(t) = l_i(t)$. Due to (13):

$$P\{\mu_i(t) = \infty\} \to 1 \text{ as } t \to \infty. \tag{15}$$

But due to lemma 1 $Y_i(n) \leq Z_i(n)$ for $t \leq n < \mu_i(t)$ providing that $Y_i(t) = Z_i(t) = l_i(t)$. Thus, taking into account (13) and (15), we get:

$$P\{Y_i(n) \to 0 | Y_i(t) = l_i(t)\} \geq P\{Y_i(n) \to 0, \mu_i(t) = \infty | Y_i(t) = l_i(t)\} \geq$$

$$P\{Z_i(n) \to 0, \mu_i(t) = \infty | Z_i(t) = l_i(t)\} \to 1 \text{ as } t \to \infty.$$

Therefore to accomplish the proof it is enough to refer to (14).■

Proof of theorem 5. We need the following lemma:

Lemma 3. *Consider two multiple urn processes $X(.)$ and $Y(.)$ which agree in a neighborhood N of a point $\theta \in (R[0,1])^m$. Then there exists an urn process $Z(.)$ with the same urn function as $Y(.)$ such that $P\{Z(t) \to \theta\} > 0$ if $P\{X(t) \to \theta\} > 0$. Also consider a neighborhood N_0 (N_1) of 0 (1); if it is reachable by $X_i(.)$, given the initial number of balls, and if the urn functions never take the values 0 (1) in that neighborhood (0 (1) excluded), then $P\{Z(t) \to 0\} > 0$ from every initial number of balls only if $P\{X(t) \to 0\} > 0$ $(P\{Z(t) \to 1\} > 0$ only if $P\{X(t) \to 1\} > 0)$.*

Proof. From almost sure convergence we have that $\exists t > 0$ and two vectors $n, t \in \mathbf{Z}_+^m$ such that

$$\mathcal{P}\left\{\begin{array}{l} X(s) \to \theta, X_i(t) = \frac{n_i}{t_i+G_i}, i = 1, ..., m, \\ \sum_{i=1}^{m}(t_i + G_i) = t + G, X(s) \in N, s > t \end{array}\right\} > 0,$$

which implies

$$\mathcal{P}\left\{\begin{array}{l} X(s) \to \theta, X(s) \in N, s > t \\ X_i(t) = \frac{n_i}{t_i+G_i}, i = 1, ..., m \end{array}\right\} > 0. \qquad (16)$$

Take $Z_i(0) = \frac{n_i}{t_i+G_i}$. Since on N $X(.)$ and $Y(.)$ agree, from (16) we have

$$\mathcal{P}\left\{Z(t) \to \theta, Z(t) \in N, t > 0\right\} > 0,$$

from which the first statement of the lemma follows.

Since N_0 is reachable $\exists \bar{t} > 0$ and $\exists(y, n, t) \in N_0 \times \mathbf{Z}_+^{2m} : \frac{n_i}{t_i+G_i} = y_i$, $i = 1, ..., m$, $\sum_{i=1}^{m}(t_i + G_i) = \bar{t} + G$ such that

$$\mathcal{P}\left\{X(\bar{t}) = y\right\} > 0. \qquad (17)$$

Take n_i, t_i+G_i as initial conditions of the process $Z(.)$. Again from almost sure convergence we have that $\mathcal{P}\{Z(t) \to 0\} > 0$ from every initial number of balls implies that, $\exists z \in N_0$ and $\exists T > 0$ such that

$$\mathcal{P}\left\{Z(s) \to 0, Z(s) \in N_0, s \geq T, Z(T) = z \in N_0\right\} > 0.$$

Given that the urn functions never reach 0 or 1 in N_0, z can be reached from y without leaving N_0 (through an appropriate sequence of 0 first and 1 afterwards), we have also

$$\mathcal{P}\left\{Z(s) \to 0, Z(s) \in N_0, Z(0) = y \in N_0\right\} > 0,$$

which implies

$$\mathcal{P}\left\{Z(s) \to 0, Z(s) \in N_0 | Z(0) = y \in N_0\right\} > 0. \qquad (18)$$

Given that on N_0 $X(.)$ and $Y(.)$ agree, we can choose the process $Z(t)$ defined on the common probability space in such a way that $X(s+\bar{t}) = Z(s)$ for any $s < \tilde{t} = \min\{t : Z(t) \notin N_0\}$. From (18) we have

$$\mathcal{P}\left\{X(s) \to 0, X(s) \in N_0 | X(\bar{t}) = y \in N_0\right\} > 0,$$

which, taking into account (17), implies that $\exists t > 0$ such that

$$\mathcal{P}\left\{X(s) \to 0, X(s) \in N_0, s \geq t\right\} > 0.$$

Convergence to 1 can be studied with similar arguments.∎

To prove the first statement of the theorem take a process $Y(.)$ with urn function:

$$d(x, .) = \begin{cases} g(x, .) \ if \ x \in \prod_{i=1}^{m}[0, \eta_i] \\ 0 \quad\quad\quad otherwise \end{cases},$$

the apply lemma 3 and lemma 1. The second statement can be proved with similar arguments. For the third statement take a process $Y(.)$ with urn function:

$$d(x, .) = \begin{cases} g(x, .) \ if \ \|x - y\| < \epsilon \\ \alpha \quad\quad\quad otherwise \end{cases},$$

then apply lemma 3 and lemma 1. The last statement can be proved with similar arguments.∎

Proof of theorem 6. Consider only the first case – convergence to 0. Without loss of generality we can assume that $\mathcal{P}\{Y_i(t) \to 0\} > 0$.

Let $Z_i(\cdot)$ be a conventional urn process with cx as the urn-function and the same initial numbers of balls. Then

$$EZ_i(t+1) \leq [1 - \frac{1-c}{t+G_i}]EZ_i(t), \ \ t \geq 1,$$

and consequently

$$EZ_i(t) \leq Z_i(1) \prod_{j=1}^{t-1}(1 - \frac{1-c}{j+G_i}) = Z_i(1)t^{c-1}[1 + o_t(1)],$$

where $o_t(1) \to 0$ as $t \to \infty$. Hence from Markov's inequality

$$\mathcal{P}\{t^{1-c-\delta}Z_i(t) < \tau\} \to 1 \ \text{as} \ t \to \infty \tag{19}$$

for every $\delta \in (0, 1-c)$ and $\tau > 0$.

For arbitrary $\sigma \in (0, \epsilon)$ and $v > 0$ there is N depending on these variables such that

$$\mathcal{P}\{\{Y_i(t) \to 0\}\Delta\{Y_i(n) \leq \sigma, \ n \geq N\}\} < v.$$

where $A\Delta B = (A\backslash B) \cup (B\backslash A)$. Also since $Z_i(t) \to 0$ with probability 1 as $t \to \infty$, we can choose this N so large that

$$\mathcal{P}\{\{Y_i(t) \to 0\}\Delta\{Y_i(n) \leq \sigma, \ Z_i(n) \leq \sigma, \ n \geq N\}\} < v. \tag{20}$$

To prove the theorem it is enough to show that

$$\lim_{n\to\infty} \mathcal{P}\{n^{1-c-\delta}Y_i(n) < \tau, \ Y_i(t) \to 0\} = \mathcal{P}\{Y_i(t) \to 0\},$$

or, taking into account that v in (19) can be arbitrary small, that

$$\lim_{n\to\infty} P\{n^{1-c-\delta}Y_i(n) < \tau,\ Y_i(n) \leq \sigma,\ Z_i(n) \leq \sigma,\ n \geq N\} =$$

$$P\{Y_i(n) \leq \sigma,\ Z_i(n) \leq \sigma,\ n \geq N\}.$$

Due to lemma 1 $Z_i(\cdot)$ majorizes $Y_i(\cdot)$ on the event $Z_i(t) \leq \sigma$, $t \geq N$, providing that these processes start from the same point. Hence,

$$P\{Y_i(t) \leq \sigma,\ Z_i(t) \leq \sigma,\ t \geq N\} \geq$$

$$\limsup_{n\to\infty} P\{n^{1-c-\delta}Y_i(n) < \tau,\ Y_i(t) \leq \sigma,\ Z_i(t) \leq \sigma,\ t \geq N\} \geq$$

$$\liminf_{n\to\infty} P\{n^{1-c-\delta}Y_i(n) < \tau,\ Y_i(t) \leq \sigma,\ Z_i(t) \leq \sigma,\ t \geq N\} =$$

$$\liminf_{n\to\infty} EP\{n^{1-c-\delta}Y_i(n) < \tau,\ Y_i(t) \leq \sigma,\ Z_i(t) \leq \sigma,\ t \geq N|Y_i(N)\} \geq$$

$$\liminf_{n\to\infty} EP\{\{n^{1-c-\delta}Z_i(n) < \tau,\ Y_i(t) \leq \sigma,\ Z_i(t) \leq \sigma,\ t \geq N|Z_i(N) =$$

$$Y_i(N)\}|Y_i(N)\} = EP\{Y_i(t) \leq \sigma,\ Z_i(t) \leq \sigma,\ t \geq N|Y_i(N)\} =$$

$$P\{Y_i(t) \leq \sigma,\ Z_i(t) \leq \sigma,\ t \geq N\},$$

i.e. (20) holds true.∎

6   References

An, M., and N.Kiefer, Local Externalities and Societal Adoption of Technologies, *J. of Evolutionary Econ.*, 5, 103–117, 1995.

Arthur, W.B., On Competing Technologies and Historical Small Events: The Dynamics of Choice under Increasing Returns, IIASA Working Paper WP-83-90 [Reprinted in W.B. Arthur (1994) *Increasing Returns and Path-Dependence in the Economy*, Ann Arbor: University of Michigan Press], 1983.

Arthur, W.B., Competing Technologies, Increasing Returns and Lock-In by Historical Events, *Econ. J.*, 99, 116–131, 1989.

Arthur, W.B., "Sylicon Valley" Locational Clusters: When Do Increasing Returns Imply Monopoly?, *Math. Soc. Sci.*, 19, 235–51, 1990.

Arthur, W.B., Y.Ermoliev and Y.Kaniovski, Generalized Urn Problem and Its Applications, *Cybernetics*, 19, 61-71, 1983.

Bassanini, A.P. and G.Dosi, Competing Technologies, Technological Monopolies, and the Rate of Convergence to a Stable Market Structure, unpublished manuscript, 1998.

Brock, W.A. and S.N.Durlauf, Discrete Choice with Social Interactions I: Theory, NBER Working Paper #5291, 1995.

Brock, W.A. and S.N.Durlauf, A Formal Model of Theory Choice in Science, *Economic Theory*, forthcoming, 1998.

Brynjolfsson, E. and C.F.Kemerer, Network Externalities in Microcomputer Software: An Econometric Analysis of the Spreadsheet Market, *Management Science*, **42**, 1627-47, 1996.

Cantwell, J., *Technological Innovation and Multinational Corporations*, Oxford: Blackwell, 1989.

Church, J. and N.Gandal, Complementary Network Externalities and Technological Adoption, *Int. J. of Industrial Organization*, **11**, 239-60, 1993.

Cowan, R., Tortoises and Hares: Choice among Technologies of Unknown Merit, *Econ. J.*, **101**, 801-14, 1991.

Cusumano, M.A., Y.Milonadis and R.S.Rosenbloom, Strategic Maneuvering and Mass-Market Dynamics: The Triumph of VHS over Beta, *Business History Rev.*, **66**, 51-94, 1992.

David, P., Clio and the Economics of QWERTY, *AEA Papers and Proceedings*, **75**, 332-7, 1985.

David, P., Heroes, Herds and Hystheres in Technological Theory: Thomas Edison and the Battle of Systems Reconsidered, *Industrial and Corporate Change*, **1**, 129-80, 1992.

Dosi, G., Technological Paradigms and Technological Trajectories, *Research Policy*, **11**, 142-67, 1982.

Dosi, G., Sources, Procedures and Microeconomic Effect of Innovation, *J. Econ. Lit.*, **26**, 1120-71, 1988.

Dosi, G., Research on Innovation Diffusion: An Assessment, in A.Grübler and N.Nakicenovic (eds.), *Innovation Diffusion and Social Behavior*, Berlin: Springer, 1991.

Dosi, G., Y.Ermoliev and Y.Kaniovski, Generalized Urn Schemes and Technological Dynamics, *J. Math. Econ.*, **23**, 1-19, 1994.

Dosi, G. and Y.Kaniovski, On Badly Behaved Dynamics, *J. of Evolutionary Econ.*, **4**, 93-123, 1994.

Dosi, G., K.Pavitt and L.Soete, *The Economics of Technological Change and International Trade*, New York: NYU Press, 1990.

Durlauf, S.N., Statistical Mechanics Approaches to Socioeconomic Behavior, in S.N.Durlauf, W.B.Arthur and D.Lane (Eds.), *The Economy as an Evolving Complex System II*, New York: Addison-Wesley, 1997.

Farrell, J. and G.Saloner, Standardization, Compatibility and Innovation, *Rand J. of Econ.*, **16**, 70-83, 1985.

Farrell, J. and G.Saloner, Installed Base and Compatibility: Innovation, Product Preannouncements, and Predation, *Amer. Econ. Rev.*, **76**, 940-55, 1986.

Freeman, C., *The Economics of Industrial Innovation*, London: Pinter, 2nd ed., 1992.

Freeman, C., The Economics of Technical Change: A Critical Survey, *Cambridge J. of Econ.*, **18**, 463-514, 1994.

Freeman, C., The National Systems of Innovation in Historical Perspective, *Cambridge J. of Econ.*, 1995.

Hill, B.M., D.Lane and W.Sudderth, A Strong Law for Some Generalized Urn Processes, *Annals of Probability*, **8**, 214-26, 1980.

Kaniovski, Y. and H.P.Young, Learning Dynamics in Games with Stochastic Perturbations, *Games and Econ. Behavior*, **11**, 330-63, 1995.

Katz, M.L. and C.Shapiro, Network Externalities, Competition , and Compatibility, *Amer. Econ. Rev.*, **75**, 424–40, 1985.

Katz, M.L. and C.Shapiro, Technology Adoption in the Presence of Network Externalities, *J. Pol. Econ.*, **94**, 822–41, 1986.

Katz, M.L. and C.Shapiro, Product Introduction with Network Externalities, *J. of Industrial Econ.*, **40**, 55–84, 1992.

Katz, M.L. and C.Shapiro, Systems Competition and Network Effects, *J. of Econ. Perspectives*, **8**, 93–115, 1994.

Krugman, P., History vs. Expectations, *Quart. J. Econ.*, **106**, 651-67, 1991a.

Krugman, P., *Geography and Trade*, Cambridge, MA: MIT press, 1991b.

Krugman, P., and A.Venables, Globalization and the Inequality of nations, *Quart. J. Econ.*, **110**, 857-80, 1995.

Lundvall, B.A. (ed.), *National Innovation Systems*, London: Pinter, 1992.

Nelson, R. (ed.), *National Systems of Innovation*, Oxford: OUP, 1993.

Oren, S. and S.Smith, Critical Mass and Tariff Structure in Electronic Communications Markets, *Bell J. of Econ.*, **12**, 467–87, 1981.

Rauch, J.E., Does History Matter Only When It Matters Little? The Case of City-Industry Location, *Quart. J. Econ.*, **108**, 843–67, 1993.

Rohlfs, J., A Theory of Interdependent Demand for a Communication Service, *Bell J. of Econ.*, **5**, 16–37, 1974.

Silverberg, G., G.Dosi and L.Orsenigo, Innovation, Diversity and Diffusion: A Self-Organization Model, *Econ. J.*, **98**, 1032-54, 1988.

Tushman, M.L. and J.P.Murmann, Dominant Designs, Technology Cycles, and Organizational Outcomes, in B.Staw and L.L.Cummings (eds.), *Research in Organizational Behavior*, **20**, Greenwich, CT: JAI press, 1998.

Venables, A.J., Localization of Industry and Trade Performance, *Oxford Rev. of Econ. Policy*, **12**(3), 52-60, 1996.

Market Organization : Noncooperative Models of Coalition Formation

Sylvie Thoron

GREQAM, University of Toulon

Abstract. I apply three noncooperative models of coalition formation to a Cournot olygopoly. In each model, each firm has to choose the coalition it wants to belong to. But each of this models is characterised by a different assumption that defines what happens to a coalition from which one or more players depart (which we shall refer to as a "depleted coalition"). In the first model proposed by Von Neumann and Morgenstern [1944], this depleted coalition is assumed to "fall apart", in the second one proposed by Hart and Kurz [1983], it is assumed to "stick together". I prove that the results depend crucially on the game of coalition formation. In the first model, the grand coalition is stable, in the second model, the unique stable structure is the structure in which all the firms are independent. In fact, The assumption that characterises the game of coalition formation has to be considered as a threat, the credibility of which has to be analysed. That is why I propose a third game in which members of a depleted coalition choose the reaction to adopt. It turns out that the members of such a coalition stick together as long as they are sufficiently numerous. As a result, the set of stable structures in this model depends on the number of firms, n. When this number is small, the grand coalition is the unique stable structure. But when the number of firms increases, asymmetrical coalition structures appear. For great value of n, stable structures appear with several coalitions, that can be of different sizes. We notice that, in this game with symmetric firms as players, the result can be asymmetric.

JEL classification: D43, C72.

Keywords: coalition formation, noncooperative games, market organization,   Cournot oligopoly.

1 Introduction

The obvious criticism that can be addressed to General Equilibrium Theory is that it represents a world in which each agent is isolated and does not take into account the actions of the others. The consistency between the choices of all the agents is ensured by the price system. One seemingly attractive way to obtain a more realistic representation seems to be the introduction of heterogeneous interacting agents. But one might ask oneself if this kind of approach is so fundamentally opposed to that of General Equilibrium Theory. Indeed, in the framework of the General Equilibrium Theory, all the agents, who are not necessarily homogeneous, are equally linked. All the agents, each of them isolated from each other, face the same price system. In classical game theory, even if direct interactions are made explicit, we have in one sense the same kind of framework, namely a framework in which all of the agents face the same rules. Now, an interesting question is about what happens when the heterogeneity is not about the agents themselves but about the links between them. Consider a world in which the interacting network does not have a uniform density. A world in which the agents have the possibility to belong to coalitions and in which the relationships linking them depends on the coalition structure. There is a different sort of relationship inside each coalition and between coalitions. In that case, it is interesting to analyse the formation of this structure.

In fact the stability of coalition structures is one of the oldest problems of game theory. But in the literature, this problem has mainly been conducted in the framework of games in coalitional form. However the founders of game theory themselves, von Neumann and Morgenstern, also proposed a noncooperative approach to this problem. In their famous book [1944] we find a noncooperative model of coalition formation in which each player has to choose the coalition to which he wants to belong. In fact such a strategy is a wish, the fulfilment of which depends on other players' wishes. Therefore knowing the strategies chosen by the players is not enough to determine the outcome of the game. That is why von Neumann and Morgenstern assume that a coalition S forms if and only if every member of S chooses the strategy : "I wish to belong to S".

Hart and Kurz [1983] use this model to construct a generalization of the Shapley value which is defined for games with coalition structures. They also introduce another game with the same strategies but in which a coalition M forms if and only if all members of the coalition choose the same strategy : "I wish to belong to S" - where S is a coalition including M. Each of these two games is characterized by an assumption that defines what happens to a coalition from which one or more players depart (which we shall refer to as a "depleted coalition"). In the first model this depleted coalition is assumed to "fall apart", in the second one it is assumed to "stick together". These two alternative models have been used by Burbidge et al. [1994] to analyse the federation of nations. They prove two results independent of the game to be used : in the case of two states, complete federation (the grand coalition) is the unique equilibrium outcome; in the case of more than two states, a coalition structure other than the grand coalition can be the unique equilibrium outcome.

In this paper, on the other hand we emphasize differences between these two models. We prove that when results are made more precise, they can be diametrically opposed in the two cases. Then we propose a new game in which the assumption about the reaction of a depleted coalition is endogenized.

We suppose that, in each game of coalition formation, players are firms and outcomes are coalitions competing in an oligopoly "à la Cournot". On the one hand we prove that the von Neumann and Morgenstern model is the most favourable to cooperation. In particular the grand coalition is stable in that model. On the other hand we prove that in Hart and Kurz's model no coalition can form. The situation in which all the firms remain independent is the unique structure that satisfies a stability criterion. These results can be easily interpreted in the oligopoly context. Indeed the profit of a player is a decreasing function of the number of competitors. Therefore, if a group of firms defects from a coalition, the most unfavourable situation for them is when the remaining members separate and the most favourable one is when they stick together.

The assumption that characterizes the game of coalition formation has to be considered as a threat, the credibility of which has to be analysed. That is why we propose a game in which members of a depleted coalition choose the reaction to adopt. It turns out that the members of such a coalition stick together as long as they are sufficiently numerous. As a result, the set of stable structures in this model depends on the number of firms. When this number is small the grand coalition is the unique stable structure. But when the number of firms increases, asymmetrical coalition structures appear. For intermediate value of n, stable coalition structures have a unique coalition grouping less than the whole. Finally, for great value of n, stable structures appear with several coalitions, that can be of different sizes.

2 Two Assumptions about Reaction

We consider an "initial" oligopoly composed of a fixed finite number of firms n. Firms have identical costs. We suppose that firms can form coalitions that will compete in a "final" oligopoly. To represent this situation we use a noncooperative model of coalition formation. Let $N = \{1,...,n\}$ be the set of players. Each player has to choose the coalition it wants to belong to. Formally, letting $\sum_i$ being player i's set of strategies we write :

$$\forall i \in N, \sum_i = \{\sigma_i = S_i / S_i \subset N \text{ and } i \in S_i\}.$$

The outcome of the game is a strategy profile $\sigma = (\sigma_1,...,\sigma_n)$ that determines a coalition structure B that is a partition of N. However, the knowledge of σ is not sufficient to characterize the coalition structure generated. Indeed if $\sigma_i = S_i$ is the coalition the player i wants to belongs to, the realisation of σ_i depends on the other players' wishes. The same thing applies for a strategy profile   which is a restriction of the strategy profile $\sigma = (\sigma_1,...,\sigma_n)$ to the coalition S. The case in which this problem does not appear is very specific. We say in that case that strategy profile is feasible.

Definition 2.1   A strategy profile $\sigma_S = (S_i)_{i \in S}, S \subset N$, is *feasible* if :

$$\forall i \in S, \forall j \neq i \text{ such that } j \in S_i, \text{ then } S_j = S_i$$

the set of feasible strategy profiles for $S \subset N, \sigma_S = (S_i)_{i \in S}$, is denoted Σ_S^f.

Let us also define another particular kind of strategy profile.

Definition 2.2   A strategy profile $\sigma_S = (S_i)_{i \in S}, S \subset N$, is *autonomous* if it is independent of other players' strategies. That is : $\forall i \in S, \forall j \in S_i, j \in S$.

Note that an autonomous strategy profile is not necessarily feasible and that a non autonomous strategy profile can be feasible. We will say that a strategic profile is *consistent* if it is autonomous and feasible. The set of consistent strategy profiles $\sigma_S = (S_i)_{i \in S}, S \subset N$, is denoted Σ_S^c .

To illustrate those notions let us consider the following example in which the set of players is $N = \{1,2,3\}$.

The autonomous strategy profiles for players 1 and 2, $\sigma_{1,2} = (\sigma_1, \sigma_2)$ are :

$(S_1 = \{1\}, S_2 = \{2\}); (S_1 = \{1, 2\}, S_2 = \{2\}); (S_1 = \{1\}, S_2 = \{1, 2\}); (S_1 = \{1, 2\}, S_2 = \{1, 2\})$.

The first and the last autonomous strategy profiles are the only ones which are both feasible and autonomous and therefore consistent. The non autonomous strategy profiles are :

$(S_1 = \{1, 3\}, S_2 = \{2\}); (S_1 = \{1, 2, 3\}, S_2 = \{2\}); (S_1 = \{1\}, S_2 = \{2, 3\}; (S_1 = \{1\}, S_2 = \{1, 2, 3\});); (S_1 = \{1, 2\}, S_2 = \{2, 3\}) ; (S_1 = \{1, 2\}, S_2 = \{1, 2, 3\}); (S_1 = \{1, 2, 3\}, S_2 = \{1, 2\}); (S_1 = \{1, 3\}, S_2 = \{1, 2\}); (S_1 = \{1, 2, 3\}, S_2 = \{1, 2, 3\})$.

Now if $S_3 = \{3\}$ no non autonomous strategy profiles can be feasible, if $S_3 = \{1, 3\}$ the first one is feasible and if $S_3 = \{1, 2, 3\}$ the last one is feasible.

Given the nature of the strategies in this coalition formation model, we have to define a special kind of coalition.

Definition 2.3   L is a *depleted coalition* generated by $\sigma = (S_1, ..., S_2)$ if σ_L is non feasible and $\forall i, j \in L, S_j = S_i = S$.

The coalition structure that a strategy profile determines, depends on the behaviour of depleted coalitions. We could assume as did von Neumann and Morgenstern that the members of a depleted coalition give up cooperation and become independent. This assumption denoted H_1 in addition to the previous specification constitutes a first model of coalition formation which we shall call model Γ. Alternatively we may assume as did Hart and Kurz that the depleted coalition still constitutes a coalition. This assumption denoted H_2 characterises a second model of coalition formation which we shall refer to as model Δ. Then from a strategy profile σ we can deduce in each case the coalition structure generated denoted respectively by $B_\Gamma(\sigma)$ or $B_\Delta(\sigma)$. Note that, in each model, the same coalition structure B can be generated by different strategy profiles but only one is feasible. We denote by $\sigma^f(B)$ this strategy profile in which, for each player, his strategy is the coalition he belongs to in B. Note that $\sigma^f(B)$ does not depend on the model to be used.

An oligopoly game "à la Cournot" between coalitions of the structure generated by the strategies determines the payments. In order to focus the analysis on strategic effects we suppose that the formation of coalitions only acts on the level of competition. In particular, there is no cost advantage to forming coalitions. This oligopoly game is symmetric. Therefore, the coalition structure can be denoted by $B = (\alpha_1,...,\alpha_k,...,\alpha_n)$, α_k being the number of coalitions each consisting of k firms and $\sum_{t=1}^{n} \alpha_t$ the total number of coalitions. Total profits earned by an S-coalition do not depend on its size[1] but only on the number of competitors in the coalition structure. Total profits earned by an S-coalition in the structure $B = (\alpha_1,...,\alpha_n)$ generated by the strategy profile σ in the μ-model where $\mu = \Delta$ or Γ are denoted :

$$\pi_S(\sigma) = \pi(\sigma), \text{ or } \pi_S(B_\mu(\sigma)) = \pi(B_\mu(\sigma)) = \pi\left(\sum_{t=1}^{n} \alpha_t\right).$$

However a player's payment depends on the size of the coalition he belongs to. Each member of a s-size coalition[2] earns :

$$\pi_S\left(\sum_{t=1}^{n} \alpha_t\right) = \frac{\pi\left(\sum_{t=1}^{n} \alpha_t\right)}{s}.$$

We consider the simple oligopoly game "à la Cournot" with zero cost, homogeneous goods, and linear demand function P = 1 - Q, where P is the price and Q is the total quantity produced, each member of an s-size coalition earns at the equilibrium:

---

[1] The size of a coalition is its cardinal.

[2] Throughout the paper, we adopt the following convention : coalitions are denoted by capital letters and their cardinal by the corresponding lower case letter.

$$\pi_S\left(\sum_{t=1}^{n}\alpha_t\right) = \frac{1}{s\left(\sum_{t=1}^{n}\alpha_t + 1\right)^2}. \tag{1}$$

Note that the payment of a player depends not only on the coalition he belongs to but on the whole structure. Therefore in the same structure coalitions are linked. This specific feature of our framework justifies the use of a strategic approach to analyse coalition formation. In this framework, the structure $B = (\alpha_1,...,\alpha_n)$ is Nash-stable if $\sigma^f(B)$ is a Nash equilibrium of the μ-model where μ = Δ or Γ. The set of Nash-stable coalition structures of the μ-model is denoted $E^\mu(N)$. In that case, no player can profit from modifing the structure. But in the model Δ or Γ, because of the definition of strategies, a player alone can only become independent. The unique structure that a player in an i-size coalition of $B = (\alpha_1,...,\alpha_n)$ can impose depends on the model to be used, it is called the *attainable structure*.

Definition 2.4 $B = (\alpha_1,...,\alpha_n) \in E^\mu(N)$ is Nash-stable in the μ-model if :

$$\forall i = 2,...,n \quad \text{such that} \quad \alpha_i \neq 0, \pi_i(B) \geq \pi_i(B_\mu'),$$

with

$$B_\Gamma' = (\alpha_1 + i,...,\alpha_i - 1,...,\alpha_n)$$

and

$$B_\Delta' = (\alpha_1 + 1,...,\alpha_{i-1} + 1,\alpha_i - 1,...,\alpha_n).$$

Proposition 2.1 In the Γ-game,

$$N^\Gamma(N) = \left\{ B = (\alpha_1,...,\alpha_n)/(\alpha_1 = n) \text{ or } \forall i = 2,...,n \text{ with } \alpha_i \neq 0, i \geq \left(\sum_{t=1}^{n}\alpha_t\right)^2\right\}$$

Proof. First note that, by the definition of the stability criterion, the structure in which all the firms are independent is always Nash-stable.

To know if a non trivial structure $B = (\alpha_1,...,\alpha_n)$ is Nash-stable, we have to determine the attainable structure of a firm for each size of coalition in B Consider the deviation of a member of an i-size coalition. After the deviation, the i-size coalition disintegrates and the oligopoly is composed of $\sum_{t=1}^{n}\alpha_t + i - 1$ competitors.

This situation is not advantageous to the deviant member if the following equality is satisfied :

$$\pi_i\left(\sum_{t=1}^{n}\alpha_t\right) = \frac{1}{i\left(\sum_{t=1}^{n}\alpha_t + 1\right)^2} \geq \frac{1}{\left(\sum_{t=1}^{n}\alpha_t + i\right)^2} = \pi_1\left(\sum_{t=1}^{n}\alpha_t + i - 1\right),$$

which leads to the following condition on the size i :

$$i \geq \left(\sum_{t=1}^{n}\alpha_t\right)^2. \qquad (2)$$

We say that the i-size coalition is profitable when i satisfies this condition.

Therefore a non trivial structure $B = (\alpha_1,...,\alpha_n)$ is Nash-stable if all its coalitions are profitable, i.e. if :

$$\forall i = 2,...,n \text{ such that } \alpha_i \neq 0, i \geq \left(\sum_{t=1}^{n}\alpha_t\right)^2. \quad \square$$

Inequality (2) means that the size of non trivial coalitions has to be large enough in relation to the number of competitors. In particular the grand coalition is always Nash-stable in the Γ-model. In the Δ-game cooperation we have the following result :

Proposition 2.2 In the Δ-game if $n > 2, E^\Delta(N) = \{(\alpha_1 = n)\}$.

Proof. In a structure $B = (\alpha_1,...,\alpha_n)$, when a member of a i-size coalition become independent the resulting oligopoly is composed of $\sum_{t=1}^{n}\alpha_t + 1$ competitors. Thus this deviation is advantageous if the following inequality is verified :

$$\pi_1\left(\sum_{t=1}^{n}\alpha_t + 1\right) = \frac{1}{\left(\sum_{t=1}^{n}\alpha_t + 2\right)^2} \geq \frac{1}{i\left(\sum_{t=1}^{n}\alpha_t + 1\right)^2} = \pi_i\left(\sum_{t=1}^{n}\alpha_t\right).$$

This inequality depends on the sign of equation of a polynomial of degree two in $\sum_{t=1}^{n}\alpha_t + 1$. We obtain that the deviation is always advantageous except when i = 2 and $\sum_{t=1}^{n}\alpha_t = 1$, i.e. when n = 2. Therefore, except in the duopoly case the unique

Nash-stable structure is the initial oligopoly in which all the firms are independent.   ☐

3 Endogeneous Reaction

Now, let us introduce in this section a model denoted by Ω in which the depleted coalition chooses its reaction. In the first step the set of players denoted by N and the set of strategies for the player i, denoted by Σ_i^1, are as in both previous models.

Therefore

$$N = \{1, \ldots, n\}$$

and

$$\forall i \in N, \Sigma_i^1 = \{\sigma_i^1 = S_i | S_i \subset N \text{ and } i \in S_i\}.$$

The outcome of the first step of the game is a strategy profile $\sigma^1 = (\sigma_1^1, \ldots, \sigma_n^1)$.

We denote by $N^f(\sigma^1)$ the set of players with feasible strategies. Therefore at the end of the first step, the players of $N^f(\sigma^1)$ know the coalition they belong to. The remaining players have to make a choice again. However in the second step of the game we suppose that the players are not the elements of $N \setminus N^f(\sigma^1)$ but the depleted coalitions generated by σ^1. Therefore in the second step of the game the set of players denoted by $M(\sigma^1)$ is a partition of $N \setminus N^f(\sigma^1)$.

What are the strategies of those coalition-players ? For each coalition-player $I \in M(\sigma^1)$ that contains i members, its strategy σ_I^2 is a consistent strategy profile in Σ_I^1. Moreover we only keep consistent strategy profiles in Σ_I^1 that satisfy assumptions H_1 and H_2. Therefore each coalition-player has to make a choice between falling apart, strategy $\{I\}$ or sticking together, strategy $\langle I \rangle$.

$$\forall I \in M(\sigma^1) \Sigma_I^2 = \{\{I\}, \langle I \rangle\}$$

Therefore the hypothesis that characterizes each of both previous models, is now a strategy for an depleted coalition. Does the depleted coalition decide to disintegrate or to stick together ? The answer is not given as an assumption but it is an outcome of the second step of the game. The outcome of the game Ω is a strategy profile (σ^1, σ^2) that determines a coalition structure $B = (\alpha_1, \ldots, \alpha_n)$. Both of the following propositions characterise the size and the number of coalitions in a Nash-stable structure, and deal with the existence question.

Proposition 3.1   Nash-stable coalition structures are the structure formed by independents and non trivial structures $B = (\alpha_1, ..., \alpha_n)$, such that :

$$\forall i = 2,...,n \text{ with } \alpha_i \neq 0, \left(\sum_{t=1}^{n}\sigma_t +1\right)^2 -1 \geq i \geq \left(\sum_{t=1}^{n}\sigma_t\right)^2 \qquad (3.1)$$

which are called *just profitable coalition structure* (j.p.c.s.).

Proof.   The unique attainable structure of a deviating firm depends on the size of the depleted coalition. Therefore given a structure $B = (\alpha_1, ..., \alpha_n)$, we have to determine the attainable structure of a firm for each size of coalition in B.

Consider the deviation of a member of an i-size coalition. What happens to the depleted coalition ? It compares its aggregated profits in two situations : when it forms a new coalition and when its members are singletons. Then, the depleted coalition forms a new coalition when it is profitable that is when :

$$i-1 \geq \left(\sum_{t=1}^{n}\alpha_t +1\right)^2.$$

Therefore members of a depleted coalition form a new coalition if they are sufficiently numerous and become singletons otherwise. L. S. Shapley made the following suggestion to Hart and Kurz in order to justify their model: the fact that a small number of players leave a coalition should not influence the others' agreement to act together. This intuition appears as a result of our model. Now, to analyse Nash-stability we have to consider three cases :

$$* \ \forall i = 2,...,n \text{ such that } \alpha_i \neq 0, i-1 \geq \left(\sum_{t=1}^{n}\alpha_t +1\right)^2.$$

In this case after all individual deviations members of the depleted coalitions react by forming a new coalition and model Δ is relevant. In this model we saw in the previous section that $(\alpha_1 = n)$ is the unique Nash-stable coalition structure as soon as there are more than two firms.

$$* \ \exists i, 2 < i < n, \alpha_i \neq 0 \text{ such that :}$$

$$\forall j \leq i, \ j-i \leq \left(\sum_{t=1}^{n}\alpha_t +1\right)^2 \text{ and } \forall j \geq i, \ j-i \geq \left(\sum_{t=1}^{n}\alpha_t +1\right)^2.$$

In this case there is no Nash-stable structure. Indeed the Δ-model, in which $(\alpha_1 = n)$ is the unique Nash-stable structure, applies to the largest coalitions.

$$* \ \forall i = 2,...,n \text{ such that } \alpha_i \neq 0, i-1 \leq \left(\sum_{t=1}^{n}\alpha_t +1\right)^2.$$

In this case, after all individual deviations members of the depleted coalition react by becoming singletons and model Γ is relevant. In this model we saw in the previous section that the Nash-stable coalition structures are the structures in which all coalitions are profitable, that is :

$$\forall i = 2,...,n \text{ such that } \alpha_i \neq 0, i-1 \leq \left(\sum_{t=1}^{n} \alpha_t + 1\right)^2.$$

Therefore structures that verify the following condition are Nash-stable :

$$\forall i = 2,...,n \text{ with } \alpha_i \neq 0, \left(\sum_{t=1}^{n} \alpha_t + 1\right)^2 - 1 \geq i \geq \left(\sum_{t=1}^{n} \alpha_t\right)^2. \quad \square$$

Denote by N_+ the set of positive integers and let $F_{n,m}$ be the set of structures formed with m non degenerate coalitions, $n, m \in N_+$. Denote by $E^\Omega(n)$ the set of Nash-stable structures in the Ω-model, when there are n firms in the "initial" oligopoly.

Proposition 3.2 $\forall n$, there exist Nash-stable coalition structures in the Ω-model. Let $\tilde{m}$ be the integer part of $n^{1/3}$, then :

$$\forall m \in N_+, m \leq \tilde{m}, \quad E^\Omega(n) \cap F_{n,m} \neq \emptyset, \text{ and}$$

$$\forall m \in N_+, m < \tilde{m}, \quad E^\Omega(n) \cap F_{n,m} = \emptyset.$$

Proof. The proof uses the following algorithm.

Consider at the beginning of the algorithm the structure in $F_{n,m}$ in which there are m coalitions of size $i_0 = 2$ and $I_0 = n - 2m$ independent firms. At each stage, take one independent and share it out between the m coalitions and repeat the procedure until coalitions are profitable.

If coalitions of size n/m are not yet profitable, then there is no Nash-stable structure with m coalitions, $E^\Omega(n) \cap F_{n,m} = \emptyset$. The algorithm is finished.

Otherwise, there exists a stage t in which the structure composed of m coalitions of size i_t and I_t independents is just profitable. But if i_t is not an integer this structure makes no sense. That means there is no Nash-stable structure with m coalitions of the same integer size. However there exists at least a Nash-stable structure with m coalitions of different integer size. The structure in which coalitions are of size $e(i_t)$ [3] or $e(i_t)+1$ is just profitable. Indeed the upper and the lower bound of the condition (3.1) are integers. Moreover it is always possible to construct such a structure since mi_t is an integer. Therefore $E^\Omega(n) \cap F_{n,m} \neq \emptyset$. The algorithm is finished. $\square$

From this algorithm we deduce that the unique case in which there is no Nash-stable structure with m coalitions is when coalitions of size n/m are not profitable,

---

[3] $e(i_t)$ is the integer part of i_t.

i.e. when n < m³. Denote by $\tilde{m}$ the integer part of $n^{1/3}$. Then, if $m \leq \tilde{m}$, there exist at least a Nash-stable structure. Therefore, since n • 2, there is always a Nash-stable structure with a unique coalition.

Note that here, contrary to both previous models, characteristics of the set of Nash-stable structures depend on n. In this way the grand coalition is not yet Nash-stable as soon as n > 5. Indeed, in the structure $(\alpha_1 = 1, \alpha_{n-1} = 1)$, comparing $\pi(2)$ and $(n-1)\pi(n)$, we can easily verify that the coalition is profitable as soon as n > 5. Thereafter, Nash-stable structures contain more and more coalitions when n increases : a unique coalition when n < 8, no more than two when 8 • n < 27, no more than three when 27 • n < 64, no more than four when 64 • n < 115,...

With Proposition 3.3 it is possible to compare Nash-stable structure to each other.

Proposition 3.3 Let $m \leq \tilde{m}$, then if we compare two kinds of individually stable structure, $B = (\alpha_1, ..., \alpha_n) \in F_{n,m}$ and $B^- = (\alpha_1^-, ..., \alpha_n^-) \in F_{n,m-1}$, we obtain the two following results :

- the number of competitors is always greater in B^- :

$$\sum_{t=1}^{n} \alpha_t^- = m - 1 + I_{m-1} > m + I_m = \sum_{t=1}^{n} \alpha_t . \tag{1}$$

- the average size of coalitions is larger in B^- :

$$\frac{n - I_{m-1}}{m - 1} > \frac{n - I_m}{m} . \tag{2}$$

Proof For all m we have :

$$m i_m + I_m = n . \tag{i}$$

Therefore, a decrease of the number of coalitions must occur with an increase of the size of coalitions and/or an increase with the number of independents. In fact the two variables increase simultaneously. The proof is in two steps. First we prove that when there is an increase of the number of independents there cannot be a non positive variation of the size of coalitions. Otherwise since coalitions are just profitable in B, coalitions in B^- are not profitable. Then we prove that when there is an increase of the size of coalitions there cannot be a non positive variation of the number of independents. Otherwise the increase of the size of coalitions is so great that coalitions in B^- are too profitable.

B_m is composed of m coalitions of size i_m and I_m independents, it is compared with B_{m-1} composed of $m-1$ coalitions of size $i_{m-1} = i_m + \Delta i_m$ and $I_{m-1} = I_m + \Delta I_m$ independents.

From (i) we deduce that:

$$mi_m + I_m = (m-1)(i_m + \Delta i_m) + I_m + \Delta I_m,$$

and then :

$$\Delta I_m = i_m - (m-1)\Delta i_m. \tag{d0}$$

If $\Delta i_m \leq 0$ and $\Delta I_m > 0$, since :

$$(m + I_m + 1)^2 + 1 \geq i_m, \tag{d1}$$

we prove that :

$$i_{m-1} \geq (m - 1 + I_{m-1})^2 \tag{d2}$$

is impossible. From (d0) and (d2) we deduce that :

$$i_m \geq \left[(m-1)(1 - \Delta i_m) + I_m + i_m\right]^2 - \Delta i_m$$

which is incompatible with (d1). Indeed, as soon as $i_m > 2$ we verify that :

$$\left[(m-1)(1 - \Delta i_m) + I_m + i_m\right]^2 - \Delta i_m > (m + I_m + 1)^2 + 1$$

If $\Delta i_m > 0$ and $\Delta I_m \leq 0$, since :

$$(m + I_m)^2 \leq i_m, \tag{d3}$$

we prove that :

$$i_{m-1} \leq (m - 1 + I_{m-1} + 1)^2 + 1 \tag{d4}$$

is impossible. From (d0) and (d4) we deduce :

$$\frac{\left|(m-1)(m + I_m + \Delta I_m)^2 + m - 1 + \Delta I_m\right|}{m} \geq i_m.$$

which is incompatible with (d3). Indeed, we c an easily verify that :

$$(m + I_m)^2 > \frac{\left|(m-1)(m + I_m + \Delta I_m)^2 + m - 1 + \Delta I_m\right|}{m} \quad \square$$

Since total profits $\left(\sum_{t=1}^{n} \alpha_t\right) \pi \left(\sum_{t=1}^{n} \alpha_t\right)$ are a decreasing function of $\sum_{t=1}^{n} \alpha_t$, we deduce from Proposition 3.3 that concentration in a Nash-stable structure increases with the number of coalitions. In this way, when n is large concentration is greater in a Nash-stable structure composed of numerous little coalitions than in a Nash-stable structure with a unique large coalition. To illustrate this proposition, consider the case in which $n = 100$ (Table 1). Concentration is greater when there are 4 coalitions of 25 members than when there is a unique grand coalition of 92 firms.

4 Coalition Deviations

The use of the Nash-stability concept in a model of coalition formation might appear to be unsatisfactory. A concept taking into account coalition deviations would be more relevant. Here, we consider the Coalition-Proof Nash Equilibrium (C.P.N.E.) concept. Using Proposition 3.3 we prove that the C.P.N.E. concept rules out the structure in which firms are all independent and keeps the Nash-stable structure with the most coalitions. We denote by E_P^Ω, the set of structures generated by a C.P.N.E. of the game Ω and we call these structures Coalition-Proof Stable Structures (C.P.S.S). We can write :

Proposition 4.1 If the only Nash-stable structures are $(\alpha_1 = n)$ and the structure with only one coalition and if the members of that coalition have the same profit in the two structures, then:

$$E^\Omega(n) = E_P^\Omega(n)$$

Otherwise, the structure in which all the firms are independent cannot be coalition-proof,

$$(\alpha_1 = n) \notin E_P^\Omega.$$

Proof. First note that the structure in which all the firms are independent cannot be a C.P.S.S if there is another C.P.S.S $B = (\alpha_1', ... \alpha_n')$ with more than one coalition. Indeed, since B is composed of profitable coalitions, the deviation from $(\alpha_1 = n)$ of all the firms forming B is credible and improving for everybody. This deviation is credible because B is a C.P.S.S. It is beneficial to everybody because individual profits of the members of a profitable coalition increase or remain the same when the coalition is formed. Moreover, when this profitable coalition disintegrates, the individual profits of its members, now independent, decrease when other coalitions collapse to form the structure in which there are only independent firms:

$$\forall i\, 2,...,n \quad \text{such that} \quad \alpha_i' \neq 0, \pi_i\left(\sum_{t=1}^n {}''\alpha_t'\right) \geq \pi_1\left(\sum_{t=1}^n {}''\alpha_t' + i\right) > \pi_1(n).$$

However, if the only other C.P.S.S. has a unique coalition, let say of size i such that we can write $B' = \left(\alpha_1' = n - i, \alpha_i' = 1\right)$, it can happen that: $\pi_i(n - i + 1) = \pi_1(n)$. In that case, and in that case only, $(\alpha_1 = n)$ can be a C.P.S.S.

Let $B^I = \left(\alpha_1^I, ..., \alpha_n^I\right)$ be a Nash-stable coalition structure different from $\left(\alpha_1 = n\right)$, and call it the initial structure. Consider a deviation from B^I, to be effective, this deviation has to be improving and credible for the deviating firms. Let $B^T = \left(\alpha_1^I, ..., \alpha_n^I\right)$ be the coalition structure reached after a deviation and call it the target coalition structure. What are the characteristics of a target coalition structure? Because of the definition of a strategy, there are only deviating firms or only non deviating firms in each coalition. Comparing the initial and the target structures two cases have to be analysed: the case in which the number of competitors is unchanged or has increased and the case in which it has decreased.

* If $\sum_{t=1}^{n} \alpha_t^T \geq \sum_{t=1}^{n} \alpha_t^I$, then, the deviation is improving if all the deviating firms are in smaller coalitions. But in this case this coalitions must no longer be profitable.

* If $\sum_{t=1}^{n} \alpha_t^T < \sum_{t=1}^{n} \alpha_t^I$, then a necessary condition for the deviation to be credible is also that all the deviating firms are in smaller coalitions. Otherwise, the coalitions of deviating firms are too profitable. But because the reaction of non deviating firms can only increase the number of competitors, it is impossible to have at the same time a decrease of the number of competitors and a decrease of the size of coalitions of deviating firms.

Therefore, no coalition deviation can be improving and credible from a Nash-stable coalition structure with non trivial coalitions. ☐

The meaning of proposition 4.1 is that, except in a very specific case, when one takes into account coalition deviations, the structure in which all the firms are independent can no longer be stable.

5 Conclusion

We point out in this paper that the analysis of coalition structures and their formation allows one to deal with three different kinds of interaction between symmetrical agents: the interaction between agents that belong to a same coalition, the interaction between different coalitions and the interaction between agents the relationship between whom is altered. Here in particular, we are interested by the latter case, treated as a threat which has to be credible. In the game of coalition formation proposed here, after a deviation, the members of a depleted coalition choose the reaction to adopt. It appears that the members of such a coalition stick together as long as they are sufficiently numerous. As a result, the set of stable structures in this model depends on the number of firms. When this number is reduced the grand coalition is the unique stable structure. Thereafter the number of stable structures and the maximal number of coalitions in a stable structure increase with the size of the initial oligopoly. For intermediate values of n, stable coalition structures have a unique coalition grouping less than the whole. Finally, for large value of n, stable structures appear with several coalitions, that can be of different sizes. This shows that even with identical agents, if interaction is complicated, asymmetric results can occur, and furthermore that in this case, it is the number of agents and not their heterogeity that is relevant.

Table 1

	$b_{100,m}$	$i \neq 1 / \alpha^m_i \geq 1$	$\sum_{i=2}^{100} i\alpha^m_i$	α^m_1	$\sum_{i=1}^{100} \alpha^m_i$
m = 1	$(\alpha_1 = 8, \alpha_{92} = 1)$	92	92	8	9
m = 2	$(\alpha_1 = 4, \alpha_{48} = 2)$,	48	96	4	6
	$(\alpha_1 = 4,$				
	$\alpha_{32} = 1, \alpha_{49} = 1)$	47, 49	96	4	6
m = 3	$(\alpha_1 = 2,$ $\alpha_{32} = 1, \alpha_{33} = 2)$	32, 33	98	2	5
	...				
m = 4	$(\alpha_{25} = 4)$	25	100	0	4
	...				

Legend :

* $i \neq 1/\alpha^m_i \geq 1$: size of coalitions.

* $\sum_{i=1}^{100} i\alpha^m_i$: number of cooperating firms.

* α^m_i : number of independents.

* $\sum_{i=1}^{100} \alpha^m_i$: number of competitors.

References

Bernheim, B.D.; B. Peleg and M.D. Whinston [1987] "Coalition-Proof Nash Equilibria, I Concepts", *Journal of Economic Theory*, Vol. 42, pp. 1-12.

Bernheim, B.D.; B. Peleg and M.D. Whinston [1987] "Coalition-Proof Nash Equilibria, II Applications", *Journal of Economic Theory*, Vol. 42, pp. 13-29.

Bloch, F. [1995] "Endogeneous Structures of Association in Oligopolies", *Rand Journal of Economics*, Vol. 26, pp. 537-556.

Burbidge, J.B., J.A. DePater, G.M. Myers, and A. Sengupta [1994] "Federation as Coalition Formation", mimeo.

Hart, S. and M. Kurz [1983] "Endogenous Formation of Coalitions", *Econometrica*, Vol. 51, n°4, pp. 1047-1064.

Kamien, M., and I. Zang [1988] "The limits of Monopolization Through Acquisition", *Quarterly Journal of Economics*, Vol. CV, n°421, pp. 465-99.

Thoron, S. [1998] "Formation of a Coalition Proof Stable Cartel", *Canadian Journal of Economics,* Vol 31, n°1.

Von Neumann J. and O. Morgenstern [1944] Theory of Games and Economic Behaviour, University Press, Princeton.

Yi, S.S. [1997] "Stable Coalition Structures with Externalities", *Games and Economic Behavior*, Vol 20, pp. 201-237.

Evolutionary Selection of Correlation Mechanisms for Coordination Games

Angelo Antoci[1], Marcello Galeotti[1], and Pier Luigi Sacco[2]

[1] DIMADEFAS, University of Florence, Via C. Lombroso 6/17, 50134 Firenze, Italy
[2] Department of Economics, University of Bologna, Piazza Scaravilli, 2, 40126 Bologna, Italy

Abstract. One of the main problems with the notion of correlated equilibrium is the lack of an explicit rationale for the correlation mechanism that is adopted. This paper investigates the conditions under which a specific correlation mechanism may be selected through a social learning process in a population of boundedly rational players that are randomly matched to play a coordination game. The selection process among correlation mechanisms is defined by replicator equations and the qualitative features of the dynamics are analyzed for the general case with n correlation devices. It is found that the dynamics generically select *one* specific mechanism among the alternative ones, thus bringing about a social standard of choice, i.e. a conventional way of correlating players' actions in anonymous interactions. This result then provides a strong evolutionary rationale for correlated equilibrium as a solution concept for coordination games.

1   Introduction

One problem with the notion of correlated equilibrium is that it provides no explanation as to how players manage to coordinate unless the correlation mechanism is given, known to all and agreed upon in advance by all participants, i.e. unless it is the object of some kind of pre-existing social convention (see e.g. [8]). [4] pointed out this problem but argued that it does not undermine the plausibility of correlated equilibrium as a solution concept. A broad discussion of the informational characteristics of correlated equilibrium is provided by [6]. [12] study the emergence of correlation under the assumption of costly computation. At any rate, as for other game-theoretic solution concepts, the sensibility of correlated equilibria as an instance of rational strategic behavior must ultimately be traced back to the existence of plausible dynamic processes (be they learning, evolutionary processes etc.) that admit them as limit outcomes.

The literature provides many different justifications in this vein. [19] explains the emergence of correlated equilibria through a process of rational deliberation undertaken by Bayesian decision makers. [18] proves that a Bayesian learning process satisfying certain technical conditions in the context of an infinitely repeated game with incomplete information necessarily leads to correlated equilibria of the game with complete information. [14]

prove a somewhat analogous result for a large class of adaptive learning processes in strategic contexts. It is also often suggested that, if players are able to communicate, they should also be able to correlate their actions if this turns out to be profitable; see e.g. [2]. No explicit model of communication has however been provided until recently; [24] has shown that correlated equilibria may indeed arise in cheap talk games with complete information. [22] provide experimental evidence about the role of strategically irrelevant information as useful and efficient correlation devices in coordination games. [20] makes a more fundamental point arguing that correlation should be *built* into any sensible economic model as an essential feature of the structure of realistic strategic interactions. In a somewhat complementary fashion, [13] show that correlation is a natural equilibrium property in a local interaction scenario.

The present paper focuses on the correlation issue from a slightly different point of view, which is related to a certain extent to some of the above mentioned points. In accordance with the 'classical' game-theoretic literature, we do not assume any preexisting source of correlation in the strategic interaction of players. However, we assume that our players, facing a standard coordination problem, will have reason to try to correlate their choices in the underlying anonymous, random matching context and will therefore focus upon possible correlation devices, as an object of choice themselves. In other words, we build an explicit evolutionary model of the social selection of a 'conventional' correlation mechanism from a set of 'feasible' alternatives addressing the following question: under what conditions the selection dynamics will yield a unique mechanism that will be taken by all players as a natural reference to correlate their strategies? If the conditions under which the answer turns out to be affirmative are weak enough, we can conclude that, in general, one can safely take correlated equilibrium as a 'feasible' strategic outcome without much further theoretical elaboration. If however such conditions are found to be pretty restrictive, one should be much more cautious when assuming that players 'can' correlate their strategic behavior if they wish to do so.

We thus aim at building an explicit model that explains how a specific correlation mechanism which is common to all players may be selected among a finite number of available ones. Time is continuous; players are randomly matched from a 'large' population to play a given coordination game. Ours is a two-population model in which players belonging to different 'populations' have different preferences as to the strict Nash equilibrium of the base coordination game; on the other hand, players are always matched to opponents from the other population and have a strong interest to coordinate their choices, as it is in the popular 'battle of sexes' example. We assume that players settle this conflict by trying to correlate their choices according to a suitable scheme. There are, however, many possible correlation devices and players are not sure about the one their opponent has in mind in any single interaction. Thus, in a sense, in our context the real strategic choice does not concern the actual strategy to be played in the base game, but rather the correlation device that determines it on the basis of the realization of a given 'extrinsic' variable. We therefore assume that players' essential concern is finding out the most convenient device to achieve successful correlation with partners from the other population. We model the aggregate selection mechanism among correlation devices by means of the replicator dynamics (see e.g. [9]), which is to be regarded as a convenient and workable 'macro' model of decentralized, imitation-based adaptive social learning process taking place in a large population of players (see e.g. [3]) who have a rather limited perception of the law of motion ruling the social dynamics. According to this specification, at the aggregate level one has that the strategic options that perform better than average are chosen by an increasing proportion of players at the expenses of less rewarding ones; as to individual players, they follow adaptive rules that prompt them to change their choice whenever they happen to meet other players whose behavior improves upon theirs at the *status quo*; of course, behaviors that are not rewarding enough at a given *status quo* could be very rewarding under different conditions (i.e. under a different profile of individual choices).

In the above framework, we find that indeed the replicator learning dynamics always generically selects only one correlation mechanism as a social standard of choice among a finite, given set of alternatives, and therefore provides a strong evolutionary foundation for correlated equilibrium as a useful solution concept for coordination games.

Before closing this introductory section, a few remarks concerning the interpretation of our result and its relationships with the existing literature are in order. There is in principle no contradiction between correlation of individual strategies and bounded rationality; in fact, the eventual selection of a common correlation mechanism at the aggregate level may be seen as the emergence of a convention in the sense of [11] and [21], i.e. as a customary, expected, self-enforcing state of things. Given that all players adopt the same mechanism and that this turns out to be a 'good' choice in that it allows successful coordination between parties, there is reason to expect that players will continue to use the same mechanism in the future, in that no player has an incentive to deviate from it. That conventions may be a natural outcome of bounded rationality has already been argued by [7], [17] and [23] among others.

Other attempts to explain the emergence of coordination through the action of some selection mechanism in an evolutionary environment may be found in the literature. For example, [16] model the selection of coordination mechanisms for common interest games in an evolutionary context with random matching, whereas [15] shows that credible cheap talk can emerge in the same context.

As anticipated, in this paper we focus on a specific coordination game, namely a classical version of the battle of sexes. To fix ideas, in the next section we deal with the simplest case in which only two alternative correlation mechanisms are present in the population of players; the next sections introduce and analyze the evolutionary dynamics for the more general case in which players can choose among n alterative correlation mechanisms for any given n.

2   The model with two correlation mechanisms

Consider the following standard version of the 'battle of sexes' coordination game:

$$
\begin{array}{c c c}
 & S & B \\
S & \gamma^M, \gamma^F & 0,0 \\
B & 0,0 & \delta^M, \delta^F
\end{array}
$$

Players must choose, say, whether to go to the stadium (S) or to the ball-room (B). There are two types of players, 'male' players (M) (row players), who prefer the (S,S) outcome, and 'female' players (F), who prefer (B,B); more precisely we have that the parameters γ^M, γ^F, δ^M, δ^F are such that $\gamma^M > \delta^M > 0$ and $0 < \gamma^F < \delta^F$. There is a continuum of both types of players, who are randomly matched to play the game; matchings are always heterogeneous (i.e., a 'male' with a 'female'). As argued in the previous section, we assume that players cope with their different preferences as to the (strict) Nash equilibrium outcome to be chosen, by trying to correlate their strategic behavior according to some tie-breaking rule. There are two possible correlation mechanisms. The first one is, say, weather conditions (W); players adopting this mechanism go to the stadium if the sun is shining, an event that occurs with probability $1 - \alpha_1$, and go to the ballroom if the sun does not shine; the probability of the latter event is of course α_1. The other mechanism has to do, say, with whether or not a new hit record (R) has been released 'the day before' in music shops (probabilities are, respectively, α_2 and $1 - \alpha_2$). If there has been a release, the player adopting this mechanism goes to the ballroom; if not, she goes to the stadium.

When a pair of players are selected to play the game, neither knows the correlation mechanism adopted by the other, in the absence of an established social standard of choice in this respect. We denote the proportion of male players adopting the two correlation mechanisms by x_1 and x_2, respectively, where x_1, $x_2 \geq 0$ and $x_1 + x_2 = 1$, and the proportions of female players by y_1 and y_2, where y_1, $y_2 \geq 0$ and $y_1 + y_2 = 1$. As anticipated, we assume that the social dynamics of the patterns of adoption evolve according to the replicator dynamics (see [25] for a discussion of the 'representativeness' of the replicator dynamics within the class of payoff-monotonic dynamics[1]).

Under such dynamic specification, the proportions x_1 and y_1 evolve according to the following pair of differential equations (remember that $x_2 = 1 - x_1$ and $y_2 = 1 - y_1$):

$$\dot{x}_1 = x_1 \left\{ \pi^M(W) - \left[x_1 \pi^M(W) + x_2 \pi^M(R) \right] \right\}, \qquad (1a)$$

$$\dot{y}_1 = y_1 \left\{ \pi^F(W) - \left[y_1 \pi^F(W) + y_2 \pi^F(R) \right] \right\}, \qquad (1b)$$

where $\dot{x}_1$, $\dot{y}_1$ indicate time derivatives of x_1, y_1; $\pi^j(W)$ and $\pi^j(R)$ are, respectively, the payoffs from the adoption of mechanisms W and R by the player type $j = M, F$. The terms in the square brackets represent the average (ex ante) payoffs for male and female populations, respectively.

The behavioral implications of (1a)-(1b) have already been discussed above. In particular, the assumption that population dynamics are ruled by ex ante payoffs is standard in evolutionary models with a random matching structure (remember that the population is large, and that therefore strategy[2] payoffs at the aggregate level are equal (with some caveat) to expected payoffs; see e.g. [25]).

We must now compute the returns to the alternative mechanisms available to players as a function of the current strategy profile. Begin with male players. Assume that the selected player adopts R. Denote moreover by mR the event 'the selected male player adopts R', by mW the event 'the selected male player adopts W', and accordingly for fR and fW as to the selected female player. Then the payoff to a male R-player is given by:

$$\pi^M(R) = \gamma^M p(S, S \mid mR) + \delta^M p(B, B \mid mR)$$

Here $p(S, S \mid mR)$ is the probability that the outcome (S, S) occurs given that the selected male player adopts R, whereas $p(B, B \mid mR)$ is the probability that (B, B) occurs under the same circumstance. Denote by A_1 the event 'the sun is shining' and by $-A_1$ the complementary event. Accordingly, denote by A_2 the event 'a new hit record is released' and by $-A_2$ the complementary event. Then one has:

$$p(S, S \mid mR) = p(fR, -A_2 \mid mR) + p(fW, A_1, -A_2 \mid mR) =$$

---

[1] An evolutionary dynamics is said to be payoff-monotonic if relatively more rewarding strategies increase their weight in the population more than relatively less rewarding ones.

[2] In what follows we will denote by 'strategies' the actual behavioral options chosen by players: this means in particular that a player's strategy has to do with the choice of a correlation device, and not with the choice of a strategy of the base game, which follows mechanically from the former.

$$= (1 - \alpha_1)(1 - \alpha_2)y_1 + (1 - \alpha_2)y_2$$

$$p(B, B \mid mR) = p(fR, A_2 \mid mR) + p(fW, A_2, -A_1 \mid mR) =$$

$$= \alpha_2 \alpha_1 y_1 + \alpha_2 y_2$$

It therefore follows that:

$$\pi^M(R) = \gamma^M \left[(1 - \alpha_1)(1 - \alpha_2)y_1 + (1 - \alpha_2)y_2 \right] + \delta^M \left[\alpha_2 \alpha_1 y_1 + \alpha_2 y_2 \right] =$$

$$= \left[\gamma^M (1 - \alpha_1)(1 - \alpha_2) + \delta^M \alpha_1 \alpha_2 \right] y_1 + \left[\gamma^M (1 - \alpha_2) + \delta^M \alpha_2 \right] y_2$$

With similar computations we obtain:

$$\pi^M(W) = \left[\gamma^M (1 - \alpha_1) + \delta^M \alpha_1 \right] y_1 + \left[\gamma^M (1 - \alpha_1)(1 - \alpha_2) + \delta^M \alpha_1 \alpha_2 \right] y_2$$

Analogously, for female players we obtain:

$$\pi^F(R) = \left[\gamma^F (1 - \alpha_1)(1 - \alpha_2) + \delta^F \alpha_1 \alpha_2 \right] x_1 + \left[\gamma^F (1 - \alpha_2) + \delta^F \alpha_2 \right] x_2$$

and

$$\pi^F(W) = \left[\gamma^F (1 - \alpha_1) + \delta^F \alpha_1 \right] x_1 + \left[\gamma^F (1 - \alpha_1)(1 - \alpha_2) + \delta^F \alpha_1 \alpha_2 \right] x_2$$

Notice that letting

$$A_M \equiv \begin{pmatrix} \gamma^M (1 - \alpha_1) + \delta^M \alpha_1 & \gamma^M (1 - \alpha_1)(1 - \alpha_2) + \delta^M \alpha_1 \alpha_2 \\ \gamma^M (1 - \alpha_1)(1 - \alpha_2) + \delta^M \alpha_1 \alpha_2 & \gamma^M (1 - \alpha_2) + \delta^M \alpha_2 \end{pmatrix}$$

and

$$A_F \equiv \begin{pmatrix} \gamma^F (1 - \alpha_1) + \delta^F \alpha_1 & \gamma^F (1 - \alpha_1)(1 - \alpha_2) + \delta^F \alpha_1 \alpha_2 \\ \gamma^F (1 - \alpha_1)(1 - \alpha_2) + \delta^F \alpha_1 \alpha_2 & \gamma^F (1 - \alpha_2) + \delta^F \alpha_2 \end{pmatrix}$$

we can write:

$$\pi^M(W) = e_1^t A_M y$$

$$\pi^F(W) = e_1^t A_F x$$

$$x_1 \pi^M(W) + x_2 \pi^M(R) = x^t A_M y$$

$$y_1 \pi^F(W) + y_2 \pi^F(R) = y^t A_F x$$

where $e_1^t = (1, 0)$, $x^t = (x_1, x_2)$ and $y^t = (y_1, y_2)$.

The following result offers a complete characterization of the dynamics for the simple two-options case:

Proposition 1. *If the correlation devices are two, the fixed points are five, namely, the four vertices (points where $x_i = y_j = 1$ for some pair i, j) and one saddle in the interior of $S^1 \times S^2$. The vertices $x_i = y_i = 1$, $i = 1, 2$, are sinks, whereas the vertices $x_i = y_j = 1$, $i \neq j$, are sources.*

The proof of proposition 1 is straightforward. Such proposition shows that the case in which only two correlation devices are present is 'well-behaved' from our point of view: apart from the special case in which the initial strategy profile lies upon the stable manifold of the interior saddle, one of the two correlation mechanisms always takes over eventually, thus providing a strong case for the social salience of the corresponding correlated equilibrium. More specifically, the mechanism that prevails is, quite intuitively, the one that is initially adopted by a 'large enough' proportion of players, both male and female.

We should now ask under if the basic features of the 'bistable', nicely behaved dynamics found above carries over to the general case. We will show that for the general case in which the correlation devices are $n > 2$ we still typically have a 'multistable' dynamics, in the sense that all the fixed points in which both male and female players follow a same, unique correlation mechanism are locally attractive and there are no other strategy profiles that are attractors.

3   The general case

The payoff structure derived in the previous section for the simple two-options case can be extended to the case of n correlation devices to obtain the replicator equations for the general model. We adopt the following notations. α_i, $0 < \alpha_i < 1$, is the probability of the event A_i, $i = 1, 2, ..., n$, that characterizes the i-th correlation device (i.e., strategy). If A_i takes place, the player adopting that strategy is willing 'to go to the ballroom', earning (provided that the opponent does the same) $\delta_M > 0$ if male, $\delta_F > 0$ if female. If $-A_i$ takes place, with probability $1 - \alpha_i$, the player is willing 'to go to the stadium', with payoffs $\gamma_M > \delta_M$ and $0 < \gamma_F < \delta_F$ according to cases. Needless to say, all convex combinations of the (strict) Nash equilibrium outcomes of the base game are correlated equilibria, and therefore all the corresponding correlation devices are eligible as socially salient coordination mechanisms. Let $p_M \equiv \frac{\gamma_M}{\gamma_M + \delta_M}$, $p_F \equiv \frac{\gamma_F}{\gamma_F + \delta_F}$, $k_M \equiv \gamma_M + \delta_M$ and $k_F \equiv \gamma_F + \delta_F$. Then $0 < p_F < 1/2 < p_M < 1$.

The replicator equations can now be written in the following form:

$$\dot{x}_i = k_M x_i \left(e_i^t A_M y - x^t A_M y \right), \tag{2a}$$

$$\dot{y}_i = k_F y_i \left(e_i^t A_F x - y^t A_F x \right), \tag{2b}$$

$i = 1, 2, ..., n$. x_i and y_i are the proportions of the male and female players adopting the i-th strategy, $0 \leq x_i, y_i \leq 1$, where $\sum_{i=1}^{n} x_i = \sum_{i=1}^{n} y_i = 1$,

$x^t = (x_1, x_2, ...x_n)$, $y^t = (y_1, y_2, ..., y_n)$, letting as usual $e_i^t = (0, ..., 1, ..., 0)$ with 1 at the i-th place. The $A_{M,F} = \left(a_{ij}^{M,F}\right)$ are symmetric square matrices of order n whose generic entry is

$$a_{ij}^{M,F} = p_{M,F}(1 - \alpha_i - \alpha_j) + \alpha_i \left[\delta_{i,j} + (1 - \delta_{i,j})\alpha_j\right]$$

$\delta_{i,j}$ being the Dirac symbol.

The dynamics (2a)-(2b) takes place in $S^1 \times S^2$, S^1 and S^2 being respectively the $(n-1)$-dimensional simplex of proportions in the male and female populations. Thus $S^1 \times S^2$ is a $2(n-1)$-dimensional 'prism'.

The following result provides the extension of the results for the $n = 2$ case.

Proposition 2. *The game under consideration is a 'rescaled partnership game* [3] *with potential function:*

$$P(x, y) = \sum_i \alpha_i(1 - \alpha_i)x_i y_i + (\sum_i \alpha_i x_i - p_F)(\sum_i \alpha_i y_i - p_M)$$

Such result can be easily deduced from theorem 27.2.1. of [9].

Proposition 2 implies in particular that:

(a) $P(x, y)$ is a monotonically increasing Lyapunov function under equations (2a)-(2b);

(b) every trajectory converges to a Nash equilibrium;

(c) 'almost every' trajectory converges to a pure Nash equilibrium;

(d) all the vertices of $S^1 \times S^2$ in which $x_i = y_i = 1$, $i = 1, ..., n$, are locally attractive [such vertices are local maxima of P];

(e) all eigenvalues at all fixed points are real; this implies that if a hyperbolic fixed point exists in the interior of $S^1 \times S^2$, then it is a saddle with a $(n-1)$-dimensional stable manifold and a $(n-1)$-dimensional unstable manifold[4].

The above results tell us that all the fixed points in which the same correlation device is followed by all (male and female) individuals are locally attractive under the dynamics (2a)-(2b)[5]. Therefore, if a 'large enough' initial proportion of male and female players adopt a given correlation mechanism, then such mechanism will eventually become conventional for all players. Furthermore, 'almost every' trajectory approaches one of such fixed points. In any case, every trajectory converges to a fixed point. Consequently, the dynamics for the general case with $n > 2$ are the 'natural' extension of those of the 'nicely behaved' $n = 2$ case.

---

[3] For the definition of 'rescaled partnership game' see [9] chapter 27.

[4] See chapters 17 and 27 of [9].

[5] This result has of course intuitive appeal, in that mechanisms are chosen in order to enhance coordination, and the best way of pursuing this goal must be looking at the same external signal.

The existence of a potential function P thus allows us to operate an equilibrium selection, by choosing the global maximizer of P (see chapter 27 of [9]). Since the only local maxima are the vertices $x_i = y_i = 1$, where $P = \alpha_i(1 - p_M - p_F)$ (up to an additive constant), the 'best' equilibrium (i.e. the best correlation device) is the i which maximizes α_i, in the case $p_M + p_F < 1$ (which amounts to asking that 'going to the ballroom' is the risk dominant equilibrium of the original coordination game), and the i which minimizes α_i, in the case $p_M + p_F > 1$ [the alternative case in which 'going to the stadium' is risk-dominant].

4   Conclusions

The model studied in this paper might be extended in many possible ways. An obvious one concerns a further broadening of the set of the available correlation mechanisms: i.e. considering an infinite or even uncountable menu of mechanisms; whether this possibility entails more room for 'complex' dynamic behavior leading away from monomorphic multi-population states is an open but far from irrelevant question.

Another promising extension has to do with an explicit characterization of the choice processes of individual players, e.g. in the spirit of [26]. A development of special interest would be that of differentiating players not only in terms of their 'strategy' choice but also in terms of idiosynchratic 'perception lags', i.e., say, players of type τ are able to observe at time t only payoffs obtained at time $t - \tau$ (and, of course, at earlier times). Alternatively, players could be only able to process information about payoffs with an idiosynchratic delay. [10] have shown that this kind of heterogeneity in players' characteristics may generate interesting as well as very complex dynamic behavior. Finally, players might be characterized by more sophisticated learning mechanisms than imitation of successful strategies or best-reply to the observed *status quo*, and in particular by expectational schemes incorporating, say, conjectures about the future unfolding of the social dynamics or spare bits of 'structural' knowledge, in the presence of adjustment costs or of other sources of 'behavioral inertia' (see e.g. [1]). All these possibilities, among others, are open to future research.

4.1   Acknowledgements

We are grateful to Peter Hammond and Josef Hofbauer for very useful comments and suggestions. A special thank to Marco Sandri for some technical advices. The usual disclaimer applies.

References

1. Antoci A., Sacco P.L. (1997), Expectations-driven inertial evolutionary dynamics, mimeo, University of Florence.

2. Aumann R.J. (1987), Correlated equilibrium as an expression of Bayesian rationality, Econometrica **55**, 1-18.
3. Bjornerstedt J., Weibull J. (1996), Nash equilibrium and evolution by imitation, in Arrow K.J., Colombatto E., Perlman M., Schmidt C. (eds.), The rational foundations of economic behavior, Macmillan, London, 155-171.
4. Brandeburger A. , Dekel E. (1987), Rationalizability and correlated equilibria, Econometrica **55**, 1391-1402.
5. Cressman R. (1996), Local stability of smooth selection dynamics for normal-form games, mimeo, Wilfrid Laurier University.
6. Forges F. (1986), An approach to communication equilibria, Econometrica **54**, 1375-1385.
7. Gilbert M. (1990), Convention, Synthese **84**, 1-22.
8. Hammond P. (1993), Aspects of rationalizable behavior, in Binmore K., Kirman A.P., Tani P. (eds.), Frontiers of game theory, Mit Press, Cambridge, Mass.
9. Hofbauer J. , Sigmund K. (1988), The theory of evolution and dynamical systems, Cambridge University Press, Cambridge.
10. Huberman B. , Hogg T. (1988), The behavior of computational ecologies, in Huberman B. (ed.), The ecology of computation, North Holland, Amsterdam.
11. Lewis D. (1969), Convention. A philosophical study, Harvard University Press, Cambridge, Mass.
12. Lipman B.L., Srivastava S. (1990), Computation as a correlation device, Games and Economic Behavior **2**, 154-172.
13. Mailath G.J., Samuelson L., Shaked A. (1995), Correlated equilibria and local interactions, mimeo, University of Bonn.
14. Marimon R. , McGrattan E. (1993), On adaptive learning in strategic games, in Kirman A.P. , Salmon M. (eds.), Learning and rationality in economics, Basil Blackwell, Oxford, 63-101.
15. Matsui A. (1991), Cheap-talk and cooperation in a society, Journal of Economic Theory **54**, 245-258.
16. Matsui A. , Rob R. (1991), The roles of public information and preplay communication in evolutionary games, CARESS Working Paper no. 91-10.
17. Miller S. (1990), Rationalising conventions, Synthese **84**, 23-41.
18. Nyarko Y. (1992), Bayesian learning in repeated games leads to correlated equilibria, mimeo, New York University.
19. Skyrms B. (1989), Correlated equilibria and the dynamics of rational deliberation, Erkenntnis **31**, 347-364.
20. Skyrms B. (1994), Darwin meets *The logic of decision*: Correlation in evolutionary game theory, Philosophy of Science **61**, 503-528.
21. Sugden R. (1989), Spontaneous order, Journal of Economic Perspectives **3**, 85-97.
22. Van Huyck J.B., Battalio R.C., Rankin F.W.(1997), On the origin of conventions: Evidence from coordination games, Economic Journal **107**, 576-596.
23. Wärneryd K. (1990), Conventions: An evolutionary approach, Constutional Political Economy **1**, 83-107.
24. Wärneryd K. (1992), Communication, correlation, and symmetry in bargaining, Economics Letters **39**, 295-300.
25. Weibull J. (1995), Evolutionary game theory, Mit Press, Cambridge, Mass.
26. Young P. (1993), The evolution of conventions, Econometrica **61**, 57-84.

The Propagation of Cooperation in a Spatial Model of Learning with Endogenous Aspirations

Paolo Lupi*

The University of York
Department of Economics and Related Studies
Heslington, York, YO1 5DD, United Kingdom

Abstract. In this paper we build a spatial, aspiration-based model of learning in the context of a quantity setting oligopoly from which we want to explore the conditions that lead to the emergence of cooperation among firms. We consider an economy consisting of many identical duopolies; each duopoly is placed on a square of a torus. The duopolists are boundedly rational agents which adopt a very simple behavioural rule: if they are earning at least average profits, they do not change their strategies; if they are earning below-average profits they imitate the strategy adopted by one of their neighbours. We consider many variations to this general setting and, in most of the cases, we get results that support cooperation among firms.

1 Introduction

The issue of the emergence of cooperation among individuals has been widely discussed by a large number of game theorists, economists, biologists and in the behavioural sciences in general. The reason for all this interest, especially by part of economists and game theorists, probably lies in the fact that cooperative behaviour is something that is frequently observable in many economic and social contexts and that, as many argue, traditional game theory fails to explain.

In the past two decades many theories have been devised to explain how and why cooperation, at least to a certain degree, may emerge as the final result of an evolutionary process. Several of these theories are grounded on the seminal work of Axelrod and Hamilton [3] and Axelrod [2] who showed, by means of computer simulations, that cooperative behaviour is the possible outcome of repeated interaction among agents that change their action following some adaptive behavioural rule. They identified the reason underlying

* The development of this paper started during the III Graduate Workshop in Computational Economics (14–29 July 1997) held at the Santa Fe Institute, whose hospitality and financial support is gratefully acknowledged. The author would like to thank John Miller, Scott Page and all workshop participants for helpful comments and suggestions. This work is part of the ESRC project "Evolution, Oligopoly and Competitiveness."

the emergence of cooperation in the fear of future retaliation by part of other individuals in case of individualistic behaviour. In Axelrod [2], in addition, it is shown that the probability of the evolution of the system towards a cooperative equilibrium is greatly increased if, in a model of imitative behaviour, a form of localisation of the players and local interaction is assumed and modelled. If, in fact, agents are placed on a spatial structure or on a network of social interactions and the probability of being matched with another agent depends on some criterion of proximity that puts higher weight on the interaction between nearer agents, then clusters of agents that adopt cooperative strategies[1] may form and propagate over the space of interaction.

More recently a few papers have appeared in the literature on evolutionary games and learning that explicitly study the implications of local interaction in games when some form of limitation on players rationality is assumed. Blume [4], for instance, considers the case of 2×2 symmetric coordination games played by agents who live on a lattice and interact only with a limited number of neighbouring agents. He finds that, under myopic best response dynamics, possibly perturbed by random choices, the risk dominant equilibrium[2] is selected in the limit; the same findings, unfortunately, not always apply to $n \times n$ games. In a similar fashion Ellison [8] studies a local interaction version of the Kandori et al. [11] model of stochastic best-reply and finds that with local interaction, convergence toward the final risk dominant equilibrium is achieved more quickly than with global interaction, and that the speed of convergence is inversely related to the size of the neighbourhood.

Anderlini and Ianni [1] study a similar setting characterised by a finite population of agents that are at every time t matched with one of their neighbours to play a pure coordination game. Agents update their strategies following a majority rule whose outcome depends on the proportion of agents playing each of the two available strategies. The agents' choice of action is also affected by some form of inertia. They find that the resulting dynamical system converges with probability one to a steady state, but since the system shows path dependence, many limiting states are possible including a state in which only local coordination occurs.

Our model differs from the literature above in several ways. The main difference lies in the fact that our unit of investigation is not the single agent, but the pair of agents. In fact, we consider a population of duopolies placed on a two-dimensional connected square lattice (a torus). Matching, as in Dixon [6] and Dixon and Lupi [7], is therefore "permanent" in the sense that agents, firms in our case, face the same competitor over time, and are not allowed to move and/or change competitor.

---

[1] That are strategies that usually perform well when played against themselves, but not so well when played against others.

[2] Which, as known, is the equilibrium with the largest basin of attraction in the space of possible mixed strategies.

Every cell on the lattice can be thought as a location or a market where two competitors face each other in duopolistic competition. The more natural interpretation of a location is of a position in a geographical space, but it may also be considered as a position in the "space of products" where neighbouring cells are occupied by firms producing a slightly differentiated product.

Firms at every duopoly adopt a very simple imitative rule based on aspirations in their decision making: at every time t they compare their actual profits with an aspiration level which is endogenously determined on the basis of the average profit in their neighbourhood. If their profits are at least equal to this aspiration level they stick to the strategy used in the previous round of action. On the other hand, if their profits fall short of the aspiration level they revise their strategy by imitating the strategy of another, randomly chosen, firm in their neighbourhood.

We consider two variations to this simple learning rule. According to the first, we let the probability of revising the strategy of unsatisfied firms vary with the difference between their current profits and the average level of profits in the neighbourhood. In other words firms for which the difference between current profits and the average level of profits in the neighbourhood is substantial will be more likely to change their strategy with respect to firms that experience a lower difference. This rule may reflect the presence of inertia in the strategy revision procedure or some form of lock-in motivated by technological reasons or by the presence of switching costs.

We have also studied a perturbed version of our model. According to this "noisy" version unsatisfied firms may, with (a small) probability ϵ make a mistake in their imitation procedure and end up choosing a new strategy at random. Noise, as customary in evolutionary models, is also introduced to test the robustness of the model.

The fact the firms can only imitate the strategies adopted by a subset of the population of firms (the firms in their neighbourhood) reflects the presence of costs of gathering information about the strategies and the performance of firms located in distant locations. This "limitation" could also be explicitly desired by firms. In fact, especially in the case where we interpret the cells of the lattice as locations or markets in a geographical space, firms may not be interested in imitating the strategy of firms far-off on the lattice, because they could think that those strategies might not be very effective in their area due to spatial differences in the "fundamentals" of the economy.

Despite the localisation of interaction, the behaviour of a firm, not only directly influences the behaviour of its direct competitor in the duopoly, but can also indirectly propagate to more distant agents by successively influencing the choices of locally interconnected neighbours via both the local average mechanism and the imitation procedure.

Even though the model is quite simple, the nature of interaction among firms is very complex. There are, as we have seen, different levels of interactions among firms: at a very local level (the location or duopoly level) firms interact with their competitors in the duopoly game, at an intermediate level they interact with the firms in their neighbourhood via the imitation mechanism and, in the case where the average level of profits is computed over the whole "economic system" there is also a global level of interaction in which every firm indirectly interacts with all the others by means of the global level of average profits.

The complexity of the interactions makes extremely difficult, if not impossible, to analyze analytically our model (a problem common to many models of spatial interaction). For this reason the analysis of the dynamical system will rely mainly on computer simulations.

We will give full account of the results of our simulations in section 3, but we can anticipate here that in almost all the simulations we got convergence to the cooperative equilibrium characterised by all firms playing the joint profit maximising strategy. This result is also robust to small levels of "noise".

The reminder of the paper is structured in the following way: in section 2 we introduce the formal model, in section 3 we report and discuss the results of the simulations, section 4 contains some concluding remarks.

2 The model

2.1 The spatial structure

Consider an "economy" of duopolies placed on a two-dimensional connected square lattice. Every cell on the lattice is the address of a pair of firms permanently tied to play a duopoly game using quantities as strategies.

We identify every duopoly by $d(x, y)$, where x and y are the horizontal and vertical coordinates of the cell on the lattice occupied by the duopoly. If the number of rows and columns is equal to K (a square lattice) we have that the duopoly space is $\mathcal{D} = \{1, \dots, K\} \times \{1, \dots, K\}$ and its cardinality $|\mathcal{D}|$ is, of course, equal to K^2.

We measure the distance $\text{dist}\,[d(x, y); d(u, v)]$ between any two cells or duopolies $d(x, y)$ and $d(u, v)$ using a modified version of the metric induced by the $\|x\|_\infty$ norm, that takes into account the fact that in our case distances are measured over a connected lattice (a torus). According to this metric we have that:

$$\text{dist}\,[d(x, y); d(u, v)] = \max\{\, \min\,[|\, x - u \,|, K - |\, x - u \,|]\, ,$$
$$\min\,[|\, y - v \,|, K - |\, y - v \,|]\}\, .$$

In other words the distance between any two duopolies is given by the minimal number of duopolies that must be crossed (in all directions, including diagonals and allowing for border-crossing) in order to go from the first to the second. We define the neighbourhood of radius ρ of duopoly $d(x, y)$, $N^\rho_{x,y}$ as the set:

$$N_{x,y}^{\rho} = \{d(u,v) \in \mathcal{D} \mid \text{dist}\,[d(x,y); d(u,v)] \le \rho\}\ ,$$

that is the set containing all cells or duopolies located within ρ distance from $d(x,y)$.[3] This formalisation of the neighbourhood relation is symmetric: for all $d(x,y), d(v,u) \in \mathcal{D}$, the fact that $d(u,v) \in N_{x,y}^{\rho}$ implies that $d(x,y) \in N_{u,v}^{\rho}$. We denote the number of duopolies in the neighbourhood of size ρ of $d(x,y)$ by $|N_{x,y}^{\rho}| = (2\rho + 1)^2$ and, since at each duopoly there are two firms we have that the total number of firms in $N_{x,y}^{\rho}$ is $2|N_{x,y}^{\rho}|$. Figure 1 shows two neighbourhoods characterised by two different values of the parameter ρ; the locations depicted as grey circles constitute the neighbourhood of the location depicted as a black circle. Every circle represents a duopoly.

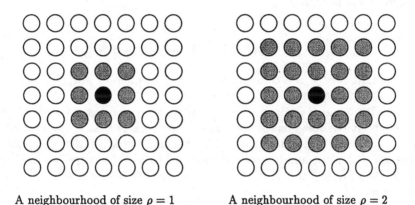

A neighbourhood of size $\rho = 1$ A neighbourhood of size $\rho = 2$

Fig. 1. The neighbourhood structure

We have, due to computational constraints, restricted the size of the square lattices to values of $K \le 10$ (corresponding to a population of $N \le 100$ duopolies), however the results of the simulations have shown that the value of K, for K sufficiently large i.e. $K \ge 6$, does not affect significantly the final outcome, at least in terms of the limiting distributions of the evolutionary processes.

Even though geographical structures such as torii (checkerboards where the edges are pasted together) do not exist in real world, we have decided to adopt these structures on the grounds of their capability to avoid "boundary effects", i.e. the ability to maintain the number of duopolies in the neighbourhood of each duopoly constant independently of the position of the duopoly on the lattice.

---

[3] The neighbourhood relation we have defined, is also known, in the theory of cellular automata, as Moore neighbourhood.

2.2 The duopoly game

The set of all firms f in the economy is denoted by $\mathcal{F}$, since at each location or duopoly $d(x,y) \in \mathcal{D}$ there are two firms, the number of the elements of the set $\mathcal{F}$ is $|\mathcal{F}| = 2|\mathcal{D}|$.

We define the index function $g(f,x,y)$ as the function that returns 1 if and only if firm f operates at duopoly $d(x,y)$ and 0 otherwise:

$$g(f,x,y) = \begin{cases} 1 & \text{iff } f \text{ is at } d(x,y) \\ 0 & \text{otherwise} . \end{cases}$$

The set $f^N \subseteq \mathcal{F}$ is the set of all firms f in the neighbourhood $N^\rho_{x,y}$ of duopoly $d(x,y)$ and it is defined as:

$$f^N = \{ f \in \mathcal{F} | g(f,x,y) = 1 \text{ and } d(x,y) \in N^\rho_{x,y} \} .$$

We say that firm f' is a competitor of firm f at duopoly $d(x,y)$ if and only if $g(f,x,y,) = g(f',x,y) = 1$.

At each location or duopoly $d(x,y)$ there are two firms f and f' playing the simplest possible quantity settings duopoly game that is assumed to be the same everywhere on the lattice. The market price $p_{x,y}$ at $d(x,y)$ is a linear function with slope and intercept normalised to 1 of the outputs q produced by the two firms f and f'. That is to say, dropping the location subscripts for convenience:

$$p = \max \left[0, 1 - q^f - q^{f'} \right] ,$$

where both q^f and $q^{f'}$ are non-negative. The profits of each firm f are therefore $\pi^f = q^f\, p$. We have not explicitly included costs in the demand function, but we can interpret the price as net of constant average production costs.

In this simple duopoly model, the outputs of the two firms are strategic substitutes (the best-response functions are downward sloping), and the payoff of each firm is decreasing (when positive) in the output of the other firm. In order to generate a finite strategy set for this model, we constructed a grid of outputs, so that each strategy is an output level. The (symmetric) $S \times S$ payoff matrix Π gives the payoffs $\pi_{i,j}$ to the firm producing output levels $i = 1 \ldots S$ when the other firm is producing output levels $j = 1 \ldots S$.

According to this specification of the demand function, the Cournot-Nash outcome occurs when both firms produce a quantity equal to 1/3 at a price of 1/3 earning a profit per firm of 1/9. The joint profit maximising outcome (JPM) occurs when both firms produce a quantity equal to 1/4 earning 1/8 profits. Table 1 shows some of the key reference points of the model.

Table 1. The duopoly model: reference points

Outcome	Output	Profits per firm
Cournot-Nash Equilibrium	$q^f = q^{f'} = 1/3$	0.1111
Joint-Profit Maximum	$q^f = q^{f'} = 1/4$	0.1250
Stackelberg	$q^f = 1/2 , q^{f'} = 1/4$	0.1250 , 0.0625
Walrasian	$1 - q^f - q^{f'} = 0$	0

The elements of set of outputs (or strategies) we use in our simulations come from a grid of evenly spaced points over the interval $[0.1, 0.6]$.[4] The granularity of the grid is 0.05 resulting in 11 output levels; we have slightly modified the grid in order to include the Cournot firm (output 0.3333). In the remainder of the paper we will indifferently refer to the 0.125 strategy as the JPM or the cooperative strategy. The outputs used in the simulations are shown in table 2. In some simulations we let the firms choose their strategies (outputs levels) from the closed interval $[0.1, 0.6]$. In this case the strategy space is $\mathcal{S} = [0.1, 0.6] \times [0.1, 0.6]$.

Table 2. Set of outputs used in the simulations

0.1	0.15	0.2	0.25[a]	0.3	0.3333[b]	0.4	0.45	0.5	0.55	0.6

[a] Joint profit maximisation output.
[b] Cournot-Nash output.

2.3 Aspirations and learning

We have modelled firms as boundedly rational agents that use a very simple behavioural rule based on aspirations in their decision making. Each firm at each duopoly has an aspiration level of profits: if it is earning at least this level of profits it continues to adopt the same strategy it was previously using, if it is earning below aspiration profits it "experiments" a new strategy by imitating the strategy adopted by one of the firms in its neighbourhood. In our model the aspiration level is endogenous and equal to the average level of profits in the neighbourhood.

According to this behavioural rule a strategy can be considered as a routine that is kept in use as far as it provides to the firm a satisfactory level of profits. It should be noted that the experimenting firm does not take into

---

[4] We have decided to restrict the range of the grid to the interval $[0.1, 0.6]$ because this restriction speeded up the simulations by leaving out many zero-profit pairs of strategies. Furthermore the outcome of the simulations is not affected by this restriction.

account any strategic consideration when revising its strategy, it simply observes a randomly chosen firm in its neighbourhood and imitates its strategy (that could be the same strategy it was using). Consequently the probability for a strategy of being imitated by an experimenting firm depends exclusively on the number of firms in the neighbourhood adopting that strategy.

If we define the profits of each firm at $d(x,y) \in \mathcal{D}$ as $\pi_{x,y}^f$, we have that the average level of profits in the neighbourhood $N_{x,y}^\rho$ of duopoly $d(x,y)$ is:

$$\bar{\pi}_{x,y} = \frac{1}{2|N_{x,y}^\rho|} \sum_{f \in f^N} \pi_{x,y}^f \ . \tag{1}$$

When $2\rho + 1 = K$, that is when the size of the neighbourhood equals the size of the lattice i.e. the interaction is global, the average level of profits is given by:

$$\bar{\pi} = \frac{1}{2K^2} \sum_{f \in \mathcal{F}} \left(\pi_{x,y}^f \right) \ . \tag{2}$$

At every time t each firm f carries out its strategy revision procedure by comparing its profits with the neighbourhood average. The outcome of this comparison determines what we call the learning state of the firm. We say, in fact, that a firm f is in learning state 0 and does not experiment if it is fulfilling its aspirations (it is earning a profit at least equal to the local average), on the other hand, a firm f is in learning state 1 and it does experiment if it is not fulfilling its aspirations (it is earning below local average profits). According to the learning state of the firms we can also partition the set of all firms into two mutually exclusive partitions $\mathcal{L}_0$ and $\mathcal{L}_1$ whose elements are defined in the following way:

$$\mathcal{L}_0 = \{f \in f^N | \pi^f \geq \bar{\pi}_{x,y}\}$$
$$\mathcal{L}_1 = \{f \in f^N | \pi^f < \bar{\pi}_{x,y}\} \ .$$

All firms in the set $\mathcal{L}_1$ (below aspiration firms) will choose the strategy to adopt in the following period by means of a simple imitative rule: they randomly sample a firm in their neighbourhood and adopt its strategy; as a consequence the probabilities of switching from any strategy to any other will depend on the frequency of adoption of each strategy in the neighbourhood: the higher the proportion of firms adopting a certain strategy, the higher the probability for that strategy of being adopted by below aspiration firms. Firms in $\mathcal{L}_0$ (above aspiration firms) will "stay."

In order to compute the switching probabilities let's first define the function $I(s,t,x,y)$ that returns the number of firms f in the neighbourhood

$N_{x,y}^{\rho}$ of duopoly $d(x,y)$ playing strategy $s \in S$ at time t. We can obtain the proportion $P_t(s)$ of firms in neighbourhood $N_{x,y}$ adopting strategy $s \in S$ at time t as:

$$P_t(s) = \frac{I(s,t,x,y)}{2|N_{x,y}^{\rho}|} \; . \tag{3}$$

We are now in a position to define the probability $\mu_{x,y}^{0,t}(s,s')$ for a firm $f \in \mathcal{L}_0$ adopting strategy s at time t of switching to strategy $s' \in S$ at time $t+1$. This probability is given by:

$$\mu_{x,y}^{0,t}(s,s') = \begin{cases} 1 & \text{if } s' = s \\ 0 & \text{otherwise} \, . \end{cases} \tag{4}$$

On the other hand, the probability $\mu_{x,y}^{1,t}(s,s')$ for a firm $f \in \mathcal{L}_1$ adopting strategy s at time t to switch to strategy $s' \in S$ at time $t+1$ is given by:

$$\mu_{x,y}^{1,t}(s,s') = P_t(s') \, . \tag{5}$$

Note that when $2\rho + 1 = K$, i.e. the size of the neighbourhood coincides with the size of the lattice, firms take their decisions on the basis of global average profits and can, if unsatisfied, imitate the strategy adopted by any other firm in the "population"; in this case our model looses its locational features becoming a model of global interaction.

As in KirchKamp [12] and Hoffman and Waring [9], we have that the localisation of action which happens at the duopoly level, differs from the localisation of learning, which happens at the neighbourhood level. In fact, it is not clear why they should coincide: in many economic situations agents apply locally strategies which are chosen on the basis of global information; learning in this model is "social" rather than strategic.

In section 3 we also explore the case where firms compute their aspiration levels of the basis of global average profits, but restrict the "pool" of firms to imitate to the local neighbourhood. This particular specification of the width of the neighbourhoods can, in a way, be used to model situations where there are some institutions, (financial markets, for instance) that centrally process and distribute information about the performance of agents. This information is then used by agents in order to assess the effectiveness of their strategies, but given the presence of costs in observing the strategies adopted by other agents, their imitation capabilities are restricted to a local level.

2.4 Differential switching

We have also explored the implications of a different behavioural rule according to which firms earning below average profits do not revise their strategy with certainty. According to this *differential* rule unsatisfied firms experiment with a probability proportional to the distance between their current payoffs and the aspiration level. The fact that below average firms have only a probability rather than the certainty of switching to a new strategy may reflect the presence of difficulties by part of the firms in the evaluation of their performance (relatively to the average level of profits) and/or the presence of switching costs. We have modeled this probability as a decreasing linear function of the current profits of the firm: each firm f in the neighbourhood $N_{x,y}^\rho$ revises its strategy at time t with a probability $\alpha_t(\bar{\pi}_{x,y}, \pi^f)$ given by (dropping the firm superscripts):

$$\alpha_t(\bar{\pi}_{x,y}, \pi^f) = \max\left[0, 1 - \frac{\pi^f}{\bar{\pi}_{x,y}}\right] . \tag{6}$$

Thus the function that generates the probabilities $\nu_t(s, s')$ of switching from strategy s to $s' \in S$ at time t takes the following form:

$$\nu_t(s, s') = \begin{cases} 1 - \alpha_t + \alpha_t P_t(s') & \text{if } s' = s \\ \alpha_t P_t(s') & \text{otherwise} . \end{cases} \tag{7}$$

2.5   Imitation with noise

The last learning rule that we consider is a simple modification of the imitative learning rule of section 2.3 that allows for some random experimentation by part of below average firms. In order to take into account this possibility into the model we have only to replace formula (5) by the following:

$$\mu_{x,y}^{1,t}(s, s') = \begin{cases} P_t(s') & \text{with probability } 1 - \epsilon \\ \frac{1}{S} & \text{with probability } \epsilon . \end{cases} \tag{8}$$

Note that in this case only below aspiration level firms can randomly switch to a new strategy, above average firms will continue to adopt the strategy used in the previous period with probability one. This "noisy" version of our basic imitative rule should take into account errors by part of the firms in observing the strategies adopted by other firms.

3   Simulation design and discussion of the results

In this section we report the results of our simulations. In particular, we explore and compare the results of the simulations of the learning processes induced by the three behavioural rules defined in sections 2.3–2.5. For each of the learning rules we consider both the case where firms choose their strategies from a discrete set and the case where firms are allowed to choose strategies continuously from the interval $[0.1, 0.6]$. Then, for each of the resulting

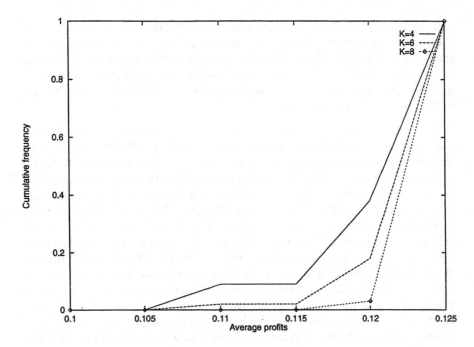

Fig. 2. Cumulative distributions of final average profits. Evolution by imitation, discrete strategies, $\rho = 1$

combinations of learning rules and strategy space type we run simulations for different values of the size K of the lattice. We have started all simulations from an initial random distribution of firms' strategies over the strategy space. In other words at the beginning of each simulation each firm at each duopoly on the torus chooses at random a strategy from the set of available strategies. At this point we let the computer carry out the evolutionary process until all the firms on the lattice satisfy their aspiration level requirement and we record the final average output which we can consider as a measure of cooperativeness among firms. For each of the considered combinations of learning rules, strategy space type and lattice size we computed 100 simulations in order to get a cumulative distribution of the final average profits.

3.1 Evolution by imitation without noise

Figure 2 shows the cumulative distributions of final average profits for different values of the size of the lattice and for a neighbourhood radius $\rho = 1$. We can observe that the cumulative distributions tend to collapse toward the 0.125 value (the level of profits associated to the joint profit maximising strategy) as the size of the lattice increases.[5] In other words the degree of cooperation among firms is positively related to the size of the lattice (and to the number of firms). When, for instance, the size K of the lattice is equal to 8, resulting in $2(8^2) = 128$ firms, we get perfect cooperation at all locations in 97% of the simulations. This percentage is sensibly higher than the one, 62%, that we get when $K = 4$.

The reason behind this relationship between neighbourhood size and degree of cooperation is fairly simple to understand. A sufficient condition for the cooperative strategy to spread over the lattice is that at time $t = 0$ there is at least a duopoly $d(x, y)$ where both firms produce the cooperative quantity $q^f = q^{f'} = 0.25$; this, in fact, ensures that both f and f' at $d(x, y)$ receive the maximal level of profits $\pi^f = \pi^{f'} = 0.125$ achievable in our simple duopoly model. As a consequence both firms f and f' at $d(x, y)$ are in learning state 0 and will never leave this state (and change their strategies) since their profits cannot, being maximal, fall below average.[6] On the other hand, all firms in the neighbourhood of duopoly $d(x, y)$ that earn below average profits can, with a strictly positive probability, imitate the cooperative strategy used by the firms at $d(x, y)$. Some of them, over time, will do it increasing, in turn, the number of cooperative duopolies in the neighbourhood, the probability of adopting the cooperative strategy, and the local average level of profits. This increase in the average profits will force some of the firms who earned profits higher than the local average, but still not cooperative to switch from learning state 0 to learning state 1. This evolutionary process will continue until all duopolies in the neighbourhood of $d(x, y)$ adopt the cooperative (JPM) strategy; finally, since all neighbourhoods are interconnected, the cooperative strategy will propagate over the entire lattice. It is now easy to understand why the size of the lattice can affect the degree of cooperation. In fact, as the size of the lattice (and the number of duopolies) increases, the probability of having at time $t = 0$ a duopoly where both firms play the JPM strategy, and in general the probability than in a certain neighbourhood more than one firm plays the cooperative strategy also increases.

Global cooperation can also be achieved when there are no duopolies where both firms play the cooperative strategy at time $t = 0$. In this case, however, the cooperative outcome is less likely to emerge and its realisation depends on the initial number of *firms* adopting the cooperative strategy. In this case, in fact, since the JPM strategy do not perform very well against

---

[5] Since the evolutionary process ends when all firms satisfy their aspirations, final average profits coincide with the final profits of each and all firms. In fact, at the end of the evolutionary process all firms end up choosing the same strategy and earning the same level of profits.

[6] The pair of strategies $q^f = q^{f'} = 0.125$ is, in fact, the global attractor of the dynamic process in the space of pairs of strategies (see Dixon [6]).

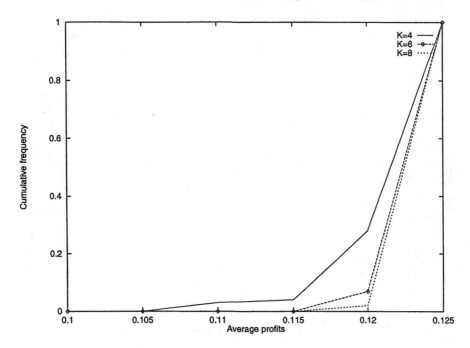

Fig. 3. Cumulative distributions of final average profits. Evolution by imitation with noise ($\epsilon = 0.1$), discrete strategies, $\rho = 1$

other strategies[7] it is very likely that it will "perish" during the initial phases of the evolutionary process. But if the JPM manages to survive, because it is able to provide above average profits to at least some of the firms f adopting it, then it is possible that, if their competitors f' earn below average profits, they will imitate the JPM strategy establishing a new cooperative duopoly. It is also possible that two below average firms at the same duopoly end up by chance imitating the cooperative strategy adopted by one firm in their neighbourhood. The likelihood of all these events is directly related to number of firms adopting the JPM strategy at the beginning of each simulation which is proportional to the size of the lattice.

It must be pointed out that if no firm adopts the JPM strategy initially, then, unless some form of mutation or random switching is introduced into the model, there is no possibility for the cooperative strategy to establish itself and propagate.

---

[7] Against the JPM strategy ($q = 0.125$), in fact, every other strategy associated to a production level $q \geq 0.25$ has a better performance as long as the market price is positive.

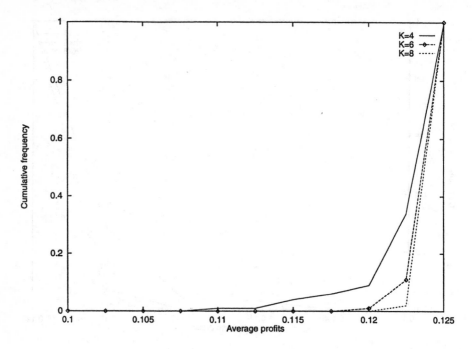

Fig. 4. Cumulative distributions of final average profits. Evolution by imitation, continuous strategies, $\rho = 1$

3.2   Evolution by imitation with noise

Figure 3 shows the case where random experimentation or mutation is introduced in the model. In particular it shows the outcome of the simulations where below average firms have a probability $\epsilon = 0.1$ of choosing a new strategy at random. The cumulative distributions of final average profits do not differ very much from the distributions relative to the no mutation case, but we can observe that when the size of the lattice is small i. e. $K = 4$ the distribution is more skewed to the right revealing an higher probability of getting the cooperative outcome at the end of the learning process. The fact that experimenting firms can randomly introduce in the "pool" of strategies, strategies (like the JPM) that at the beginning of the simulation were not sufficiently represented or not represented at all or strategies that during the evolutionary process went "extinct" can increase to a great extent the probability of establishing a cooperative duopoly.

In Figure 4 we can observe what happens when we allow firms to choose strategies continuously from the interval $[0.1, 0.6]$. In this case too, the fact that at time $t = 0$ are "generated" $S = 2(K^2)$ different strategies and that some new strategies can come to life by random switching seems to increase tendency toward cooperation in small populations of duopolies.

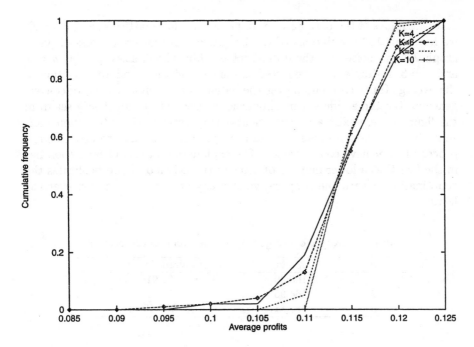

Fig. 5. Cumulative distributions of final average profits. Evolution by imitation, differential rule, $\rho = 1$

3.3   Evolution by imitation, differential rule

Figure 5 reports the results of the simulations relative to the differential switching rule. As we can immediately observe, this rule, by introducing inertia in the strategy revision process of the firms reduces significantly the final degree of cooperation among firms. In fact, according to this rule below average firms can continue to adopt the same unsatisfactory rule with a positive probability. The effect of inertia is amplified when the size of the lattice is relatively small; the reduced rate of imitation do not allow to more cooperative strategies to spread over the lattice increasing the number of duopolies where both firms play non-cooperative strategies.[8]

3.4   Neighbourhood size effects

In order to explore the effect of neighbourhood size on the time necessary to the evolutionary process to achieve convergence we have run simulations for

---

[8] For the simulation of the evolutionary processes characterised by differential switching we adopted a slightly modified stopping rule. According to this rule, the evolutionary processes ended when no firm for 10 consecutive periods changed its strategy.

different values of the parameter ρ. In particular, for a lattice size of $K = 10$, we have run 100 simulations of the imitative evolutionary process of paragraph 2.3 (no noise) for three different neighbourhood sizes: $\rho = 1$, $\rho = 2$ and $\rho = 3$. In Table 3 are reported the mean and the standard deviation of the average times (computed over the batches of 100 simulations) of convergence for the three different neighbourhood sizes. As we can clearly see from the figures, there exist a positive relationship between the interaction horizon (given by the parameter ρ) and the time necessary for the evolutionary processes to achieve convergence.[9] The explanation of this phenomenon lies in the fact that a lower number of firms in the neighbourhood facilitates the coordination toward the cooperative strategy and its propagation over the lattice.

Table 3. Average converge time of the evolutionary processes

ρ	Mean	Standard deviation
1	100.40	26.91
2	164.95	57.88
3	287.81	200.40

4   Conclusions

In this paper we study an evolutionary model of local interaction where agents (duopolists) adopt simple aspiration-based behavioural rules in their decision

---

[9] In order to statistically test this relationship, we have tested for the pair of evolutionary processes where $\rho = 1$ and $\rho = 2$ and then for the pair of processes where $\rho = 2$ and $\rho = 3$, the one side hypothesis that the mean of convergence times of the process with the bigger horizon is greater than the mean of converge times of the process with the smaller horizon. We therefore have applied the statistic

$$\frac{\bar{X}_1 - \bar{X}_2}{\sqrt{\frac{s_{X_1}^2}{n} + \frac{s_{X_2}^2}{n}}} \sim t_{n-1} , \tag{9}$$

where $\bar{X}_1$ and $\bar{X}_2$ are the two means, $s_{X_1}^2$ and $s_{X_2}^2$ their sampling variances and n the size of the sample, to each pair of means. The value of the statistic calculated over the means of the first two processes ($\rho = 1$ and $\rho = 2$) is 10.112, while the value of the same statistic calculated over the last two processes ($\rho = 2$ and $\rho = 3$) is 5.789; since both values are bigger than 1.98, the critical value of a t distribution with $n = 100 - 1 = 99$ degrees of freedom at a significance level of 0.01, we can conclude that the mean of the $\rho = 3$ evolutionary process is significantly bigger than the mean of the $\rho = 2$ evolutionary process, which is, in turn, significantly bigger than the mean of the $\rho = 1$ evolutionary process.

making. In our setting at each location on a torus there are two firms that repeatedly play a Cournot game and revise their strategies according to some imitative rule.

We find that under the general imitative rule and all its variations we study, the limiting distributions are characterised by most (and some times, almost all) firms playing the cooperative strategy (the strategy that maximises joint profits). We also find that the size of the learning neighbourhood does not affect this result: both global and local imitation lead to cooperation among firms. But local interaction may affect the *degree* of cooperation among firms, with cooperation increasing with size of the lattice and the number of firms. We also observe that local interaction affects the time path towards equilibrium by sensibly accelerating it. These results are in accordance with the theoretical results of Dixon [6] and the numerical results of Dixon and Lupi [7].

A   Appendix

All simulations were run on a Sun SPARCstation 5. All computer code[10] was written by the author in Gauss ver. 3.2.18 for Solaris 2.4. In almost all cases the output of Gauss was post-processed with Octave ver. 2.0.5 and then plotted with Gnuplot ver 3.5.

References

1. Luca Anderlini and Antonella Ianni. Path dependence and learning from neighbours. *Games and Economic Behavior*, 13(2):141–177, 1996.
2. Robert Axelrod. *The evolution of cooperation*. Basic Books, New York, 1984.
3. Robert Axelrod and William D. Hamilton. The evolution of cooperation. *Science*, 211:1390–96, 1981.
4. Lawrence E. Blume. The statistical mechanics of strategic interaction. *Games and Economic Behavior*, 5:387–424, 1993.
5. David Canning. Average behavior in learning models. *Journal of Economic Theory*, 57:442–472, 1992.
6. Huw D. Dixon. Keeping Up with the Joneses: Competition and the evolution of collusion in an oligopolistic economy. Research Papers in Economics 1810, Center for Economic Policy Researh, 1998.
7. Huw D. Dixon and Paolo Lupi. Learning with a known average: a simulation study of different learning rules. Discussion Papers in Economics 97/18, University of York, 1997. Presented at the III International Conference on Computing in Finance and Economics. Stanford, June 1997.
8. Glenn Ellison. Learning, local interaction, and coordination. *Econometrica*, 61(5):1047, 1993.
9. R. Hoffmann and N. Waring. The localization of interaction and learning in the repeated prisoner's dilemma. Technical report, Santa Fe Institute, 1996.

---

[10] All programs are available from the author upon request.

10. N. Jonard and M. Yildizoglu. Thecnological diversity in an evolutionary indus-try model with localized learning and network externalities. *Mimeo University Louis Pasteur – Strasbourg*, 1997.
11. Michihiro Kandori, George J. Mailath, and Raphael Rob. Learning, mutation, and long run equilibria in games. *Econometrica*, 61(1):29–56, Jan 1993.
12. Oliver Kirchkamp. *Evolution and Learning in Spatial Models*. PhD thesis, University of Dusseldorf, 1996.
13. Ramon Marimon. Learning from learning in economics. In David M. Kreps and Kenneth F. Wallis, editors, *Advances in Economics and Econometrics: Theory and Applications*, volume I of *Econometric Society Monographs*, chapter 9, pages 278–315. Cambridge University press, Cambridge UK, 1997.
14. Ramon Marimon and Ellen McGratten. On adaptive learning in strategic games. In Alan Kirman and Mark Salmon, editors, *Learning and Rationality in Economics*, chapter 3. Blackwells, 1995.
15. Sidney Siegel. Level of aspiration and decision making. *Psychological review*, 64(4):253–262, 1957.
16. Herbert A. Simon. *Administraive Behaviour: a Study of Decision-making Processes in Administrative Organizations*. MacMillan, 1947.
17. Herbert A. Simon. *The Science of the Artificial*. MIT press, Cambridge, Massachussets, third edition, 1996.

Expectation Formation in a Cobweb Economy: Some One Person Experiments*

Cars Hommes[1], Joep Sonnemans[1,2], and Henk van de Velden[1]

[1] University of Amsterdam, Center for Non-linear Dynamics in Economics and Finance (CeNDEF), Roetersstraat 11, 1018 WB Amsterdam, The Netherlands
[2] University of Amsterdam, Center for Research in Experimental Economics and Political Decision-Making (CREED), Roetersstraat 11, 1018 WB Amsterdam, The Netherlands

Abstract. In economics expectations play an important role. In making decisions agents form expectations about future values of variables. Therefore, in any dynamic economic model, agents beliefs about the future have to be modeled. Do people form expectations using a simple rule of thumb or do they use a continually updated forecasting rule? Can people learn a *rational expectations equilibrium*? This paper describes experiments where we investigate how people form expectations in the simplest dynamic economic model, the cobweb model, without any knowledge of the underlying market equilibrium equations. We found that only about 35% of the subjects seemed to be able to learn the unique *rational expectations* equilibrium. We also found that many individuals deviate from *rational expectations* for long periods of time, sometimes with 'systematic forecasting errors'.

1 Introduction

In making optimal decisions agents often have to form expectations about future values of variables. Although much research has been done concerning theoretical models of expectation formation and learning, it is still not clear how agents form expectations in real markets. The currently leading paradigm in expectation formation in economics still seems to be the *Rational Expectations Hypothesis*, introduced by Muth [11]. However, this hypothesis has been criticized a lot in the last decade or so, especially in the *bounded rationality* literature; see for example, the surveys by Sargent [13] and Evans and Honkapohja [4]. One reason for the criticism is that rational expectations assumes unrealistic high computing powers of the agents within the model. Another critique is that rational expectations assumes perfect knowledge of underlying market equilibrium equations. As an alternative the rational agents may be replaced by boundedly rational agents who behave like

---

* Paper presented at the third workshop on Economics with Heterogeneous Interacting Agents, Ancona, May 29-30, 1998. We would like to thank the participants of the workshop for useful comments. We also would like to thank Jan Tuinstra for his comments on previous drafts.

econometricians using time series observations to form expectations. Boundedly rational agents use their own model of the world and they estimate the parameters as more observations become available.

The objective of this paper is to investigate how agents form expectations in an experimental cobweb economy, without knowledge of the underlying market equilibrium equations. In the experiment prices were generated by a non-linear cobweb model, with expectations formed by individual participants. In this experimental setting of what is perhaps the simplest dynamic economic model, we address the following questions: 'Do agents use simple habitual rule of thumbs or do they form expectations some other way?' and 'Do agents learn the unique *rational expectations equilibrium?*'.

The paper is organized as follows. Section 2 briefly recalls the price dynamics of the nonlinear cobweb model for different expectation schemes. In section 3 the experimental setting is explained, while section 4 gives a description of the results. Section 5 concludes and contains some remarks about future experimental work.

2   The Cobweb Model

In the thirties the cobweb model was introduced into economic theory, see for example Ezekiel [5]. Since then the cobweb model has been one of the benchmark models in economic dynamics. The cobweb model describes the price behavior in a single market with one non-storable good taking one unit of time to produce. The demand, q_t^d, for the produced good depends upon the price of the good, p_t. Since it takes one period to produce the good the production decision of the suppliers depends on the expected price, p_t^e, that will prevail in the market. The actual price is determined by market clearing, that is the equality of total supply and total demand. The model can thus be represented by the following three equations:

$$q_t^d = D(p_t) \tag{1}$$
$$q_t^s = S(p_t^e) \tag{2}$$
$$q_t^d = q_t^s. \tag{3}$$

Throughout this paper we will use the following specifications of demand and supply functions:

$$D(p_t) = a - bp_t \tag{4}$$
$$S(p_t^e) = tanh(\lambda(p_t^e - c)) + 1. \tag{5}$$

The demand curve is linear and decreasing in price, whereas the supply curve is non-linear and increasing in the expected price. Notice that a non-linear increasing supply curve is consistent with profit maximizing firms. The reason for choosing a non-linear supply curve is that, for instance with adaptive expectations, the non-linear cobweb model can generate chaotic price fluctuations. An important question is whether in the corresponding experimental cobweb economy agents will be able to learn the (unstable) rational expectations steady state equilibrium price. From (1-3), using demand (4) and supply (5), one easily finds that the market equilibrium price p_t is given by:

$$p_t = \frac{1}{b}[a - tanh(\lambda(p_t^e - c)) - 1] \tag{6}$$

From this equation it is clear that the price, p_t, depends upon the expectations of the agents. In the experimental cobweb economy prices will be generated by the unknown market equilibrium equation (6), with expectations being formed by participants of the experiment. In the following we first recall how the dynamics depends upon the different kind of expectation schemes, studied in the literature.

Naive Expectations

The first expectation scheme we will consider is naive expectations. If producers have naive expectations then they expect today's price to be equal to yesterday's realized price, that is,

$$p_t^e = p_{t-1}$$

It is well known that the cobweb model with naive expectations and monotonic demand and supply curves yield only three types of long run dynamic behavior: (i) convergence to a stable steady state equilibrium, (ii) a (stable) period two cycle and (iii) unbounded price oscillations. In our setting, the latter possibility can not occur, since the supply curve (5) is bounded. Notice also that in the case of a 2-cycle, agents make 'systematic forecasting' errors, in the sense that the actual price will be high (low) when expected price is low (high).

Adaptive Expectations

Adaptive expectations means that the expected price is a weighted average of yesterday's price and yesterday's expected price, that is,

$$p_t^e = wp_{t-1} + (1 - w)p_{t-1}^e$$

Nerlove [12] introduced adaptive expectations into the linear cobweb model and showed that it has a stabilizing effect on the price fluctuations. More recently Chiarella [3] and Hommes [7] investigated the cobweb model with adaptive expectations and a non-linear (but monotonically increasing) supply curve and found that price cycles of any period and even chaotic price fluctuations can arise. To show what happens we make use of a bifurcation diagram. A bifurcation diagram shows the long run price dynamics as a (multi-)

valued function of a parameter. In the bifurcation diagram, figure 1, below
we see that a shift of the demand curve can result in a steady state price, a
stable k-cycle ($k = 2, 4, ..$) or chaotic price oscillations.

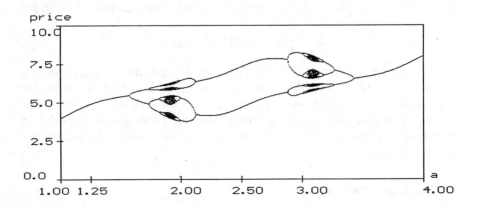

Fig. 1. Bifurcation diagram for cobweb economy with adaptive expectations w.r.t.
shifting the demand curve upwards, other parameters are $\lambda = 2, b = 0.25, c = 6, w = 0.5$.

In figure 2 we see what will happen to the price dynamics if we change
the weight factor, w, from zero to one.

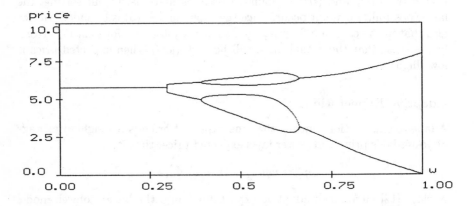

Fig. 2. Bifurcation diagram for cobweb economy with adaptive expectations w.r.t
the expectations weight factor w, other parameters are $a = 2, \lambda = 2, b = 0.25, c = 6$

This figure demonstrates that the introduction of adaptive expectations into the cobweb model has a stabilizing effect, it dampens the amplitude of the price oscillations. However adaptive expectations also introduces the posibillity of chaotic or a-periodic price fluctuations.

Learning

In the theoretical bounded rationality literature, much attention has been paid to learning schemes where agents update parameters. There are different kind of expectations schemes that involve learning rules. A well-known example of a learning rule is Ordinary Least Squares-learning (OLS-learning). Bray and Savin [2] showed convergence to rational expectations in the cobweb model with OLS-learning. Another related adaptive learning rule, Sample AutoCorrelation-learning (SAC-learning) where agents constantly update the parameters of their forecasting function according to the sample average and the sample autocorrelation coefficient, was recently introcued by Hommes and Sorger [9]. Learning leads to convergence to the rational expectation equilibrium steady state price.

3   An Experimental Cobweb Economy

In this section we will describe the experiments. In the next section we will present the results of the experiments and we will show how these results fit the theoretical framework, presented above.

3.1   The Experimental Design

We conducted four experiments. The participants in experiments 1a and 1b had to predict a 'value' between zero and ten while participants in experiments 2a and 2b were asked to predict a 'price' between zero and ten. We started the experiment when everybody had finished reading their instructions. The experiments lasted 50 periods, every period lasted 30 seconds. We will call the participants predictions the *predicted value/price* and the realized value/price the *real value*. At the end of every period the participants were informed about the *real value*. Nothing was said about how this *real value* was calculated or if it was calculated. So the only information the participants had were the previous *real values* and that their prediction should lie between zero and ten. The better the participant predicted the more he would earn. Every period the participants could earn up to 1300 points[1]. At

---

[1] The payment of each prediction is based upon a quadratic payoff function $1300 - 260(X - Y)^2$ where Y is the predicted value and X is the real value. The expected value of this function is maximized by $Y = EX$. Negative payoffs were not used; earnings were 0 if $|X - Y| > \sqrt{5}$. At the end of the experiments the points were exchanged to Dutch guilders at a rate 1300 points = 1 guilder (is approximately \$0.50).

the end of every period the participants screen was updated. Figure 3 below shows a typical screen the participants saw during the experiment.

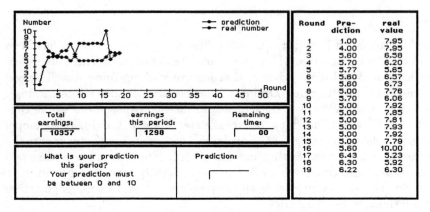

Fig. 3. Typical computerscreen of participants during the experiment

3.2   The Different Conditions

We report the findings from 4 experiments using the design parameters listed in Table 1.

Table 1. design parameters of the experiments

experi-	periods				shock
ments	1-15	16-28	29-40	41-50	(ϵ_t)
exp. 1a	$a_t = 2$	$a_t = 3$	$a_t = 1.25$	$a_t = 2.5$	U(-0.2,0.2)
exp. 1b	$a_t = 2.3$	$a_t = 2.3$	$a_t = 2.3$	$a_t = 2.3$	N(0,0.5)
exp. 2a	$a_t = 2$	$a_t = 3$	$a_t = 1.25$	$a_t = 2.5$	U(-0.2,0.2)
exp. 2b	$a_t = 2.3$	$a_t = 2.3$	$a_t = 2.3$	$a_t = 2.3$	N(0,0.5)

Participants were not informed about the market equilibrium equation which generated the price as a function of the expected price. The real value was generated to be the market equilibrium price in the cobweb economy in section 2, with expectations formed by a single participant, i.e.,

$$p_t = \frac{a_t - tanh(2(p_t^e - 6)) - 1}{0.25} + \epsilon_t, \qquad (7)$$

where ϵ_t is an (unknown) exogenous shock. There are three main differences between the experiments. Firstly, as can be seen in Table 1, in experiments 1b and 2b the parameter a is the same for fifty periods, so that there are no large demand shocks. In contrast, in the other two experiments 1a and 2a four different values of the parameter a are used, implying that there are three (large) demand shocks (three shifts of the demand curve) within the 50 periods of the experiment. Participants have no information about any shocks occurring; in fact, as stated before, participants do not even know that the time series are generated by an underlying cobweb model with feedback from their own expectations. The second difference between the experiments is the difference between the permanent shocks (ϵ_t). In experiments 1a and 2a there are small permanent shocks, drawn from a uniform distribution. In experiments 1b and 2b there are medium size permanent shocks, drawn from a normal distribution. The third difference is that in experiments 1a and 1b the participants had no market information at all, but where simply asked to predict a 'value' or 'number' between 0 and 10. In contrast, in experiments 2a and 2b the participants had some general market information, and were asked to predict the price in a market. In the latter case, participants knew that they had to predict 'some kind of price sequence', but they were not informed that this price sequence was generated by a demand-supply model with feedback from their own expectations. The question now arises how these differences in the experiments affect the participants predictions.

4   The Results of the Experiments

In this section we will give the results of the experiments. We will show the differences and similarities of the results between the different experiments.

4.1   Experiments 1a and 2a: Three Large Exogenous Shocks

Large differences between the participants occured. Some of the participants earned up to 52000 points (40 guilders) while others earned nothing. An obvious reason for this is that participants used different kind of expectation rules. For a good examination of the results we categorized the participants into three categories by looking at their time series. The three categories we obtained are:

1. participants who seem to have some kind of adaptive expectations or AR(1) learning
2. participants who seem to have some special form of naive expectations, which we call markov expectations
3. participants who did not seem to use a systematic forecasting rule

Table 2 shows how the participants in experiments 1a and 2a are distributed over the different categories. The average amount of money in guilders earned

Table 2. earnings of participants of experiments 1a and 2a

experiment 1a	category 1	category 2	category 3	total
participants	8	5	7	20
average earn.	28.99	10.94	6.29	16.54
experiment 2a	category 1	category 2	category 3	total
participants	4	11	4	19
average earn.	25.85	8.97	9.33	12.60

by a subject in that category is also shown. From the table we see that participants in category 1 earned most money, while the difference between participants in categories 2 and 3 is less obvious. Even though the participants in experiment 2a had some general market information their average earnings are somewhat less than those of the participants in experiment 1a. Overall this suggests that general market information does not improve prediction performance. Note that the participants with naive expectations or markov expectations who according to the theory will always make systematic forecasting errors did earn some money. An explanation for this is that the theoretic cobweb model with naive expectations and parameters as in the experiment, leads to the stable equilibrium value in periods 29-40 .

Figure 4 shows the time series of participant 31 (experiment 1a), a typical example of category 1.

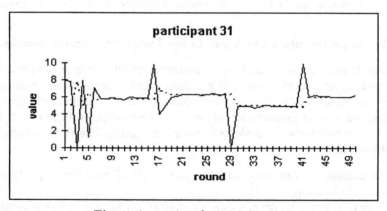

Fig. 4. time series of participant 31

The dotted line represents the participants' *predicted value* and the black line represents the *real value*. From figure 4 we see that around period eight the participant predicted the equilibrium price. At period sixteen the (un-expected) exogenous shock takes place (the parameter a changes from 2 to 3) causing the *real value* to become almost ten. At period 17 the participant adapts his *predicted value* too much in the direction of the *real value* caus-ing the *real value* to decline sharply. But from that moment on he adapts with smaller steps and within four periods he has found the new equilib-rium again. After the second (period 29) and the third (period 41) exogenous shock he finds the equilibrium price/value even faster. Participant 31 is able to learn the unique rational expectations steady state within 8 periods, without any knowledge of the market equilibrium equations. After a large exogenous shock, participant 31 is able to find the new rational expectations steady state quickly.

Simulations with Experiment 1a and 2a

We did some simulations to show how our results relate to the theory. In figure 5 below we see that in the case the expectations or forecasting rule is adaptive expectations with weight factor $w = 0.2$, the generated time series is similar to the time series for participant 31 in the actual experiment. This suggests that participant 31 has been using some kind of adaptive expecta-tions forecasting rule with a small weight factor.

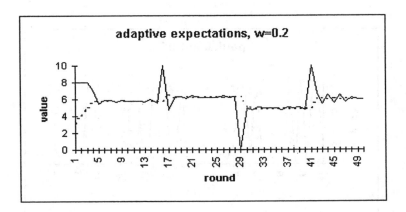

Fig. 5. simulated time series with adaptive expectations with expectations weight factor $w = 0.2$.

4.2   Experiments 1b and 2b: Permanent Medium Shocks

The difference between these experiments and the former experiments is that
in this experiment there are no large shifts of the demand curve, but instead
there are permanent medium exogenous shocks $\epsilon_t \sim N(0, 0.5)$. Table 3 shows
the results for experiments 1b and 2b.

Table 3. earnings of participants of experiments 1b and 2b

experiment 1b	category 1	category 2	category 3	total
participants	7	9	6	22
average earn.	21.63	0	4.63	8.14
experiment 2b	category 1	category 2	category 3	total
participants	6	5	5	16
average earn.	29.18	0.32	6.96	13.22

Again we see that the participants who we put in category 1 earned the most
money. Notice that in this case general market information does lead to some
prediction improvement and therefore to higher average earnings. Figure 6
shows the time series of participant 102 (experiment 2b), a typical example
of category 2.

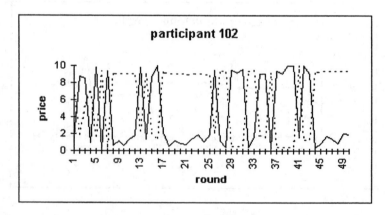

Fig. 6. time series of participant 102

It is easy to see that this participant only expected a high or a low price.

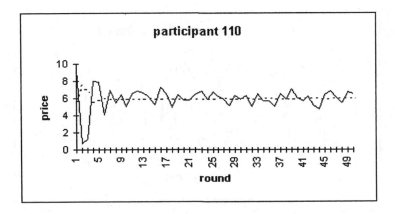

Fig. 7. time series of participant 110

Since in these experiments the equilibrium price was 5.92 this participant did not earn any points at all. On the other hand participant 110 from group 1 predicted the price very well as we can see in figure 7.

Simulations with Experiments 1b and 2b

We now present a simulation with markov expectations. Markov expectations means that a participants' *predicted value* is either his last *predicted value* or the last *real value*, with some probability of switching between these two. This leads to the following time series.

From a qualitative viewpoint, figure 8 is similar to the time series of participant 102. Some individuals in the experiments thus seem to use some kind of markov expectations rule.

Finally, Figure 9 shows the time series of a simulation with SAC-learning. Despite the medium sized permanent demand shocks, the learning algorithm converges to the unique steady state equilibrium. This time series is similar to the time series of participant 110 (category 1). SAC-learning thus seems to be a reasonable description of some of the individual forecasting rules.

5 Summary and Concluding Remarks

In this paper we have built an experimental environment to investigate expectation formation in a cobweb economy, and in particular to investigate

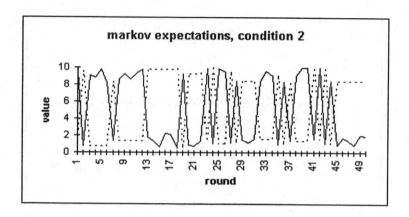

Fig. 8. simulated time series with markov expectations, transition probabilities of 0.25 and 0.75.

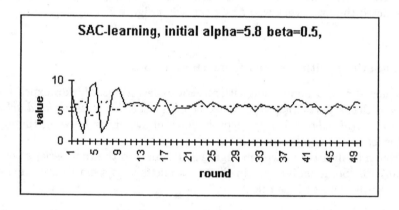

Fig. 9. simulated time series with SAC-learning, $\alpha = 5.8$ and $\beta = 0.5$.

whether agents are able to learn rational expectations in an unstable market when market equilibrium equations are not known. We found that around 35% of the participants was able to learn the rational expectations equilibrium price/value. These participants seemed to use adaptive expectations with a small weight factor w. They adapted their predictions with small steps into the direction of the realized price. Also in some cases SAC-learning or OLS-learning describes expectation formation reasonably well. In contrast, one of the main results of these individual experiments is that a large fraction of the participants was not able to learn the unique rational expectations equilibrium price/value, not even within 50 time periods. This result is remarkable since we are dealing with what is perhaps the simplest dynamic economic model. Although there is a unique rational expectations equilibrium many agents are not able to learn it when market equilibrium equations are unknown.

In order to get insight into expectations in real markets, much more work remains to be done. A controlled experimental environment seems to be very useful in addressing the problem of expectation formation. An important shortcoming of the present paper is that so far we have focussed entirely on individual experiments, that is, in all experiments described above the realized price/value is fully determined by the expected price of a single individual. It is much more interesting to consider group experiments, where the realized price/value will be determined by an equilbrium equation with simultaneous expectation feedback from many, different individuals. Does *aggregation* of expectations improve convergence to the rational expectations steady state, or is instability of rational expectations equilibria in a many agent world, with many different forecasting rules being used, even more likely? We intend to run such group experiments for the cobweb model in the CREED laboratory of the Unversity of Amsterdam in the near future. The individual experiments described in this paper should be useful as a benchmark to address the issue whether aggregation in expectations is stabilizing or destabilizing.

The market institution will also be important in determining whether aggregation of expectations will be stabilizing or not. In future work, we hope to consider different institutional settings, e.g. by applying our experimental setup to other underlying market equilibrium models such as financial asset pricing, exchange rate or inflation models.

References

1. Arrow, K.J., Nerlove, M. (1958): A note on expectations and stability. Econometrica 26, 297-305
2. Bray, M.M., Savin, N.E. (1986): Rational Expectations Equilibria, Learning and Model Specification. Econometrica 54, 1129-1160
3. Chiarella, C. (1988): The cobweb model. Its instability and the onset of chaos. Economic Modelling, 377-384
4. Evans, G.W., Honkapohja, S. (1999): Learning Dynamics. In: Taylor, J.B., Woodford, M. (Eds.): Handbook of Macroeconomics. North-Holland, Amsterdam
5. Ezekiel, M. (1938): The cobweb theorem. Quarterly Journal of Economics 52, 255-280
6. Hey, J.D. (1994): Expectations formation: Rational or adaptive or...? Journal of Economic Behavior & Organization 25, 329-349

7. Hommes, C.H. (1994): Dynamics of the cobweb model with adaptive expectations and non-linear supply and demand. Journal of Economic Behavior & Organization 24, 315-335
8. Hommes, C.H. (1998): On the consistency of backward looking expectations. The case of the cobweb. Journal of Economic Behavior & Organization 33, 333-362
9. Hommes, C.H., Sorger, G. (1998): Consistent expectations equilibrium. Macroeconomic Dynamics 1998
10. Marimon, R., Spear, S.E., Sunder, S. (1993): Expectationally driven market volatility: an experimental study. Journal of Economic Theory 61, 74-103
11. Muth, J.F. (1961): Rational expectations and the theory of price movements. Econometrica 29, 315-335
12. Nerlove, M. (1958): Adaptive expectations and cobweb phenomena. Quarterly Journal of Economics 72, 227-240
13. Sargent, T.J. (1993) Bounded rationality in macroeconomics, Clarendon Press, Oxford.
14. Smith, V.L., Suchanek, G.L., Williams, A.W., (1988): Bubbles, crashes, and endogenous expectations in experimental spot asset markets. Econometrica 56, 1119-1151

Fecund, Cheap and Out of Control: Heterogeneous Economic Agents as Flawed Computers vs. Markets as Evolving Computational Entities

Philip Mirowski and Koye Somefun

Deapartment of Economics, University of Notre Dame, Notre Dame, IN 46556, USA
(e-mail: philip.e.mirowski.1@nd.edu)

Abstract. Our objective in this paper is to try and clarify what we perceive to be two major approaches to the problem of heterogeneous interactive economic agents, and argue in favor of the option which we feel has suffered relative neglect. The first option, perhaps best represented by the work of Alan Kirman, but found throughout the avant garde of the profession, tends to characterize agents as flawed automata or limited computational entities. Exercises in this tradition tend to produce simulations of specific economic situations. While there is much to admire in this program, we maintain that invoking a gestalt reversal which regards markets as computational devices, or literal formal automata, would achieve many of the same goals as the former research program, but would foster a rich and viable evolutionary economics to boot, one which would encourage both mathematical rigor and historical relevance, while avoiding many of the mechanistic excesses of neoclassical theory. Because the second path is the road less traveled, we survey what we call a computational understanding of markets, in order to provide a framework for incorporation of automata theory into a consciously evolutionary approach. For after all, what is the purpose of acknowledging the heterogeneity of agents, if not to then subject them to some form of selection process? We work through an explicit example of the automata theory approach, using two papers by Gode & Sunder [1993, 1997] to illustrate how some recent literatures could be recast into this novel approach. We close with the suggestion that it is experience with real-time markets being run as automata on computers, and not just some academic simulations, which will induce both economists and market participants to come to an appreciation of this kind of evolutionary economics.

1. Waiting for a Little Spontaneous Order

The effect of the computer upon modern developments in economic theory is a topic still in its infancy. All manner of novel and imaginative research programs owe their genesis to the spread of the computer throughout the whole gamut of postwar sciences: Artificial Intelligence, Artificial Life, bounded rationality, cognitive science, information theory, nonlinear dynamics, genetic algorithms, simulation exercises, and so forth. Situated in the midst of this eruption of innovations, it is more than a little difficult to discern the main lines of development inherent in present trends, in part because nascent formations get conflated and confused with other parallel trends, such as the relative health or debilitation of the neoclassical orthodoxy, changing cultural images (evolution, maximum entropy) of the iconic instantiations of social order, sufficient grasp of the implications of intellectual innovations in other sciences, and so on. We broach this issue, not because we believe we can supply answers to these big questions in this paper (we can't!), but rather because we have been struck by the diversity and incompatibility of theoretical exercises which have been suggested at the Santa Fe Institute, the Society for Computational Economics meetings, and at the Ancona conference. Too often, the computer in its protean manifestations has provided yeoman service as the lone common denominator which permits all manner of theorists to pronounce on where economics is going in one others' presence, without taking into account the importance of rival programs, empirical commitments, or scientific constraints. The purpose of this paper is to lay out two very different trends in modern theory in stark outline, both owing their very conceptual essence to the computer, and yet each individually imposing an entirely alternative framework upon the economic phenomenon. Both champion the point of departure of their new economics upon acknowledgement of heterogeneous interactive economic agents, and both can be described as descending from John von Neumann's invention of the theory of automata; but beyond that, they are as different as night and day. We shall dub these alternatives 'agents as flawed computers' versus 'markets as evolving computational entities'.

Although there are many eminent representatives of the first category, we shall take Alan Kirman's lecture "The Emergency of Market Organization" as an admirable summary of many of the objectives of this program.[1] Kirman begins by diagnosing the failure of the neoclassical Walrasian orthodoxy in achieving an understanding of market processes. First in the bill of indictment is the penchant for treating all rational agents as fundamentally alike; next, there is the confusion of rationality with omniscience; and then there is the problem that "too much interdependence destroys the possibility of moving from the micro level to the macro level". The prescription to cure these ills is to keep the orthodox notion of market equilibrium more or less entact, but to loosen up on the specification of individual rationality. Of necessity, this requires devoting greater theoretical attention to the psychological makeup of the economic agents. Kirman suggests that this implies paying closer attention to formats of information processing; this might mean more

---

[1] This is the lecture presented as the plenary at the Ancona conference.

realistic specifications of the modification of individual expectations, or else the resort to imitation of other agents to solve short-term calculational shortcomings, or it may just mean treating the agent more like a computer handicapped with various computational limitations. These modelling choices find their counterparts in techniques such as cellular automata, spin glasses on lattices, stochastic graph theory, and other formalisms pioneered primarily in computer science, but also in the physical sciences. Taking into account the heterogeneity of agent rationalizations and giving due consideration to agent learning does raise the issue of the existence at the macro level of regularities with anything approaching a law-like character. Kirman believes that acknowledgment of the cognitive limitations of individuals leads inexorably to an appreciation of the role of institutional structures in market coordination. As he himself has practiced what he preaches, this involves looking at the sequential character of markets, their closing rules, distributions of realized price dispersions, and other phenomena often overlooked by neoclassical theory.

Although we applaud each and every one of the improvements which Kirman urges over the neoclassical orthodoxy, we do feel impelled to question the extent to which the project is firmly grounded in issues of computation and the externally given identity of individual intentionalities. There is also the troubling question of what the theoretical acknowledgement of the fundamental heterogeneity of agents is intended to achieve. We fully admit that people really do diverge dramatically in terms of their notions of rationality and their cognitive capacities; but the deeper question is why and how this should matter for economics.

As is well known, the Walrasian project took as its givens tastes, technologies and endowments, because it sought to reduce all causal relations to those putatively 'natural' determinants. The very notion of "equilibrium" as appropriated from physics makes little sense without this very important proviso (Mirowski, 1989). The first three generations of neoclassicals did not seek to explain psychological regularities, since they wished to treat their postulates concerning utility as universal abstractions of human rationality. They were not bothered by the fact that they were formally treating everyone as identical; indeed, for them, this was a vindication of their scientific aspirations (however much it might clash with the ideology of individual freedom of choice, or indeed, any notion of free will). The purpose of "equilibrium" was to portray the market as using prices to balance the natural givens to an exquisitely precise degree: hence the sobriequet of "marginalism".

Once economists relinquish this particular framework in the interests of allowing for agent heterogeneity, this project tends to lose its rationale. Indeed, this is one way of understanding the significance of the Sonnenschein/Mantel/Debreu theorems. There it has been demonstrated that the project of Walrasian equilibrium largely 'works' when everyone is identical, but generally comes acropper when individual differences are analytically acknowledged. The "no-trade" theorems likewise show that with full rationality but the possibility of differential information, rational agents would abjure participation in the market due to strategic considerations. Indeed, these and other developments have been some of the major motivations behind the new-found fascination with older traditions of bounded rationality, finite automata playing games, machine learning and the like (Mirowski, forthcoming).

Nevertheless, there persist deeper contradictions adhering to attempts to import computational and psychological considerations into the orthodox equilibrium program. The most apparent incongruity is that most exercises which are promoted as advocating agent homogeneity in fact rarely live up to their billing. Instead, agents are frequently equipped with only the most rudimentary algorithmic capacities, perhaps differing only by a parameter or two, and then the model is deployed to demonstrate certain aggregate stochastic regularities. While this does reveal a different approach to bridging the micro-macro divide, it does not begin to acknowledge the analytical significance of true diversity in the population; nor does it lead to guidelines for a theoretically informed empiricism about the nature and importance of agent diversity. What generally happens is that economic theorists end up strenuously avoiding cognitive science and behavioral psychology in the interests of producing tractable equilibrium models. In practice, the ritual adherence to methodological individualism turns out to consist largely of empty gestures.

The second contradiction of this newer work is that, while most of its findings are based to a greater or lesser extent upon formalisms developed in the sciences most heavily influenced by the computer, these economic models predominantly avoid any incorporation of formal theories of computation. For instance, agents may be treated as relatively simple automata; but there is no consideration of why certain limitations are imposed (say, limited memory capacity) whereas other obvious limitations are transcended (say, infinite precision in computation). Fundamental barriers to algorithmic rationality such as the halting problem are rarely if ever addressed. This channels the work of modeling away from analytics and towards *simulation*, as discussed below. A nagging weakness of the program then becomes the palpable absence of any widely agreed-upon criteria of what would constitute a good or superior simulation.

The third contradiction of this trend is that it never stops to consider why the heterogeneity of agents is so very important for economics, as opposed to the conundra of late Walrasianism. Here we might suggest that the major difference between a science predicated upon physics-- be it classical or statistical mechanics-- and one informed by biology, is that the latter recognizes the central significance of heterogeneity as allowing for the possibility of selection, and therefore evolutionary change. Formal acknowledgement of agent heterogeneity is rather unavailing if the outcome of the modeling exercise is for everyone to end up as effectively identical, as frequently happens in the learning and 'evolutionary' game literature. A deeper lesson to be learned from the persistence of heterogeneity is that it is fundamentally opposed to the very notion of equilibrium bequeathed from the physical sciences. Heterogeneity of entities or organisms, when coupled with various selection mechanisms, maintains a diverse population which then displays a capacity in the aggregate to adapt to multiple fluctuating environments.

It is our contention that the issues of computation, heterogeneity of agents and concepts of evolution have been given cogent interpretations in economics in the era since World War II, but that economic theorists have remained relatively deaf to these discussions. It seems that intellectual clarification of the issues is not a matter of spontaneous order, but rather that economists sometimes have to have their memories jogged by a little history. We would suggest that the two major incarnations of the computational approach in economics can be associated with the names of Herbert Simon and John von Neumann, respectively. While the former is most closely associated with appeals to "bounded rationality" in economic theory (Conlisk, 1996), and the latter is honored as the progenitor of game theory, neither doctrine sufficiently represents or captures the manner in which these figures strove to combine computation and evolution into a single framework. A survey of their complete corpus, which in both cases encompasses numerous works outside the narrow ambit of economics, reveals that each has provided a framework for a formal theory of evolution which abstracts away the 'wet' details of biology; both are predicated upon the computer as both exemplar and instantiation of how evolution is thought to work. Yet, even though they both began from very similar aspirations, their respective frameworks are so different that they can stand as contrasting rival research programs. Indeed, von Neumann sought to subsume evolution under a general theory of "automata" (1966), whereas Simon believed it could be treated under the heading of the 'sciences of the artificial' (1981), or what we shall call here a theory of "simulacra".

1.1 Simon's Simulacra versus von Neumann's Automata.

Before venturing into a more detailed discussion of what is entailed with a computational understanding of markets we will use this subsection to give a more explicit account of Simon's theory of simulacra and von Neumann's theory of automata. Since this might be a fruitful way to deepen our understanding of an evolutionary economics along modern information processing lines, which --we think-- should be based upon a computational understanding of markets.

It is not widely appreciated that after the publication of the *Theory of Games and Economic Behavior*, von Neumann did very little further on games, instead devoting most of his prodigious intellectual energies in the last decade of his life to the development of the computer and the theory of automata.[2] This theory of automata was to claim as its subject any information-processing mechanism which exhibited self-regulation in interaction with the environment, and hence resembled the newly-constructed computer. Beyond any pedestrian exploration of parallels, von Neumann envisioned this theory as a province of *logic*, beginning with Shannon's theory of information; it would proceed to encompass the formal theory of computation by basing itself on Alan Turing's theory of the universal calculation machine. Experience had shown that information processors could be constituted from widely varying substrata, all the way from vacuum tubes to the McCulloch-Pitts neuron to mechanical analogue devices. Hence it was the task of a theory of automata to ask: what were the necessary prerequisites, in an abstract sense, for the self-regulation of an abstract information processor? Once that question was answered, the theory would extend Turing's insights into this realm to inquire after the existence of a "universal" constructor of information processors. Biology would make an appearance at this juncture, since the question could be rephrased as asking: under what formal conditions could a universal constructor reconstruct a copy of itself? The logical problems of self-reference initially highlighted by Godel were then brought to the fore. What was it about this system which endowed it with the capacity to resist degradation or "noise" in successive rounds of self-reproduction? Interestingly enough, von Neumann thought the solution to the paradox was a function of the introduction of the irreversible passage of time.[3] Once the conditions for successful repeated reproduction were stated, then the theory of automata would address itself to the theory of evolution. If an automaton could reproduce itself in a second automaton of equal complexity, what, if any, further conditions were required for the same automaton to produce an 'offspring' of greater complexity than itself?

Even from this extremely truncated description, it should be possible to appreciate that von Neumann sought to distill out the formal logic of evolution in a theory of sweeping generality. In this theory, very simple micro-level rule-governed structures interact in mechanical, and even possibly random, manners. Out of their interactions arise higher-level regularities generating behaviors more complex than anything observed at the lower

---

[2] On this seachange, see (Mirowski, forthcoming, chap.3). Von Neumann was very concerned with the question of the extent to which human reasoning could be replaced by mechanisms; as one set of commentators put it, he "thought that science and technology would shift from a past emphasis on the subjects of motion, force, energy and power to a future emphasis on the subjects of communication, organization, programming and control" (Aspray & Burks, 1987, p.365).

[3] Von Neumann wrote: "There is one important difference between ordinary logic and the automata which represent it. Time never occurs in logic, but every network or nervous system has a definite time lag between the input signal and output response... it prevents the occurence of various kinds of more or less vicious circles (related to 'non-constructivity,' 'impredicativity' and the like) which represent a major class of dangers in modern logical systems" (in Aspray & Burks, 1987, p.554).

micro-levels. The characterization of relative "complexity" is predicated upon the information-processing capacities at each level of the macro-structure. The ability to maintain information transmission relative to noise in a structure of reproduction is a characteristic attribute of an automaton; the appearance of enhanced abilities to operate at higher levels of complexity is the hallmark of evolution. Although intended as a general theory of both living and inanimate entities, most of the formalisms are expressed within the framework of the computer and a theory of computation. Von Neumann justified this dependence upon the computational metaphor because, "of all automata of high complexity, computing machines are the ones we have the best chance of understanding. In the case of computing machines the complications can be very high, and yet they pertain to an object which is primarily mathematical and which we understand better than most natural objects" (1966, p.32). For precisely this reason, von Neumann did *not* believe a theory of automata should be predicated upon the actual organic architecture of our brains. The theory of automata was *not* intended as a surrogate for a theory of human psychology. If anything, von Neumann personally sought a theory of the genesis and maintenance of *organizations*. Furthermore, in contrast to modern orthodox economics, he deemed that his own theory of games played no role in his nascent theory of automata, essentially because it was not sufficiently firmly grounded in logic and in computer architectures.

Herbert Simon's theory of simulacra is also intimately related to the computer, but in a manner orthogonal to that of von Neumann. Beginning as a theorist of administration and management, his experience with computers at RAND led him to develop a general theory of systems which could apply indifferently to individual minds and organizations, and prompted him to become one of the progenitors of the field of Artificial Intelligence. He also found inspiration in the ideas of Alan Turing, but by contrast with von Neumann, he did not ground his theory in mathematical logic, but instead in the idea of the "Turing test". For Turing the problem of defining intelligence threatened to bog down in endless philosophical disputes, and so he proposed to cut the Gordian knot by suggesting that a machine was 'intelligent' if it could not be distinguished from a live human being after a suitable interval of interaction with a qualified interlocutor. Simon follows Turing in asserting that the simulation of a mind or an organization using simple modular and hierarchical protocols is "good enough" for understanding how that entity behaves, if it tracks the behavior of the entity so closely that the simulacrum cannot be distinguished (within some error margin) from the original.

If mere simulation were all there were to his theory of systems, then it would be difficult to credit it with much novelty; but Simon went further in insisting that the very structure of computer programs tells us something very important about the structure of the world.

Simon maintains that the modularity of programs in conventional computer architectures[4] mirrors an important fact about our methods of dealing with out own cognitive limitations. If human memory, attention span, and computational capacities are all finite, and control and communication activity between humans is likewise limited, then humans must have developed mechanisms to circumvent these limitations. The primary instrumentality for overcoming these obstacles is to sort and isolate phenomena into decomposable modular structures, which are then reintegrated into a whole through levels of hierarchical interactions. This is the context of the theory of bounded rationality. The resemblance, as he admits, is to the flow chart of a computer program. At the individual level, behavior is not so much substantively as procedurally "rational", breaking down problems into smaller sub-problems which can be attacked using heuristics and rules-of-thumb. At the level of the organization, repetitive problems are dealt with at lower levels, with more vexing unique problems passed up through chains of command and well-specified lines of authority.

Hierarchies of imperfectly decomposable subsystems are for Simon the primary index of "complexity": the more interconnected are the modules, the more complex the phenomenon. Complexity is significant because, given human limitations, it is the major reason certain classes of problems lay beyond our ken. However, it also becomes the bridge to Simon's theory of evolution. He maintains (1973; 1981, pp.202) that evolution, or at minimum natural selection, is "speeded up" when organic systems make use of relatively autonomous sub-components. Organisms, like information processors, are asserted to be solving problems; and if those problems are divided up along modular lines, then the organism itself can become a hierarchical structure, dealing with more complex problems than those addressable by its lower-level sub-components.[5] However, this is not intended as an explanation of the actual physiological structure of the brain, much less the morphological layout of the mammal or the organization chart of the M-form corporation, although it is primarily published in psychology journals. Because Simon believes that simulations do provide access to the understanding of complex phenomena, we gain insight into the general problem of information processing by building simulacra of problem-solving exercises.

---

[4] Which exclude any sorts of newer parallel computational architectures. It is for this reason that Simon is often categorized as a proponent of 'older' AI, characterized by sequential symbol processing, treating thought as "problem solving".

[5] One notable way in which Simon diverges from von Neumann is that the latter saw his theory as explaining how automata could triumph over the second law of thermodynamics, whereas Simon declines to make any statements about the possible relationship between entropy and evolution (1981, p.204).

Although both the "automata" and "simulacra" approaches intersect at numerous points, from dependence upon computer metaphors to algorithmic implementation to shared concern with complexity and evolution, it will be important for our subsequent argument to pay close attention to the critical ways in which they diverge. Von Neumann's automata are squarely based upon the abstract theory of computation for their formal basis, whereas Simon's simulacra usually avoid all reference to the formal theory of computation. Von Neumann regarded computational intractability as a significant component of any theory of automata, whereas Simon appears to believe that heuristic search through hierarchies 'solves' the problem of computational intractability (1981,p.35). Von Neumann did not regard the standard sequential-architecture of his computers as an adequate or even approximate model of the mind; Simon has predicated his entire career on the thesis that computer simulations of psychology are "good enough".[6] Von Neumann tended to stress the processes of interaction between the automaton and its environment as comprising the logic of its operation, while Simon has tended to blur the environment/organism distinction in his own writings, perhaps because his notion of hierarchy 'internalizes' interactions as representations of problems to be solved within the processor.

Although both von Neumann and Simon have been notorious in their disdain for orthodox neoclassical economic theory over the course of their careers, it is our impression that it has been Simon's simulacra approach which has attracted the bulk of attention and elaboration by economists relative to von Neumann's theory of automata, even among those who find themselves out of sympathy with the neoclassical orthodoxy.[7] While the reasons are undoubtedly many and varied, it might be conjectured that Simon's theory of bounded rationality appeared to hold out the promise that it could potentially be reconciled with the general neoclassical approach to economic theory, especially ignoring his doctrines concerning hierarchies. After all, Simon appears to remain resolutely methodologically individualist, treating market coordination largely as a problem of individual cognition; his simulacra approach resonates with the orthodox position that people act 'as if' they were rational maximizers, eschewing any commitment to actual empirical psychology. Indeed, much modern effort has been expended recasting bounded rationality as itself the outcome of a constrained optimization with scarce cognitive

---

[6] There is some evidence that Simon pursued the computer/ brain analogy in his early work *because* von Neumann had warned against taking it too seriously. On this incident, see (Sent, forthcoming).

[7] See, for example (Hodgson, 1993; Egidi, 1991; Conlisk, 1996).

resources.[8] The end product has not resulted in much in the way of distinctly evolutionary propositions or theories, either because of the relatively superficial treatment of evolution in Simon's own writings, or else because of the tendency of neoclassical theorists to access a conception of selection resembling earlier notions of a convergence to a fixed equilibrium or teleological imperative.

We should like to suggest that the options for the possible development of an evolutionary economics along modern information-processing lines would gain in clarity if Simon's simulacra were juxtaposed with von Neumann's automata. In particular, if Simon fosters a project which involves building little simulated problem solvers who internalize evolution, von Neumann initiated an intellectual project which constructs markets as algorithms which then evolve in the direction of increased computational complexity.

2. The Computational Approach to Markets

"The economic system can be viewed as a gigantic computing machine which tirelessly grinds out the solutions of an unending stream of quantitative problems" (Leontief, 1966, p.237).

While comparisons of markets to computers are thick on the ground in the history of economics, explicit explications of the operation of markets in formal computational terms are much less common. Here we briefly endeavor to lay out the prerequisites of the treatment of markets as automata in the spirit of von Neumann.

2.1 What a Computational Understanding of Markets Entails

One of the main effects of the neoclassical school on economic thought was a stress on the desires of the agent to the detriment of consideration of the mechanics of individual market operations. Yet recent developments in a number of seemingly unrelated areas-- experimental economics, finance, incentive structure designs, automated trading devices, law and economics-- have increasingly focused upon the definition of a market as a set of

---

[8] (Conlisk, 1996) surveys this literature. He is commendable in that he points out the paradox of self-reference which bedevils this project: How can someone carry out a constrained maximization to decide that a constrained maximization was not 'worth it'? This is a subset of the larger problem of positing neoclassical 'costs' of information: Who sets the prices of the price system, and who sets the prices of the prices of...? The contrast with von Neumann is stark: he directly confronts the logical problem of Godellian self-reference.

rules which facilitate the conduct of exchange and the conveyance of information between buyers and sellers. This shift in perspective is salutary from the viewpoint of a computational approach, since it permits the reconceptualization of markets as a set of procedures which terminate in a given goal or output.

The paramount goal from the viewpoint of neoclassical economists has been some version of the notion of allocative efficiency. Whereas the Walrasian approach tended to define a state of Pareto optimality for the 'generic' market devoid of procedural specification, research in the area of experimental economics began to raise the question of differential degrees of allocative efficiency in different types of market rule-structures. In particular, (Smith, 1991) has claimed that that the Double Auction market (DA) dominates most other market formats (such as, say, the sealed-bid auction) in producing high allocative efficiency in controlled experiments. Abstaining for the moment from accepting Smith's particular characterization of the goal or end-state of the market, and postponing a detailed description of the DA market, his work does propose the valuable idea of *ranking different market procedures according to their relative success in achieving a particular end-state*. This realization has been carried further in the work of Gode & Sunder (1993,1997), and for that reason, we shall opt to translate their work into more explicit computational terms in section 3 below. The valuable insight of Gode & Sunder is that it is possible to produce a ranking of differential market procedures by abstracting away from the cognitive capacities of the market participants, at least as a first approximation. Where we shall diverge from Gode & Sunder is that we show that the categorical arrangement of market procedures (or, perhaps better, 'institutions') in some hierarchy can be generalized for any given goal or end-state, and that the principle of categorization is provided by computational theory.

Hence, in the computational approach, particular market institutions possess a certain computational capacity independent of the computational capacity of the agents participating in the market, and this capacity can be deduced from an enumeration of the rules that constitute the specific market. Interesting examples of this approach can be found in Miller (1986). He employs first order logic in order to give a mechanical description of a DA market. Given an input of type of agent (buyer, seller), type of action (bid, ask) and quantitative proposed price, the set of rules generates an outcome, namely, an allocation of goods. Miller demonstrates that modeling of the sorts of optimality conditions favored by neoclassical economics goes well beyond this mechanical specification, requiring, for instance, the use of second-order logic.

Thus, there exists substantial precedent for attributing a certain computational capacity to types of markets predicated upon the set of market rules that describe a repetitive procedure. In the theory of computation, a procedure which contains a finite set of instructions or rules is called an algorithm. An algorithm may be described as a finite sequence of instructions, precisely expressed, that -- when confronted with a question of some kind and carried out in the most literal-minded way-- will invariably terminate, sooner or later, with the correct answer (Lewis & Papadimitriou, 1981, p.36). We would argue that the authors cited above, and indeed many other economists, are conceptualizing markets as algorithms without being fully aware of the implications of that activity. In particular, the notion of market as algorithm is entirely separable from whatever one conceives as the *purpose* of the market. For Smith, the output of the algorithm is a particular proportional realization of his definition of pre-existent consumers' surplus. For others, as in the incentive compatibility literature, it may be some notion of allocative efficiency conditional upon precise specification of agent preferences. Simpler end-state conditions might alternatively be posited, such as the clearing of a market in a certain time frame, or the output of a set of prices obeying the no-arbitrage condition.

If the individual market rules meet the criteria for an algorithm, then this constitutes the formal content of the widespread impression that the market system is a giant computer. The central lesson for an evolutionary economics is that multiple criteria for end-states justify the existence of multiple types of market/algorithms, and that these can be arrayed along a continuum of computational capacities.

2.2 Hierarchies and Classes of Automata

Automata theory is a familiar framework within the larger theory of computation, permitting a more formal specification of the informal notion of an algorithm. There exist a number of introductions to the theory of automata and computation (Lewis & Papadimitriou, 1981; Davis et al, 1994); they are the sources for our brief summary characterization below. We shall define an automaton as a restricted and abstract formal model of a computer. Algorithms can be processed on abstract automata of various capacities and configurations.

The standard theory of computation proposes a hierarchy of automata of various capacities (in increasing order) to handle strings of inputs: finite automata, pushdown automata, and Turing machines. All automata possess a finite set of internal states (including an initial state), a well-defined finite alphabet, an input (and) output device, and a transition function which carries the automaton from one state to its successor. A deterministic automaton has only one successor state for each given active state, whereas a nondeterministic automaton may have more than one successor state. The primary array of relative computational capacities of the hierarchy of automata are determined by the amount and kind of memory to which the machine has access. A Turing machine has no restriction on its memory, in the sense that there always exists the opportunity to expand its capacity. Pushdown automata also have unlimited memory, but is restricted to the process of stacking data -- last in first out -- and finite automata lack any storage device. Turing machines occupy the pinnacle of the computational hierarchy because, ignoring for the moment issues of efficiency in computation, a Turing machine can simulate the operation of any other machine, and therefore, in an abstract sense, all Turing machines are equivalent in computational capacity. "Church's Thesis" states that because Turing machines can carry out any computation that can be successfully prosecuted on any other type of automata, the Turing machine captures the intuitive content of the notion of an algorithm.

2.3 How Automata Diverge from Conventional Economics

Because of the preoccupation of orthodox economics with the characterization of the market as a manifestation of what some agent or agents *think* about it, it may require some stretch of the imagination to realize that the evolutionary automata approach (at least initially) pushes the cognitive states of the agents to the margins and focuses upon the mechanics of the processing of messages. In this framework, a market accepts well-formed sentences as inputs (orders, bids, asks, reservation schedules), grinds through the set of states implied by those messages, and produces output messages (realized prices, quantities). These messages may correspond to actions or activities (conveyance of goods, payments of currency, assumption of debts, etc.), but then again, *they may not*. One might regard this analytical separation as a projection of the standard distinction between syntax and semantics; but it proves much more far-reaching in this framework. Critical assumptions about the topology of commodity space, the 'smoothness' of preferences, independence of irrelevant alternatives, and all the rest of the standard armamentarium of the mathematical economist play no role here. A well-known result in computational theory suggests that an abstract Turing machine can be realized in a myriad of underlying physical configurations of automata; thus the physical attributes of economic activity (such as technologies or 'endowments') can be readily placed in a different class of theoretical abstractions, those effectively removed from general considerations of market operation and efficiency, but of course relevant to specific historical circumstances and social structures. Instead of the orthodox habit of imagining an atemporal generic phenomenon called a "market" (or "human rationality") fully and equally present in all of human history, the automata approach posits an abstract category of information processor which then evolves into variant formats of *plural* markets depending upon local circumstances and some generic notions of *computational* complexity and efficiency.

2.4 Some Immediate Implications of the Automata Approach for an Evolutionary Economics

Already at this very early stage, the theory of evolutionary automata bears very specific economic content. Turing machines may (ideally) possess infinite "tape" or memory, but they are restricted to a finite number of internal states and a finite alphabet. The motivation behind this inflexible requirement is that we are enjoined to adhere to a "constructivist" approach to mathematics, showing how an answer is arrived at deploying prosaic sets of rules without appeal to intuition or insight.[9] For technical reasons, it follows that our machine must restrict itself to a discrete alphabet, or when calculating, restrict its operations to the set of countable numbers (e.g., natural numbers). Far from being a nuisance, this restriction embodies an empirical generation about the history of markets: prices have always and invariably been expressed as rational numbers (i.e., ratios of natural numbers), and further, they have been denominated in monetary units which are discrete and possess an arbitrary lower bound to the smallest possible negotiable value. The appeal of the mathematical economist to the real orthant has no correspondence to economic history. This empirical regularity is not an artifact of "convenience" or some notion of costs of calculation; it is a direct consequence of the algorithmic character of markets.[10]

A salutary influence of the computational approach to markets is that it forces the analyst to be much more precise in specification of *how* the market operates, by demanding the enumeration of the sequence of steps that carries the automaton from its initial state to the final output of a sequence of prices and quantities. It is no longer acceptable to build a model simply to identify a supposed equilibrium configuration, leaving aside the question of the 'dynamics' of putative convergence until a later exercise. Indeed, it was only with the dual pressures of the automation of real-time markets, combined with the need to algorithmically specify the details of the computerized experimental protocols in the promulgation and standardization of the nascent experimental economics, that the economics profession was induced to confront the fact that there exist plural structures of market institutions, and that differences in configurations might lead to differential price-

---

[9] The constructivist approach to mathematics is best contrasted with the "Bourbakist" approach which has dominated work on Walrasian general equilibrium in the postwar period. For a nice discussion of this distinction, see (Velupillai, 1996); the history of the Bourbakist incursion into economics is described in (Weintraub & Mirowski, 199x).

[10] One could also pursue a similar inquiry into the interplay of market evolution and the invention and definition of quantitative commodity identities along the lines of (Kula, 1986), an inquiry we must bypass here. Nevertheless, the requirement that one specify the algebra over which computations are performed dictates an intrindically *monetary* theory of markets, in sharp contrast with the real/nominal dichotomy of neoclassical microeconomic theory.

quantity outcomes. Although there has been a pronounced tendency to focus attention upon the "double auction" market (one of which we shall be equally guilty), probably due to its resonance with certain neoclassical models, it has now become commonplace to admit that microeconomics should provide a taxonomy of market forms, along the lines of that in Figure I ((Friedman & Rust, 1993, p.8).

It is noteworthy that the diagram in Figure I resembles a phylogenetic tree, a device commonly used to demonstrate descent with modification in evolutionary biology. We do not claim that this particular diagram captures any such evolutionary phylogeny-- indeed, orthodox economics possesses no means by which to judge whether one abstract form could or could not descend from another, much less the historical curiosity to inquire whether it actually happened.

Our major thesis is that the automata approach does supply the wherewithal to prosecute this inquiry. Once the algorithm which characterizes a particular market format is identified and represented as a specific automata, then it becomes possible to bring von Neumann's project back into economics. First, from examination of the algorithm, one would inquire whether and under what conditions the algorithm halts. This would include questions about the conditions under which the algorithm is regarded as arrivingat the "correct" answer. Is the desideratum of the algorithm to "clear" the market in a certain time frame? Or is it simply to provide a "public order book" in which information about outstanding bids and offers is freely and accurately available to all? Or, alternatively, is it to produce a simple quantifiable halt condition, such as the absence of arbitrage possibilities within a specific time frame? Or is it constructed to meet a certain specific welfare criterion? It is of paramount importance to keep in mind that the objectives to be attained by market automata are multiple, some potentially complementary and some in conflict. The mix of objectives is geographically and temporally variable: the first prerequisite of an evolutionary situation.

Second, the analyst would rate the basic computational capacity of the specific market format relative to the previously identified objective. Is a simple finite automaton, or something more powerful, approaching the capacity of a Turing machine? If it qualifies as the latter, can it then be arrayed in order of the complexity of the inputs it is expected to handle? Additionally, one could compare and contrast automata of the same complexity class by invoking standard measures of time complexity in the theory of computation-- can the "worst case" computation be carried out in polynomial time (Garey & Johnson, 1979; Scott, 1995)? Given a suitable complexity index, one would then proceed to tackle Von Neumann's question, namely, under what set of conditions could a market of a posited level of complexity give rise to another market form of equal or greater complexity? In what formal sense is market evolution possible?

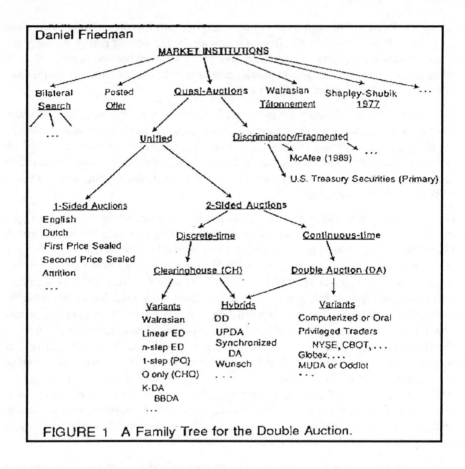

Daniel Friedman

MARKET INSTITUTIONS

Bilateral Search / Posted Offer / Quasi-Auctions / Walrasian Tâtonnement / Shapley-Shubik 1977 / ...

Unified / Discriminatory/Fragmented

McAfee (1989) ...

U.S. Treasury Securities (Primary)

1-Sided Auctions
English
Dutch
First Price Sealed
Second Price Sealed
Attrition
...

2-Sided Auctions

Discrete-time / Continuous-time

Clearinghouse (CH) / Double Auction (DA)

Variants
Walrasian
Linear ED
n-step ED
1-step (PQ)
Q only (CHQ)
K-DA
BBDA
...

Hybrids
DD
UPDA
Synchronized DA
Wunsch
...

Variants
Computerized or Oral
Privileged Traders
NYSE, CBOT, ...
Globex. ...
MUDA or Oddlot
...

FIGURE 1 A Family Tree for the Double Auction.

2.5 The Problem of Reproduction

It may be that it is here, at the idea of a specific market structure "giving rise" to another, that economic intuition may falter. What could it mean for a market automaton to "reproduce"? Here is where the abstract computational approach comes to dominate an "embodied" conception of markets. Market institutions spread in an extensive or embodied manner by simple replication of their rules, say, at another geographic location. This does not qualify as von Neumann reproduction, since it was not the market algorithm that produced the copy of itself, Market automata "reproduce" when they can imitate the abstract operation of other markets as a part of their own algorithm, incorporating a simulation of the operation of the specific market format into their own, different market format.

The simplest example of this "universal" capacity is markets for derivatives. When agents trade in the futures market for grain contracts, they are attempting to simulate the outputs of a different market, namely, that of the spot market for actual grain. It is of special importance to recognize that the spot market (say, an English auction) can and frequently does operate according to distinctly divergent algorithms than does the futures market (say, a double auction); hence one automaton is "reproducing" an altogether different automaton. It is the appearance of this "self-referential" aspect of automata that creates the possibility of a hierarchy of computational complexity, and hence "evolution" in the von Neumann sense. Market forms may "spread" relative to one another (say, fixed-price storefronts replace itinerant haggling peddlers), and as such may be subject to a particularly crude kind of "selection"; but since nothing profoundly novel arises from this process, there is no phylogeny and no evolution as such. The system only displays a phylogeny and therefore a distinct arrow of time when market automata begin to emulate the operation of other such automata, resulting in calculations of ever-higher complexity.

In this evolutionary automata approach, many economic terms undergo profound redefinition. Markets are no longer environments within which agents operate; it is within the ecosystem of the multiform diversity of agents and cultures in which markets calculate and evolve. Since the first prerequisite of an evolutionary theory of 'natural selection' is that the entity which encapsulates the inheritance principle displays greater inertia than the surrounding environment, for the first time economists may escape the Lamarckian indictment which has bedeviled the efforts of theorists like Nelson and Winter (1982). Moreover, "market failure" no longer indicates some disjunction between an imaginary optimum of utility and the equilibrium identified by the analyst; it now refers to a real and easily identifiable phenomenon, that where a market algorithm fails to halt within the parameters of operation of the specific automaton. Since it is a theorem of the theory of computation that there is no general algorithm for deciding whether or not a Turing machine will halt, market failure is understood to be an endemic and inescapable fact of life. Examples of such phenomena are market "crashes", price free-falls, markets unable to conduct arbitrage operations, markets incapable of conveying order information to other markets, cascading shortfalls and macroeconomic contractions. "Efficiency" likewise becomes decoupled from any prior specification of the desires of the individuals involved. An 'efficient market' now becomes an automaton that can handle a wide diversity of messages emanating from people with differing beliefs, desires, cognitive skills and cultural backgrounds as inputs, and produce price and quantity outputs meeting fixed prior desiderata (market clearing, arbitrage, etc.) in finite, and preferably polynomial, time. Furthermore, the age-old theme of the benefits of the division of labor, so vanishingly present within the Walrasian tradition, enjoys a revival within the computational tradition. There need be no presumption that market automata are restricted to be sequential symbol processing devices; as markets necessarily become more interconnected, accepting as inputs the price and quantity outputs of other market automata, it becomes helpful to regard clusters of market automata as constituting a distributed processing device, mimicking connectionist architectures (Barbosa, 1993). This concatenation of multiple processors at a lower level into a novel entity at a macro level may mirror the transitions between levels of organization found in the biological record (Smith & Szathmary, 1995).

3. A Concrete Example of the Evolutionary Automata Approach.

We have argued that the evolutionary automata approach (at least initially) should relegate the cognitive states of the agents to a subordinate status and focus upon the mechanics of the processing of messages and information. Elements of this research project can already be found in the economic literature (e.g., Miller (1996), DeVany & Walls(1996), Cason & Friedman(1997), and Gode & Sunder(1993;1997)). To give some idea of the extent to which this literature can be synthesized and expanded within the automata approach suggested in the previous section, we here opt to translate the work of Gode&Sunder (henceforth G&S)--specifically, parts of their 1997 paper-- into our automata framework. By so doing, we do not intend to endorse their claim that Marshallian consumer surplus is the single correct index of allocative efficiency, nor do we necessarily agree with their assertions concerning discovery of the attributes of success true for all markets, whatever their structure. Our objective is rather to provide an illustration of how one goes about formulating an abstract market structure as an automaton, and to reveal (in a manner they did not) that there exists a computational hierarchy along which different markets can be ranked, as a prelude to full prosecution of von Neumann's program of formalizing evolution as the temporal unfolding of increased complexity.

We can identify at least three aspects of the work of G&S that render it suitable to be encompassed by our suggested evolutionary automata approach.

[1] The analytical distinction between market (automata) and the agents' cognitive skills is an issue already rendered salient by the experimental economics literature. This distinction was initiated by the work of Smith (1991), which reports strikingly high allocative efficiency of experiments conducted in a DA market. G&S (1993) resorted to simulated Zero Intelligence (ZI) traders submitting bids and asks in a computerized market setting explicitly to "zero out" all cognitive considerations and highlight the primary determinants of this standard finding of high allocative efficiency in the DA market. They show that almost all of this efficiency is due to the algorithmic aspects of

the market alone, i.e., the market closing rules and the restriction that the bid/asks are only effective when they conform to a budget constraint.[11] Thus they make explicit the key analytical distinction between market automata and environment (i.e., agents' cognitive skills) which we claim is central to the automata approach and permits our distinctive conception of evolution.

[2] The 1993 paper also shows that ZI simulations with budget constraints mimic the results of human experiments fairly closely. This suggests the idea that certain market formats are relatively robust in performance relative to different environments consisting of people of diverse cognitive skills. This idea echoes our discussion (in sections 2.3-4) of different markets possessing different levels of computational capacity arrayed in order of their robustness (here provisionally defined as stability of outputs in different environments) as a first step towards the introduction of von Neumann's project into economics.

[3] The 1997 paper begins to deal with a hierarchy of different market rules in an explicit ZI environment, with the idea of quantifying incremental improvements in the efficiency measure and attributing them to specific rules. This work takes the largest strides toward treating different markets as different types of automata, although G&S do not motivate it in this manner. It also begins to entertain more explicitly the idea of arraying the different markets along some continuum of complexity, and testing that continuum against a controlled environment, thus opening up the possibility of a von Neumann-style definition of evolution.

Our exercise assumes the following format. G&S provide models of three classes of market rules: their so-called "Null Market" (random matching of good to buyer); a simple first-price sealed bid auction; and a synchronized double auction (DA). Real markets are much more complicated than such sparse characterizations, so the abstractions of G&S provide us with a convenient opportunity to encode this much simpler set of rules as automata. We show that their definitions of sealed-bid and DA fall into different classes of computational capacity, viz., different types of automata. Our initial contribution to an evolutionary approach is to show that a DA can mimic a sealed-bid auction but that the converse is not true. This intransitivity has not previously been a topic of commentary in the economics literature, and can only become obvious when both markets are redefined in an automata framework. The DA requires extra memory capacity that makes it impossible for the sealed bid market to mimic the DA market. This suggests that, for certain given objectives, the DA is formally a "descendant" of the sealed bid market, and

---

[11] It is not completely obvious that the latter is part of the market automata under consideration. But what is important is that it is not necessarily part of the agents cognitive skill.

can therefore handle more complex information processing tasks. This formal result can then be brought to bear in the future on a "natural history" of markets, to research the possible ways in which these particular market forms have evolved relative to one another.

3.1 The Work of G&S.

In a sequence of papers G&S (1993;1997) address the question why the experimental economics literature reports high allocative efficiency for DA markets. Allocative efficiency-- the ratio of the actual to the potential gains from trade-- is one of the criteria used by the experimental literature to analyze the working of markets in general, and the DA in particular. Allocative efficiency in this definition is high if the consumers who value a good the most manage to buy their units from the lowest cost producers.

G&S (1993) report a market experiment in which human traders are completely replaced by "zero-intelligence" (ZI) agents. These ZIs are in practice simulation programs that randomly choose their bids and asks subject to market rules. The ZIs generate an allocative efficiency close to 100% once their bids and asks are forced to conform to their budget constraints. Thus, by introducing ZIs, G&S are able to "zero out" all cognitive considerations and highlight the primary causes of the standard finding of experimental economists that the DA market achieves high level of allocative efficiency. In G&S (1997) they further elaborate upon this striking result. This paper shows that starting with a base situation of almost no market rules (their Null Market) and then recursively adding procedural rules to the simulation will improve its expected allocative efficiency. The trading environment remains specified as ZI traders that choose randomly subject to market rules, whereas the market rules determine the bid/ask range within which traders choose subject to a uniform probability distribution. They show that recursively adding market rules will further limit the possible price range in which the good can be traded by extramarginal traders, consequently increasing the expected allocative efficiency. The work of G&S demonstrates that almost all of the observed allocative efficiency is due to the algorithmic aspects of the market, independent of cognitive considerations.

The work of G&S (1997) therefore seems to justify the conclusion that much of the computational capacity required to conduct trade is incorporated in certain repetitive market rules, where the market itself can be interpreted as an algorithm. To render this assertion more precise we will use several of the rules analyzed by G&S to provide a sketch of the automaton to which the markets--that are constituted by these rules--can be encoded.

Note that throughout this analysis we will make the simplifying assumption that in every trade round only one unit is under consideration by the agents. This is an artifact of the translation of G&S's exercise. Additionally, bids and asks are encoded in a "convenient" way, which for our purpose is an unary notation (e.g., bid=10 is represented as a string of 10 ones denoted as I). Thus, for purposes of illustration, we limit the construction of the machine to the encoding of the market rules. This assumption is justified by the fact that we are only interested in comparing the computational complexity of markets constituted by certain commensurate rules, i.e., all markets are assumed to have the same auxiliary capacity to encoded bids and ask in an unary input string.

3.2 Null Market Encoded on a Finite Automaton.

The base case of our analysis will be the Null market described in Gode & Sunder (1997, p.612); this market is deficient of rules. The machine that represents this market is exceedingly trivial, something which the name already seems to imply. The only thing that the machine needs to do is recognize if both a bid and ask are submitted; after this condition is satisfied, it will arbitrarily halt or read the next available input. This requires so little computational capacity that this market can be modeled by a nondeterministic finite automaton. A nondeterministic finite automaton is a quintuple $M=(Q, \Sigma, \Delta, q_0, F)$, where Q is a finite set of which its elements are called states; q_0 is a distinguished element of Q called the start state; Σ denotes an alphabet; $F \subseteq Q$ is the set of final states, and Δ, the transition relation, is a finite subset of $Qx\Sigma^*xQ$. (Σ^* is the set of all strings--including the empty string--over Σ.) The rules according to which the automaton M picks its next state are encoded into the transition relation. For example, if $(q,a,q') \in \Delta$, M may read of a and move to state q'. Note, that this automata is called nondeterministic because Δ does not (necessarily) uniquely determines the machine's next configuration. Given that a machine is in state q, Δ can have, for example the instructions: read of an arbitrary number of $a's$, $a \in \Sigma$, and go to state q' or do not read of any element of the input string and go to state q''. The essential feature of finite automata is that it is a language recognizer. It reads of an input string, $\sigma \in \Sigma^*$ (scanning the string from left to right) and if after reading of the whole string it reaches a final state $q \in F$ then the input sting is considered to be accepted. The language accepted by the machine is the set of strings it accepts.

We can encode the Null market onto a finite automaton M_0 by using only four states where $Q=\{ q_0, q_1, q_2, q_3\}$, $\Sigma=\{a, b, I\}$, $F=\{q_3\}$ and the essential transitions in Δ are (q_0, a, q_1), (q_1,b, q_3), (q_0, b, q_2), and (q_2, a, q_3). We adopt the convention that the symbol "a" proceeds the unary input if it is an ask and "b" if it is a bid. Now, M_0 constitutes an and-gate that ensures, that at least one bid and offer are submitted before the machine halts. In constructing the automaton we ignored details highlighted by G&S, such as what mechanism determines the probability that a transaction takes place. By extending its design, and introducing probabilistic matrices that encode the probability of a certain transition-taking place, we can simulate the interaction of Null market. To do so we need to add an extra element to the machine such that we have the sextuple $M_0'=(Q, \Sigma, \Delta, q_0, F, \{A(x)\})$, where only $\{A(x)\}$ differs from the original machine M_0. $\{A(x)\}$ is a finite set containing $|\Sigma|$ square stochastic matrices of the order $|Q|$ where $x \in \Sigma$ and a matrix $A(x)$ is stochastic if all the entries of its row vectors are greater than or equal to 0 and sum up to 1. ($|.|$ denotes the cardinality of a set.) M_0' is a probabilistic finite automaton. We first introduced M_0 in order to draw an explicit distinction between an algorithmic analysis of market rules and the more conventional approach that begins with behavior without specification of context.

3.3 A Sealed Bid Auction Encoded on a Two-Headed Pushdown Automaton

In the previous subsection we completed our sketch of the automaton of the Null market, M_0. Before continuing we want to emphasis that automaton M_0 has very little computational capacity as its only real computation-- with respect to calculating a market price-- is the and-gate which ensures that at least one bid and ask are submitted before a final state is reached. The first thing we need to introduce in order to encode a market with a more substantial computational capacity on a machine M is to introduce a more sophisticated halting condition. A halting condition gives the circumstances under which a machine M reaches a final state and ceases computation. In the previous case, the halting condition was that at least one bid and ask need to be submitted. Henceforth, the condition for a machine to halt will be that a submitted bid is greater than or equal to a submitted ask. This apparently simple condition already requires a machine substantially more powerful than a finite automata. The reason for this is that the machine needs to be able to accept the following types of string,

$L=\{I^m b I^n a : m \geq n\}$,

where $a, b, I \in \Sigma$ and $I^m b$ encodes a bid of magnitude m in denary notation (e.g., $I^m b$ where $m=10$ gives a bid of \$10). Thus L defines the language that M needs to accept. First note that we do not put any a priori restrictions on the size of a bid and ask, this implies that L is an infinite language. Therefore we can show that L cannot be accepted by a finite automaton, using for instance one of the *pumping theorems* for Finite Automata (Lewis & Papadimitriou 1981, chapter 2). The intuition here is that, since finite automata have no storage capacity, they can only handle strings of arbitrary length that have very limited complexity.

In order to encode this halting condition onto a machine we need to introduce appropriate storage capacity. This can be done by restricting the data structure to a stack--last in first out--i.e., we can use a pushdown automaton to encode the halting condition. A pushdown automaton is a quintuple $M=(Q, \Sigma, \Gamma, q_0, F)$, where Q is a finite set of states, $q_0 \in Q$ is the start state, Σ is an alphabet (the input symbols), Γ is an alphabet (the stack symbols), $F \subseteq Q$ is the set of final states, and Δ, the transition relation, is a finite subset of $(Q x \Sigma^* x \Gamma^*) x (Q x \Gamma^*)$. Intuitively, if $((q,a,\omega),(q',\theta)) \in \Delta$ then whenever M is in state q with ω on top of the stack it may read a from the input tape replace ω by θ on the top of the stack and enter state q'. The essence of M is that it stores an encoded ask, and if a bit is submitted starts crossing out I's. If the stack is emptied before the complete bid string is read it will reach a halting state $q \in F$ and halts (after reading the remaining element of b).

We will now add the following two rules to the halting condition (taken from Gode & Sunder (1997, p.610)):

1. *Binding contract rule: bids and asks are binding, i.e., buyers must pay what they bid; and sellers must sell at what they ask.*

2. *Price priority rule: higher bids dominate lower bids, and lower asks dominate higher asks.*

Rule 1 enjoins the market participant to bid in accordance with their budget constraint, and rule 2 makes it more likely that buyers with the highest redemption value and sellers with the lowest cost will trade. These two rules, in combination with the halting condition, can give rise to a Sealed-Bid market.[12] Two essential features of this institution are: the one-sidedness of the auction, dictating that for a given fixed supply only bids are submitted; and the restriction that traders have no knowledge of or influence upon other bids being submitted.

For simplicity, we will consider a single-unit sealed-bid auction (only one unit is offered). This institution can be encoded on a pushdown automaton, where only the *minimum ask*-- the price below which the supplier is not willing to trade--needs to be stored in the automaton. The automaton will halt as soon as a bid exceeds this minimum price. Given this very simple structure of the auction rule 2 is automatically satisfied by the halting condition, because the machine halts as soon as a bid exceeds the minimum ask. It is not equally straightforward if the binding contract rule (rule 1) should also be encoded on the market automaton. A possibility might exist that traders are enjoined to keep a deposit accessible by the auction mechanism so that the credibility of every bid can be checked. However, it is more likely that rule 1 is enforced outside of the immediate framework of

---

[12] Note that above rules in combination with that halting condition ensures that only voluntary trade will occur, hence satisfying all three conditions for a Sealed Bid market stated by Gode&Sunder.

the auction, by either the law, or some other separate institution such as the banking system, gilds of individual traders, credit-rating services, or any combination of these structures. Henceforth, we will assume that rule 1 is enforced outside the market institution under consideration. Hence the most important aspect of a pushdown automaton M_1 --that gives rise to a single-unit sealed-bid auction-- is the halting condition.

Appendix I presents the essential features of a pushdown automaton that accepts the language $L=\{l^m b l^n a : m \geq n\}$. That is the halting condition-- a bid has to exceed an ask before the machine reaches a final state-- is encoded on this machine. Henceforth we will call this automaton the halting machine, M_H. This halting machine can be best portrayed as a subroutine of the machine M_1. Additionally, M_1, needs to have an extra head to restore the minimum ask (below which the supplier is not willing to trade) on to the stack. (See appendix II for the pseudo-code and a more formal definition of a k-headed push down automaton.)

Note that M_1 is a machine with minimum computational complexity upon which such an auction can be encoded. The computational capacity of a pushdown automaton with two heads is larger in magnitude than an automaton with one stack. This is due to the fact that elements stored earlier have to be deleted before elements that are stored later are accessible. In other words, to read an ask in order to compare it with a bid, it is necessary for machine M_H to delete the stored ask while checking if the halting condition is satisfied. Moreover, both heads only move from left to right scanning the input tape on which the submitted bids are encoded. Once a bid is scanned the head cannot return to this particular bid. Therefore M_1 needs an additional head to restore the minimum ask on top of the stack, so that it can compute the subroutine M_H an arbitrary number of times.

The complexity of the sealed bid auction discussed above can be increased by adding one more rule that needs to be encoded on the machine (Gode & Sunder 1997, p.610):

3. *Accumulation rule: the highest bid (and the lowest ask if it is a double auction) are chosen only after all bids (and asks) have been collected.*

Rule 3 ensures that the market no longer automatically clears as soon as a bid exceeds a ask. Now it will be the case that, under a certain regime, all bids (and asks if it is a double auction) submitted within a certain time frame are collected before the market clears. To encode the machine M_2 with the additional rule 3 requires the machine--in addition to the functions it inherit from M_1 --to store the highest bid that has been registered of the input string so far. Additionally, the machine now needs to keep track of who submitted the stored bid and ask. Implicitly, the machine needs to keep track of the order in which bids and asks are scanned. Although, M_2 is a more complex machine than M_1 it can still be encoded on a two headed pushdown automaton (see appendix II). We can be more precise with our notion of complexity by arguing in this instance that in the worst case scenario, it will take M_2 longer to halt than M_1.

3.4 The Double Auction Encoded on a Three-Tape Pushdown Automaton

The last rule we will introduce in this paper is:

4. *Double Auction rule: buyers can bid as well as sellers can ask.*

Rules 1 to 4 give rise to a rudimentary double auction (DA). To encoded the DA on a machine M_3 it is necessary to deploy an automaton of a different computational complexity class. It is impossible for the DA to be encoded on a two-headed pushdown automaton that stores both the highest bid and lowest ask and simultaneously keeps track of the number of bids and ask that preceded a stored bid or ask (in order to know who submitted the bid or ask). For simplicity, we will still assume that only one good per trading round is traded/offered, but now both bids and asks can be submitted. M_3 uses M_2 as a subroutine; only now two additional heads are needed (head 3 and 4). The two additional heads are needed to first store the minimum ask on top of the stack. Next M_2 is used as a subroutine to determine the maximum bid and if this bid exceeds the minimum.

3.5 Concluding Remarks

For the purpose of illustration of our discussion of a von Neumann-style definition of evolution as a progression through increasing degrees of complexity, we accessed the definitions by Gode & Sunder of a Null market baseline, a sealed-bid market and a DA market. We demonstrated that all three "markets" can be characterized by automata of differing computational complexities. The Null baseline can be described as a simple finite automata; the sealed bid market can be encoded on a two headed push down automaton; and the double auction market needs at least the computational capacity of a four headed pushdown automata, primarily because both sides of the market are active. As a direct corollary of this result, it follows that it is (in general) impossible for the sealed-bid market to mimic the operation of the DA, but the converse is not true since a sealed-bid market can be encoded as a subroutine of the DA.

The implications of this exercise for an evolutionary economics are immediate and striking. Gode & Sunder have argued that these three market formats underwrite a progressively greater degree of allocative efficiency, admittedly gauged by their single criterion. We have demonstrated that these three formats display an increasing degree of computational complexity when viewed as automata, independent of the cognitive capacities of the market participants. Thus, given some specific goals or criteria for success, it is now possible to provide a formal characterization of the hierarchy of the diversity of market forms in terms of their complexity, defined relative to that specific goal. Further, "reproduction" is now given an unambiguous interpretation as one market format mimicking the operation of another. With the recognition of multiple goals and their attendant complexity hierarchies, *for the first time* there exists the outlines of a formal economic model of the modern conception of evolution as a dynamic selection of information processors which is not itself a metaphorical projection of the attributes of biological entities. It is a revival of the project of von Neumann, not that of Darwin. It is an "evolutionary economics" where the stress is on the noun, not the adjective.

In contrast to previous competing versions of evolutionary economics, the computational approach has one historical trend in its favor, which suggests that it will eventually transcend mere academic interest. Already, automated markets and artificial agents are playing an ever-increasing role in real-world economic transactions (Anon, 1997; Miller, 1996). Specialists are employed today to program the automata we have described. Market participants will not have to stretch their imaginations to conceptualize the automata approach to economics, for they will increasingly find it all around themselves in their everyday activities.

Appendix I:

The halting condition.

The halting condition that a bid needs to exceeds an ask can be captured by the language

$L=\{l^m b l^n a : m \geq n\}$.

This language can be accepted by a pushdown automaton $M_H=(Q, \Sigma, \Gamma, \Delta, q_0, F)$, where

Q is a finite set of states, $q_0 \in Q$ is the start state, Σ is an alphabet (the input symbols), Γ is an alphabet (the stack symbols), $F \subseteq Q$ is the set of final states, and Δ, the transition relation, is a finite subset of $(Q x \Sigma^* x \Gamma^*) x (Q x \Gamma^*)$.

The essential transitions of a (nondetermenistic) pushdown automaton that accepts this language are

1. $((q_0,a,e),(q_1,a))$ push (add) a on top of the stack

2. $((q_1,I,e),(q_1,I))$ push (add) I on top of the stack

3. $((q_1,b,e),(q_2,e))$ switch states

4. $((q_2,I,I),(q_2,e))$ pop (replace) I from the stack

5. $((q_2,I,\#),(q_f,e))$ reach final state q_f, since bid>ask,

where all 5 transitions are an element of Δ, the transition relation. Transition 1 recognizes an ask and puts the machine in state q_1 the state in which an ask is stored. The storage is completed by transition 2, which has the ones, I, stored. (Remember that $I...I$ denotes the size of bids and asks in unary notation.) Transition 4 checks if a bid exceeds the stored ask by crossing out ones and if a blank symbol--denoted by #--is reach first on the stack then the bid is bigger then the ask, hence the machine reaches the final state q_f (transition 5).

Appendix II:

More formally we can describe a push down automaton with multiple heads as follows.

A k headed push down automata (henceforth k-PDA) is a sextuple $M=(Q, \Sigma, \Gamma, \Delta, q_0, F)$, where Q is a finite set of states; Σ is an alphabet (the input symbols); Γ is an alphabet (the stack symbols); $q_0 \in Q$ is the initial state; $F \subseteq Q$ is the set of final states; Δ, the transition relation, is a mapping from $Q \times (\Sigma \cup \{e\})^k \times \Gamma$ to finite subsets of $Q \times \Gamma^*$, where Γ^* denotes the set of all strings over the alphabet Γ and $(\Sigma \cup \{e\})^k$ abbreviates $(\Sigma \cup \{e\}) \times ... \times (\Sigma \cup \{e\})$; the k symbols (possible the empty symbol/string denoted by e) read by the k-heads.

Let M be a k-DPA, p and q be two state in M, u an input symbol, γ and β stack symbols and $((p,u,e,...,e, \beta),(q,\gamma)) \in \Delta$. Then M, whenever it is in state p with β on top of the stack, may read u from the input tape with head I, read nothing with the other heads, replace β by γ on top of the stack, and enter state q. A symbol is deleted whenever it is popped from the stack and a symbols is stored whenever it is pushed onto the stack. M for example pops (deletes) β from the stack with the transition $((p,u,e,...,e,\beta),(q,e))$ and pushes (stored) β with the transition $((p,u,e,...,e,e),(q,\beta))$. M is said to accept a string $\pi \in \Sigma^*$ if and only if (q_0,π,e) yields (p,e,e) for some state $p \in F$ and a sequence of transitions. The language accepted by M, denoted $L(M)$, is the set of all strings accepted by M.

In this appendix we show that a sealed bid can be encoded onto a 2-PDA automaton. Machine M_1 gives rise to the sealed-bid market with only the price priority rule. M_1 is a pushdown automaton with two heads, 1 and 2, respectively and elements of M_H as a subroutine.[13] The pseudo-code of M_1 is the following.

1. Push the minimum ask on top of the stack, using head I.

2. Compare stored ask with the next submitted bids using head I. If ask >bid then recover ask by adding bid to remainder of ask, using head II. Otherwise, push bid onto stack, using head II.

3. Repeat step 2 until Ask≤Bid or the end of input tape is reached. When the latter happens the automaton terminates without reaching a final state.

Thus M_1 halts as soon as it detects a bid that exceeds the minimum ask. The last bid scanned by M_1 gives the price for which the offered good will be traded. Machine M_2 gives rise to a sealed-bid auction with price priority rule and accumulation rule. M_2 is again a pushdown automaton with two heads, 1 and 2, respectively. M_2 is very similar to M_1 only now the machine will only halts if all bids within a certain trading round are read of. M_2 contains M_1 plus the following additional steps.

4. Compare stored bid with bid currently scanned by head I. If stored bid ≥ scanned bid recover stored bid by adding scanned bid to remainder of stored bid, using head II. Otherwise, pop remainder of stored bid and push currently scanned bid onto stack, using head II.

5. Repeat step IV until the end of the input tape is reached, after which the machine reaches a final state. The essential transitions of M_2 are: [14]

1. Push the minimum ask on top of the stack using head I.

      1.1 $(q_0,a,a,e),(q_1,a)$ push a on top of stack.

      1.2 $(q_1,I,e,e),(q_1,I)$ push I on top of stack.

      1.3 $(q_1,b,b,e),(q_2,e)$ switch states as soon as the next bid is encountered.

2. Compare minimum ask with scanned bid using head I.

    2.1 $(q_2,I,e,I),(q_2,e)$ pop I from stack.

    2.2 $(q_2,I,e,a),(q_f,b)$ bid exceeds ask.[15]

---

[13] Strictly speaking M_H, defined in appendix I, is not really a subroutine of M_1 because it is a 1-PDA whereas M_1 is a 2-PDA. The real issue is that M_1 incorporates the essential computational features of M_H as a subroutine.

[14] For simplicity we omitted all transactions related to reaching the end of the input tape

2.3 $(q_2,b,e,a),(q_{f+1},b)$ bid equals ask (see footnote 15)

2.4 $(q_2,b,e,I),(q_3,e)$ ask exceeds bid.

3. Recover minimum ask by using head II and go to step 2 again.

3.1 $(q_3,e,I,e),(q_3,e)$ push I on top of stack.

3.2 $(q_3,e,b,e),(q_2,e)$ switch states (the minimum ask is restored).

4.1 Have head I completely scan remainder of the currently scanned bid.

4.1 $(q_f,I,e,e),(q_f,e)$ scan input tape with head I.

4.2 $(q_f,b,e,e),(q_{f+1},e)$ switch state (head one reaches the next bid).

4.2 Recover highest bid scanned using head II.

4.3 $(q_{f+1},e,I,e),(q_{f+1},I)$ push I onto top of stack.

4.4 $(q_{f+1},e,b,e),(q_{f+2},e)$ switch state (bid is stored onto stack).

4.3 Compare stored bid with the bid scanned next by head I.

4.5 $(q_{f+2},I,e,I),(q_{f+2},e)$ pop I from stack.

4.6 $(q_{f+2},I,e,b),(q_{f+1},e)$ stored bid exceeds scanned bid.

4.7 $(q_{f+2},b,e,b),(q_{f+1},e)$ stored bid equals scanned bid.

4.8 $(q_{f+2},b,e,I),(q_{f+1},b)$ scanned bid exceeds stored bid (see footnote 15).

5. The last three transitions already incorporate the final step of repeating step 4.

References

Anon. 1997. "Intelligent Agents Roboshop," *The Economist*, June 14:72.

Aspray, W. & Burks, A. eds. 1987. *The Papers of John von Neumann on Computing and Computer Theory*. Cambridge: MIT Press.

Badii, R. & Politi, A. 1997. *Complexity: Hierarchical Structures and Scaling in Physics*. Cambridge: Cambridge University Press.

---

[15] b is pushed on top of the stack to mark the end of a stored bid.

Barbosa, Valmir. 1993. *Massively Parallel Models of Computation*. New York: Horwood.

Cason, Timothy & Friedman, Daniel. 1997. "Price Formation in Single Call Markets," *Econometrica*, (65):311-45.

Chang & Keisler.

Conlisk, John. 1996. "Why Bounded Rationality?" *Journal of Economic Literature*, (34):669-700.

Davis, M.; Sigal, R. & Weyuker, E. 1994. *Computability, Complexity and Languages.* San Diego: Academic Press.

Dennett, Daniel. 1995. *Darwin's Dangerous Idea.* New York: Simon & Schuster.

Depew, David & Weber, Bruce. 1995. *Darwinism Evolving.* Cambridge: MIT Press.

de Vany, A. & Walls, x. 1996.

Egidi, M. et al. 1991. *Economics, Bounded Rationality and the Cognitive Revolution.* Aldershot: Elgar.

Friedman, D. & Rust, J. eds. 1993. *The Double Auction Market.* Reading: Addison-Wesley.

Garey, M. & Johnson, D. 1979. *Computers and Intractability.* New York: WH Freeman.

Gode, D. & Sunder, S. 1993. "Allocative Efficiency of Markets with Zero-Intelligence Traders," *Journal of Political Economy*, (101):119-137.

Gode, D. & Sunder, S. 1997. "What Makes Markets Allocatively Efficient?" *Quarterly Journal of Economics*, (105): 603-30.

Hirshleifer, Jack. 1978. "Natural economy versus political economy," *Journal of Social and Biological Structures*, (2):319-337.

Hodgson, Geoffrey. 1993. *Economics and Evolution.* Ann Arbor: University of Michigan Press.

Kay, Lily. 1997. "Cybernetics, Information, Life," *Configurations*, (5):23-91.

Kula, Witold. 1986. *Measures and Men.* Princeton: Princeton University Press.

Leontief, Wassily. 1966. *Essays in Economics.* Oxford: Oxford University Press.

Lewis, Alain. 1985. "On Effectively Computable Realizations of Choice Functions," *Mathematical Social Sciences*, (10):43-80.

Lewis, Harry & Papadimitriou, Christos. 1981. *Elements of the Theory of Computation*. Englewood Cliffs: Prentice Hall.

Miller, Ross. 1986. "Markets as Logic Programs," in L. Pau, ed., *Artificial Intelligence in Economics and Management*. Amsterdam: North Holland.

Miller, Ross. 1996. "Smart Market Mechanisms: from practice to theory," *Journal of Economic Dynamics and Control*, (20):967-978.

Mirowski, Philip. 1989. *More Heat than Light*. New York: Cambridge University Press.

Mirowski, Philip. forthcoming. *Machine Dreams*. Durham: Duke University Press.

Mirowski, Philip & Somefun, Koye. "Markets as Evolving Computational Entities," Journal of Evolutionary Economics, (8):329-356.

Murphy, M. & O'Neill, L. eds. 1995. *What is Life? The Next 50 Years*. Cambridge: Cambridge University Press.

National Science Board. 1996. *Science and Engineering Indicators, 1996*. Washington: US Government Printing Office.

Nelson, R. & Winter, S. 1982. *An Evolutionary Theory of Economic Change*. Cambridge: Harvard University Press.

Page, Scott E. 1995. *"Two measures of Difficulty,"* California Institute of Technology working paper.

Sent, Esther-Mirjam. forthcoming. "A Simon Who Is Not All that Simple" University of Notre Dame working paper.

Simon, Herbert. 1973. "The Organization of Complex Systems," in H. Patee, ed., *Hierarchy Theory*. New York: George Braziller.

Simon, Herbert. 1981. *The Sciences of the Artificial*. rev. ed. Cambridge: MIT Press.

Smith, John Maynard & Szathmary, Eors. 1995. *The Major Transitions in Evolution*. Oxford: WH Freeman.

Smith, Vernon. 1991. *Papers in Experimental Economics*. New York: Cambridge University Press.

Velupillai, Kumaraswamy. 1996. "The Computable Alternative in the Formalization of Economics," *Kyklos*, (49):251-272.

von Neumann, John. 1966. *Theory of Self-Reproducing Automata.* Urbana: University of Illinois Press.

Weintraub, E.R. & Mirowski, P. 1994. "The Pure and the Applied," *Science in Context*, (7):245-272.

Yockey, Hubert. 1992. *Information Theory and Molecular Biology.* New York: Cambridge University Press.

Druck: Strauss Offsetdruck, Mörlenbach
Verarbeitung: Schäffer, Grünstadt

Lecture Notes in Economics and Mathematical Systems

For information about Vols. 1–295
please contact your bookseller or Springer-Verlag

Vol. 296: A. Börsch-Supan, Econometric Analysis of Discrete Choice. VIII, 211 pages. 1987.

Vol. 297: V. Fedorov, H. Läuter (Eds.), Model-Oriented Data Analysis. Proceedings, 1987. VI, 239 pages. 1988.

Vol. 298: S.H. Chew, Q. Zheng, Integral Global Optimization. VII, 179 pages. 1988.

Vol. 299: K. Marti, Descent Directions and Efficient Solutions in Discretely Distributed Stochastic Programs. XIV, 178 pages. 1988.

Vol. 300: U. Derigs, Programming in Networks and Graphs. XI, 315 pages. 1988.

Vol. 301: J. Kacprzyk, M. Roubens (Eds.), Non-Conventional Preference Relations in Decision Making. VII, 155 pages. 1988.

Vol. 302: H.A. Eiselt, G. Pederzoli (Eds.), Advances in Optimization and Control. Proceedings, 1986. VIII, 372 pages. 1988.

Vol. 303: F.X. Diebold, Empirical Modeling of Exchange Rate Dynamics. VII, 143 pages. 1988.

Vol. 304: A. Kurzhanski, K. Neumann, D. Pallaschke (Eds.), Optimization, Parallel Processing and Applications. Proceedings, 1987. VI, 292 pages. 1988.

Vol. 305: G.-J.C.Th. van Schijndel, Dynamic Firm and Investor Behaviour under Progressive Personal Taxation. X, 215 pages.1988.

Vol. 306: Ch. Klein, A Static Microeconomic Model of Pure Competition. VIII, 139 pages. 1988.

Vol. 307: T.K. Dijkstra (Ed.), On Model Uncertainty and its Statistical Implications. VII, 138 pages. 1988.

Vol. 308: J.R. Daduna, A. Wren (Eds.), Computer-Aided Transit Scheduling. VIII, 339 pages. 1988.

Vol. 309: G. Ricci, K. Velupillai (Eds.), Growth Cycles and Multisectoral Economics: The Goodwin Tradition. III, 126 pages. 1988.

Vol. 310: J. Kacprzyk, M. Fedrizzi (Eds.), Combining Fuzzy Imprecision with Probabilistic Uncertainty in Decision Making. IX, 399 pages. 1988.

Vol. 311: R. Färe, Fundamentals of Production Theory. IX, 163 pages. 1988.

Vol. 312: J. Krishnakumar, Estimation of Simultaneous Equation Models with Error Components Structure. X, 357 pages. 1988.

Vol. 313: W. Jammernegg, Sequential Binary Investment Decisions. VI, 156 pages. 1988.

Vol. 314: R. Tietz, W. Albers, R. Selten (Eds.), Bounded Rational Behavior in Experimental Games and Markets. VI, 368 pages. 1988.

Vol. 315: I. Orishimo, G.J.D. Hewings, P. Nijkamp (Eds.), Information Technology: Social and Spatial Perspectives. Proceedings 1986. VI, 268 pages. 1988.

Vol. 316: R.L. Basmann, D.J. Slottje, K. Hayes, J.D. Johnson, D.J. Molina, The Generalized Fechner-Thurstone Direct Utility Function and Some of its Uses. VIII, 159 pages. 1988.

Vol. 317: L. Bianco, A. La Bella (Eds.), Freight Transport Planning and Logistics. Proceedings, 1987. X, 568 pages. 1988.

Vol. 318: T. Doup, Simplicial Algorithms on the Simplotope. VIII, 262 pages. 1988.

Vol. 319: D.T. Luc, Theory of Vector Optimization. VIII, 173 pages. 1989.

Vol. 320: D. van der Wijst, Financial Structure in Small Business. VII, 181 pages. 1989.

Vol. 321: M. Di Matteo, R.M. Goodwin, A. Vercelli (Eds.), Technological and Social Factors in Long Term Fluctuations. Proceedings. IX, 442 pages. 1989.

Vol. 322: T. Kollintzas (Ed.), The Rational Expectations Equilibrium Inventory Model. XI, 269 pages. 1989.

Vol. 323: M.B.M. de Koster, Capacity Oriented Analysis and Design of Production Systems. XII, 245 pages. 1989.

Vol. 324: I.M. Bomze, B.M. Pötscher, Game Theoretical Foundations of Evolutionary Stability. VI, 145 pages. 1989.

Vol. 325: P. Ferri, E. Greenberg, The Labor Market and Business Cycle Theories. X, 183 pages. 1989.

Vol. 326: Ch. Sauer, Alternative Theories of Output, Unemployment, and Inflation in Germany: 1960–1985. XIII, 206 pages. 1989.

Vol. 327: M. Tawada, Production Structure and International Trade. V, 132 pages. 1989.

Vol. 328: W. Güth, B. Kalkofen, Unique Solutions for Strategic Games. VII, 200 pages. 1989.

Vol. 329: G. Tillmann, Equity, Incentives, and Taxation. VI, 132 pages. 1989.

Vol. 330: P.M. Kort, Optimal Dynamic Investment Policies of a Value Maximizing Firm. VII, 185 pages. 1989.

Vol. 331: A. Lewandowski, A.P. Wierzbicki (Eds.), Aspiration Based Decision Support Systems. X, 400 pages. 1989.

Vol. 332: T.R. Gulledge, Jr., L.A. Litteral (Eds.), Cost Analysis Applications of Economics and Operations Research. Proceedings. VII, 422 pages. 1989.

Vol. 333: N. Dellaert, Production to Order. VII, 158 pages. 1989.

Vol. 334: H.-W. Lorenz, Nonlinear Dynamical Economics and Chaotic Motion. XI, 248 pages. 1989.

Vol. 335: A.G. Lockett, G. Islei (Eds.), Improving Decision Making in Organisations. Proceedings. IX, 606 pages. 1989.

Vol. 336: T. Puu, Nonlinear Economic Dynamics. VII, 119 pages. 1989.

Vol. 337: A. Lewandowski, I. Stanchev (Eds.), Methodology and Software for Interactive Decision Support. VIII, 309 pages. 1989.

Vol. 338: J.K. Ho, R.P. Sundarraj, DECOMP: An Implementation of Dantzig-Wolfe Decomposition for Linear Programming. VI, 206 pages.

Vol. 339: J. Terceiro Lomba, Estimation of Dynamic Econometric Models with Errors in Variables. VIII, 116 pages. 1990.

Vol. 340: T. Vasko, R. Ayres, L. Fontvieille (Eds.), Life Cycles and Long Waves. XIV, 293 pages. 1990.

Vol. 341: G.R. Uhlich, Descriptive Theories of Bargaining. IX, 165 pages. 1990.

Vol. 342: K. Okuguchi, F. Szidarovszky, The Theory of Oligopoly with Multi-Product Firms. V, 167 pages. 1990.

Vol. 343: C. Chiarella, The Elements of a Nonlinear Theory of Economic Dynamics. IX, 149 pages. 1990.

Vol. 344: K. Neumann, Stochastic Project Networks. XI, 237 pages. 1990.

Vol. 345: A. Cambini, E. Castagnoli, L. Martein, P Mazzoleni, S. Schaible (Eds.), Generalized Convexity and Fractional Programming with Economic Applications. Proceedings, 1988. VII, 361 pages. 1990.

Vol. 346: R. von Randow (Ed.), Integer Programming and Related Areas. A Classified Bibliography 1984–1987. XIII, 514 pages. 1990.

Vol. 347: D. Ríos Insua, Sensitivity Analysis in Multiobjective Decision Making. XI, 193 pages. 1990.

Vol. 348: H. Störmer, Binary Functions and their Applications. VIII, 151 pages. 1990.

Vol. 349: G.A. Pfann, Dynamic Modelling of Stochastic Demand for Manufacturing Employment. VI, 158 pages. 1990.

Vol. 350: W.-B. Zhang, Economic Dynamics. X, 232 pages. 1990.

Vol. 351: A. Lewandowski, V. Volkovich (Eds.), Multiobjective Problems of Mathematical Programming. Proceedings, 1988. VII, 315 pages. 1991.

Vol. 352: O. van Hilten, Optimal Firm Behaviour in the Context of Technological Progress and a Business Cycle. XII, 229 pages. 1991.

Vol. 353: G. Ricci (Ed.), Decision Processes in Economics. Proceedings, 1989. III, 209 pages 1991.

Vol. 354: M. Ivaldi, A Structural Analysis of Expectation Formation. XII, 230 pages. 1991.

Vol. 355: M. Salomon. Deterministic Lotsizing Models for Production Planning. VII, 158 pages. 1991.

Vol. 356: P. Korhonen, A. Lewandowski, J . Wallenius (Eds.), Multiple Criteria Decision Support. Proceedings, 1989. XII, 393 pages. 1991.

Vol. 357: P. Zörnig, Degeneracy Graphs and Simplex Cycling. XV, 194 pages. 1991.

Vol. 358: P. Knottnerus, Linear Models with Correlated Disturbances. VIII, 196 pages. 1991.

Vol. 359: E. de Jong, Exchange Rate Determination and Optimal Economic Policy Under Various Exchange Rate Regimes. VII, 270 pages. 1991.

Vol. 360: P. Stalder, Regime Translations, Spillovers and Buffer Stocks. VI, 193 pages . 1991.

Vol. 361: C. F. Daganzo, Logistics Systems Analysis. X, 321 pages. 1991.

Vol. 362: F. Gehrels, Essays in Macroeconomics of an Open Economy. VII, 183 pages. 1991.

Vol. 363: C. Puppe, Distorted Probabilities and Choice under Risk. VIII, 100 pages . 1991

Vol. 364: B. Horvath, Are Policy Variables Exogenous? XII, 162 pages. 1991.

Vol. 365: G. A. Heuer, U. Leopold-Wildburger. Balanced Silverman Games on General Discrete Sets. V, 140 pages. 1991.

Vol. 366: J. Gruber (Ed.), Econometric Decision Models. Proceedings, 1989. VIII, 636 pages. 1991.

Vol. 367: M. Grauer, D. B. Pressmar (Eds.), Parallel Computing and Mathematical Optimization. Proceedings. V, 208 pages. 1991.

Vol. 368: M. Fedrizzi, J. Kacprzyk, M. Roubens (Eds.), Interactive Fuzzy Optimization. VII, 216 pages. 1991.

Vol. 369: R. Koblo, The Visible Hand. VIII, 131 pages.1991.

Vol. 370: M. J. Beckmann, M. N. Gopalan, R. Subramanian (Eds.), Stochastic Processes and their Applications. Proceedings, 1990. XLI, 292 pages. 1991.

Vol. 371: A. Schmutzler, Flexibility and Adjustment to Information in Sequential Decision Problems. VIII, 198 pages. 1991.

Vol. 372: J. Esteban, The Social Viability of Money. X, 202 pages. 1991.

Vol. 373: A. Billot, Economic Theory of Fuzzy Equilibria. XIII, 164 pages. 1992.

Vol. 374: G. Pflug, U. Dieter (Eds.), Simulation and Optimization. Proceedings, 1990. X, 162 pages. 1992.

Vol. 375: S.-J. Chen, Ch.-L. Hwang, Fuzzy Multiple Attribute Decision Making. XII, 536 pages. 1992.

Vol. 376: K.-H. Jöckel, G. Rothe, W. Sendler (Eds.), Bootstrapping and Related Techniques. Proceedings, 1990. VIII, 247 pages. 1992.

Vol. 377: A. Villar, Operator Theorems with Applications to Distributive Problems and Equilibrium Models. XVI, 160 pages. 1992.

Vol. 378: W. Krabs, J. Zowe (Eds.), Modern Methods of Optimization. Proceedings, 1990. VIII, 348 pages. 1992.

Vol. 379: K. Marti (Ed.), Stochastic Optimization. Proceedings, 1990. VII, 182 pages. 1992.

Vol. 380: J. Odelstad, Invariance and Structural Dependence. XII, 245 pages. 1992.

Vol. 381: C. Giannini, Topics in Structural VAR Econometrics. XI, 131 pages. 1992.

Vol. 382: W. Oettli, D. Pallaschke (Eds.), Advances in Optimization. Proceedings, 1991. X, 527 pages. 1992.

Vol. 383: J. Vartiainen, Capital Accumulation in a Corporatist Economy. VII, 177 pages. 1992.

Vol. 384: A. Martina, Lectures on the Economic Theory of Taxation. XII, 313 pages. 1992.

Vol. 385: J. Gardeazabal, M. Regúlez, The Monetary Model of Exchange Rates and Cointegration. X, 194 pages. 1992.

Vol. 386: M. Desrochers, J.-M. Rousseau (Eds.), Computer-Aided Transit Scheduling. Proceedings, 1990. XIII, 432 pages. 1992.

Vol. 387: W. Gaertner, M. Klemisch-Ahlert, Social Choice and Bargaining Perspectives on Distributive Justice. VIII, 131 pages. 1992.

Vol. 388: D. Bartmann, M. J. Beckmann, Inventory Control. XV, 252 pages. 1992.

Vol. 389: B. Dutta, D. Mookherjee, T. Parthasarathy, T. Raghavan, D. Ray, S. Tijs (Eds.), Game Theory and Economic Applications. Proceedings, 1990. IX, 454 pages. 1992.

Vol. 390: G. Sorger, Minimum Impatience Theorem for Recursive Economic Models. X, 162 pages. 1992.

Vol. 391: C. Keser, Experimental Duopoly Markets with Demand Inertia. X, 150 pages. 1992.

Vol. 392: K. Frauendorfer, Stochastic Two-Stage Programming. VIII, 228 pages. 1992.

Vol. 393: B. Lucke, Price Stabilization on World Agricultural Markets. XI, 274 pages. 1992.

Vol. 394: Y.-J. Lai, C.-L. Hwang, Fuzzy Mathematical Programming. XIII, 301 pages. 1992.

Vol. 395: G. Haag, U. Mueller, K. G. Troitzsch (Eds.), Economic Evolution and Demographic Change. XVI, 409 pages. 1992.

Vol. 396: R. V. V. Vidal (Ed.), Applied Simulated Annealing. VIII, 358 pages. 1992.

Vol. 397: J. Wessels, A. P. Wierzbicki (Eds.), User-Oriented Methodology and Techniques of Decision Analysis and Support. Proceedings, 1991. XII, 295 pages. 1993.

Vol. 398: J.-P. Urbain, Exogeneity in Error Correction Models. XI, 189 pages. 1993.

Vol. 399: F. Gori, L. Geronazzo, M. Galeotti (Eds.), Nonlinear Dynamics in Economics and Social Sciences. Proceedings, 1991. VIII, 367 pages. 1993.

Vol. 400: H. Tanizaki, Nonlinear Filters. XII, 203 pages. 1993.

Vol. 401: K. Mosler, M. Scarsini, Stochastic Orders and Applications. V, 379 pages. 1993.

Vol. 402: A. van den Elzen, Adjustment Processes for Exchange Economies and Noncooperative Games. VII, 146 pages. 1993.

Vol. 403: G. Brennscheidt, Predictive Behavior. VI, 227 pages. 1993.

Vol. 404: Y.-J. Lai, Ch.-L. Hwang, Fuzzy Multiple Objective Decision Making. XIV, 475 pages. 1994.

Vol. 405: S. Komlósi, T. Rapcsák, S. Schaible (Eds.), Generalized Convexity. Proceedings, 1992. VIII, 404 pages. 1994.

Vol. 406: N. M. Hung, N. V. Quyen, Dynamic Timing Decisions Under Uncertainty. X, 194 pages. 1994.

Vol. 407: M. Ooms, Empirical Vector Autoregressive Modeling. XIII, 380 pages. 1994.

Vol. 408: K. Haase, Lotsizing and Scheduling for Production Planning. VIII, 118 pages. 1994.

Vol. 409: A. Sprecher, Resource-Constrained Project Scheduling. XII, 142 pages. 1994.

Vol. 410: R. Winkelmann, Count Data Models. XI, 213 pages. 1994.

Vol. 411: S. Dauzère-Péres, J.-B. Lasserre, An Integrated Approach in Production Planning and Scheduling. XVI, 137 pages. 1994.

Vol. 412: B. Kuon, Two-Person Bargaining Experiments with Incomplete Information. IX, 293 pages. 1994.

Vol. 413: R. Fiorito (Ed.), Inventory, Business Cycles and Monetary Transmission. VI, 287 pages. 1994.

Vol. 414: Y. Crama, A. Oerlemans, F. Spieksma, Production Planning in Automated Manufacturing. X, 210 pages. 1994.

Vol. 415: P. C. Nicola, Imperfect General Equilibrium. XI, 167 pages. 1994.

Vol. 416: H. S. J. Cesar, Control and Game Models of the Greenhouse Effect. XI, 225 pages. 1994.

Vol. 417: B. Ran, D. E. Boyce, Dynamic Urban Transportation Network Models. XV, 391 pages. 1994.

Vol. 418: P. Bogetoft, Non-Cooperative Planning Theory. XI, 309 pages. 1994.

Vol. 419: T. Maruyama, W. Takahashi (Eds.), Nonlinear and Convex Analysis in Economic Theory. VIII, 306 pages. 1995.

Vol. 420: M. Peeters, Time-To-Build. Interrelated Investment and Labour Demand Modelling. With Applications to Six OECD Countries. IX, 204 pages. 1995.

Vol. 421: C. Dang, Triangulations and Simplicial Methods. IX, 196 pages. 1995.

Vol. 422: D. S. Bridges, G. B. Mehta, Representations of Preference Orderings. X, 165 pages. 1995.

Vol. 423: K. Marti, P. Kall (Eds.), Stochastic Programming. Numerical Techniques and Engineering Applications. VIII, 351 pages. 1995.

Vol. 424: G. A. Heuer, U. Leopold-Wildburger, Silverman's Game. X, 283 pages. 1995.

Vol. 425: J. Kohlas, P.-A. Monney, A Mathematical Theory of Hints. XIII, 419 pages, 1995.

Vol. 426: B. Finkenstädt, Nonlinear Dynamics in Economics. IX, 156 pages. 1995.

Vol. 427: F. W. van Tongeren, Microsimulation Modelling of the Corporate Firm. XVII, 275 pages. 1995.

Vol. 428: A. A. Powell, Ch. W. Murphy, Inside a Modern Macroeconometric Model. XVIII, 424 pages. 1995.

Vol. 429: R. Durier, C. Michelot, Recent Developments in Optimization. VIII, 356 pages. 1995.

Vol. 430: J. R. Daduna, I. Branco, J. M. Pinto Paixão (Eds.), Computer-Aided Transit Scheduling. XIV, 374 pages. 1995.

Vol. 431: A. Aulin, Causal and Stochastic Elements in Business Cycles. XI, 116 pages. 1996.

Vol. 432: M. Tamiz (Ed.), Multi-Objective Programming and Goal Programming. VI, 359 pages. 1996.

Vol. 433: J. Menon, Exchange Rates and Prices. XIV, 313 pages. 1996.

Vol. 434: M. W. J. Blok, [===] 193 pages. 1996.

Vol. 435: L. Chen, Interest Rate Dynamics, Derivatives Pricing, and Risk Management. XII, 149 pages. 1996.

Vol. 436: M. Klemisch-Ahlert, Bargaining in Economic and Ethical Environments. IX, 155 pages. 1996.

Vol. 437: C. Jordan, Batching and Scheduling. IX, 178 pages. 1996.

Vol. 438: A. Villar, General Equilibrium with Increasing Returns. XIII, 164 pages. 1996.

Vol. 439: M. Zenner, Learning to Become Rational. VII, 201 pages. 1996.

Vol. 440: W. Ryll, Litigation and Settlement in a Game with Incomplete Information. VIII, 174 pages. 1996.

Vol. 441: H. Dawid, Adaptive Learning by Genetic Algorithms. IX, 166 pages.1996.

Vol. 442: L. Corchón, Theories of Imperfectly Competitive Markets. XIII, 163 pages. 1996.

Vol. 443: G. Lang, On Overlapping Generations Models with Productive Capital. X, 98 pages. 1996.

Vol. 444: S. Jørgensen, G. Zaccour (Eds.), Dynamic Competitive Analysis in Marketing. X, 285 pages. 1996.

Vol. 445: A. H. Christer, S. Osaki, L. C. Thomas (Eds.), Stochastic Modelling in Innovative Manufactoring. X, 361 pages. 1997.

Vol. 446: G. Dhaene, Encompassing. X, 160 pages. 1997.

Vol. 447: A. Artale, Rings in Auctions. X, 172 pages. 1997.

Vol. 448: G. Fandel, T. Gal (Eds.), Multiple Criteria Decision Making. XII, 678 pages. 1997.

Vol. 449: F. Fang, M. Sanglier (Eds.), Complexity and Self-Organization in Social and Economic Systems. IX, 317 pages, 1997.

Vol. 450: P. M. Pardalos, D. W. Hearn, W. W. Hager, (Eds.), Network Optimization. VIII, 485 pages, 1997.

Vol. 451: M. Salge, Rational Bubbles. Theoretical Basis, Economic Relevance, and Empirical Evidence with a Special Emphasis on the German Stock Market.IX, 265 pages. 1997.

Vol. 452: P. Gritzmann, R. Horst, E. Sachs, R. Tichatschke (Eds.), Recent Advances in Optimization. VIII, 379 pages. 1997.

Vol. 453: A. S. Tangian, J. Gruber (Eds.), Constructing Scalar-Valued Objective Functions. VIII, 298 pages. 1997.

Vol. 454: H.-M. Krolzig, Markov-Switching Vector Auto-regressions. XIV, 358 pages. 1997.

Vol. 455: R. Caballero, F. Ruiz, R. E. Steuer (Eds.), Advances in Multiple Objective and Goal Programming. VIII, 391 pages. 1997.

Vol. 456: R. Conte, R. Hegselmann, P. Terna (Eds.), Simulating Social Phenomena. VIII, 536 pages. 1997.

Vol. 457: C. Hsu, Volume and the Nonlinear Dynamics of Stock Returns. VIII, 133 pages. 1998.

Vol. 458: K. Marti, P. Kall (Eds.), Stochastic Programming Methods and Technical Applications. X, 437 pages. 1998.

Vol. 459: H. K. Ryu, D. J. Slottje, Measuring Trends in U.S. Income Inequality. XI, 195 pages. 1998.

Vol. 460: B. Fleischmann, J. A. E. E. van Nunen, M. G. Speranza, P. Stähly, Advances in Distribution Logistic. XI, 535 pages. 1998.

Vol. 461: U. Schmidt, Axiomatic Utility Theory under Risk. XV, 201 pages. 1998.

Vol. 462: L. von Auer, Dynamic Preferences, Choice Mechanisms, and Welfare. XII, 226 pages. 1998.

Vol. 463: G. Abraham-Frois (Ed.), Non-Linear Dynamics and Endogenous Cycles. VI, 204 pages. 1998.

Vol. 464: A. Aulin, The Impact of Science on Economic Growth and its Cycles. IX, 204 pages. 1998.

Vol. 465: T. J. Stewart, R. C. van den Honert (Eds.), Trends in Multicriteria Decision Making. X, 448 pages. 1998.

Vol. 466: A. Sadrieh, The Alternating Double Auction Market. VII, 350 pages. 1998.

Vol. 467: H. Hennig-Schmidt, Bargaining in a Video Experiment. Determinants of Boundedly Rational Behavior. XII, 221 pages. 1999.

Vol. 468: A. Ziegler, A Game Theory Analysis of Options. XIV, 145 pages. 1999.

Vol. 469: M. P. Vogel, Environmental Kuznets Curves. XIII, 197 pages. 1999.

Vol. 470: M. Ammann, Pricing Derivative Credit Risk. XII, 228 pages. 1999.

Vol. 471: N. H. M. Wilson (Ed.), Computer-Aided Transit Scheduling. XI, 444 pages. 1999.

Vol. 472: J.-R. Tyran, Money Illusion and Strategic Complementarity as Causes of Monetary Non-Neutrality. X, 228 pages. 1999.

Vol. 473: S. Helber, Performance Analysis of Flow Lines with Non-Linear Flow of Material. IX, 280 pages. 1999.

Vol. 474: U. Schwalbe, The Core of Economies with Asymmetric Information. IX, 141 pages. 1999.

Vol. 475: L. Kaas, Dynamic Macroelectronics with Imperfect Competition. XI, 155 pages. 1999.

Vol. 476: R. Demel, Fiscal Policy, Public Debt and the Term Structure of Interest Rates. X, 279 pages. 1999.

Vol. 477: M. Théra, R. Tichatschke (Eds.), Ill-posed Variational Problems and Regularization Techniques. VIII, 274 pages. 1999.

Vol. 478: S. Hartmann, Project Scheduling under Limited Resources. XII, 221 pages. 1999.

Vol. 479: L. v. Thadden, Money, Inflation, and Capital Formation. IX, 192 pages. 1999.

Vol. 480: M. Grazia Speranza, P. Stähly (Eds.), New Trends in Distribution Logistics. X, 336 pages. 1999.

Vol. 481: V. H. Nguyen, J. J. Strodiot, P. Tossings (Eds.). Optimations. IX, 498 pages. 2000.

Vol. 482: W. B. Zhang, A Theory of International Trade. XI, 192 pages. 2000.

Vol. 483: M. Königstein, Equity, Efficiency and Evolutionary Stability in Bargaining Games with Joint Production. XII, 197 pages. 2000.

Vol. 484: D. D. Gatti, M. Gallegati, A. Kirman, Interaction and Market Structure. VI, 298 pages. 2000.